Death Customs

An Analytical Study of
Burial Rites

By

E. BENDANN

Ph. B., University of Chicago (1914), A.M. Columbia University (1914)

NEW YORK
ALFRED A. KNOPF
1930
Republished by Omnigraphics ● Penobscot Building ● Detroit ● 1990

Library of Congress Cataloging-in-Publication Data

Bendann, E. (Effie)
    Death customs : an analytical study of burial rites / E. Bendann.
       p. cm.
    Reprint. Originally published: New York : Knopf, 1930.
    Includes bibliographical references.
    ISBN 1-55888-844-6 (lib. bdg. : alk. paper)
    1. Funeral rites and ceremonies. I. Title.
    GT3150.B35   1989
    .393—dc20
                                      89-63007
                                           CIP

♾ This book is printed on acid-free paper meeting the ANSI Z39.48
Standard. The infinity symbol that appears above indicates that the
paper in this book meets that standard.

Printed in the United States of America

INTRODUCTION

MISS EFFIE BENDANN'S book, Death Customs, *is what it purports to be : An Analytical Study of Burial Rites. With commendable courage the author launches into a comparative investigation of a type which for some time has been out of fashion. There is, however, no lack of critical safeguards. In a historical Introduction the author deals rather cavalierly with some out-standing representatives, living and dead, of anthropological theory. Spencer, Tylor, Frazer, Bastian, Durkheim, Lévy-Bruhl, Graebner, and Rivers come in for their share of judicious criticism. Then the author plunges into* medias res. *The study is based on an intensive. investigation of burial rites and associated ideas in Melanesia, Australia, Northeast Siberia, and India, where the Vedic conceptions receive particular attention. Here and there, as when commenting upon the universality of the notion that death is unnatural, the author draws her material from a much wider geographical range.*

The book falls into two main sections : Part I, in which the similarities in rites and ideas are considered ; and Part II, in which the differences are subjected to a similar analysis. In her conclusion to Part I, the author is able to point out, by way of summary, how complex the sources and motivations of mourning ceremonies can be shown to be. With justice she stresses, in opposition to Westermarck, that the " natural condition of sorrow " at a death has little to do with the elaborate ritual. The author would have found striking confirmation of this in Malinowski's recent book, Sexual Life of Savages, *where ceremonial mourning is shown to vary in inverse ratio with actual or probable sorrow.*

In a conclusion to the section dealing with differences, the author is able to show, to her own and the reader's satisfaction, that psychological factors apart, the specific content of the burial complex in the different areas depends upon "rank, sex, age, social organization, status, environmental, moral, religious differences, and myth conceptions, the location of the realms of the dead, the physical condition of the deceased, totemic considerations, and the kind of life after death."

The book is well done, carefully documented, and readable. Its real value, of course, consists in the fact that a new chapter has thus been added to the story of human culture of which the end is not yet, showing the complexity of the stuff culture is made of, the unceasing mutations of motives, the overhanging veil of rationalizations, and, before and after all, man's all-pervading tendency to pour old wine into new bottles—or to serve new wine in old ones.

ALEXANDER GOLDENWEISER.

Washington, D.C.
April, 1930.

PREFACE

*T*HE subject of this investigation was suggested to me by
Professor James Shotwell. In pursuance of this idea and
under the stimulating influence of Professor A. V. W. Jackson,
I studied the Death Customs of India, with special emphasis
upon Rig-Vedic literature. Then Roman death-rites came in
for a share of attention and it was in a seminar conducted by
the late Professor Botsford, whose masterful leadership and
sympathetic attitude greatly contributed to my interest in the
subject, that I presented a survey of Roman Death Customs.
However, up to this time my approach was purely historical
and comparative. I was thoroughly imbued with the evolutionary
point of view, and like the scientific gossip, I was engaged in a
strenuous but futile search for ultimate origins. It was then
that Professor Shotwell indicated the feasibility of working along
anthropological lines. A survey of the anthropological field
convinced me that such an idea as I had in mind was only a
visionary conception, furthered by an unscientific attitude
toward the problem.

To say that I owe a special debt of gratitude to Professor
Shotwell and to Dr. A. A. Goldenweiser, is a faint expression
of my appreciation ; to the former for having opened up the
vista by making me realize the possibilities of the development
of this study, and to Dr. Goldenweiser who made me cognizant
of the limitations of my approach. His suggestive lectures,
his brilliant interpretation of ethnological phenomena, and his
inspiring discussions pointed out the way to an approach other
than that to which I found myself committed by my former
standpoint.

PREFACE

Finally I came to the conclusion that the complexity of the death-situation was such that psychological and deductive methods alone could not account for some of its various and intricate phases. The method of procedure was indicated by Dr. Goldenweiser. With this confession, I now place the result of my investigation before the public.

EFFIE BENDANN.

Columbia University.

CONTENTS

PART ONE

SIMILARITIES

PART TWO

DIFFERENCES

A Connection between the Myths of Origin and
the Disposal of the Dead ; A Connection between
the Myths of Origin and the Orientation of the
Dead. A Connection between the Myths of
Origin and the Land of the Dead, and the
Orientation of the Dead.—A Connection between
the Myths Relating to Totemic Ancestors and
Tree Burial. Dependent upon the Kind of Death.
—Influenced by Moral Considerations.—A Con-
nection between the Method of Burial and the
Worship of the Sun.—Disposal of the Bones
Related to Animal Beliefs.—Connected with
Social Infractions.—Connected with the Reputa-
tion of the Deceased.—Connected with Divina-
tion.—Associated with Ethical Considerations.—
Ceremonies Connected with Social Status.—
Method of Burial Influenced by Environmental
Conditions.—Affected by the Physical Condi-
tions of the Deceased.—Orientation of the Dead
Correlated with Their Original Home.—Connec-
ted with the Birthplace of the Deceased.—
Burial Dependent upon the Exigencies of the
Occasion.—Manner of Digging the Grave
Dependent upon the Conception of the Resting-
place of the Deceased.—Affected by the
Location of the Realms of the Dead.

Explanations for Abbreviations of Journals used in Footnotes

A.A.	American Anthropologist
A.J.S.	American Journal of Sociology
A.R.W.	Archiv für Religionwissenschaft
B.A.R.	Breasted, Ancient Records
F.L.	Folk-Lore
Int. Arch.	Internationales Archiv für Ethnographie
J.A.F.L.	Journal of American Folk-Lore
J.A.I.	Journal of the Anthropological Institute of Great Britain and Ireland
J.A.O.S.	Journal of the American Oriental Society
J.A.S.B.	Journal of the Asiatic Society of Bengal
J.N.P.E.	Jesup North Pacific Expedition
J.R.A.S.	Journal of the Royal Asiatic Society
R.H.R.	Revue d'Histoire des Religions

DEATH CUSTOMS

AN
ANALYTICAL STUDY OF BURIAL RITES

INTRODUCTION

THE GENERAL PROBLEM

ANTHROPOLOGISTS, sociologists, and historians have been most zealous in their efforts to show that similar ideas are common to man in all parts of the world ; nor would it be too much to say that this similarity in mental manifestations in societies culturally different has been the starting point of all those who have wished to trace the evolution of civilization, including especially such specific developments as those of material culture, art, religion, social organization, and other phases of culture.

THE COMPARATIVE METHOD OF SPENCER AND TYLOR NON-COMPARABILITY OF THE DATA

Our problem is how to approach the subject of death customs. Some old writers, such as Spencer and Tylor, would have used the comparative method to the exclusion of all other lines of approach as a basis for such a study. The total inadequacy of this method, when it does not consider the cultural phases, is so well known to ethnologists, that there is no need to discuss its unreliability. Thus, both in Australia and Siberia we find the practice of killing individuals before they arrive at the age of decrepitude. Whereas in Australia the motives which actuate such a proceeding are the desire to get rid of the old for fear they may become burdensome to the tribe, or because of their inability to cope with the perils of a dangerous journey or on account of their

concern lest the feeble fall into the hands of the enemy ; in Siberia the idea is, that since life in the future world is a continuance of the same kind of existence as experienced here, it would be non-judicious to allow the deceased to perpetuate such an impaired condition of life. Again, we find cremation practised in all the areas under consideration. In the Vedic and Siberian regions the belief is accentuated that if the flames go straight upward, the spirit will reach heaven ; but in the Australian and Melanesian areas, one of the main objects of cremation is to prevent the spirit of the dead from shivering, or to light its way to the other world. Here we have the same custom with entirely different motives actuating the performers. Thus, the general cultural setting must be known before we can draw our conclusions. Although the comparative method has given us generalized laws for thought development in human societies, yet this investigation shows the weakness of approaching an analysis of a complex by this method alone, inasmuch as ofttimes the laws indicated are based upon non-comparable data. To quote Boas : " One of the fundamental points to be borne in mind in the development of anthropological psychology is the necessity of looking for the common psychological features, not in the outward similarities of ethnic phenomena, but in the similarity of psychological processes as they can be observed or inferred ".[1] Before us is always the problem that diverse phenomena frequently emanate from similar psychic processes, and care must be taken against making wrong deductions from anthropological phenomena culturally similar. One of the great faults of workers in the field of anthropology, such as Spencer and Frazer, has been their failure to realize the non-comparability of the data used in arriving at their deductions. The illustrations given are sufficient to show that phenomena outwardly similar are often compared and classified as if their nature were identical, no consideration being given to the historical development. This study has led us to the conclusion which it is advisable to stress at the start, that rites, different in nature and origin, often manifest external resemblances and that their interpretation is often beset by insurmountable difficulties.

[1] Boas, " Mythology and Folk-Tales in North America ", *A.A.*, Vol. XVI, (1914), p. 620.

A Psychological Explanation not Always Sufficient to Account for Cultural Phenomena

Spencer and his followers in accounting for the development of institutions and customs first utilized a deductive and psychological method in constructing a series of probable successive stages through which such institutions must pass. Then, because of their evolutionary position, which insists upon one line of development, they apply a comparative method by taking illustrations from all over the world, without looking for historical succession. The material thus utilized in this comparative approach is non-psychological and non-cultural, inasmuch as the historical and cultural background is lost sight of.

The reasons prompting death ceremonials have been discussed by Spencer and Tylor. They attempt to explain the death-situation from the psychological viewpoint, with their evolutionary tendency always in evidence. Despite the fact that Tylor recognizes the possibility of diffusion,[1] he does not apply it. Then again, although he explains some things through the agency of independent development, yet in other instances he resorts to diffusion where the modern evolutionist would apply independent development.[2] Although a psychological explanation is the only one that can be offered, to explain many similar customs, such as for instance, in the Melanesian, Australian, African, and North American areas where we find stories showing the connection of the moon with death, the waning and waxing of the moon naturally suggesting life, death, and resurrection, yet a mere psychological explanation is not sufficient in itself. The changing of the skin, too, figures in many tales. Such a conception is also due to psychological factors, but then we have yet to account for the fact as to why the stories connected with the changing of the skin are found in one area, as in Melanesia, and why other tales asserting that death is due to the decision of two personages, are met with in the entire region of the eastern

---

[1] Whenever we find a continuous, not intermittent, distribution of certain traits over a certain geographical area, we may assume that diffusion has taken place.

[2] Thus in his *Researches into the Early History* he ascribes the curious custom of couvade to diffusion, an interpretation that few modern ethnologists would countenance.

foot-hills from the Rocky Mountains. Here we must recognize the process of diffusion also.

One of the chief weaknesses of the evolutionary method is that it assumes parallel development whenever similarities of culture occur. However, such deductions are of doubtful value unless proof can be given. Those who are advocates of this psychological mechanism take it for granted that all similar phenomena are due to similar causes. Thus all culture is brought within the restricted limits of psychology. Such evolutionists would have us believe that because many conceptions of future life have developed from dreams and hallucinations, all such ideas have the same origin. This we know to be entirely at variance with facts in the case, for such ideas may be due to many other causes. From analysis of the concrete material we find that in some tribes of aborigines their conception of future existence was due to the appearance of the white man, inasmuch as many of the natives of Melanesia and Australia think that a white man is a ghost of some departed tribesman, or again, the concept of life after death was influenced by certain myths, or the nature of the place of sojourn after departure from this life was due to environmental conditions, or punishment in the future world was attributed to certain social infractions.

Customs and beliefs themselves are not the ultimate objects of research and our object is to study the history of their development and the processes by means of which certain stages of culture have developed.[1]

Thus we have attempted to sound a note of warning in regard to the validity of applying a psychological explanation for all cultural phases. Long since anthropologists have been unanimous in their opinion that ultimate psychological explanations are visionary conceptions, furthered by an unscientific attitude toward the problem. Not only have we often to disentangle the psychological setting from the historical determinants, but cognizance must be taken of the fact that the psychic processes of the individual have been directly influenced by social factors.[2] Brinton's attempt to explain all ceremonies as due to the psychic unity of mankind,

---

[1] Boas, " Limitations of the Comparative Methods of Anthropology", *Science*, Vol. IV (1896), p. 905.

[2] Lowie, " Psychology and Sociology", *A.J.S.*, Vol. XXI (1915), p. 229.

suffers a rude collapse. According to his conception, customs, even those identical among tribes in the closest proximity to each other, are attributable to psychological similarities, not to a common historical setting.[1]

Bastian has attempted to prove that man universally develops the same elementary ideas. He does not say definitely what these fundamental basic ideas, which he calls *Elementargedanken*, are, but he insists that they are permanent and always appear because of the constitution of the nervous system. Although these may be modified by social and environmental conditions, thus resulting in *Volkergedanken*, their essential character remains unchanged. Since these basic ideas do not evolve, development is due to the reaction between culture and environment. Bastian's attitude is peculiar in so far as he denies the comparability of cultures since they are geographically determined, and hence there are different lines of development in different cultures ; however, he regards the psychic content of the individual as comparable. We may add that an analysis of the death-situation shows that the conception of Bastian that the common ideas found all over the world are presumably due to the same cause, is erroneous. Another illustration will be fitting here. In some areas, the object of feasts is commemorative, in others, there is the desire to feed the dead so that he can survive in the future world. Among some primitives we find the belief that they wish to eat with the dead to continue the human relations which have been cut off.

The more we examine different types of ideas, the more we become conscious of the great complexity of the subject matter. The mere occurrence of these ideas does not in itself explain either the psychological processes which produced them or the reasons for their persistency. We must not only know the psychological setting for a ceremonial or custom, but the psychological sources for its origin. A great weakness of the comparative method is that it assumes a similarity in development.

We, too, must account for psychological differences. In his discussion of "Ceremonialism in North America", Lowie has shown conclusively that the occurrence of certain ceremonial elements, even in the simplest form of society, seems

[1] Brinton, *The Myths of the New World*, pp. 172-173.

to indicate that "variations in ceremonial development are not so much correlated with psychological differences, as with the way of combining and multiplying elements of general distribution ".[1] Even when a ceremony seems to be entirely transmitted it becomes different from what it was, because of the difference in culture of the group which transmits and the tribe which borrows. The definite relation of the newly introduced ceremonies to the cultural phases of the group must be taken into consideration. Even peoples with similar customs and ideas may have totally different conceptions in regard to the transmitted ceremony.[2] Hence, a ceremony may become metamorphosed because of a complicated and new environment. In support of this theory Lowie cites the characteristic potlatch ceremonies of the Tlingit and Haida, representing a single cultural phenomenon with the corresponding disparity between the significance of such a ceremonial ; whereas, among the Haida, the ceremony was performed by a chief in the interest of his own moiety for the acquisition of prestige, among the Tlingit it was performed in behalf of the opposite division, merely to manifest respect for the dead.[3]

DURKHEIM'S METHOD—NON-ADVISABILITY OF CONSIDERING ONE AREA

Durkheim and his school, in accounting for the death complex, would have made an intensive study of one area only, perhaps of Australia with its high diversified burial rites, and generalized from it, as he did in his *Les Formes élémentaires de la Vie religieuse*. We regard such a law as unjustifiable, since law cannot be deduced from a study of one historic complex.[4]

THE WEAKNESS OF THE SOCIO-PSYCHOLOGICAL METHOD

Although Durkheim goes a step beyond some of the representatives of the French Sociological School in accentuating

[1] Lowie, "Ceremonialism in North America ", *A.A.*, Vol. XVI (1914), p. 606.
[2] Lowie, *Ibid*, p. 611.
[3] Swanton, "Social Conditions, Beliefs and Linguistic Relationships of the Tlingit Indians", *Twenty-sixth Annual Report, Bureau American Ethnology* (1908), p. 434, et seqq, p. 155, et seqq, p. 162.
[4] Goldenweiser, "Totemism, An Analytic Study", *J.A.F.L.*, Vol. XXIII 1910), pp. 179-293.

the influence of the social group, yet the socio-psychological approach is not historical, for he does not consider the cultural phase in which we are interested and which we shall attempt to prove is inextricably bound up with our problem. When Durkheim states that nature as such cannot inspire the religious emotion which he claims can originate only through a crowd, he is not only oblivious to the experiences of ancient and modern man in all parts of the world, but he also eliminates the individual in favour of the social. Different crowd situations produce emotions of varied intensity and character. Our concepts have other origins outside of the religious and social.[1]

LÉVY-BRUHL'S APPROACH

That we cannot interpret a complex ceremonial as such is so self-evident, that no explanation is necessary. If, however, such an intricate ceremonial is divided into a number of disparate elements, the problem is to explain the process by which some of these seemingly non-related elements have become united. A study of complexes shows that concepts not related according to our mode of thinking are related in the savage mind. This seems to disprove the theory of Lévy-Bruhl who discusses at length the illogical character of primitive mentality. He claims that whereas our mentality represents a collective, socialized product, due to our physical and mental environment, the mentality of the savage must necessarily be different because his social environment differs radically from that of civilized man ; as a result we would expect different concepts, an association of different things. Our deductions yield but a partial endorsement of the views of the author of *Les Fonctions mentales dans les Sociétés inférieures*, whose central thesis is that the primitive's mental picture of the world is totally different from that of civilized man.

In considering the "Law of Participation", Lévy-Bruhl regards the formation of chains of associations along irrational channels ; these associations are so related that they are

---

[1] For a discussion of Durkheim see Goldenweiser, Vol. XVII (1915), pp. 719-735 ; Goldenweiser, " Religion and Society, A Critic of Emil Durkheim's Theory of the Origin and Nature of Religion ", *The Journal of Philosophy, Psychology and Scientific Methods*, Vol. XIV (1917), No. 5, pp. 113-124.

almost identical. He next applies a further extension of the "Law of Participation", when he says that primitive man does not construct things as we see them. According to his conception, there is a specific association in the mind of the savage between various objectively non-related objects and actions. Our investigation demonstrates that although this is sometimes true, yet it certainly does not apply in all instances. Such limitations as he suggests are likewise common to our own society, where, too, very different cycles of participation are in evidence.

The automatic character of actions must also be taken into consideration, for a study of the functions of social units shows the important rôle which the unconscious element plays ; indeed, emotionalism is often reduced to a minimum, in fact, we have seen its complete elimination. This is a fact which Durkheim and Lévy-Bruhl have overlooked in their discussion of primitive mentality. To illustrate : After a death the aborigines of Australia and Melanesia indulge in the most exaggerated forms of weeping, wailing, heart-rending cries, and display other manifestations of emotional excitement seemingly because of grief for the departed, but at the end of a certain designated interval they cease with metronomic precision, and the would-be mourners indulge in laughter and other forms of amusement, ill-befitting the occasion.

THE THEORY OF DIFFUSION—THE MECHANISTIC THEORY OF GRAEBNER

In our discussion we cannot use the method of Ratzel, the originator of the diffusion theory, inasmuch as he applies a different criterion to material than he does to spiritual culture. He does not believe in fundamental development, and although he would acknowledge that cultural similarities are correlated in certain psychic dispositions, yet he begs the psychic unity of mankind theory, merely contenting himself with the conception that there is no deep-rooted differences in the make-up.[1] Just as we have voiced an objection against the procedure of those who insist upon a psychological method at the expense of all other avenues of approach, so we are

[1] Ratzel, "Uber den anthropologischen Wert ethnographischer Merkmale", *Anthropogeographie*, Vol. II, pp. 577-631 ; *Die Geestige Generatio Alquivoca*, pp. 706-710.

not in sympathy with the method of those who, like Ratzel and his disciples, start out with the assumption that geographical environment is a most important factor in determining the nature of the culture. Investigation shows that people living under identical physical conditions practise diversified customs and ceremonies.

Despairing of the psychic unity of mankind theory and evolution, Graebner[1] and those of his school proceed by a mechanistic method and explain all similarities in culture as due to diffusion, reaching their conclusion by a purely hypothetical line of approach. Although diffusion may account for many similar tales dealing with the origin of death and the same burial rites and mourning practices, yet such similarities in different cultures may be ascribed to other influences. No more hypothetical than the changes due to diffusion are those evolutionary changes brought about by internal factors.

However, in some instances, diffusion is the only possibility. Thus when the entire area from the eastern hills of the Rocky Mountains to California as far northward as the Lillooet, we find the origin of death due to a decision of two personages, one of whom wishes man to be mortal, the other immortal, and that this idea takes two forms, a western one where the decision is made by a council, and another in which it is due to divination, we certainly must see that diffusion has taken place.

The assumption of Graebner that at one time there was no differentiation in the mental make-up of primitives is entirely hypothetical and his argument that convergence can occur only under identical cultural conditions in the last analysis resulting from identical environmental settings, is not borne out by an investigation of the death-situation. For instance, hair cutting and its association with mourning is found in Melanesia, Australia, India, the Israelitish regions, Rome, America, and Japan, but not in Siberia. Here we have various areas representing entirely different cultural development where diffusion is not at all probable, but the same custom is in vogue with almost identical stipulations regarding the details. In this case we can argue for the validity of independent development which cannot be proved, but only assumed. Although the environmental-cultural explanation

[1] Graebner, *Methode der Ethnologie*, pp. 104-125.

10   INTRODUCTION

may be advanced to account for the absence of hair cutting
in Siberia, inasmuch as the climate in this region is not conducive to cropped hair or shaven heads, yet such an explanation
certainly could not be advanced to explain such a custom
in the areas just designated. Again, lacerations following
a death are found in Melanesia, Australia, in ancient Rome,
in the Indian areas of North America, among the Israelites
of Biblical times, etc. But in this case, too, it is in Siberia
where climatic conditions are such that the blood would
probably congeal and thus the object of such a practice be
defeated, that we note the absence of this specific phase of
mourning rites. We must not lose sight of the fact that
although in Siberia where environmental and cultural conditions are totally different from the other areas under consideration, we likewise, as in them, have other mourning customs.
In this category are taboos consisting of the abstinence from
the ordinary activities of life, of the avoidance of the name
of the dead, and other practices connected with death, such
as the removal from a hut after a death, the reversal of the
order of the funeral procession or as we see in India, the carrying out of a corpse by an exit other than that of the ordinary
entrance as in Melanesia, India, parts of France, Germany,
Switzerland, the British Isles, Africa, Tibet, Greenland, among
the Eskimo of Hudson Bay, and other areas. Other similar
expedients are resorted to to prevent the return of the spirit
as are found in widely diversified cultural areas and the same
general attitude toward a dead body is likewise manifested.
Here again we must assume independent development to have
taken place.*[1]

According to the convergence theory first suggested by
Ehrenreich, a culture complex which is the same among
different groups may have had diverse origins.[2] Graebner

* Our leading ethnologists have manifested a tendency to explain
identity of traits by independent development rather than by diffusion, being
influenced by European political conditions and Darwinism, which emphasizes
development as an aspect of culture. (See Wissler's discussion of " Theories
of Culture Origin " in *The American Indian*, p. 342.)

[1] Ehrenreich, " Zur Frage der Beurtheilung und Bewehrthung ethnographischer Analogien," *Correspondenz Blatt der deutschen Gesellschaft für
Anthropologie*, Vol. XXXIV (1903), pp. 176-180.

[2] By convergence we mean " the independent development of psychologically similar cultural traits from dissimilar or less similar sources in two
or more cultural complexes." Goldenweiser, " Principle of Limited
Possibilities ", *J.A.F.L.*, Vol. XXVI (1913), p. 269.

neglects the historical phase when he does not seem to recognize the fact that in many instances we have definite proof that the same development is brought about through entirely different channels.[1] Thus in the death situation we meet with numerous taboos. In some areas food taboos have been instituted because of the desirability of supplying the deceased with a sufficient quantity of the favourite food, again abstinence from certain food stuffs has been enjoined because a specified article of diet, such as a pomegranate, is the same colour as blood, regarded by primitives as one of the main sources of impurity ; again, in other tribes certain fish are tabooed during mourning periods because of the susceptibility of special fish, especially salmon, to the influence of dead bodies ; in some tribes cooked food is denied the mourners because since food undergoes a transformation when cooked, and as such changes are looked upon with awe or suspicion, it would be inadvisable to partake of such a diet on account of this uncanny aspect. The forbidden fruit in this case is a unit—that of taboo, despite the fact that its psychological origins are totally at variance. To illustrate our point further : In all of the areas under consideration, cremation is -practised. Sometimes its object is to prevent the wild beasts from devouring any portion of the body of the deceased ; again, the fire is regarded as a benefit to the ghost ; then, fire is looked upon as a purifying agency ; again, it may be a means of lighting the spirit of the departed to the other world ; then it may be the agency through which the complete dissolution of the body from the soul may be effected. A note of warning must be given to those who are most zealous advocates of the theory of the independent development of cultural traits at the expense of all other methods. These representatives hold that the unity of the human mind is sufficient to account for cultural similarities if the environment is the same. Investigation of the customs of various areas shows us that different people, even though they are influenced by identical conditions, come to many solutions of the same problem.

Again, it must be borne in mind that similar ideas may rise

---

[1] Graebner, " Methode der Ethnologie," *Kriterien der Kulturbeziehungen*, pp. 104-125 ; Lowie, " On the Principle of Convergence in Ethnology," *J.A.F.L.*, Vol. XXV, (1912), pp. 24-42.

from diverse sources and that social environment may cause the development of psychologically similar traits from dissimilar or less similar sources in two or more cultural complexes. This may in our opinion explain some of the phases of the death situation.[1]

RATZEL AS A DIFFUSIONIST AND ENVIRONMENTALIST

Ratzel's attempt to explain all similar cultures on the basis of similarities in geographical environments cannot be substantiated by the facts in the death-situation. Again, very dissimilar geographical settings may produce identical results. Not only is this true of the death-complex, but of other cultural phenomena. As we have indicated before, many similar customs in connection with burial rites and mourning observances are found both in Siberia and India, where climatic conditions are entirely at variance. Although environment plays an important rôle in the development of a culture, yet it cannot be regarded as a basic determinant.

RIVERS AS AN EVOLUTIONIST AND DIFFUSIONIST

Rivers in his *History of Melanesian Society* has applied a well-articulated, logical method in making his deductions ; indeed, his work marks an important epoch in theoretical approach. In this volume he appears first as an evolutionist, his method having for its foundation the theory of survivals. Soon he assumes the rôle of diffusionist. After he has made a study of the various methods of burial practised in Melanesia, he attributes such differences in the disposal of a dead body to the various burial practices of different and successive immigrants, representing the dual, kava, and betel peoples. He also suggests Micronesian and Polynesian influence. Thus, like Graebner, he advances a diffusion interpretation, introducing a purely hypothetical method without attempting to prove his case. Again, we have occasion to emphasize the fact that, whereas independent development may be assumed, diffusion must be proved.[2] Rivers himself states that the chief aim of the *History of Melanesian Society* is

---

[1] For discussion of Convergence see Goldenweiser, " Principle of Limited Possibilities ", *J.A.F.L.*, Vol. XXVI (1913), p. 270, et seqq.

[2] See Goldenweiser, " Critique of the History of Melanesian Society ", *Science*, Vol. XLIV (1916), pp. 824-828.

"to show how social institutions and customs have arisen as a result of the interaction between two peoples, the resulting compound resembling that produced by a chemical mixture in that it requires a process of analysis to discover its composition ".[1] It may be added that in many countries and even in the same tribe we find numerous ways employed to dispose of the dead, with no indication or proof of any kind that such are traceable to immigrant peoples, but that the varied methods of getting rid of a dead body are dependent upon rank, sex, age, ethical, environmental, and other considerations. Thus we have no justification in claiming that the many different ways of disposing of a corpse found in one area are due to various immigrant strata unless we can adduce proof that such is the case. Again, to use another example from Rivers. In accounting for the religious societies of the Island of Mota, the author of the *History of Melanesian Society* attributes their gradations in rank, their number, and their secrecy to an immigrant people. Now, other religious societies in different parts of the world manifest the same characteristics without any intimation that an immigrant people are responsible for such results. Indeed, rank considerations play such a conspicuous rôle in the death-situation as well as in other complexes, that it would be unreasonable to assume that this phase has been the outcome of various immigrations. Again, secrecy is such a common feature not only in " secret societies ", but in every form of ceremonial and ritualistic activity, that it seems improbable that this characteristic is always due to a foreign element. Although Rivers acknowledges the possibility of an alternate interpretation, he rejects it in favour of diffusion. Nevertheless, he is alive to the importance of the psychological aspects of culture, a phase which Graebner has overlooked.

OUR METHOD

In burial rites we have a phenomenon of world wide distribution, connected with certain common human elements such as death itself, the various attitudes towards it, the fear of the ghost, the significance of burial, the specific attitude toward the corpse, and the problem of life after death. As before intimated, it is evident that many of these features have

[1] Rivers, *History of Melanesian Society*, Vol. II, p. 585.

been developed independently and they will be found again and again as our concrete material shows. Then we find some elements associated with burial rites which suggest other ethnological phenomena. Among them may be mentioned name, food, and sexual taboos, lacerations, wailings, and injunctions relating to hair, the use of an exit or entrance other than that of the ordinary one, retirement to a hut or lodge, feasts, dancing ceremonies, and purification rites. As the subsequent discussion illustrates, these phenomena are associated with various complexes. We feel perfectly justified in assuming then that, as different phases of culture developed, there was an association in local peculiarities and other aspects of culture. Since the deceased was in the realm of the unfathomable and incomprehensible, a corpse was associated with everything mysterious and uncanny and was placed in the same category as thunder, lightning, earthquakes, spirits, and other phenomena of nature and magic. Hence, arose the necessity of propitiating such a spirit, otherwise, it might bring disaster upon the living. At first, perhaps, hair cutting in conjunction with mourning was unknown. But as magical practices developed in a special group, and when the belief in sympathetic magic was in the ascendency, it is easy to conceive how hair began to be looked upon as a " pars pro toto " of the deceased ; no wonder then of its connection with mourning customs ; or again, since it might have been observed that hair keeps growing even after death, there might have arisen in the mind of the savage a belief in the efficacy and strength of hair. Naturally, then, it became identified with death, one of the two supreme crises in the life of an individual. Then, because of its great power it might have become connected with other events of moment such as when a vow was to be taken or at times of special danger. Again, we are not surprised to find the head conceived of as the seat of life, the use of hair as a charm, the various restrictions after hair cutting regarded by many tribes as a sacred event and the dedication of hair to a god. There is no reason why these associations should not have taken place, each developed independently of the other.

Again, another illustration of a different type to show how customs are often a reflex of the cultural setting. Thus, in all the areas selected as a basis for this study, we find numerous

instances where the manner of disposal of a dead body is
dependent upon the rank of the deceased. Not so, however,
in Siberia. The reason is very evident. Since the Chukchee
and Koryak represent the simplest form of social organization
with the family as the unit, rank is unknown, and hence rank
considerations would not figure in the burial rites. However, in other areas, such as Australia and Melanesia, where
the forms of social organization are far more complicated,
the rank of an individual is of prime importance, and as a
result we find many examples of rank distinctions in connection with burial. Analysis reveals the fact that many
characteristics, which at first glance may seem to be identified
with the death complex alone, are by no means peculiar to
it. Just as Dr. Goldenweiser, in his diagnosis of totemism,[1]
has shown that the so-called classical attributes of totemism
are by no means common to all totemic complexes, but may be
intimately identified with rites not at all connected with totemism, so an attempt shall be made to prove by an intensive
study of certain areas (since an exhaustive study of all is not
possible) that the same holds good of the death situation,
though in a form perhaps less marked. Although an analysis
of such features may show the independence of some of the
constituent phases of the death complex of each other,
there are characteristics of the "just so" death situation
which are so identified with it, that they must be regarded as
parts of its very essence. What has been attempted then,
is to explain the death-situation by identifying it whenever
possible, with the culture of the group we are considering, and
thus to trace the sources of the death-situation complex.
Although we agree with the writer of the article in *Science*.[2]
that the ideal of such a treatise "would be to state where,
among whom, and under what conditions, these elements
were associated with the present complex", yet we cannot,
because of the paucity of our information in certain instances,
always find a solution along such ideal lines.

As we are interested in processes by means of which certain
stages of culture have developed, we have endeavoured to

---

[1] Goldenweiser, "Totemism, an Analytical Study", *J.A.F.L.*, Vol.
XXIII (1910), pp. 179-292.
[2] Wissler, "Psychological and Historical Interpretations for Culture ",
Science, Vol. XLIII (1916), p.194.

ascertain the history of definite phenomena by a purely inductive method. Actual history, then, forms the basis of our deductions. Although we see the limitations of the old comparative method, yet we recognize the results obtained through such an approach if the comparability of the material is tested. In this case, the processes of growth must be compared to see if there is uniformity.

The idea is to make an intensive investigation of several areas, the Melanesian, Australian, North-East Siberian, and Indian areas of Asia,* especially stressing the Vedic conceptions, and then, by the use of the comparative method, to make a generalized statement of the death conceptions of the world. "The history of the case is necessary and this cannot be reconstructed from an ensemble of culture traits, however minutely they may be described in psychological terms ".[1]

The material utilized in this study is not presented, as in Frazer's works, from heterogeneous sources, but from the special areas under consideration. Not only would such a study be undesirable, even well-nigh impossible, because of the lack of scientific data, but the object is not to write a book of mortuary customs. That the conclusions are tentative, and that much remains to be done along the lines already laid out, is well known to the writer.

However, when such a phenomenon as the idea of the unnatural character of death is shown to be common to all primitive tribes, such an attitude has been explained, not only by a study of the special areas under consideration, but by some heterogeneous material introduced to show that such a phenomenon exists almost universally.

After making such an analysis as indicated of complexes connected with burial rites, a comparison reveals the fact that there are certain common features in all areas, such as the causes of death, the significance of burial, the dread of the spirit, the specific attitude toward the corpse, mourning rites, taboos, the potent power of the name, and feasts for the dead. Some of the elements have evidently developed through

---

* These areas have been chosen inasmuch as knowledge of the territories specified is such as to warrant satisfactory results.

[1] Wissler, " Psychological and Historical Interpretations for Culture ". *Science*, Vol. XLIII (1916), p. 194.

psychological channels, and in many cases we may assume independent development to have taken place. Perhaps the particular form which certain burial rites and subsequent taboos and ceremonies assume, may be attributed to the development of a certain pattern adopted by the group. The investigation shows that such a form is different in Siberia from in India, and the same may be said of the other areas. Thus certain social units become moulded into an organized ceremony which becomes a model or pattern along the lines of which other observances are developed. The traits which enter the cultural complex from without finally become identified with such a pattern. Thus many beliefs and ceremonies often follow such patterns which are usually few and well defined.[1]

If we look into the question of complex ceremonialism, for instance, and note the paucity of group ceremonial observances in some areas, such as the Mackenzie and Plateau areas of North America, and their intensive use in others, as in the South-West, we might at first, as Lowie[2] intimates, ascribe this difference to psychological variations between tribes. However, mention merely can be made that such a fact might be accounted for by the diffusion of the cultural traits in some areas, and not in others, and that the pattern already organized from within might also be a potent factor toward contributing toward the result. It may be added in connection with burial rites that they often assume a far more pronounced character in some areas than in others.

Part II in this study is concerned with the differentia of the death-situation. Here an attempt has been made to explain the variation in burial rites by the peculiarities of the specific cultures and by drawing into the burial-complex features which are not psychologically derivable from it.

Thus, although disposal of the dead is such a common feature in the death situation that it can be said to exist universally, yet we note that the methods of such disposal are often dependent upon certain attitudes which are reflections of the cultural background. Naturally then, since burial

---

[1] Goldenweiser, " Principle of Limited Possibilities ", *J.A.F.L.*, Vol. XXVI (1913), p. 270.
[2] Lowie, " Ceremonialism in North America ", *A.A.*, Vol. XVI (1914), p. 620.

rites are so universally practised, we would expect numerous phases of the culture of a group in evidence in these differences. An attempt will be made to correlate the variations in observances and ceremonies with the general culture. All those phases of culture which are of sufficient import will be studied and their connection with the general death situation, as well as the persistency with which they enter the complex, will be shown. Hence, many elements seemingly foreign to the death situation will necessarily be drawn in to prove that certain social and physical determinants must be considered before any scientific conclusion can be reached.

PART I
SIMILARITIES

CHAPTER I

ORIGIN OF DEATH

IF we take a glance into the tales regarding the origin and the causes of death, we will perceive that all of them emphasize most strikingly its unnatural character.

CASTING OF THE SKIN

MELANESIA.

In the Shortland Islands, the people relate that the great foremother of the race sloughed her skin at intervals and remained eternally young. The catastrophe of death occurred because she was once disturbed in the operation by the screaming of her child, and it was thus that death made its appearance.[1]

NEW POMERANIA

The Wise Spirit ordained that snakes should die, but men should slough their skins and live forever. His brother reversed the decree.[2] We find parallel accounts of the origin of death in Saa, Banks Islands, and New Hebrides.

BANKS ISLAND STORY

At first men never died, but when they advanced in life they cast their skins like snakes and crabs and came out with life renewed. After a time a woman, growing old, went to a stream to change her skin. According to some she was the

[1] "Haddon's Review of Ribbe's Zwei Jahre unter den Kannibalen der Salomo-Inseln", *F.L.*, Vol. XVI (1905), p. 115.

A similar story to that related in the Shortland Islands is told by the Baluba on the border of the Congo State, but here the operation is interrupted by the woman's fellow-wife.

Similar stories are found in the Admiralty Islands. Meier, 'Mythen und Sagen der Admiralitatsinsualaner", *Anthropos*, Vol. III (1908), p. 193, among the Vuatom of Bismarck Archipelago, among the Nias who occupy an island off Sumatra, the Arawaks of British Guinea, the Tamanchiers, an Indian tribe on the Orinoco. (Quoted by Frazer,* pp. 70-71.)

[2] Foy, "Melanesier", *Archiv für Religionswissenschaft*, Vol. X (1907), p. 308.

(* When " quoted by Frazer " is mentioned in this manner, Volume I of his *Belief in Immortality* is referred to.)

mother of Iat, according to others, Wetamarama, change-skin of the world. After throwing off her old skin in the water she returned home to her child. But the child refused to acknowledge her rejuvenated parent, and the mother then decided to don the old skin. From this time on mankind refused to cast their skins and death followed. In another Banks Island story this woman is Iro Puget, Bird's-Nest-Fern, the wife of Mate, Death. At Saa, as at Banks Island and New Hebrides, Death is ascribed to an old woman who after changing her skin, made use again of the slough which had been caught upon a reed.

One of the many other stories accounts for Death because of the inconvenience of the permanence of property in the same hands while men changed their skins and lived for ever.[1]

LEPERS' ISLAND

Here the origin of death is said to be due to the disuse of the power of changing the skin, and to a defect in nature, which has not given men that power. Once a woman and a crab disputed, the woman claiming that the crab was better than men since it had the power to change its skin. But we note that the story is told in varying forms in Solomon Islands, the Banks group, and New Hebrides. According to these versions, men had in former times the ability to change their skins. An old woman had two grandchildren who one day were attempting to block back the water of a little brook, when the stream washed down a chestnut. One of the boys gave the nut to his grandmother to roast, but the other lad, who pretended to hate it, stole a march on his companion and ate the nut. When the defeated boy saw what a trick had been played on him he scolded his grandparent for her neglect. Thereupon she replied : "You two don't wish to live forever, but should rather that we should not live". She had just come from changing her cast-off skin in the stream which the boys were blocking. They had seen the skin, picked it up with a stick, and thrown it out of the water. The old woman finally reached the bank where the skin was lying, and donned it again. Since then mankind have been unable to change their skins and death has been the result.[2]

---

[1] Codrington, *Melanesians*, pp. 265-266.
[2] *Ibid*, pp. 283-284.

ORIGIN OF DEATH 23

CASTING OF THE SKIN AND REVERSAL OF A DECREE

At Araga, Pentecost, we have another story about the changing of the skin. A man who had two boys living with him, used to change his skin daily when he worked with them. One day he put on his old skin, and the boys killed him because they had been deceived. All men would have had everlasting life had he not died.[1]

They say that the Kambinana, the Good Spirit, loved men and wished to make them immortal, but he hated the serpents and wished to kill them. So he called his brother To-Korvuvu and said : " Go to men and tell them the secret of immortality. Tell them to cast their skins every year. By this means death can be warded off and renewal of life will be possible, but tell serpents that death must be their lot ". However, To-Korvuvu reversed the message, and revealed to the serpents the secret of immortality. Since then men have been mortal, and serpents, by casting their skins, immortal.[2]

INDIA

We find a similar tale in Annam. They say that Ngochoang sent a messenger from heaven to men to say that when they reached old age they should change their skins and live forever, but when advanced old age was attained, serpents must die. The messenger then came to earth and repeated the message as directed, much to the indignation of the serpents, who declared that unless the decree were reversed, they would bite him. Whereupon the order was repeated thus : " When he is old, the serpent shall cast his skin, but when man is old he shall die and be laid in a coffin."[3]

---

[1] *Ibid*, p. 287.

[2] Kleintitschen, *Die Küstenbewohner der Gazellehalbinsel*, p. 334, quoted by Frazer, p. 69.

[3] Landes, " Contes et Légendes Annamites Cochinchne francaise " *Excursions et Reconnaissances*, no. 25, p. 108, quoted by Frazer, p. 70.

The stories such as Frazer has placed in the category of the two Messengers (Frazer, *The Belief in Immortality and the Worship of the Dead*, Vol. I, pp. 61-63), are common in Africa, especially among the Bantu tribes. The principle of diffusion would account for the prevalence of such stories found among tribes living in such close proximity to each other.

The contiguity of such stories can be seen among the Bechuanas (Chapman, *Travels in the Interior of South Africa*, Vol. I, p. 47), the Basutos (Caralis, *The Basutos*, p. 242), and the Ngori (Elmslia, *Amongst Wild Ngori*, p. 70).

With variations the same story is found among the Akamba of British East Africa, the Togos of German West Africa and the Ashantees of West Africa (Frazer, pp. 62-63).

The Chams of further India saw a female figure in the moon. She was a goddess who restored the dead to life until the great sky-god, chagrined with this interference with eternal laws, transported her to the moon.[1]

AUSTRALIA

Among the Kaitish and Unmatjera there is a belief that formerly when men were buried they came to life again in three days. The Kaitish believe that permanent death was due to an old man who was tired of this arrangement and wanted to die once for all. This desire was secured by kicking into the sea the body of one who had just died and was temporarily buried.[2]

MOON TALES

MELANESIA

CAROLINE ISLANDS

They say that long, long ago, death was unknown, or rather it was a short sleep, not as long as it is now. Men died on the last day of the waning moon and came to life again on the first appearance of the new moon, just as if they had awakened from a refreshing slumber. But an evil spirit once contrived that when men slept the sleep of death they should sleep no more.[3]

FIJI ISLANDS

They say that once upon a time the moon contended that men should be like himself (for the Fijian moon seems to be a male) ; that is, just as he grows old, disappears, and comes in sight again, so men, grown old, should vanish for a while and then return to life. But the rat, who is a Fijian god, would not hear of it : " No ", said he, " let men die like rats ". And he had the best of it in a dispute, for men die like rats to this day.[4]

AUSTRALIA

Arunta Tale

Before there was a moon in the sky a man died and was buried. When the people ran away from him he followed,

---

[1] Cabaton, *Nouvelles Researches sur les Chams,* p. 19.
[2] Spencer and Gillen, *Northern Tribes of Central Australia,* pp. 513-514.
[3] *Lettres Edifiantes et Curieuses, Nouvelle Edition,* p. 305, quoted by Frazer, p. 67.
[4] Williams, *Fiji and the Fijians,* Vol. I, p. 205.

calling that if they fled they would have no hope of resurrection, while he would die and rise again in the sky.[1]

From a Wotjobaluk story we learn that when people died the moon used to say : " You, up again ", but the old man said, " Let them remain dead ", and since then none has ever come to life again except the moon.[2]

RESULT OF DISOBEDIENCE TO THE DIVINE COMMAND
MELANESIA

Some of the Fijians account for deaths as follows :

When the first man, the father of the human race, was being

---

[1] Spencer and Gillen, *Northern Tribes of Central Australia*, p. 249 ; *Native Tribes of Central Australia*, p. 564.

[2] Howitt, *The Natives of South-East Australia*, p. 429.

The Indians of San Juan Capistrano, in California, used to call together all the young men on the day when the new moon first appeared and make them run about while the old men danced in a circle saying, " As the moon dieth, cometh to life again, so we also having to die, will again live." (Father G. Boscano, " Chinigchinich ", in *Life in California, by an American*, p. 298.) Quoted by Frazer, p. 68.

An old writer narrates that in the Congo district, at the appearance of every new moon, the natives clapped their hands and cried out, sometimes falling on their knees, " So may I renew my life, as thou art renewed. (Merolla, " Voyage to Congo," in *Pinkerton's Voyages and Travels*, Vol. XVI, p. 273.)

Hottentot Story. The Namaquas or Hottentots say that once the moon charged the hare to go to men and say : " As I die, and rise to life again, so shall you die and rise to life again." So the hare went to men, but either out of forgetfulness or malice he reversed the message, and said : " As I die, and do not rise to life again, so you shall also die and not rise to life again." Then he went back to the moon and she asked him what he had said. He told her, and when she heard how he had given the wrong message, she was so angry that she threw a stick at him, and split his lip, which is the reason why a hare's lip is still split. So the hare ran away, and is still running to this day. Some people, however, say that before he fled he clawed the moon's face, which still bears the marks of the scratching, as anybody may see for himself on a clear moonlight-night. So the Hottentots are still angry with the hare for bringing death into the world. (Alexander, *Expedition of Discovery into the Interior of Africa*, Vol. I, p. 129.)

In another Hottentot version we note the appearance of two messengers, an insect and a hare. The insect is charged by the moon with a message of resurrection to men ; but the hare persuades the insect to let him bear the tidings, which he perverts into a message of destruction. Here the type of the two messenger stories corresponds to the moon type (Bleek, *Reynard the Fox in South Africa*, pp. 69-74 ; five versions of the story are given here.)

Masai story (East Africa). They narrate that in early days a god told a man that if a child were to die he was to throw away the body and say : " Man die, and come back again ; moon die, and remain away." Soon afterwards, a child died, but it was not one of the man's own children, so when he threw the body away he said : " Man die, and remain away ; moon die and return." Afterwards one of his own children died, and when he threw away the body he said : " Man die, and return ; moon die and remain away." But God said to him, " It is of no use now, for you spoilt matters in the other child." That is why down to this day when a man dies he returns no more, but when the moon dies, she always comes to life again. (Hollis, *The Masai*, p. 271.)

buried, a god passed by the grave and inquired what it meant, for he had never seen a grave before. Upon receiving the information from those about the place of interment that they had just buried their father, he said : " Do not bury him, dig up the body again ". " No ", they replied, " we cannot do that. He has been dead for four days and smells ". " Not so ", entreated the god, " dig him up and I promise you that he will live again ". But they refused to carry out the divine injunction. Then the god declared, " By disobeying me, you have sealed your own fate. Had you dug up your ancestor, you would have found him alive, and you yourselves when you passed from this world should have been buried as bananas are for four days, after which you shall have been dug up, not rotten, but ripe. But now, as a punishment for your disobedience, you shall die and rot ". And whenever they hear this sad tale the Fijians say : " Oh, that those children had dug up that body " !¹

AUSTRALIA

Among various tribes in New South Wales it is said that men were supposed to live forever. They were forbidden to approach a certain tree where the wild bees made a nest. Despite many warnings, some women who coveted the honey attacked the tree with tomahawks. Whereupon out flew a bat which was Death. From now on it could claim all whom it could touch with its wings.[2*]

MISCELLANEOUS TALES

MELANESIA

In a Fijian tale death is due to the rebellion of the gods instigated by Hikuleo, the evil one.[3]

AUSTRALIA

When man first began to exist there were two beings, a male and a female, Walleyneup and Doronop. Their son, Bindir-

[1] Williams, *Fiji and the Fijians*, Vol. I, p. 204.
[2] Smyth, *The Aborigines of Victoria*, Vol. I, p. 428.
* The Yaos and Wayisa of East Central Africa attributed death to lizards. It was originally brought into the world by a woman who taught two men to go to sleep. One day while they were sleeping she held the nostrils of one of them until his breath was no more and then he died. (Macdonald, " East Central African Customs," *J.A.I.*, Vol. XXII (1893), pp. 111-112.)
[3] Fison, *Tales from Old Fiji*, pp. 139-161.

woor, received a deadly wound for which there was no cure. Thereupon the father declared that all who came after him should die. But he did not remain in the grave and went to the unknown land of spirits across the sea. His parents who went after him were unable to persuade him to return so they remained with him ever since.[1]

INDIA

At first no Todas died. After a time a man died and the people wept bitterly. While they were taking the body to the burial place, the goddess Teikirzi took pity on them and came to bring him back to life. But while some wept, others seemed to rejoice. Whereupon the goddess changed her mind and instead of resurrecting the dead man, decreed that the funeral ceremony should take place.[2]*

In many of the stories cited as identified with our area, the moon plays a conspicuous part in the legends, and so others have been introduced to show how different persons connect the moon with death. Although the common use of this idea in various parts of Australia in districts in proximity to each other, and in many almost contiguous areas in Africa, may suggest historical contact between the individual tribes in Australia with each other, as well as those in Africa with one another, yet a reason must be adduced to account for the persistency of such ideas in regions as far apart as Australia, Africa, Melanesia, and America. Here a psychological explanation is deemed sufficient, inasmuch as the observation and meditation of the phases of the moon naturally suggest death and restoration to life. The cycle of death

---

[1] Thomas, *The Natives of Australia*, p. 245.

[2] Rivers, *The Todas*, p. 400.

* When Baldur of Scandinavian fame was slain, the goddess Hel promised to release him if all things wept for his death. (*Hastings*, Vol. IV, p. 412.) The idea that death is due to a decision of two personages, one of whom wishes man to be mortal, the other immortal, is frequently met with in North America (Boas, " The Origin of Death," *J.A.F.L.*, Vol. XXX (1918), No. 118, pp. 486-491). This takes two forms ; a western one, where the decision is made by a council and another in which it is due to divination. Prof. Boas points out that in the western version all the typical forms of the story end with the incident that the child of the person who instituted death dies, and then the decision cannot be rescinded. He shows how this idea is found in a continuous area from California northward as far as the Lillooet. The divination version is found among the Athapascan tribes, the Arapaho, the Blackfoot, the Cheyenne, the Comanche, the Jicarilla Apache, and Navajo, thus including the entire area from the eastern foot hills of the Rocky Mountains. (*Ibid*, p. 490.)

and resurrection after three days so often found, was suggested by the monthly disappearance and reappearance of the moon.[1] From this we do not wish it to be inferred that the resurrection idea itself is attributable to the influence of the moon alone, for we are fully cognizant of the many reasons that can be adduced to account for the supposed resurrection of the dead to life.*

If we examine the first Hottentot tale given we shall see that therein is combined the stories of the Moon and the Reversal of the Decree Type, with an explanation element added. This explanatory phase is evidently no part of the original story, but here we have the principle of secondary association. The unrelated elements certainly could have had no connection with the primary tale. The explanatory element then must be considered a recent adaptation of the story, influenced by the specific cultural setting and the tendency for explanations. In such a case the myth bears evidence of an historical development, its original form having been modified by influences from various sources.

The Masai story also shows the combination of the moon tale with the Reversal of a Decree story; in the second Hottentot narrative we see the coupling of the moon idea with the Two Messengers Type. We may add that we cannot find in our special areas any stories which Frazer characterizes as of the Banana type.[2]

We note that in the stories mentioned referring to the inhabitants of the Shortland Islands, New Pomerania, and the Aruntas, death is accounted for by the fact that the sloughing of the skin operation by women was interrupted. Perhaps we are justified in assigning the following psychological reasons for the similarity in such tales.

(1) The desire for long life is one of the prominent life values.

(2) Such a longing for restoration of youth is especially

---

[1] Frazer, *Belief in Immortality*, Vol. I, p. 67.
* Some causes which may account for the persistency with which the moon figures in different phases of primitive life.
   1. It shines by night as well as by day.
   2. General phases in the moon's appearance, its waning or waxing.
   3. Moisture connected with the moon.
   4. Tidal effect of the moon.
   5. Growth identified with the waxing moon.
[2] Frazer, *Belief in Immortality*, Vol. I, p. 73.

characteristic of women, especially since females show marks of age before males.

(3) Age becomes first evident in facial and other lines, hence measures must be employed to eradicate them.

However, we have been unable to find any evidence to account for the interruption of the process other than that such would be a most natural and convenient way of explaining such a phenomenon. Change of actors, such as we see in the two stories, is characteristic of many tales. The explanations we have in these narratives, dealing with the origin of death, can be looked upon as recent developments, and furthermore we have no evidence as to what the stories were in their original form.

The shedding of the skin, which is a common element in the Saa, Banks Islands, and the New Hebrides tales, is easily explainable by the fact that such a deduction was made after concrete experiences, and observation which passed through the psychic channel. Thus, the phenomenon of the change of skin, with its accompanying effects, must have been often noted by the natives of these islands. Here not only observation, but generalization, is involved.

Again, in several of the tales cited, those belonging to the Aruntas, the Todas, and the Scandinavians, we note that restoration could not be effected unless all individuals bewailed the loss of the dead, and a unanimous judgment must therefore be secured before restoration could be an established fact.

Although the appearance of similar stories relating to the origin of death in a fairly contiguous area seems to point to the diffusion theory in Australia and Africa, yet we must remember, as we have endeavoured to show, that the simple reaction of the imagination is not due in all cases to a common historical source. These ideas expressed in the tales we have cited have naturally developed into similar incidents, and their interpretation must often be looked for in psychological processes, which result in a convergent development of certain phases of the stories.

" The desire to see the dead restored to life seems a sufficient explanation to account for the origin of death. Naturally we should expect to find the sentiment everywhere

in evidence that there should be no death. The mere occurrence of stories of the origin of death in one place due to the miscarriage of a message conveyed from an animal, in others of a bet or quarrel between two beings, is not a proof of common origin. This proof requires identity of the stories. We can even understand how, under these conditions, stories of the same literary type may become almost ·identical in form without having a common origin."[1]

[1] Boas, "Mythology and Folk Tales of the North American Indians," *J.A.F.L.*, Vol. XXVII (1914), pp. 409-410.

CHAPTER II

CAUSES OF DEATH

AUSTRALIA

(1) *South-East Australia*

(*a*) Gringai County. Before the body was lowered into the grave, the medicine man, standing at the head, spoke to find out who caused its death, and he received an answer from another medicine man at the foot of the grave.[1]

(*b*) Port Stephens. Before placing the corpse in the grave two men held it on their shoulders, while a third, standing at the side, struck the body lightly with a green bough, at the same time calling out loudly the names of the acquaintances of the deceased as well as of others. The belief was that when the name of the person who had caused his death was spoken, the deceased would shake and the corpse bearers would do the same. Then revenge was sought.[2]

(*c*) Wiradjuri. A strange belief is found among the Wiradjuri. When a man is near death he is supposed to see the shadow of the person who is causing his death by evil magic. Under such circumstances he will say to those about him, " Get out of my way, so that I may see who it is who has ' caught ' me ".

We find the same belief elsewhere, as for instance, in the Jupagalk tribe. Howitt also recalls a case among the Kurnai, that when a member of this tribe was dying, his friend who was with him asked repeatedly, " Can you see who it is ? " and was greatly disconcerted when the dying man was unable to tell him.[3]

(*d*) Jupagalk. When a Jupagalk man died, all the men went out of the camp at dusk and watched carefully to see the gulkangulkan of the man who killed him (that is, by

[1] Howitt, *Native Tribes of South-East Australia*, p. 464.
[2] *Ibid*, p. 465.
[3] *Ibid*, p. 466.

31

magic) peeping out of the bush about the camp. After they ascertained the culprit they organized a sneaking party and went quietly and killed him.[1]

(e) Chepara tribe. If a man becomes ill in the Chepara tribe, it is believed that a man of another tribe has " caught " him ; for instance, by giving him a possum rug made deadly by magic. This fact the sick man communicates to his fellow-tribesmen, and they adopt measures later to avenge him. The medicine-man in his dreams will see the culprit, and also the immediate cause of death, which has been in the gift flying back to the river.[2]

(f) Herbert River tribes. No one is believed by the tribes of the Herbert River to die from any cause but the magic of some neighbouring tribe.[3]

(2) *Wimmera District (Victoria)*

The clever men and the relatives watch the corpse over night. They see the wraith of the slayer approach with stealthy steps to view the result of its machinations. After having seemingly satisfied itself, it disappears in the direction of the hunting grounds of its own people and the relatives of the deceased know upon what tribe to wreak their vengeance.[4]

(3) *North Australia*

It not infrequently happens that with the assistance of the medicine-men, the Gammona learns who really was the cause of his Ikuntera's death. It is then his duty to organize an avenging party to kill the guilty person.[5]

(4) *Warramunga*

A mound of earth is raised on the exact spot where a man has died. A few days after the death a visit is paid to this spot to see if the tracks of any individual or living creature can be found. By such marks the totem of the culprit is found.[6]

---

[1] Howitt, *Native Tribes of South-East Australia*, p. 455.
[2] *Ibid*, p. 468.
[3] *Ibid*, p. 474.
[4] Hartland, *Hastings Encyclopedia*, Vol. IV, p. 413.
[5] Spencer and Gillen, *Native Tribes of Central Australia*, p. 51.
[6] Spencer and Gillen, *Northern Tribes of Central Australia*, p. 526.

(5) *Central Australia*

" No such thing as natural death is realized by the native ; a man who dies has of necessity been killed by another man, or perhaps even by a woman, and sooner or later that man or woman will be attacked. In the normal condition of the tribe every death meant the killing of another individual ".[1]

(6) *Western Australia*

(*a*) " The natives do not allow that there is such a thing as a death from natural causes ; they believe that if it were not for murderers, and the malignity of sorcerers, they might live forever ; hence when a native dies from the effects of an accident, or from some natural cause, they use a variety of superstitious ceremonies to ascertain in which direction the sorcerer lives whose evil practices have brought about the death of their relative ; this point being satisfactorily settled by friendly sorcerers, they then attach the crime to some individual, and the funeral obsequies are scarcely concluded ere they start to avenge their supposed wrongs ".[2]

(*b*) Watch-an-die tribe. They possess the comforting assurance that nearly all diseases, and consequent deaths, are caused by the enchantments of hostile tribes, and were it not for the malevolence of their enemies they would (with few exceptions) live for ever. Consequently, on the first approach of sickness, their first endeavour is to ascertain whether the Boollia (magic) of their own tribe is not sufficiently potent to counteract that of their foes. Should the patient recover, they are proud of the superiority of their enchantment over that of their enemies, but should the Boollia within the sick man prove stronger than their own, as there is no help for it, he must die, and the utmost they can do in this case is to revenge his death.[3]

But the same writer also states : " It is not true that the New Hollanders impute all deaths to the Boollia of un-friendly tribes, for in most cases of persons wasting visibly before them, they do not entertain the idea. It is chiefly in cases of sudden death, or where the body of the deceased is

---

[1] Spencer and Gillen, *Native Tribes of Central Australia*, p. 48.
[2] Grey, *Journals of Two Expeditions of Discovery in North-West and Western Australia*, Vol. II, p. 238.
[3] Oldfield, " The Aborigines of Australia ", *Transactions of the Ethnological Society of London*, N.S., Vol. III (1865), p. 236.

fat or in good condition, that this belief prevails, and it is only in such contingencies that it becomes an imperative duty to have revenge ".

(c) Kamilaroi tribe of New South Wales. " In some parts of the country a belief prevails that death through disease is in many, if not in all, cases the result of an enemy's malice. It is a common saying when illness or death comes, that some one has thrown his belt at the victim. There are various modes of fixing upon the murderer. One is to let an insect fly from the body of the deceased and see toward whom it goes. The person thus singled out is doomed ".[1]

Reference has before been made to the fact that all primitives regard death as an unnatural occurrence. Among the causes assigned for death, the following stand out most prominently :

I—Death as Due to the Antagonism of Some Individual Exercising Magical Rites

Melanesia

(1) *British New Guinea*

(a) The natives of Mowat or Mowatta in British New Guinea, do not believe in a natural death, but attribute even the decease of an old man to the agency of some enemy known or unknown.[2]

(b) Hood Peninsula. A belief here that no one dies a natural death. Every death is due either to the sorcery of a living or dead relative.[3]

(2) *Solomon Islands*

The natives of New Georgia, one of the Solomon Islands, think that when an individual is sick or dies he must be bewitched by a man or woman, since natural sickness is impossible.[4]

(3) *New Britain*

Amongst the Melanesians few, if any, are not killed in war, they are supposed to die from the effects of witchcraft

---

[1] Ridley, *Kamilaroi*, p. 159.
[2] Beardmore, "The Natives of Mowat, British New Guinea ", *J.A.I.*, Vol. XIX (1890), p. 461.
[3] Guise, " Out-Tribes Inhabiting the Mouth of the Wanigela River, New Guinea," *J.A.I.*, Vol. XXVIII (1899), p. 216.
[4] Ribbe, *Zwei Jahre unter den Kannibalen der Salomo-Insel*, p. 268.

or magic. Dr. Brown's account applies to the natives of New Britain and especially to those of the neighbouring Duke of York Islands.[1]

(4) *Gazelle Peninsula*

All deaths are attributed to the agency of witchcraft, and a sorcerer is called to find out who by evil magic has done the deed.[2]*

At Kai in German New Guinea " sorcery is regarded as the cause of all deaths. All men without exception die in consequence of the baneful arts of these sorcerers and accomplices ".[3]

II—Death Attributed to the Action of Evil Spirits

We must not lose sight of the fact, as Frazer suggests,[4] that there is a difference between death due to direct action of spirits, and death attributed to the indirect influence of sorcerers. If the death is caused by witchcraft, the guilty one must be found and killed, whereas, if it is brought about by the action of a demon it cannot be avenged.

(1) North-West Australia

In the North-Western part of Australia every illness is ascribed to the djuno, an evil spirit otherwise known as the warrunga or warruga.[5]

(2) Siberia

(a) The Chukchee have little conception of death by natural means. When a man dies he is supposed to be killed by the spirits, or by an evil shaman, through the influence of his charms. One of the chief features of the funeral ceremony is the cutting open of the abdomen of the corpse, especially

---

[1] Brown, *Melanesians and Polynesians*, p. 176.

[2] Kleintitschen, *Die Küstenbewohner, der Gazellehalbinsel*, p. 344. Quoted by Frazer, p. 48.

* The Baganda attribute natural deaths either to sorcery or to the action of a ghost. The illness of a king is due to ghosts because no man dares to practice magic on him. (*Roscoe, The Baganda*, pp. 98, 100, 101, 268.)

[3] Keysser, "Aus dem Leben des Kaliente," in Neuhauss' *Deutsch New Guinea*, Vol. III, p. 134.

[4] Frazer, *The Belief in Immortality*, Vol. I, p. 27.

[5] Clement, "Ethnographical Notes on the Western Australian Aborigines" *Archives Internationales*, Vol. XVI (1904), p. 8.

the liver, to discover if possible, which spirit or shaman may have killed the deceased.[1]*

(b) The Koryak conceive of the kalau as malevolent beings that are hostile to mankind, and correspond to the Chukchee kelet which sometimes appears as an invisible being, killing people by supernatural or other invisible means, while at other times he is represented as a common cannibal.[2] The kala itself pulls the soul out of the human body and sets it free to go off to the sky to possess himself of the body and the other souls of the deceased.[3] From a Koryak tale we learn that the Big-Raven sends the kalau down to the people that they may die so that he can create others.[4]

Among the other reasons assigned for death is that naïve explanation that the deceased sent a kala to kill the inhabitants of a village because the young people used to play at night and disturbed the old people.[5]

A similar practice of dissecting the body to that found among the Chukchee is also practiced among the Koryak. The Reindeer Koryak of the Palpal Ridge dissect bodies before burning them to ascertain the cause for their death, and undoubtedly this custom was likewise practiced by other Koryak. The usage which is common among the Reindeer Koryak of the Taigonos Peninsula and the Maritime Koryak of Penshina Bay of piercing the abdomen of a corpse with a knife when it is lying on the pyre, and of stuffing the wound with some rags, in cases where death was caused by some internal disease, is regarded by Jochelson as a survival of this custom. The Koryak explain this practice by saying that it is done to protect the child, who later receives the soul and name of the deceased, against the malady from which the departed is supposed to have died.[6]

---

[1] Bogoras, *Chukchee*, *J.N.P.E.*, Vol. VII (1905), p. 298.

* Peoples as far apart as Balong and the Koryaks make a post-mortem examination (Hartland, Article in *Hastings*, Vol. IV, p. 413). Evil spirits steal away the soul for the purpose of eating it and they fatten before feasting on it. (Bogoras, *Chukchee Materials*, p. 17.) We find this conception in a clearer form among the Yahut. The evil spirits eat the soul, which is one of the three souls of men.

[2] Jochelson, *The Koryak*, *J.N.P.E.*, Vol. VI (1908), p. 27.

[3] *Ibid*, p. 101.

[4] *Ibid*, p. 27.

[5] *Ibid*, p. 103.

[6] *Ibid*, p. 113.

We also read that shamans frequently inflict disease upon men.[1]*

III—DEATH AS CAUSED BY OLD AGE

(1) MELANESIA

Of the Roro-speaking tribes it is said that " except in the case of old folk, death is admitted to occur without some obvious cause as a spear thrust ".[2]

(2) AUSTRALIA

Among the Port Lincoln tribes in South Australia, we find the belief that death by old age and from wounds is recognized as natural. " In all cases of death that do not arise from old age, wounds, or other equally palpable causes, the natives suspect that unfair means have been practised ".[3]

(3) VEDIC INDIAN

(a) Death is frequently mentioned in the Rig-Veda.[4] The Atharva-Veda is full of charms to avert death.[5] Seven times did the sages keep off death by effacing their footsteps.[6] From these accounts we learn that only one kind of death, that caused by old age, is natural. Any death before one hundred years is due, according to the early Indian conception, to the inadequate propitiation of the spirits that have man's life under their jurisdiction, or to the non-performance of a certain very intricate ceremony, which only the initiated could control. In Caland's treatise we are told of the Indian conception of avoiding night death, or of death in the dark half of the moon, or again of death in the dark season.[7] A most elaborate and complicated ceremony must be performed to

---

[1] Jochelson, *The Koryak, J.N.P.E.*, Vol. VI (1908), p. 101.
* A Persian conception of the Avestan period is that every creature dies when the demon of death comes to it. (*Av.* 40.)
    The natives of Guiana believe that death may arise from a wound or concussion or may be brought about by want of food, but in other cases it is the work of the " Yauhahu," or evil spirit. (Brett, *The Indian Tribes of Guiana*, p. 357.)
[2] Seligman, *The Melanesians of British New Guinea*, p. 279.
[3] Schürmann, *The Aboriginal Tribes of Port Lincoln in South Australia*, p. 279, in *Native Tribes of South Australia*, p. 237.
[4] *Rv.* VII, 59, 12 ; X, 13, 5 ; X, 48, 15.
[5] *Av.* I, 30, 3 ; II, 28, 1 ; VIII, 2, 17 ; XI, 6, 11.
[6] Bloomfield, " The Interpretation of the Veda," *American Journal of Philology*, Vol. XII (1891), p. 416n.
[7] Caland, *Altendische Todten Gebraucher*, p. 6.

prevent such a catastrophe as departure from life at these specified times. We hear from Vedic literature that the allotted time of man's sojourn on earth is one hundred years.[1]* However, the loss of physical strength and the evils of old age are clearly recognized.[2]

IV—DEATH DUE TO VIOLENCE

(1) MELANESIA

(a) In the Island of Nvalso, one of the New Hebrides, we hear of the belief firmly established in the minds of the natives that nobody dies a natural death except as a result of violence, poison, or sorcery.[3]

(b) At Saa the term " akalo " is used for the soul of a living person and the ghost of an ordinary individual. The " akalo " which departs from the body in dreams and returns in death never finds its way back. After a natural death it leaves the body ra'e, after a violent death, lalamoa.[4]

(2) AUSTRALIA

South-East Australia

(a) The Turrbal attributed all deaths other than those caused by violence or in battle, to magic.[5]

(b) Among the Unghi, when a young man has met with a violent death it is the custom to wash the body and let his kinsmen carry it out. The reason assigned for this custom is that he has died before his time, and therefore could not rest in his grave.[6]

V—DEATH SOMETIMES ASCRIBED TO THE ESCAPE OF THE SOUL FROM THE BODY

As Hartland suggests,[7] from Siberia to Australia, from Puget Sound to the Islands of the Eastern Archipelago, means are

---

[1] *Rv.* I, 64, 14 ; 89, 9.

* Likewise the Old Testament tells us that man's existence on earth shall be three score years and ten. The weakness of old age as the cause of death is a belief amongst the Wadjagga of Central Africa (*Globus*, Vol.LXXXIX (1906), p. 198).

[2] *Rv.* I, 71, 10 ; 179, 1..

[3] Deniau, " Croyances religieuses et moeurs indigenes l'ile Malo," *Missions Catholiques*, Vol. XXXIII (1910), p. 315, quoted by Frazer, p. 48.

[4] Codrington, *Melanesians*, p. 260.

[5] Howitt, *Native Tribes of South-East Australia*, p. 469.

[6] *Ibid*, p. 468.

[7] Hartland, article in *Hastings' Dictionary*, Vol. IV, p. 412.

employed to prevent the soul from wandering and to bring it back to the body. The permanent loss of the soul means nothing more than death.

(1) MELANESIA

The soul, talegi or atai, goes out of the body in some dreams, and if for some reason it does not come back, the man is found dead in the morning. In true death the separation of the body and the soul is complete.[1]

(2) AUSTRALIA

The Marup, Yambo, Bulalong represent during life the self-consciousness of the individual. Its supposed ability to depart from the body during sleep leads naturally to the belief that death is caused by its disability to enter permanently its former body. This, as before pointed out, is brought about by the evil magic of some enemy. Thus it is that the belief is current that the individual continues his existence even after death, although it cannot gain access to its original body.[2]

VI—DEATH ATTRIBUTED TO A CURSE OR SPELL

AUSTRALIA

The Wakelbura of South-East Australia believe that no strong black would die unless someone had placed a spell on him.[3]*

Despite the fact that the unnatural character of death fills such an important function in the lives of primitives, yet we find sufficient instances of voluntary death or death by suicide in our areas. Among them we might mention the following conspicuous examples.

.   .   .   .   .   .

Among the other causes assigned we may specify death as a result of being killed in war, as is the belief of some of the tribes of New Britain and those of the Duke of York Islands.[4] We also find a similar conception among the Sioux and Omaha

[1] Codrington, *Melanesians*, p. 266.
[2] Howitt, *Native Tribes of South-East Australia*, p. 440.
[3] Howitt, *Ibid*, p. 471.
* An Eskimo tale accounts for death as the outcome of a quarrel between two men, one of whom desires to be mortal, the other wishes individuals to be immortal. Their words are regarded by Hartland as probably spells. (Rink, *Tales*, p. 41.)
[4] Brown, *Melanesians and Polynesians*, p. 176.

tribes. Death as due to the infraction of a taboo and neglect to offer sacrifice is illustrated in the case of the Koryak.[1]

In discussing the North-West Queensland Aborigines, Roth tells us of the death bone, the pearl plate and death powder, all of which are supposed to cause death. We likewise read of the bone pin which produces venereal and allied diseases which may be fatal or not. Drowning is thought to be due to a water snake, and a bogie man is responsible for a sudden disappearance. Death is regarded as a penalty and " were an individual always to remain good, he would, barring the munguni (death bone) or accident, or death by actual physical violence (spar boomerang), probably live for ever ; only a child can die by itself ".[2]

Although our investigation shows us that the unnatural character of death is universally recognized by savage tribes, yet we find a few isolated instances of primitives conceiving of its natural character too, other than voluntary death. Thus some of the Melanesians of New Hebrides and other parts of Central Melanesia believe that any serious sickness is caused by ghosts and spirits, whereas common complaints such as fever and ague are due to natural causes. " To say that a savage is never ill without supposing a supernatural cause, is not true of the Melanesians ".[3] The belief that death may be due to a natural cause is the conception of the natives of New Britain and of those of the Duke of York Islands.[4]

Fraser tells us that in New South Wales when a native is killed in battle or is so severely wounded that he dies, or is crushed to death by the falling branch of a tree, or dies from some other visible cause, his comrades do not wonder because the manner of the death is manifest, but it is otherwise when a man sickens and dies from no obvious cause.[5]

Curr has stressed the fact that the natives of Australia regard every death as due to old age or sorcery.[6]

---

[1] Jochelson, *The Koryak, J.N.P.E.*, Vol. VI (1905), p. 101.

[2] Despite the fact that the unnatural character of death fills such an important function in the lives of primitives, yet we find instances of voluntary death or death by suicide. (Roth, *Ethnological Studies among the North-West Central Queensland Aborigines*, pp. 152-161.)

Numerous cases of death by suicide also occur in the Siberian area.

[3] Codrington, *Melanesians*, p. 194.

[4] Brown, *Melanesians and Polynesians*, p. 176.

[5] Fraser, *The Aborigines of New South Wales*, p. 78.

[6] Curr, *The Australian Race*, Vol. I, p. 48 ; Vol. III, p. 27.

We have seen that death from old age is regarded as natural by some of the tribes of Melanesia and Australia, and by the Vedic Indian. The instances cited not only demonstrate the conception of the primitives in regard to the unnatural character of death, because of the non-recognition on the part of the savage of a natural law controlling phenomena, but they show us the potent power of magic and sorcery relative to the death-situation. However, we wish to emphasize that such a view is not common to the death-complex alone, but is intimately identified with every form of activity of the tribe. Indeed, so powerful is the rôle of magic and sorcery among all savage tribes, that it permeates every phase of their life. If we look into the problem, we see that nearly every death must be avenged. " In the normal condition of the tribes every death meant the killing of another individual ".[1] We can readily understand that this would have a most appreciable effect upon the numbers of a tribe, and this in turn would influence the cultural setting of the group.

An examination of the material at our disposal shows us that death in the Melanesian and Australian areas, in practically all instances, is due to witchcraft or sorcery, whereas in the North Siberian district it is invariably brought on by the action of a spirit. In the Australian and Melanesian territory death may be due to the influence of an ordinary individual exercising magical acts, but in Siberia it is often supposed to be caused by the power of a shaman, as among the Koryak and the Chukchee. From our study of the Melanesian region we see that death may be attributed to an individual who may be either a living or dead relative.[2] But among the Australians death is in nearly all instances caused by an individual of another tribe. This conception is illustrated in the case of the Chepara tribe,[3] the Herbert River tribes, who make a member of a neighbouring tribe responsible for the death,[4] the Wimmera district tribes of Victoria, who hold an individual of another tribe as the cause

---

[1] Spencer and Gillen, *Native Tribes of Central Australia*, p. 48.
[2] Guise, " On the Tribes Inhabiting the Mouth of the Wanigela River," *J.A.I.*, Vol. XXVIII (1899), p. 216.
[3] Howitt, *Native Tribes of South-East Australia*, p. 468.
[4] *Ibid*, p. 474.

of the death,[1] and the Watch-an-dies, who regard death as due to the action of a hostile tribe.[2]

In the Australian and Melanesian areas the service of a medicine-man is nearly always brought into requisition to ascertain the cause of the death of the deceased. The medicine-man is importuned in the Gringai County, Australia,[3] he is supposed to see the culprit if a death occurs in the Chepara tribe,[4] he is credited with the ability to detect the guilty among some tribes of North Australia[5]; a friendly sorcerer is consulted by tribes of West Australia.[6] If we compare this method with that of the inhabitants of North Siberia, we shall find that the supposed cause of the death is detected by entirely different means. Here a post-mortem examination is conducted, both among the Koryak and the Chukchee to discover what spirit or shaman killed the deceased.

The function of the sorcerer in the Australian and Melanesian death-situation is so important in contrast with the other areas under consideration, that we cannot afford to lose sight of its significance. This attitude seems to me to be a direct result of the historical cultural setting, for we know from our study that the rôle of the medicine-man is most conspicuous in the social life of these districts. However, if we will contrast this with conditions found among the Koryak we shall find that the part which the shaman plays in this area is reduced almost to a minimum. " I did not find a single shaman in the settlements of the Maritime Koryak along Pershina Bay. The old men of these settlements told me that many men had died among them during an epidemic of measles which had ravaged these regions before my arrival, because there were no shamans to drive away the disease ".[7]

Although we find an insignificant number of both family and professional shamans among the Koryak, yet there was a time when this tribe had all the varieties of shamans which still exist among the Chukchee.[8]

---

[1] Hartland, article in *Hastings*, Vol. IV, p. 413.
[2] Oldfield, " Aborigines of Australia ", *Transactions of the Ethnological Society of London*, Vol. II (1865), p. 236.
[3] Howitt, *Native Tribes of South-East Australia*, p. 64.
[4] *Ibid*, p. 468.
[5] Spencer and Gillen, *Native Tribes of Central Australia*, p. 51.
[6] Grey, *Journal of Two Expeditions of Discovery in the North-West and West Australia*, Vol. II, p. 238.
[7] Jochelson, *The Koryak*, *J.N.P.E.*, Vol. VI (1905), p. 48.
[8] *Ibid*, p. 48.

Despite the fact that professional shamanism has developed from family shamanism, yet the functions of the professional shaman resemble those of the priests, which are brought about by contact with a higher civilization. Hence, we would not expect to find the shaman exercising the same function as in Australia, for the function of the priest would be concerned with prayers and incantations to prevent death, but not to detect the guilty one who had caused the death. It is interesting to note that among the Yahut, representing a more advanced type of culture, the influence of the family shaman has declined with Christian teaching, which, according to Trostchansky, was formerly practiced among them, rather than that of professional shamanism. Even at the present, professional shamans can be found everywhere among the Yahut.[1]

The fact that death in the Siberian area is supposed to be due to spirits rather than to magic, finds a part reflection in the cultural setting, for the Reindeer Koryak on the Taigonos Peninsula say that the Master-on-High sends the kalau to people when they do wrong, just as the Czar sends his Cossacks against those who are disobedient.[2]

The question which we have asked ourselves and in some cases have attempted to solve, is whether the myth connected with the death ritual is primary, or whether it can be regarded as a secondary explanation of the pre-existing ceremony. Naturally we have to approach with caution the statements of natives when they derive a ceremony from a myth accounting for its origin. Although such reasons cannot be taken as objective historical fact, yet we are unwilling to concede to the position assumed by Lowie who, in criticising Swanton and Dixon's *Primitive American History*, declares "I cannot attach to oral tradition any historical value whatever, under any conditions whatsoever".[3] We might cite here our sympathy with the view of Dr. Goldenweiser, who regards such a position as depriving anthropology of an important heuristic tool. Despite the fact that with archæological, linguistic, and anthropological evidence at our command, traditional accounts

---

[1] Jochelson, *The Koryak*, *J.N.P.E.*, Vol. VI (1905), p. 48, note.
[2] *Ibid*, p. 27.
[3] Lowie, "Critical Comment on Dr. Swanson and Dr. Dixon's Primitive American History," *A.A.*, Vol. XVII (1915), p. 598.

would lose their potency, there seems to be no justification for rejecting them as of no significance. Indefinite and doubtful evidence should not be eliminated until further investigation gives more reliable data.[1]

It is interesting to look into the deductions of Boas, who, by intensive examination of the North Pacific data, has shown the predominence of diffusion in establishing the persistency of complex tales. He has demonstrated conclusively that the myths of primitive tribes are not only influenced by the historical setting, but by assimilating material from various sources.[2] Boas does not agree with Bastian and Wundt, who consider the question of how tales originate of comparative insignificance, because the same psychological processes govern material independently created and diffused.[3] The tales dealing in the shedding of the skin and the moon stories and certain other myths cannot be explained as a direct reflex of the contemplation of nature. Supernatural occurrences such as death, which represent ideas contrary to the daily experience of the primitives, have been interpreted by exaggerations of imagination.[4] Such itales are associated first in a phenomenon of nature, and an interpretative meaning is then given.[5]

[1] Goldenweiser, ' The Heuristic Value of Traditional Records, "*A.A.*, Vol. XVII (1915), p. 763.
[2] Boas, *Indianische Sagen von der Nord Pacifischen Küste Amerikas*, p. 329.
[3] Wundt, *Volkerpsychologie*, Vol. II, part 3.
[4] Boas, " The Development of Folk-Tales and Myths," *Scientific Monthly* Vol. III (1916), pp. 335-343.
[5] For a discussion of the explanatory element in folk-tales, see Watermann, " The Explanatory Element in the Folk-Tales of the North American Indians," *J.A.F.L.*, Vol. XXVII (1914).

CHAPTER III

DISPOSAL OF THE DEAD

SIGNIFICANCE

THE great importance attached to the disposal of the body seems to be universal. We may state that the principle is invariably the same—the dead would "walk" unless the body is disposed of with appropriate ceremony. The natural tendency of the deceased, then, was to find his way back to the place which had been his haunt in life.

MELANESIA

Burial is regarded as a benefit to the ghost ; if a man is killed anywhere, and his body is not buried, his ghost will haunt the region ; when a man's head has been taken and his skull has been added to some chief's collection, the ghost for a time at least, prowls about.[1] The natives of New Britain think that possession and burial of a body is very important.[2]

AUSTRALIA

In some tribes there is a belief that the souls of those whose bodies have been left unburied wander about the earth especially near the place of death, and are intent upon harming the living. Again, life beyond the grave will be denied them and their bodies will be devoured by crows and dogs.[3]

The presence of almost every conceivable method of disposal of the dead in Australia certainly emphasizes the desire of the natives to get rid of the corpse.

HINDU

The Hindus lay special stress upon burial, cremation, and other ceremonies connected with the disposal of the body.

[1] Codrington, *The Melanesians*, p. 255.
[2] Brown, *Melanesians and Polynesians*, p. 193.
[3] Brough-Smyth, *Aborigines of Victoria*, Vol. II, p. 280.

If we pass from Vedic times to the period when Asvalayana and other collections of domestic rules were composed (the Grihya-Sutras), we find that the funerals are more elaborate. Undoubtedly, one of the most interesting subjects with which the Grihya-Sutras deal is that of the funeral rites. Cremation, Caland says, was considered a sacrament. " On this day I shall go to my father and fulfill the sacrament of the cremation ".[1]

The funeral service of the Hindu seems to have a double purpose, both for the individual and for the community, for are we not told that the children of the one cremated who do not obey the injunctions relative to the observances of the funeral rites shall die of starvation ? Twice in the narrative is starvation the punishment intimated for the non-observance of certain definite funeral ceremonies. Again, if any of the funeral rites were neglected, the restless spirit of the dead was supposed to hover in this world because of its inability to reach the blissful realms. Thus every possible device was resorted to to propitiate the departed spirit and to prevent its return. We find the allusion in Vedic literature to pouring water to chase away the spirit,[2] a strong evidence, it seems to me, in support of this theory. Likewise in the ceremony performed previous to the presentation of oblations to the gods and to the Manes, we read of the extinguishing of the Rakashoghna or lighted lamp, which served the purpose of expelling evil spirits. Among the Kurns of India there is a belief that if there is no propitiation the restless spirit of the deceased will walk among them, bringing sickness, want, and ravages of wild animals.[3] An article by Monier-Williams shows us the pronounced Hindu attitude toward ghosts.[4] Although he is describing a Sraddha celebration in India in 1876, yet an examination of very ancient sources finds the same belief accentuated. When a man dies, his body is cremated and buried, but the soul always hovers in the vicinity. This is his ghost, and since it has no real body, it is uncomfortable, restless, perpetually longing to wander, and being possessed

---

[1] Jolly, *Recht und Sitte*, p. 155.

[2] *Rv.*, X, 14, 9.

[3] Colebrooke, *Life and Essays*, Vol. II, p. 205.

[4] *Indian Antiquary*, Vol. V, pp. 200-204.

with an insatiable desire to frequent its old haunts.[1] If
he dies away from his kindred and because of ignorance of
of his death they are unable to perform the funeral rites, he
becomes a pisacha or foul wandering ghost with a strong
inclination to take revenge upon the living by many violent
acts. Williams says that in 1876 he heard it remarked that
there were fewer ghosts in India than formerly. The natives
explained that this was due to the fact that means of communication were so rapid that few died without their deaths
being known.

The Vedic Hindu when cremating their dead cried out,
" Away, go away, O Death ! Injure not our sons and our
men ".[2] The Nāyars of Malabar believe that the removal
of the bones and ashes of the dead bring peace to his spirit
and free the survivors from injury.[3]

Perhaps it might be well to mention a word here not only
about the importance of the specific observance of burial
rites, especially by a son, but also the sacrifices in honour
of departed ancestors. Since extinction of the family in
India prohibits offerings to the dead, the Hindu is naturally
much concerned about dying without male descendants, and
the birth or adoption of a son cannot be divorced from his
religion.[4]

Among the Khasis when one has died at a distance from
home whose body has not been burned according to prescribed rules, it is a custom for a clan member or the
children of the deceased to take three or four seeds or
cowries to a place where three roads meet. Throwing the
seeds into the air, they say, " to alle noh ba ngin sa lum sa
kynshew noh ia phi ".—" Come, now we will collect you ".
(The seeds representing the bones of the departed.) If

---

[1] The Iroquois have a belief that unless the designated burial rites are
performed, the spirit will wander on earth and have a most unhappy existence ;
for this reason these Indians take significant measures concerning the recovery
of the bodies of their clain warriors. (Morgan, *League of the Iroquois*, Vol. I,
p. 165.) The Nāyars of Malabar are of the opinion that the disposition of
a corpse is conducive to the happiness of the spirit. (Fawcett, " The Nāyars
of Malabar," in *Madras Government Museum's Report*, Vol. III, p. 245.)

[2] *Rv.*, X, 18, 1 .

[3] Fawcett, in the *Madras Museum's Report*, Vol. III, p. 251.

[4] In Egypt it was the duty of a son to arrange the material equipment
of his father for the life beyond. This is represented in the Osiris myth as
to the duty of Horus to Osiris. (Breasted, *Development of Religion and
Thought in Ancient Egypt*, p. 63.)

possible, a portion of the dead man's clothing is buried with the seeds.[1]

NORTH SIBERIA

If a man of the Reindeer Chukchee walks along the country, and suddenly meets a corpse lying in the road, he incurs great danger. But if he turns back and endeavours to retrace his steps the corpse will soon pass ahead of him, barring his way.[2] A complete stranger when passing a graveyard where a corpse is exposed may assure himself of the protection of the deceased provided he be deferential and give proper offerings in crumbs of meat and tobacco.[3]*

Thus not only primitives, but others, shared this attitude.

[1] Gurdon, *The Khasis*, p. 137.

[2] Borgoras, *The Chukchee*, *J.N.P.E.*, Vol. VII (1907), p. 518.

[3] *Ibid*, p. 336.

* In the Old Testament we find great emphasis laid upon burial. The Biblical narrators express most scathingly their denunciation of the unburied body. " Thou are cast out of their grave like an abominable branch or the raiment of those slain, thrust through with a sword that goes down to the stones of a pit like a carcass trodden under foot. Thou shalt not be joined with them in burial because thou hast destroyed thy land and slain thy people.

They shall die grievous deaths, neither shall they be lamented ; neither shall they be buried." (*Jeremiah* xvi, 4.)

The Greeks and the Romans likewise manifested the same attitude toward unburied bodies. The Greeks believed that the soul could not enter the Elysian Fields until buried. (Tertullian, *De Anima*, LVI.) We find the shade of Elpenor earnestly imploring Odysseus to bury his body. (*Odyssey*, XV, 66.) Is not the picture of Patroclus mourning for the body of Hector familiar to all of us ? Again, we have been much moved by the sight of Priam going to Achilles to beg the body of his son. Indeed, so pronounced was the feeling of the Greeks and Romans against non-burial that they considered it a religious duty to throw earth upon a body which they chanced to find unburied. (Horace, *Carm.*, I, 28 ; Horace, *Od.*, I, 28.)

The Greeks even regarded the gods as the instigators of burial. (Sophocles, *Antigone*, 454 et seqq. ; Euripides, *Supplices*, 563.) Not only did these people of classical antiquity think it incumbent upon them to bury their own dead, but they also gave up the bodies of their enemies so that their foes would not have burial rites denied them. (Schmidt, *Die Ethik der alten Griechen*, Vol. II, p. 100, et seqq.) Lysander was regarded as especially derelict of his duty when he did not bury Philocles and four thousand prisoners whom he killed. (Pausanias, IX, 32, 9.) From Pausanias we learn that it was " a sacred and imperative duty to cover with earth a human corpse " and from the same authority we read that the Athenians themselves buried the Persians who had fallen at Marathon. (Pausanias, I, 32, 5.)

If the body of any member of a family was known to be unburied, an empty tomb was raised to his memory and his heir was obliged each year to sacrifice a victim termed Porca Praecidanea to Tellus and Ceres, to free himself and his kinsmen from pollution. According to the Roman conception, if the deceased had not been properly buried, descent into the lower world was impossible, and as a consequence, he roamed the earth disconsolately and

The Chaldeans believed that since the spirit of the unburied dead had no resting place or means of sustenance, its only thought was to harass and attack the living. It wandered through town and country occupied only with the thought of robbing the living.[1]

According to the Assyrian-Babylonian belief, to be left unburied was one of the greatest misfortunes which could befall one. The *Gilgamesh Epic* after giving a picture of those whose spirit remains at rest because of appropriate burial, refers to the awful fate of those who are denied fitting burial rites.

---

with an evil will. (Fowler, *Religious Experiments of the Romans*, p. 85.) We learn that one of the most sacred duties of the Greeks and Romans was to give the body burial rites. (Aust, *Die Religion der Römer*, p. 226.) Plautus gives us a very interesting story of a ghost whose soul was compelled to wander because due burial rites had not been accorded to it. (Plautus, *Mostellaria*.) Because the body of Caligula was not buried with appropriate ceremony, " the soul was not at rest, but continued to appear to the living." As a result, the corpse was disinterred and reburied according to prescribed form (Suetonius, *Caligula*, 59). In ancient times the dreadful punishment of denial of burial was meted out to those guilty of great crimes (Fustel de Coulanges, *The Ancient City*, p. 19).

A large house in Athens was rendered uninhabitable by a ghost which haunted it every night. The spirit appeared in the form of an emaciated old man making a thundering racket with chains which were attached to his hands and feet. Athenodorus, a philosopher, had the courage to confront the apparition ; suddenly it disappeared in the court. The following day, the spot was unearthed, and a skeleton in chains was found. After appropriate burial rites had been performed the ghost never again made its appearance. This story was believed by Pliny who narrated another. (Friedlander, *Life and Manners in the Early Roman Empire*, Vol. III, p. 305.)

In Egypt the recovery of the body that it might be embalmed was highly desirable ; otherwise, the deceased might lose prospect of life beyond the grave. (Breasted, *Ancient Records*, Vol. I, pp. 362-374.) Often such a recovery was attended with great danger as in the case of Sebni of Elephantine, who penetrated the territory of the most dangerous southern tribes to obtain the body of his father.

Among the Samoans an unburied body caused great concern. Cere-monies took place on the battlefield if the body could not be recovered, and along the banks of the river if the deceased were drowned. (Turner, *Samoa, A Hundred Years and Long Before*, p. 150.) Such bodies haunted the survivors everywhere ; crying out, " Oh, how cold ! " (Turner, *Nineteen Years in Polynesia*, p. 233.) The Batakso of Sumatra think that there is no greater disgrace than to be deprived of burial. (Westermarck, *Origin and Development of Moral Ideas*, Vol. II, p. 521.) The negroes of Accra believe that happiness depends upon power, courage, wealth, and appropriate burial. (Westermarck, *Origin and Development of Moral Ideas*, Vol. II, p. 521.)

Confucius identified the immediate disposal of the dead with the great virtue of submission and love for superiors. (de Groot, *Religious System of China*, Vol. II, book 1, p. 659.) In China no more righteous act could be conceived than of burying stray bones and covering up exposed coffins. (Westermarck, *Origin and Development of Moral Ideas*, Vol. II, p. 522.)

[1] Maspero, *Dawn of Civilization*, p. 689.

But he whose corpse remains in the fields,
As you and I have seen,
His spirit has no rest on the earth.
The one whose spirit is not cared for by any one
As you and I have seen,
He is consumed by gnawing hunger, by a longing for food
That is left on the street he is obliged to eat.[1]

True, other motives except that of fear seem to prompt the primitive to take every precaution not only to dispose of the bodies of the dead, but also to perform suitable burial rites. It is in this case, as elsewhere, at first glance the desire to benefit the ghost may appear to be the main object, and even in several instances such is distinctly stated, but the motive which instigates such an attitude is that unless such solicitude be shown, the restless, disgruntled, discontented spirit, deprived of a resting-place and means of sustenance, will return to haunt the survivors.

The wide prevalence of cremation makes us ponder the reasons for this method of disposal of the dead. Some of the motives actuating such a practice which seem to appear are :

(1) Cremation is the most effective way of preventing the possible return of the dead.
(2) This method dispels the pollution caused by death.
(3) It protects the body from wild beasts.
(4) Burning removes the deceased from the machinations of the evil spirits.
(5) This process is a means of securing warmth and comfort in the future world.
(6) Burning eliminates the process of transformation, a process detrimental to the living and the dead.

Burial, too, seems to have for its main object the prevention of the ghost from tormenting the living. As intimated elsewhere, this method of disposal must be supplemented by other practices to render the survivors safe from the spirit of the dead. It is here as elsewhere, burial may be resorted to with the idea of preventing the deceased from falling into

---

[1] Jastrow, *Religion of Babylon and Assyria*, p. 512, quoting from the *Gilgamesh Epic*. The unburied or disentombed assume the form of demons and afflict the living. (*Ibid*, p. 602.)
To the Roumanian peasant the inability of relatives to perform the customary burial rites is one of the greatest tragedies of the Great War. (Murgoci, "Customs Connected with Death and Burial among the Roumanians", *F.L.*, Vol. XXX (1919), p. 89.)

the hands of an enemy, of protecting the body from wild beasts, and as the most convenient way of disposal.

Although our object is not to give in detail the various methods practised to dispose of a dead body which we find in vogue in all primitive areas and which in themselves would afford material for an extensive study, yet a few pertinent remarks can be made upon some general theories advanced to explain why such a diversity exists.

After listing twelve different ways of disposing of the dead in New South Wales,[1] Fraser comes to the conclusion that the great variety of these modes of burial seems a strong proof that the Australian race is very mixed since a homogeneous race is very conservative in regard to burial rites. He furthermore points out that these various methods are identified with different localities, except the first three which are found in the same tribe, the Kurringgai. Then follows what Fraser considers a plausible explanation and he suggests that burial in a hollow tree or raised stage prevents the body from coming in contact with the earth, a reminder of the tower of silence. According to the Mafulu Mountain People, the graves of chiefs, chiefs' wives, members of their families, and other persons of special importance are platforms or tree graves.[2] Sir William Macgregor found it in the mountains of the Vanapa Water Shed.[3] Thomson records it as occurring among the low waters of the Kemp Welsch River.[4] Among the Semango of the Malay Peninsula and the Andamanese, although now they employ a simple form of interment, yet

[1] (1) interred at full length ; (2) lying on its side with the lower part of the legs from the knee folded up behind ; (3) trussed up in a bundle ; (4) erect in the grave ; (5) laid in a side cavity dug in the earth from the bottom of a pit ; (6) place the body in a hollow tree and leave it there, closing up the aperture with a sheet of bark ; (7) place the body on a high raised platform, and afterwards gather the bones of the skeleton or leave them on the stage or scattered on the ground ; (8) the bones are carried about for some time and interred ; (9) they do not inter the body, but merely lay it on the surface of the ground and cover it with logs, or they cover it with a mound of earth and mark some tree nearby with a peculiar blaze ; (10) they fix the body over a slow fire and thus desiccate it and smoke it until it is quite hard ; they carry it about with them awhile and afterwards bury it. The oils and juices which the fire brings from the body are rubbed on their own bodies ; (11) they eat the dead body ; (12) in some districts the body is burned. (Fraser, *The Aborigines of New South Wales*, p. 80.)
[2] Williamson, *The Mafulu Mountain People of British Guinea*, p. 263.
[3] *Annual Report* (1897-1898), pp. 22-23.
[4] Thomson, *British New Guinea*, p. 53 ; quoted by Williamson, p. 257.

formerly the distinguished members of their community, the great magicians, were exposed on trees, whereas ordinary laymen were interred in the ground.[1] In the Guanaco area of South America we find that the dead were placed upon platforms.[2] The Yukaghir formerly placed their dead on platforms raised on posts.[3]

Rivers, too,[4] is of the opinion that the various ways of disposing of dead bodies in Melanesia are not original with the population, but must have been brought by their ancestors from foreign regions. Although he assumes this to be so, yet in specific instances he does not give any proof of diffusion. Rivers' deductions are hypothetical and he insists upon diffusion at the exclusion of all other lines of development.

In his *Contact of Peoples* he points out that the complexity and variety of the burial customs of the Australian natives stand out in marked contrast to the uniformity of their social organization and physical type.[5] He then suggests that these revolutionary changes in such a conservative phase of culture where the emotional element is so much in evidence, would be contemplated only with the greatest reluctance and it is impossible to suppose that these people could have been guilty of such a deviation from a prescribed custom. True, he advances a step beyond Frazer when he devises a mechanism for his theory, but we certainly cannot endorse his line of argument when he says : " If the funeral customs of Australia have been introduced from without, they have been the outcome of permanent settlements of strangers who lived and died in such close relationship with those among whom they settled, that the visitors were able to prescribe how their own bodies should be treated and were so honoured if not reverenced, and the customs they have introduced have become established and time honoured practices ".[6] Thus we see that he bases his theory upon the idea that these diverse rites were introduced by small bodies of immigrants

[1] Skeat and Blagden, *Pagan Races of the Malay Peninsula*, Vol. II pp. 89-91.

[2] Wissler, *American Indian*, p. 235.

[3] Jochelson, *The Koryak*, J.N.P.E., Vol. IV (1908), p. 104.

[4] Rivers, *History of Melanesian Society*, Vol. II, 258 et seqq.

[5] Rivers, *Contact of People in Essays and Studies Presented To Wm. Ridgeway*, pp. 480-481.

[6] *Ibid*, pp. 481-482.

who represented a cultural strata far in advance of their own. He again offers no proof but gives us an assumption that cannot be supported by the history of the case.

No definite concrete evidence indicates that cave and mountain burial in Melanesia was, as Rivers supposes, due to certain conditions of interaction between the neighbouring people.[1] Nor can it be proved that the presence of preservation in the house in Oceania is correlated with cave burial in this same region.* Again it does not seem that extended interment and cave burial in Oceania are different modes of expressing the ideas of a people who believe in preservation in rocky tombs. However, because of environmental conditions this idea is put into execution into different ways.[2] In Indonesia we have shown (see Part II) that a certain definite connection exists between myths of origin and cave burial. However, we are fully cognizant that this is not the only reason which may account for the disposal of the body in this manner.

In this connection we may state our endorsement of the views of Rivers who also suggests that the practice of burial in caves and mountain hollows may be merely the outcome of the desire of the immigrants to remove their dead from all possible injury.[3] Thus in Melanesia the bones of the dead are used in the preparation of bows and arrows or they figure in magical rites.[4] Here we have a great incentive for stealing such valuable objects. In Marquesas, Polynesia, we also find cave burial practised, for here the idea prevails that the skull might be stolen by the enemy and preserved as a trophy.[5] At Tahiti, fish hooks, bones, and chisels are made from the bones.[6] Rivers is of the opinion that cave burial in some Polynesian districts whose location is known only

---

[1] Rivers, *History of Melanesian Society*, Vol. II, p. 271.

* What might be interpreted as a survival of cave burial is seen among some of the Pueblo people of Arizona and New Mexico. When the caves were occupied as dwellings the dead were buried in the farthest recesses and these rock shelters have been retained as a most fitting burial place of the deceased members of a community. Cushing, *Thirteenth Annual Report, Bureau of Ethnology*, 1896, p. 348.

[2] Rivers, *History of Melanesian Society*, Vol. II, pp. 286-287.

[3] *Ibid*, p. 271.

[4] Joly, *Bulletin de la Soc. d'Anth.* (1904), series, p. 369.

[5] Chaval, *Les Marquisiens*, p. 45.

[6] Ellis, *Polynesian Researches*, Vol. I, pp. 524-525.

to a few might likewise be due to the fear on the part of the survivors of desecration by enemies of the deceased. Here, he claims, we need not consider the motive as influenced by any culture or cultures.

The great fear of the dead is such that this expedient is resorted to for propitiation to mitigate the awfulness of the malign influence of a departed tribesman. Frequently in tribes representing the lowest degrees of culture where such preservation is common, the horror of the dead is most apparent. Other elements though may enter into the question of house preservation. Thus the bodies of children are often buried in the house to facilitate rebirth, the body of a chief is thus kept, for such an individual, because of his power, is supposed to wreak most vengeance upon the survivors if this seeming respect be not shown. Here we have a method of disposal dependent upon rank. Again we read of the Pygmies and Papuans,[1] " Though the people bring their skulls into their homes they show no real respect for them and they are eager to part with them when a chance occurs ". When Allen makes the statement,[2] that " during the first stage (referring to preservation in a hut or cave where the family dwell) the attitude of a man toward his dead is chiefly one of affectionate regard. The body is kept at home and tended ; the skull is carried about as a beloved object. But in the second stage which induces the practices of burial a certain fear of the dead becomes notoriously apparent. Men dread the return of the corpse or ghost and strive to keep it within prescribed limits ", he does so without supporting his hypothesis by any definite evidence to show that the successive stages which he indicates took place. To the historian who cannot let mere assumptions stand without proofs, such deductions are valueless.

It may be said that even though the corpse is kept in the house, such preservation may be prompted by a dread attitude and not by affection. Although at Murna the bones are handed to the nearest relative who keeps them as a sacred trust, yet at the end of nine months they are placed in a cleft of a cliff.

True, an affectionate attitude may sometimes account

---

[1] Wollaston, *Pygmies and Papuans*, p. 140.
[2] Allen, *The Solution of the Idea of God*, pp. 53-54.

for preservation of bones or skull in a house, but as we have seen, this motive is by no means invariably present.[1]

Rivers also suggests that there is a possibility that interment is associated with the belief in a home of the dead underground. He likewise declares that although there is no evidence for this in Melanesia,[2] Dr. Landtman records the fact that in the Fly River region of New Guinea the grave is supposed to be a means of passage to the underworld.[3] We cannot ascribe to the idea that this belief is the only motive underlying inhumation, nor can we agree to the conclusion of Rivers who is of the opinion that whatever the motives which prompted interment in the contracted position, we can be certain that these are so at variance with those which produced preservation and can be definitely assigned to different cultures.[4]

In other countries, such as India, Italy, and Greece, different methods of disposing of the body exist side by side and there is no proof to show that such were due to various cultures. Thus in India, in the Rig-Vedic period, both burial and cremation were practiced, although in India, as in Greece, burial was less favoured ; indeed it was regarded with disapproval. However, burial was not, as some suppose, rare in the Rig-Vedic period,[5] and we have an interesting hymn describing the ritual accompanying it. The apparent inconsistency between burial and burning so often stressed by Vedic scholars, is dismissed by Oldenberg[6] as unnecessary.* We may add that burning and burial existed at precisely the same time in Greece for many years, and we find numerous instances of such parallel methods of disposing of the body, not only among innumerable primitive tribes, but we also have this practice to-day among most progressive natives, the same being prompted by no cultural setting due to migration. We may add that in the Atharva-Veda we find two other modes of disposing of the body, casting out and exposure

[1] Seligmann, *Melanesians*, p. 728.
[2] Rivers, *History of Melanesian Society*, Vol. II, pp. 274-550.
[3] Westermarck, *Festskrift tillëgnad*, p. 73, quoted by Fraser.
[4] Rivers, *History of Melanesian Society*, Vol. II, p. 274.
[5] *Rv.* X, 18.
[6] Oldenberg, *Religion des Veda*, p. 57.
* To remove the apparent discrepancy between burning and burial by assuming that the references to burial are to the burial of the bones as does Oldenberg, is not necessary. (See *Vedic* Index, Vol. I, p. 8.)

of the dead. Zimmer considers that casting out is parallel with the Indo-Iranian custom of throwing out the dead to be devoured by wild beasts, or that this refers to the old who are exposed when helpless.[1] Before we have mentioned the fact that from the Grihya-Sutras we learn that all but children two years old are to be cremated. And so we could cite very many other instances to show that different methods of disposal of the body not only exist at the same time, but that such are instigated by varied motives specifically attributable to many causes, and not representing the different cultural standards due to successive migrations.

This does not mean that we wish to refute the statement of Rivers, who claims that the preservation practice in Melanesia was the result of the transmission of a practice from generation to generation, and which in the opinion of the immigrants was merely a means to an end. Naturally, the original purpose of such a custom might have been eliminated in the process of transmission.

For supplementary reading on this subject see Sir Baldwin Spencer, *Wanderings in Wild Australia*, Vol. II, Chapter on "Death, Burial and Mourning Ceremonies of the Warramunga," pp. 476-495.

[1] Zimmer, *Altindisches Leben*, p. 402.

CHAPTER IV

DREAD OF THE SPIRIT

As we see universally demonstrated, burial is not considered a sufficient precaution against the return of the ghost. Other devices must be practised to exclude the dead. There seems no other conclusion to come to in regard to the various attentions bestowed upon the dead of all ancient and primitive peoples than the view of Frazer, who says that they sprang not so much from the affections as from the fears of the survivors. " It is the way of all ghosts from Britanny to Samoa ".[1]

CARRYING OUT THE CORPSE

The custom of carrying out the corpse by some other way than that of the ordinary door is very common. We find evidence of this custom from South Africa to the farthest limits of Asia, from the Indian Archipelago to the Islands of the Southern Ocean. Although a very few specific instances of this custom can be found in the definite areas under consideration, yet the practice is common enough to merit our consideration, especially in connection with discussing the universal attitude of dread toward the spirits of the deceased.

MELANESIA

It is a custom of the Fiji Islands to break down the side of the house to carry out a dead body, although the door is wide enough.[2]

INDIA

In some areas the corpse is passed out in a seated posture through an opening in the wall. The hole is closed after the

---

[1] Frazer, " On Certain Burial Customs, an Illustration of the Primitive Theory of the Soul ", *J.A.I.*, Vol. XV (1885-1886), p. 64; Turner, *Samoa*, p. 150; Williams (Monier), *Religious Life and Thought in India*, p. 239.

[2] Williams, *Fiji and the Fijians*, Vol. I, p. 197.

ceremony.[1] It is still a custom among Hindu castes that when a death has occurred on a non-auspicious day, not to remove the corpse through the door, but through a temporary hole in the wall.[2] The corpse is carried out feet foremost, so that the ghost may not find its way back to the house.[3]

A death under an unlucky or disgraceful circumstance often occasions a special mode of conveyance of the dead body. This is usually effected by means of an opening other than that of the ordinary house door, and is resorted to among modern Hindus only when people have died on inauspicious days.[4]

The Banjâras of Khândesh reverse the process. Instead of the ordinary door they make another entrance, for the usual way of exit is supposed to be polluted by the passage of the spirit of the dead.[5] A similar custom is found among the Maghs of Bengal. When the friends return from the funeral, in the event of the death of the master of the house, the ladder leading up to the house is thrown down, and an entrance is made by cutting a hole in the back wall.[6]

In the Kabui settlement in the Valley of Manipur it is usual to carry out the body through the small door at the side of the house, or even through a small aperture made for the purpose. Such an opening is closed after the removal of the body.[7]*

SIBERIA

Among the Koryak it is the custom to carry out the dead body by raising the corner of the tent. The Chukchee carry out the body not through the entrance of the tent, but through the roof or from under the folds of the tent cover. Every trace of this improvised exit is obliterated to prevent recogni-

[1] Sonnerat, *Voyage aux Indes Orientales et à la Chine*, Vol. I, p. 86.
[2] Dubois, *Hindu Manners, Customs and Ceremonies*, Vol. II, p. 505.
[3] Crooke, *The Natives of North India*, p. 217.
[4] Frazer, *Belief in Immortality*, Vol. I, p. 458.
[5] Crooke, *Popular Religion and Folk-Lore of Northern India*, Vol. II, p. 56.
[6] *Ibid.*
[7] Hodson, *The Naga Tribes of Manipur*, p. 147.
* When a death has taken place among the Indians of north-west North America, the body is at once taken out of the house through an opening in the wall from which the boards have been removed. (Boas, *Sixth Annual Report of the Committee on North-Western Tribes of Canada*, p. 231 ; special reprint from *Report of the British Association for the Advancement of Science*, Leeds Meeting, 1903.)

tion of his old haunts by the deceased.[1] The head of the sled on which the dead body is placed is pointed to the house, the rear in the direction in which it is to be taken.[2] The so-called double dead are overturned with the sled, and fall face downward.[3]

These illustrations are sufficient to show the prevalence of the custom of carrying out the corpse by other than the ordinary means of exit.* We may add the following reasons in explanation of such a custom :

(1) The practice of throwing open the windows is sometimes observed before death for the purpose of easing the departure of the soul, for escape is impossible if the way be obstructed. It is important to bear in mind that in such a case the window is permitted to remain open only for an instant for fear the soul might return.[4]

---

[1] Jochelson, *The Koryak*, *J.N.P.E.*, Vol. VI (1905), pp. 110-111.

[2] Bogoras, *The Chukchee*, *J.N.P.E.*, Vol. VII (1907), p. 525.

[3] *Ibid.*

* The use of an exit different from that of the ordinary one is not confined to carrying out the corpse. Among the Kwakinee Indians girls during the adolescent period at the time of uncleanliness depart from and enter their room through a hole in the floor. (Boas, *First General Report of the Indians of British Columbia*, p. 42.) In the same tribe men who are contaminated because of eating human flesh for four months are not permitted to go out except by a secret door in the rear of the house.

[4] Bogoras, *The Chukchee*, *J.N.P.E.*, Vol. VII (1907), p. 517.

Among the Sakalava and the Antimerina of Madagascar, when a sorcerer or prince dies within the enclosure of the King's palace the body is carried out not through the door, but by a breach made in the wall. (Van Gennep, *Tabou et Totémisme à Madagascar*, p. 65, quoting Dr. Catat.) The Tlingit carry out a corpse through an opening in the rear corner of a house, such a passage-way being made by removing a wall plank. (Swanton, " The Tlingit," *Twenty-sixth Annual Report of Ethnology* (1908), p. 420.)

The Algonkins carry out a dead body through a hole opposite the door. (Brinton, *Myths of the New World*, p. 279.)

In the British Isles and different parts of Europe it is usual to throw open the doors and windows. Such a precaution was resorted to in England (1890), upon the death of a dignitary of the Church of England. (*Notes and Queries*, seventh series, Vol. X (1890), p. 170, quoted by Hartland, article in *Hastings*, Vol. IV, p. 415). A survival perhaps of the idea that the greatest amount of danger from death pollution emanates from those most sacred. It is significant to note in this connection that the Matse tribe of Ewhe carry out the body of a priest through a hole in the wall. (Speith, *Die E'we-Stämme*, p. 756). Here again we see that defilement is especially connected with those regarded as most sacred.

A common custom in France, Germany, and Switzerland is to take the tile off the roof with the object of easing the departure of the soul. (*Ztsch. des Verims für Volkskunde*, Vol. XI (1901), p. 267.)

The Hottentots, Bechuanas, Marotse, Barongo, and many tribes of South and West Africa, never carry a corpse through a door, but always by a special opening in the wall. (Kolben, *The Present State of the Cape of Good Hope*, Vol. I, p. 316 ; Thunberg, "An Account of the Cape of Good Hope," in

(2) There is a fear of pollution from the corpse.

(3) The main object is to prevent the dead from finding his way back.

Pinkerton's Voyages and Travels, Vol. XVI, p. 142.) A similar custom is found among the Tlingit and Haida. (Boas, *Sixth Report of the Committee on the North-Western Tribes of Canada*, p. 23), Swanton, " Contributions to the Ethnology of the Haida ", *J.N.P.E.*, Vol. V, pp. 52-54.

Sometimes the soothsayers of Tangut say that it is not good luck to carry out a corpse by the door, and they often break a hole in the wall to carry out the deceased. (Yule, *Travels of Marco Polo*, Vol. I, p. 209, n6.) The Siamese not only break an opening through the side of the house wall, but after the body is out, they hurry it at full speed, three times round the house. (Tylor, *Primitive Culture*, Vol. II, p. 26.)

If a death occurs within a house among the Eskimo of Hudson Bay, the dead body is carried out through a hole which is then closed to prevent the return of the spirit. (Turner, " Ethnology of the Ungava District, Hudson Bay Territory ", *Eleventh Annual Report of the Bureau of Ethnology* (1894), p. 191.)

It is a Norse custom that a corpse should not be carried out by the door but by a hole made in the wall which is located at back of the dead man's head ; the deceased is taken out backwards ; again, a hole is sometimes dug in the ground under the south wall, and the body of the deceased is drawn through it. (Weinhold, *Altnordisches Leben*, p. 476.)

In Greenland the body is carried out through a window if the death has occurred in the tent and the skins are unfastened in the rear of the corpse. A woman placed behind the dead body waves a lighted chip and says, " There's nothing more to be had here ". (Cranz, *History of Greenland*, Vol. I, p. 237.)

We read that in certain parts of Umbria, such as Perugia and Assizi, an opening elevated some feet above the ground and known as the " Door of the Dead ", was very common. (Yule, *Travels of Marco Polo*, Vol. I, p. 209, n6.) A bricked doorway called the " Corpse Door " existing in many farm houses of Jutland, has been recently discovered by Feilberg. (*F.L.*, Vol. XVIII (1907), p. 364.) The corpse door is still to be seen near Amsterdam. (Frazer, " On Certain Burial Customs ", *J.A.I.*, Vol. XV (1885-1886), p. 70.)

In a certain district of Central Tibet the dead bodies of members of the family are taken through the door, while the corpse of another person is carried through the window or smoke hole or a hole in the wall. (Yule, *Travels of Marco Polo*, Vol. I, p. 219, n6.)

The Hottentots remove the dead from the hut by a special opening. (Bastian, *Mench*, Vol. II, p. 323 ; quoted by Tylor, *Primitive Culture*, Vol. II, p. 26.)

A common custom among the Lolos of Western China is to make a hole in the roof of a house to enable the soul to escape. (Henry, " The Lolos and Other Tribes of Western China ", *J.A.I.*, Vol. XXXIII (1903), p. 103.)

For discussion of the Corpse Door, see Yule, *Marco Polo*, p. 209. Frazer, *On Certain Burial Customs*, p. 70.

Formerly the Cheremiss of Russia carried out a corpse through a breach in the north wall to prevent the return of the ghost. (Kusnezow, " Uber den Glauben vom Jenseits und den Todtencultus der Tscheremissen ", *Internationales Archiv für Ethnographie*, Vol. IX (1896), p. 157.)

The Eskimo about Bering Strait raise a corpse through a smoke hole in the roof ; never do they carry a dead body through a doorway. If such a hole is too small to permit the corpse to be carried through, an entrance is made in the rear of the house. Such an opening is immediately closed. (Nelson, " The Eskimo About Bering Strait ", *Eighteenth Annual Report, Bureau of Ethnology* (1899), p. 311.)

The Hupa Indians carry out a corpse, not through the door, but by means of the wall. (Goddard, *Life and Culture of the Hupa*, p. 70.)

Melanesia

In the Solomon Islands the return of the funeral cortege is
by a road other than that by which the corpse was carried,
lest the ghost should follow.[1]   On the return from the burial
of one of the natives of Florida, the mourners take a
different road than that by which they carried the corpse to
the grave.[2]

Hindu

When the Vedic Indian proceeded to the place of interment,
the eldest came first and the youngest last in the funeral
procession,[3] but the order was reversed on the homeward
march.

Siberia

After the performance of burial rites among the Chukchee
the order of the funeral procession is reversed to prevent
pursuit by the dead.[4]

Driving Away the Ghost

Melanesia

After a deceased member of the Roro-speaking tribes
has been placed in his grave, a near relative strokes it twice
from head to foot with a branch for the purpose of driving
away the dead man's spirit.   In Yule Island when the ghost
has thus been brushed away it is pursued by two men waving
sticks.   This is kept up all along the route from the village
to the forest, and here with a final curse, they hurl the sticks
and torches after him.[5]   If unusual noises and creakings are
heard coming from the dead man's deserted house, special
measures might be taken to drive the spirit away.[6]

In the Banks Islands it is thought that the ghost does not
at once leave the neighbourhood of his old body.   He manifests
his presence by noises in the house and lights on the grave.

---

[1] Codrington, *Melanesians*, p. 254.
[2] Frazer, *Belief in Immortality*, Vol. I, p. 347.
[3] Caland, *Albindische Todken Gebraucher*, p. 19.
[4] Bogoras, *The Chukchee*, *J.N.P.E.*, Vol. I (1907), p. 528.
[5] Seligmann, *The Melanesians*, p. 275n.
[6] *Ibid*, p. 277.

On the fifth day his relatives drive him away with shouts and the blowing of conch shells or the sound of bull roarers.[1]

It is a custom among the Torres Straits Islanders that after a lapse of several days following a death, the relatives return to the body, mourn, and beat the roof of the bier, while they raise a shout with the object of driving away any part of the man's spirit which might chance to remain. This is especially significant at this moment, for the time has arrived for the severing of the head of the deceased. They think that this could not be easily accomplished if the spirit were still lurking in the body. Naturally the dead man is unwilling to part with so valuable an asset as his head.[2]

The inhabitants of North Melanesia are very much afraid of ghosts and do all in their power to drive them away. At the conclusion of a feast which consists of the body of their victim, these cannibals shout, brandish spears, beat the bushes, and indulge in all sorts of fantastic cries with the object of expelling from the village the ghost of any man who has been murdered and eaten.[3]

The ceremony of expelling the ghost forms a conspicuous part in the rites of the Sulka, a tribe of New Britain to the south of the Gazelle Peninsula. The time for the expulsion is decided in secret lest the spirit should hear. Cocoanut leaves are gathered the evening preceding the ceremony and the next morning the performance begins. Then they beat the walls, shake the posts, set fire to the cocoanut leaves, and then rush out into the paths.[4] After the Fijians had buried a man alive these savages used to make a thundering noise with bamboos, trumpets, shells and other articles to drive away the spirit.[5]

The ghost of the dead wife is specially feared by the widower in British New Guinea. Everywhere he goes about in mourning and armed with an axe to defend himself against her spirit. In addition he is subject to many restrictions and has to follow a life like an outcast from society for the members

---

[1] Codrington, *Melanesians*, p. 267.
[2] Cambridge, *Anthropological Expedition to Torres Straits*, Vol. XV, p. 250.
[3] Frazer, *Belief in Immortality*, Vol. I, p. 396.
[4] Rascher, "Die Sulka ein Bertrag zur Ethnographie Neu Pommern," *Archiv. für Anthropologie*, Vol. XXIX (1904), p. 214.
[5] Jackson, in *Erskine's Journal of a Cruise Among the Islands of the Western Pacific*, p. 477; quoted by Frazer, p. 415.

of the community are afraid to come in contact with such a dangerous individual.[1] The Mafulu at the head of the St. Joseph River in British New Guinea believe that at the death of one of the natives the human spirit departs from the body and becomes an evil ghost. Hence they resort to the device of driving it away with shouts.[2] In the Hood Peninsula in British New Guinea, special precautions are taken by man-slayers. Among them may be mentioned the beating of floors, and the kindling of fires for the purpose of expelling the ghost if he should be lurking in the neighbourhood.[3] It may be added that the spirits of slain men, unchaste women, and women who have died in childbed, are especially feared.[4]

Formerly it was a custom of the Mabuiag to tie the things of a dead man together and also his great toes. The body was then wrapped in a mat which was either sewed or fastened with a skew. The corpse was carried out of the camp feet foremost lest the ghost should find its way back and trouble the survivors.[5]

In German New Guinea the Yabim drive away a ghost with shouts and the beating of drums.[6] Some days after the burial of one of the Papuans of Dutch New Guinea, about sunset, an awful noise in all the houses of the village may be heard. The yelling, screaming, and throwing of sticks are supposed to compel the ghost to take his exit.[7]

AUSTRALIA

The women of the Alice Springs Group join in the dancing and shouting connected with the funeral ceremony and beat the air with their hands in the direction away from the body with the object of driving away the spirit from the old camp which it is supposed to haunt. After the dancing is over, all the participants in the performance direct their steps to

---

[1] Guis, Les Canaques, "Mort-deuil," *Missions Catholiques*, Vol. XXXIV (1902), p. 208, et seqq, quoted by Frazer.

[2] Williamson, *The Mafulu Mountain People of British New Guinea*, pp. 244-255.

[3] Guis, Les Canaques, "Mort-deuil," *Missions Catholiques*, Vol. XXXIV (1902), p. 213 et seqq, quoted by Frazer.

[4] Williams, *Fiji and the Fijians*, Vol. I, p. 241.

[5] Cambridge, *Anthropological Expedition to Torres Straits*, Vol. V, p. 248.

[6] Vetter, *Komm herüber und hilfuns*, Vol. II, p. 7 ; Vol. III, p. 24 ; quoted by Frazer, p. 248.

[7] Van Hasselt, *Die Papuastämme an der Geelvinkbai*, quoted by Frazer p. 305.

the burial place with a run. The leader of the procession makes a circuit away from his associates, perhaps to prevent the spirit from returning to his usual haunts. When the grave is reached the leader jumps upon it and dances wildly. All the rest follow suit except the Mia, Uwinna, and Mura women, who dance backwards and forwards beating the air downward as if to drive the spirit into the grave.[1] In the Melville Islands men rush to the grave yelling and throwing spears ahead of them to drive away the spirit.[2]

HINDU

Allusion has before been made to the pouring of water during the Vedic funeral services with the avowed object of chasing away the spirit, or the lighting of the Rakshoghna which was supposed to expel evil spirits.

SUNDRY DEVICES

MELANESIA

At Mabuiag the corpse is carried out feet foremost, otherwise the mari (ghost) would find its way back and trouble the survivors.[3]

AUSTRALIA

When the Urpmilchima is practised by the Arunta, the widow, decorated with a chaplet of beads, goes to the grave. In the midst of wild lamentations and trampling of boughs she and the other relatives cut themselves, both to indicate their grief and to show that appropriate mourning has been done. Otherwise the spirit of the dead might return to take its vengeance upon the survivors for neglect. After the performance of these rites the deceased must return to the Alcheringa camp and leave them in peace.[4] In the Warramunga tribe we find that certain ceremonies must be performed to display respect for the dead, for otherwise the ghost would feel great chagrin and thus would make it most uncomfortable for the living relatives.[5]

[1] Spencer and Gillen, *Native Tribes of Central Australia*, p. 506.
[2] Spencer, *Native Tribes of the Northern Territory of Australia*, p. 233.
[3] Cambridge, *Anthropological Expedition to Torres Straits*, Vol. V, p. 248.
[4] Spencer and Gillen, *Northern Tribes of Central Australia*, p. 508.
[5] *Ibid*, p. 519.

The natives of some tribes of the Central Australian Group believe that unless a certain amount of grief be displayed, the survivors will be harmed by the offended spirit of the dead man.[1] Among the Alatunja of the Alice Springs Group, it is the custom of the widow to paint herself white to attract the attention of the spirit.[2] The ghost is supposed to watch the proceedings from the bottom of the grave. When he sees that his widow is painted white and wears the chimurilia, he realizes that he is sufficiently mourned for. The object in painting the body white is for the purpose of attracting the spirit's attention.[3]

The Ngarigo practice was to cross a river after burying a body to prevent pursuit by the ghost. Howitt recounts an instance which came to his notice. A leading man of the Ngarigo tribe died at the Snowy River and was buried there. The survivors who had camped not far away, were much alarmed at night by what they thought was the ghost of the deceased haunting the camp, as one of the relatives expressed it, " coming after his wife ".[4]

The Wakelbura also take measures to ward off the ghost. They mark all the trees in a circle round the burial place, so that when the deceased rises from his grave in pursuit of the survivors he will direct his steps in accordance with the marks on the trees, and thus will always find himself at his starting point. Furthermore, to fortify themselves more strongly against possible pursuit, they put coals in the ears of the dead man, supposing by this means that the ghost would remain in his body until they had advanced sufficiently far. Again, they would light fires and put bushes in the trees with the intention of enticing the deceased to tarry in the bushes and warm himself by the fires.[5]

Among the Dieri is a custom to tie the big toes of the corpse together. The Blanch-water section stand in awe of the dead and adopt measures to prevent the dead from rising by tying the toes together and the thumbs behind the back. If any footprints are in evidence about the grave they come to

---

[1] *Native Tribes of Central Australia*, p. 510.

[2] *Ibid*, pp. 503-507.

[3] Spencer and Gillen, *Native Tribes of Central Australia*, p. 507.

[4] Howitt, *Native Tribes of South-East Australia*, p. 461.

[5] *Ibid*, p. 473.

the conclusion that the deceased is dissatisfied with his resting place, and they bury him a second time.*

Among the Narrang-ga, the Wotjobaluk, the Mukjarawaint, the Ngarigo tribes, as well as in the Victorian area and in the Gringai country, the body is usually buried bound with heavy cords, the knees doubled up, either reaching the chest, or the face with the elbows often fast to the sides.[1] This seems a device resorted to to prevent the return of the ghost to its familiar haunts by preventing its escape from the tomb.[2]

The Kukata place digging sticks at the grave to keep the spirits away,[3] and so many other expedients were adopted to facilitate the journey of the deceased to the other world, and to interfere with his return to this one.

At the burial ceremonies of a Kakadu native the deceased is addressed thus : " You lie down quietly, do not come back, lie down all right ; if the children see your spirit later on, they will be sick ".[4] It is also a custom among the Kakadu tribe to place the body face downward, the legs bent back at the knees.[5]

In one part of Queensland the dead are buried face downward and in another part the knee-cap of the deceased is removed.[6] In Cooper Creek we note a custom also found in other sections of Australia. The ground round a grave is swept to obliterate all footprints.[7]

Perhaps the climax of the dread attitude is reached by the Kwearriburra tribe on the Lynd River in Queensland. Whenever a person dies, they cut off his head, roast it in a fire on the grave, and when it is thoroughly charred they smash it into minute pieces and leave the fragments in the hot coals. They calculate that when the ghost arises from the grave to follow the survivors he would miss his head, and go groping about for it until he scorches himself in the fire and is glad to return to his cramped quarters.[8]

---

* When an important man dies in Olaro, the two big toes are tied together. (Dennett, *Nigerian Studies*, p. 30.)

[1] Howitt, *Native Tribes of South-East Australia,* pp. 450-461.

[2] Curr, *The Australian Race,* Vol. I, p. 87.

[3] *Ibid.,* p. 450.

[4] Spencer, *Native Tribes of the Northern Territory of Australia,* p. 241.

[5] *Ibid.*

[6] Thomas, *The Natives of Australia,* p. 200.

[7] Smyth, *The Aborigines of Victoria,* Vol. I, p. 119.

[8] Urquhart, " Legends of the Australian Aborigines," *J.A.I.,* Vol. XIV (1885), p. 88.

INDIA

Before burial a clog was tied to the foot of the Vedic Indian
to prevent the return of the deceased.[1] We learn that round
the thumbs and big toes are twined one or two white threads
tied with fringe or grass. Stones are given to the survivors
and they are also placed between the village and the place
of cremation to ward off the return of the dead. Care is taken
to obliterate all footprints and those who are in the funeral
procession are requested not to look back. It is significant
to note that at the funeral ceremony plants are selected whose
names have a protective sense. The Kurmi caste also practice
the custom of tying the thumb and great toe.[2]*

The menial tribes of India bury their dead face downward
and fill the grave with thorns. Sometimes the corpse is bound
with cords or interred in the crouched position.[3]† When a
member of the Kurmi caste dies, the route along the funeral
procession is strewn with thorns.[4]‡ The Aheriya of Duâb
bury their dead face downward.[5]

In the Kunbi caste the chief mourner walks round the
corpse dropping streams of water all the way.[6] Among the
Aheriya in Duâb and the Bhangi in Hindustan, the survivors
throw sticks and stones behind them after interring the
corpse.[7]

[1] *Av.*, V, 19, 12 ; Bloomfield, *American Journal of Philology*, Vol. XII,
p. 416.
[2] Russell, *Tribes and Castes of India*, Vol. IV, p. 74.
* Tying of the limbs is a very common device to prevent walking. We
find this custom practised by the Hudson Bay Eskimo. (Turner, *Report,
Bureau of Ethnology*, Vol. XI, p. 191), by the Pimas of Arizona (Yarrow,
Introduction to the Mortuary Customs of the North American Indians, Vol. I,
p. 98), by the Tupinambas of Brazil, etc. (Southey, *History of Brazil*, Vol. I,
p. 248.) The expedients of tying the toes and thumbs together, bending the
knees, fastening the elbows to the sides, bending the head down, enveloping
the body in a net, attaching a clog to the foot, the extraction of the knee-cap,
are among the methods employed to prevent " walking."
At childbirth the hands of a Kurmi woman are tied with a cotton thread
so that the spirit cannot arise and trouble the living. (Russell, *The Tribes
and Castes of the Central Provinces of India*, Vol. IV, p. 78.)
[3] Crooke, *Popular Religion and Folk-Lore of Northern India*, Vol. II,
pp. 58-60.
† The wrapping of the dead body in clothes and nets, the placing of
stones and logs over a corpse, the putting of snakes across the coffin perhaps
are also devices for preventing the dead from walking.
[4] Russell, *Tribes and Castes of India*, Vol. IV, p. 78.
‡ Among some negro tribes thorns are put in the paths to keep away
demons. (Spencer, *Principles of Sociology*, Vol. I, p. 173, quoting Bastian.)
[5] Crooke, *The Tribes and Castes of the North-West Provinces*, Vol. I, p. 44.
[6] *Ibid*, Vol. IV, p. 35.
[7] *Ibid*, Vol. I, pp. 45-287.

Among the Nāyars those who carry the corpse to the pyre are dressed as women.[1]

When the Aheriyas of the Northern Provinces burn the corpse, they fling pebbles in the direction of the pyre to prevent the spirit accompanying them.[2] In the Himâlayas, when a man returns from the funeral services of a relative, he places a thorny bush on the road whenever it is crossed by another path. It is incumbent upon the nearest male relative when he sees this to put a stone upon it, and press it down with this feet, praying to the spirit of the dead man not to molest him. Among the Dhângars and Bason of the North-Western Provinces we meet with a strange custom. After they have sacrificed a hog, which is regarded as the representative of the dead man, they bury the trunk in the grave, and pile thorns and stones to keep the ghost down.[3] The Dwanwār carry a corpse to the grave on a cot turned upside down.[4] If a man cannot afford a bier of planks, the Kurmi place the deceased on his cot turned upside down, and carry it out with the legs pointing upward.[5]

North Siberia

Among the Chukchee, the idea of the deceased doing harm is much more in evidence than the possible good he might do. Fear of the dead and the necessity of adopting precautionary measures to prevent their return is so deeply ingrained in the mind of the natives, that this idea is even conspicuous in the children's play.[6] We might mention among some of the devices to prevent the return of the dead: directing the head

---

[1] Thurston, *Castes and Tribes of Southern India*, Vol. V, p. 359.

[2] Crooke, *Popular Religion and Folk-Lore of Northern India*, Vol. II, p. 57.

[3] *Ibid*, p. 58.

[4] Russell, *The Tribes and Castes of the Central Province of India*, Vol. II, p. 495.

It is a common custom through Europe to stop all clocks in the house or to cover all mirrors, and to turn them with their faces to the wall. This is said to be done to prevent puzzling or misleading the ghost in its efforts to leave the house. (Hartland, article in *Hastings*, Vol. IV, p. 415.)

An Ojibway widow springs over the grave and runs zigzag behind the trees as if fleeing from some one. She thus dodges the ghost of her husband to prevent it from haunting her. (Jones, *Ojibway Indians*, p. 99.)

[5] Hartland, article in *Hastings*, Vol. IV, p. 74.

In Scotland and Germany when the coffin was lifted up, the chairs on which it rested were carefully turned upside down for fear the ghost might be sitting on them. (Frazer, " On Certain Burial Customs ", *J.A.I.*, Vol. XV (1885-1886), p. 67.)

[6] Bogoras, *The Chukchee*, *J.N.P.E.*, Vol. VII (1907), p. 518.

of the corpse toward the exit,[1] the Reindeer Koryak custom of placing the reins of the reindeer, which convey the dead body to the cremation place, over the right shoulder, the reverse of the usual way,[2] and among the Chukchee we note that when the reindeer intended for the dead are being slaughtered, the collars are placed over their right shoulders, contrary to their usual custom.[3]* Before, allusion has been made to the reversal of the order of the funeral procession on its homeward march, to interfere with possible pursuit by the dead. We likewise hear of incantations being practised to prevent the spirit from following the survivors. Sometimes the summer after the death of the Chukchee the chief of the funeral procession would wade through the water in a pool exclaiming " I am not a man ; I am an eiderduck ".[4] The "followers" in the funeral procession of a Reindeer Koryak caw like ravens and bark like foxes. This is done three times to conceal their identity and make it appear that they are ravens or foxes.[5] Again there is an injunction against beating a drum for three nights during the time of the death ceremony, for this might call the dead back to life.[6] Among the Reindeer Chukchee, cutting the throat of a corpse is regarded as indispensable. This is done to prevent the spirit of the deceased from following the funeral cortege.[7] The same people practise the enchanting of an iron sheet which serves as a net into the holes of which the deceased would be caught if he attempted to return to his home. Such a sheet is placed under one of the skins of bedding in the sleeping room.[8]

A deceased Koryak is dressed in his funeral garments just before the corpse is taken out. The arrangement of the clothes is peculiar, to indicate, Jochelson suggests, that the dressing of the dead is different from that of the living.[9] But

---

[1] Bogoras, *The Chukchee*, J.N.P.E., Vol. VII (1907), p. 522.
[2] Jochelson, *The Koryak*, J.N.P.E., Vol. VI (1905), p. 110.
[3] Bogoras, *The Chukchee*, J.N.P.E., Vol. VII (1907), p. 526.
* Dogs are not allowed to drag a sled which conveys a dead body to the place of interment. (Boas, " Central Eskimo ", *Sixth Annual Report of the Bureau of Ethnology* (1888), p. 613.)
[4] Bogoras, *The Chukchee*, J.N.P.E., Vol. VII (1907), p. 532.
[5] *Ibid*, pp. 526-527.
[6] *Ibid*, p. 521.
[7] *Ibid*, p. 528.
[8] *Ibid*, p. 528.
[9] Jochelson, *The Koryak*, J.N.P.E., Vol. VI (1905), p. 110.

it seems that this practice must have another object—namely, to confuse the ghost by a reversal of an ordinary custom.

We read that the left-hand mitten is put on the right-hand, and the right-hand one on the left-hand. The cap is put on with its front toward the back. When hitching the reindeer which carry the dead body to the place of cremation, the reindeer Koryak puts the collar over the right shoulder of the animal which ordinarily is placed over the left. After the body is put on a sledge, it is tied with straps to prevent its getting up.[1]

Methods are adopted among the Koryak of preventing the spirits of the deceased from entering other houses. As soon as a death occurs, a messenger ascends to the entrance of each house, and calls: "Set a noose!" The messenger is asked by those within the house, "Who is dead?" and after the desired information is communicated, the messenger departs. Then a blade of grass or a splinter is placed near the head of the ladder. One of the relatives of the deceased holds the head of the dead man on his knees until the entire village is informed. Little children are held in their mother's or grandmother's arms. After the news of the death has been told to all the natives, the deceased is placed on his bed.[2]

An interesting story is told of a Koryak who was taken ill while travelling and who died in a Russian village near Gishiga. The Russians buried him in his travelling clothes. The relatives of the deceased did not then know what to do with his funeral costume which among the Koryak is always prepared in advance of the death. As they feared he might come to get it, they decided to send it to the Russians of the house where the man died, and thus performed their duty to the deceased. However the Russians were unwilling to accept it, but the Koryak messenger left it on the floor of the house and drove away.[3]

Other practices in the funeral rites of the Koryak demonstrate the same attitude toward the spirits of the dead. Jochelson has given us a very significant account of a funeral ceremony which he witnessed among the Koryak. We are just going to recount those details which directly concern the point

[1] Jochelson, *The Koryak, J.N.P.E.*, Vol. VI (1905), p. 111.
[2] *Ibid*, p. 104.
[3] *Ibid*, p. 108.

under consideration. After the burning of the child's clothes, and appearance of the child's head, the grandfather took a pole and thrusting it into the body exclaimed : " Of yonder magpie pricked ". He then imitated the actions of the magpie in the world of the dead with the object of indicating to the deceased that she was passing into another world and must not return to the house. The rest of the performance had the same end in view. As the flames were about to become extinguished he took some twigs from the nearby bushes and placed them round the pyre. These were supposed to represent a dense forest. The grandfather went round the pyre, first from right to left, then from left to right, to eradicate his tracks and thus prevent the spirit from following. After this, as he stepped away from the place of cremation, drawing a line across the snow, he jumped over it and shook himself. The line represented a river which separated the village from the place where the funeral rites were enacted.[1] The desire that water should intervene between the place of burial and the abode of the deceased is also characteristic of the funeral ritual of the Chukchee. The carriers of the corpse of a Maritime Koryak are often replaced en route to the burial place presumably with the object of circumventing the dead in case of pursuit.[2]*

From these concrete instances and from a study of the motives which seem to have actuated the performers of these ceremonies, we must come to the conclusion that dread of the evil influence of the deceased, their impurity, and their possible interference with the survivors is everywhere apparent. This theory is entirely at variance with the view expressed by Rivers, who declared that such an attitude is not characteristic of the natives of Melanesia. Why then, we ask, should such elaborate ceremonies as those described by Codrington for expelling ghosts be resorted to, if the dread idea is not a paramount conception relative to the death-situation of the inhabitants of these islands ? Ghosts in Melanesia, according to Codrington, are not only believed to haunt their burial

[1] Bogoras, *The Chukchee*, *J.N.P.E.*, Vol. VII (1907), p. 476.

[2] *Ibid*, p. 535.

* The Roman who put the torch to the funeral pyre of his relative did so with averted eyes (Virgil, *Aeneid*, VI, 224), for we are told that the spirits were eager to gain recruits. (Granger, *The Worship of the Romans*, p. 70.)

places and to partake of the feast prepared for them, but at night they are everywhere in evidence, dancing, shouting and blowing pipes.[1] The return of the funeral procession by another route than that along which the corpse was carried[2] seems further to corroborate our hypothesis.

It is said that the tribes of the Hood Peninsula have no belief in any good spirit, but in a great number of evil spirits, including those of their dead ancestors. The natives are continually on their guard not to offend these hostile spirits by the least provocation.[3]

Although among the Kori of British New Guinea the spirits of the dead are supposed to go to Mount Idu, it is often their custom to return to their native villages and haunt the burial place. On such visits a most hostile spirit is displayed by these ghosts, and the dread of the ghost among this tribe is so pronounced that they commonly desert a house where a death has occurred.[4]

Among the Roro-speaking tribes of British New Guinea, already referred to, when a death takes place, the female relatives mutilate their bodies in all sorts of conceivable ways, until they are overcome with pain and fatigue. Then, too, a fire is kept burning on the grave for a very long period, with the purpose, so the account goes, of warming the ghost.[5] As Frazer suggests,[6] this, after a cursory glance, might be regarded as a mark of great affection, but when we consider the subsequent harsh methods adopted in expelling the supposed evil spirits from the vicinity of the burial place, we must be of the opinion that the dread of the deceased is the main consideration of the survivors.

The numerous devices practised in the Australian area for expelling the spirits of the dead and for warding off their evil influence are at all times much emphasized. At first sight some of the customs followed might, too, be interpreted as marks of devotion, but a more careful study reveals the fact that such is not the case.

---

[1] Codrington, *Melanesians*, p. 255.
[2] *Ibid*, p. 254.
[3] Frazer, *Belief in Immortality*, Vol. I, p. 203.
[4] *Ibid*, p. 195.
[5] Jouet, *La Sociètè des Missionaires du Sacré Coeur dans les Vicariats Apostoliques de la Mélanésie et de la Micronésie* (1877), p. 30, quoted by Frazer, p. 197.
[6] Frazer, *Belief in Immortality*, Vol. I, p. 197.

The tribes of the Herbert River bury a man with all the paraphernalia which belonged to him in life. Furthermore, they build a hut on his grave, supplying him with a drinking vessel, and at the same time putting food and water at the burial place. If we were not informed of the cruel and brutal treatment later accorded the corpse we might think that most sympathetic and humane motives prompted the survivors. That the spirit of the deceased should not haunt the camp, the father or brother or husband of the dead takes a club, and maltreats the corpse to such an extent that ofttimes the bones are broken. He even breaks both the legs so that wandering would be impossible. To add to the discomfort of the ghost he bores holes in the lungs, stomach and other organs, and places stones in these openings with the object of so weighing down the deceased that he cannot travel far.[1] Thus the object of these mutilations seems to be to render the ghost harmless.

The fear attitude toward the dead finds expression among the Narrinyeri of Australia. These people believe that the souls of the deceased live in the sky, but descend at night to earth to annoy the living. Among them there is little or no trace of affection toward their departed.[2] Although seemingly the most excessive grief is displayed which takes the form of wailing and cutting yet it is the opinion of Taplin " that fear has more to do with these exhibitions than grief ", and he says that " for one moment a woman will appear in the deepest agony of grief and tears ; a few minutes after the conventional amount of weeping having been accomplished, she will laugh and talk with the merriest ".[3] If this sorrow were not manifested, the deceased would not think that he is sufficiently mourned for, and hence would take vengeance upon the survivors.

The Warramunga suppose that the spirit of the dead person, called " ungwulan ", hovers about the tree where the corpse has been deposited and sometimes visits camp to see if the widow is mourning sufficiently ; occasionally it can be heard making a whistling sound.[4]

[1] Howitt, *Native Tribes of South-East Australia*, p. 474.
[2] Frazer, *Belief in Immortality*, p. 135.
[3] Taplin, " The Narrinyeri," in *Native Tribes of South Australia*, pp. 20-21.
[4] Spencer and Gillen, *Northern Tribes of Central Australia*, p. 530.

From a study of our Siberian data it is also evident that the deceased is regarded as a spirit unfriendly to the living. The conceptions which we have submitted are without doubt proof of the attitude of dread manifested toward the spirits of the dead by the inhabitants of this region. Although Jochelson says that he did not hear of any tales of direct transformation of a dead person into an evil spirit yet such tales are found among the Chukchee and also among North American and Siberian tribes in many parts of the world.[1] These transformed evil spirits are particularly pernicious to the relatives of the deceased.*

Our investigation into Vedic literature leads us to the deduction that dread of the evil influence of the deceased was certainly far more accentuated in their funeral ceremonies than was any regard or affection for the departed. Reference has before been made to the various devices which were employed to prevent the return of the spirits of the dead. It is not without interest that many of the regulations of the Sutras find present day parallels among Indian tribes.

If we examine the data presented we shall find the belief that water acts as a barrier between man and his ghostly pursuer among the Chukchee, the Koryak, the Australian tribes, and the Hindus.† For some reason ghosts are unable to cross water, and we also hear of water being thrown along the route of the funeral procession.‡

The spirit of the deceased is frequently represented as thirsty, and in the Indian area a thread is stretched which serves the departed as a ladder to reach the drink suspended

---

[1] Jochelson, *The Koryak, J.N.P.E.*, Vol. VI (1905), pp. 112-113.

* In this connection he mentions the Tupilaq of the Eskimo ; (Boas, *Central Eskimo*, p. 591 and *Baffin Land Eskimo*, p. 131). Similar conceptions are held by the Yahut (Trotschansky, *The Evolution of the Black Faith of the Yahut*, pp. 82-87 ; Jochelson, *Wandering Tribes*, p. 34) ; the Buryat (Agapitoff and Khangaloff, *Materials for the Study of Shamanism of Siberia*, p. 24) ; the Altaiana (*Potanin Sketches of North-West Mongolia*, Vol. IV, p. 130) ; and Mongolia (Mikhailovsky, *Shamanism*, p. 17). The above references quoted by Jochelson, *The Koryak, J.N.P.E.*, Vol. VI (1905), p. 113.

† We find the same belief among the Omaha (Fletcher, *Twenty-seventh Annual Report Bureau of Ethnology* (1911), p. 591.

‡ In Greece all the water stored along the route of the funeral procession is thrown out. (Politis, " On the Breaking of Vessels as a Funeral Rite in Modern Greece," *J.A.I.*, Vol. XXIII (1894), pp. 35-41.) It was a Greek idea that water would ease the burning pains of the dead, but this is interpreted as probably a later and Christian explanation. (Hartland, article in *Hastings*, Vol. IV, p. 427.) However, I can find no trace of such a conception in the areas under consideration.

by it.[1] Among the high-caste Hindus a jar of water is hung
on a Pipal tree for the refreshment of the spirit.[2]

The Kutaba tribe of Australia think that the ghost may
be thirsty, so they leave a drinking vessel on the grave that
he may quench his thirst.[3] The ghosts of the natives of the
Maranoa river were likewise represented as thirsty souls, and
vessels of water were suspended for their use over the grave.[4]

Here we might call attention to the enormous rôle played by
water in religious ceremonies, for we well know its use is by
no means confined to the death-situation. In the history of
many peoples, although water has its nymphs, nixen, and its
protecting gods, yet it is the water itself which always remains
sacred, divine, mighty. The immediate valuation of the
elements finds expression in the Persian religion, where the
practical use of water is connected with its worship. Water
is kept " pure ", first, because of its divine character, and then
because of its " human " character, and, what to us is more
important, its human character survives even after the
divine has been eliminated. In his comment upon the religion
of the Todas, King says : " The transformation of practical
acts into religious ones, through the medium of habit, has
no more striking illustration than that furnished by the
Todas with their daily religion. When the worth of an
object is once established in a group's practical or social life
it thereby gains through eternal momentum to go on increas-
ing, in relative independence of practical social interests ".[5]

The use of fire, too, plays a most important part in the death
ceremonies of all peoples, not only as regards cremation, but
in connection with leaving fires at the place of interment
and stepping over fire after a burial.* Mention has been made
of the fact that the Wakelbura tribe of Australia, as a precaution, light fires with the idea that the ghost would tarry
long enough at the fire so that the living could effect an escape.
However, we do not wish it to be inferred that dread was
always the only motive which influenced the survivors.
Doubtless, at times a certain regard is shown for the comfort

---

[1] Caland, *Altendische Todten Gebraucher*, p. 88.
[2] Crooke, *Popular Religion and Folk-Lore of North India*, Vol. II, p. 61.
[3] Howitt, *Native Tribes of South-East Australia*, p. 450.
[4] *Ibid*, p. 467.
[5] King, *Development of Religion*, pp. 117-121.
* Roman mourners returning from a funeral stepped over a fire. (Festus,
s.v. *Aqua et Igne*.)

and convenience of the ghost. Among the natives of Australia the custom of lighting a fire at the grave to afford comfort to the ghost seems to have been practised.* In West Victoria the aborigines kept up fires all night for this purpose,[1] and we also hear that sometimes these fires were kept burning for an entire month. The Gournditchmara of Australia used to make fires at the grave with the idea of warming the ghost.[2] When a member of any tribe located within thirty miles of Maryborough, South-East Australia, died, one or more fires were lighted on the grave, not only to allow the departed to warm himself, but also to ward off the ghosts of other tribes and of bad men of his own tribe. The greater the number of fires, the more affection is supposed to be displayed. Fires were also lit by Wiimbaio and Wotjobaluk natives to enable the ghosts of the dead to warm themselves.[3] At the grave of a Mabuiag native was always a fire, "for dead man he cold".[4] Among the Roro-speaking tribes of British New Guinea a fire is kindled at the grave and is kept burning almost a month with the object of preventing the ghost from shivering.[5] At Tubetube in British New Guinea on the day when the body is buried, a fire is kindled at the grave and kept continually burning until the feast of the dead is held. The reason assigned for this custom is that the ghost is enabled to get warm when it rises from the grave.[6] A fire is kindled at the grave of a deceased Papuo-Melanesian of British New Guinea and kept burning for nine days so that the ghost may not shiver.[7] In the Hood Peninsula after a manslayer performs several ceremonies as a precaution to ward off the ghost of his victim, fires are kindled with the object of driving away the ghost. If a chief known for his bravery dies in the Duke of York Islands, the women make

---

* The Omaha had a custom of kindling fires at the burial place to cheer the dead. (Fletcher, " The Omaha ", *Twenty-Seventh Annual Report, Bureau of Ethnology* (1911), p. 592.)

For barriers of fire and water see Frazer, " On Certain Burial Customs ", *J.A.I.*, Vol. XV (1886), p. 76-81.

[1] Dawson, *Australian Aborigines*, p. 50.
[2] Howitt, *Native Tribes of South-East Australia*, p. 455.
[3] *Ibid*, p. 452.
[4] Cambridge, *Anthropological Expedition to Torres Straits*, Vol. V, p. 249.
[5] Jouet, *La Société des Missionaires du Sacré Coeur dans les Vicariats Apostoliques de la Mélanésia et de la Micronésie*, p. 30.
[6] Field, quoted by Brown, *Melanesians and Polynesians*, p. 442.
[7] Chalmers, "Notes on the Natives of Kiwai Island, British New Guinea ", *J.A.I.*, Vol. XXXIII (1903), p. 120.

fires that his ghost might warm himself at them.[1] The natives of Vaté or Efat, one of the New Hebrides, kindled a fire on the grave to enable the soul of the deceased to rise to the sun. According to Turner, if this custom were not observed, the soul went to the wretched regions of Pakasia in the lower world.[2] This is doubted by Frazer, who says that he does not recall any other instance of the souls of the Melanesians ascending to the sun, since the usual custom was for them to descend to the earth. The fire, he claims, was probably for the purpose of warming the ghost.[3] Some of the natives of Murua light a fire on the grave which the parents of the deceased look after for two weeks and on a specified day the fire is put out.[4] For the first four nights after a Koita burial, fires are lit on and round the grave near which the dead man's wife and near relatives sleep, while his other relatives and friends sleep in his house.[5]*

In India there is a belief that if, at the time of cremation, the flames ascend directly upward, the deceased gains heaven. Among the Kabīrpanthis a lamp is burnt and the soul is supposed to mingle with the flames and thus to become absorbed into the deity, Kabīr.[6]

Summing up our evidence, the following seem to be some of the possible motives which suggest the use of fire in connection with the death-situation :

(1) To warm the ghost.
(2) To drive away ill disposed beings.

---

[1] Brown, *Melanesians and Polynesians*, p. 389.
[2] Turner, *Samoa, A Hundred Years and Long Before*, p. 335.
[3] Frazer, *Belief in Immortality*, Vol. I, p. 360n.
[4] Seligmann, *Melanesians*, p. 727.
[5] *Ibid*, p. 161-162.

* The Hupa light fires at the grave. (Goddard, *Life and Culture of the Hupa*, pp. 70-72.) The Ashira tribe, the Krumen in Africa, the natives of Kingsmill Islands, keep a fire burning near a corpse. (Smyth, *Aborigines of Victoria*, Vol. I, p. 122.) The Iroquois build a fire near a grave to enable the spirit to prepare its food. (Morgan, *League of the Iroquois*, Vol. II, p. 175.) The Macusi of South America light a fire before the hut in which a corpse is lying to scare off both the ghost and the evil spirit which caused the death. (Koch, " Zum Animus der Südamerikanischen Indianer ", *Int. Arch.*, Vol. XIII (1900), Supplement, p. 88.)

The Yabim of German East Africa believe that the fire which is lit on the grave directs the ghost to the door of the man who killed him by sorcery. (Frazer, *Belief in Immortality*, Vol. I, p. 246.)

The Algonkins and the Mexican maintain a fire on the grave for four days with the object of lighting the spirit upon its journey. (Brinton, *Myths of the New World*, p. 281.)

[6] Russell, *The Tribes and Castes of India*, Vol. I, p. 241.

(3) For lighting the spirit of the deceased to the other world.

(4) For purification.

(5) The belief that if the flames go straight upward, the dead gain heaven.

(6) We must also consider fire and its association with the practical. The effect of fire must have been observed with its connection with heating, lighting, foodstuffs.

(7) To hasten dissolution.

(8) To detect the sorcerer who caused the death.

Noise, too, is a potent factor in driving away ghosts. Thus wailing, drum beating, stone clinking, and brass rattling are practised to ward off the evil effects which the spirits of the deceased might have upon the living. Dances, too, are often instituted with the same object in view.

Wailing is a common form of lamentation in connection with the ceremonies at Bank Islands, at Saa,[1] and at the Shortland Islands.[2] It is likewise a form of lamentation of the Tongaranka tribe,[3] the Kurnai,[4] the Kamilaroi,[5] the Wakelbura,[6] the Warramunga,[7] the Weimbaio, the Wotjabaluk, and the Tongaranka tribes.[8] After the final bone ceremony practised by the Mara tribes, the wailing is kept up the entire night.[9] Among the Koryak we find that it is forbidden to wail for the deceased until he has been taken out of the house.[10]

It was the custom for the youngest son at the funeral ceremony of a Vedic Indian to utter loud, mournful cries which remind us of the " conclamatio " of the Romans.* In the

[1] Codrington, *Melanesians*, pp. 261-267, 270.
[2] Brown, *Melanesians and Polynesians*, p. 211.
[3] Howitt, *Native Tribes of South-East Australia*, p. 451.
[4] *Ibid*, p. 459.
[5] *Ibid*, p. 466.
[6] *Ibid*, p. 471.
[7] Spencer and Gillen, *Across Australia*, Vol. II, p. 426.
[8] Howitt, *Native Tribes of South-East Australia*, p. 451.
[9] Spencer, *Native Tribes of the Northern Territory of Australia*, p. 255.
[10] Jochelson, " The Koryak," *J.N.P.E.*, Vol. VI, 1 (1905), p. 110.
* The Roman mourners repeatedly called upon the names of the deceased with loud cries (Ovid, *Met.*, X, 62; Lucan, *Phars.*, II, 22; Catullus, CI). We also read that calling the name of the dead three times at burial was done because the survivors wished that the departed might live happy underground. Three times they said to him, " Fare thee well. May the earth rest lightly upon thee". They wrote upon his tomb that the man rested there. (*Il.*, XXIII, 221; *Pausanias*, II, 72; Virgil, *Aeneid*, III, 68; *Catullus*, 98-110; Ovid, *Trist.* III, 3-43.) We also learn that the Romans had paid mourners to chant the funeral wail. Loud lamentation, groaning, wailing and beating of the breasts were characteristic of the Greek ritual for the dead. (Lucian, *de Luctu*, 12.)

areas we have considered we can find only one instance in which the wailing indulged in at the death ceremonies is not supposed to drive away the ghost of the departed. Among the inhabitants of Lepers' Island we find that the wailing commences after death begins. Codrington describes the last solemnity rites connected with the death of a man of prominence. On this occasion all the people assemble in the middle of the village ; a man of the waivung division to which the deceased did not belong, mounts a tree, and calls the names of the departed. This is followed by silence and all listen very attentively for a sound. If none is forthcoming, they utter a wailing cry, because they will hear the voice of the dead man no more. They have no thought in this instance of driving away the ghost.[1]

Ten days after a death the Maritime Koryak beat the drum, thus expressing their grief for the deceased, whereas the Reindeer Koryak beat the drum immediately after the funeral.[2] Among the Chukchee, there was an interdiction against beating the drum for three nights during the time of the burial ceremony, for this might call the dead back to the house.[3] Here, as we see illustrated, are two conceptions, one that the ghost was frightened by noise, and the other, that the spirit of the deceased would frequent his old haunts, if a drum were beaten a short time after death. But nevertheless, the idea, after all, is the same,—the departed was not wanted in the realms of the living as he was dreaded by the survivors.*

---

[1] Codrington, *Melanesians*, p. 285.
[2] Jochelson, *The Koryak*, *J.N.P.E.*, Vol. VI (1905), p. 113.
[3] Bogoras, *The Chukchee*, *J.N.P.E.*, Vol. VII (1907), p. 521.
* We also find a ritualistic wailing and dirge common to the Israelitish cult (Zechariah, XII, 10-15). When Micah depicts the fall of Samaria he declares : " Therefore will I wail and howl ". (Micah, I, 8.)
It is chiefly at the time of the Pomniki, or ceremonies in honour of the dead, that the Prichitaniya, or lamentations for the departed, are to be heard. (Ralston, *Songs of the Russian People*, pp. 342-343.) Fauriel gives us an interesting account of the myrologia of modern Greece in his *Chants populaires de la Grèce Moderne*. "The myrologion", he says, is a "poetic, improvisation, inspired by grief". The improvisation is done by women and in Asiatic Greece and in the Islands are professional myrologists whose functions are almost parallel with those of the Russian wailers.
The Skazki stories of the Russian people bear frequent witness to the fact that the dead spirits are regarded as vampires or werwolves, thirsting for human blood. The only ghosts which sometimes are regarded as friendly are those of parents evincing sympathy with a child by intending to do it a service. (Ralston, *Songs of the Russian People*, p. 335.)
Among the Romans we find the fear attitude so emphasized that because of this feeling toward the dead, men would pine and go mad. (Fasti, V,

The dread idea seems to have prompted the Dieri and the Herbert River tribes of South-East Australia, the Warramunga of Central Australia, the Koita tribe of British New Guinea, and the Chukchee either to shift camp or to desert the house in which a death occurred.

It is very interesting to note that the procedure followed in the disposal of a dead body among the Koryak is identical with the episodes narrated in the Magic Flight Tales. The express object in imitating the actions of the magpie in the world of the dead is to inform the deceased that he is passing into another world and must not return to his old haunts, since he is looked upon as a spirit hostile to the survivors.[1]

As Jochelson suggests, the question why dead persons are supposed to radiate such danger especially upon those to whom they have been most attached and dearest in life, is one of the most difficult problems for the ethnologist to attempt to solve.[2] Although we have throughout this treatise stressed the conception which universally prevails among all peoples regarding the evil influence of the deceased upon the living, yet we are not insensible to the fact that other factors sometimes contribute which cause the performance of certain rites. Thus in the Solomon Islands in Florida, when a man dies, his relatives and friends cut down the dead man's fruit trees, as a mark of respect and affection, not because they think that these will be of advantage to him in the ghost world;[3] likewise in Saa, a man's cocoa-nut and bread-fruit trees are cut down after his death, which act the natives interpret as an evidence of respect.[4] Among the Koita tribe of British New Guinea, there is a belief that residence in the spirit land depends upon the length of time their names and memories survive in the land of the living. However, even here the idea of the spirits of the dead haunting the realms of this world is the paramount conception. We have before alluded to the kindly motive which sometimes prompts the lightings

---

p. 429, et seqq.) The Greeks too were afraid of their dead ; their heroes were regarded as very irritable and evil. (Rohde, *Psyche,* pp. 177-225 n4.)

The ancient Greeks beat brass to drive away the spirits. (Rohde, *Psyche,* II, 77.)

[1] Jochelson, *The Koryak, J.N.P.E.,* Vol. VI (1905), p. 112.

[2] *Ibid.*

[3] Codrington, *Melanesians,* p. 255.

[4] *Ibid,* p. 263.

of fires at a grave. In German New Guinea we find the belief that ghosts are supposed to help as well as to harm the living, assisting in the cultivation of the land. But here, too, the predominant motive is that of fear of the spirits of the dead.[1] We feel firmly convinced that although the various propitiatory offerings may be actuated by motives not altogether selfish, yet the dread attitude is so emphasized everywhere that we cannot afford to lose sight of its potency.

If we examine our data we shall see that the custom of driving away spirits is far more in evidence in the Melanesian and Australian areas than in the Siberian region, although we learn from the Chukchee texts[2] that beating the air was a common device for getting rid of spirits. We would certainly expect that the performance of driving away the spirits would be more conspicuous among peoples where magic plays such an important rôle, than in communities where its rôle is comparatively insignificant. Thus we have seen that in the Melanesian and Australian areas where many magical rites are practised, means of driving away spirits are inseparably connected with death customs. The differentiation which Codrington has so aptly characterized between the ideas of the natives of the New Hebrides and Banks Islands to the East and those of the inhabitants of the Solomon Islands to the West, seems to me also to hold good when applied to the Australian and Siberian areas. Whereas the religious ideas of the natives of New Hebrides and the Banks Islands are directed toward spirits rather than ghosts, those on the West are primarily concerned with ghosts, and they address themselves almost wholly to them. This, Codrington says, goes with a greater development of the sacrificial system in the West than in the East and with a certain advance in the arts of life.[3] We likewise find that in Australia where the sacrificial system is developed, we have ghosts playing a most important part in the religious ceremonies, but in the Siberian area where there is practically no system of sacrifice, the inhabitants concern themselves with spirits.

---

[1] Vetter, *Komm herüber und hilfuns*, Vol. III, pp. 19-24. In Mitteilungen der *Geographischen Gesellschaft zu Jena*, Vol. XII (1893), p. 96, et seqq., quoted by Frazer, p. 247.

[2] Bogoras, *Chukchee Mythology*, *J.N.P.E.*, Vol. VIII (1913), p. 130.

[3] Codrington, *Melanesians*, p. 122.

Our study demonstrates the universality of the beliefs connected with the spirits of the deceased in the Melanesian, Australian, Hindu, and Siberian areas. We are of the opinion that these beliefs are the outcome of the just-so death-situation, and are evolved independently of any outside source. It is not necessary in this instance, we claim, to attribute such ideas either to diffusion or to historical contact of any sort whatever. We voice here the sentiment of Boas[1] who is of the opinion that psychological conditions may bring about similarity of ideas without an underlying historical connection. These similar beliefs may be explained by similarities in the reactions of the mind. In this case we must take issue with Wissler who does not think that a psychological explanation is valid for cultural phenomena.[2]

[1] Boas, "Mythology and Folk Tales", *J.A.F.L.* (1914), p. 408.
[2] Wissler, "Historical Interpretation for Culture", *Science*, Vol. LXIII (1916), p. 193.

CHAPTER V

GENERAL ATTITUDE TOWARD THE CORPSE

THE influence which our investigation reveals as the most fundamental is not the non-recognition on the part of the savage of conceiving of death as a fact, but the awfulness felt to attach to the dead body itself. Here, we are in accord with Marett[1] who thinks, " We have the cause of a definite assignment to a passing appearance such as the trance image of real and permanent existence in relation to a dead owner ". However, real as the thrill of ghost-seeing may be, according to this view it is insignificant in comparison to the very horror of a human corpse instilled into man's body by the self-preservation instinct. The mass of evidence dealing with the use of human remains for the purpose of offensive or protective magic seems to support this view. The acquisition of a dead man's scalplock, his bones, his hair, insures the possession of mana to the recipient.

Since the ghost is in the realm of the mysterious and uncanny, it is naturally saturated with danger. " The potency of the mysterious is the fundamental historical basis of religion." Even " in ghost stories the victim is transfixed with horror ''.[2] The very awfulness of contact with a dead body makes one show respect and reverence to the departed and to perform acts of service to propitiate the ghost. As there is a pronounced tendency to personify the supernatural and unfathomable, and at the same time to resort to every possible expedient such as conciliation, communion, and self-restraint to appease such a formidable power, we must expect to find this attitude emphasized in the mystery of death, encircled as it is by such an imaginative setting.

An examination of the concrete material shows that a " perfect pandemonium centres around the corpse ".[3] Although in the areas with which we are concerned only a few

[1] Marett, *The Threshold of Religion*, p. 23.
[2] Shotwell, *The Religious Revolution of To-Day*, pp. 111-122.
[3] Farnell, *Evolution of Religion*, p. 134.

examples of a specific attitude toward the corpse as such can be found, yet the presence of innumerable mourning customs, death taboos, purification rites, and various devices adopted to prevent the return of the deceased, point to a confirmation of Marett's and Farnell's views.

The universal attitude toward the corpse is mystical and supernatural, and the contact from it is alarming. Not only do we find this emphasized in the Iranic Sacred Books, in the Old Testament, among the Grecians and Romans, but wherever we turn we see society replete with examples of this conception.

The author of the *Evolution of Religion* has voiced a most characteristic utterance when he says that the " Zend-Avesta regards the whole universe as an over-charged battery of spiritual electricity, where a single careless act of accidental uncleanliness is a common catastrophe ".[1] That a corpse is regarded as uncanny, and that it is supposed to contain a certain power for evil, is emphasized most significantly in the Sacred Book of the Persians. Since the corpse is supposed to be saturated with danger for mortals, it is regarded as taboo. The amount of influence which a dead body can radiate, is often in proportion to the rank and sanctity of the deceased. Thus in the Zend-Avesta, the defiling power is most potent in the case of a priest, less in a warrior, and least in a husbandman.[2] The sacred person can defile the most because he is looked upon as being charged with the greatest amount of spiritual electricity. A striking instance of this is seen in the Old Testament. When the ark was being conveyed to Jerusalem the cart shook, and the person who struck it fell.[3] Uzziah thus came in contact with Deity and died of terror.[*]

[1] Farnell, *Evolution of Religion*, p. 104.
[2] *Vd.* V, 25.
[3] This same principle is illustrated by the Roman concept.
[*] After Augustus had conveyed the body of Agrippa into the Forum he pronounced over it a funeral oration with a curtain drawn before him because the eyes of a pontiff might not look upon the body of a corpse. (Merivale, *History of Rome*, Vol. IV, p. 166.) The idea is explained by Seneca in relation to a similar scene forty years later. (*Cons. ad Marc.*, 5.) Again, a cypress bough was placed over the door of a noble family to give warning to any pontiff who chanced to pass, that he was not to enter.
At Hierapolis no man could enter the great temple of Astarte on the same day when he viewed a corpse. However, the next day he was permitted to go in provided he had first purified himself. But kinsmen were not allowed to enter until thirty days after a death and then not without shorn heads.

MELANESIA

A person in the Fiji Islands because of the defilement caused by touching the corpse of one who died a natural death is yambo and as a consequence is not allowed to touch food with his hands for several days.[1] In Fiji, too, a man who has dug the grave of a chief is unclean for a year.[2]*

Among the Koita any men not closely related to the dead man may bear him to his grave, but these attendants give place to others at almost every pace since the body is now highly aina. This indicates a contagious quality which is harmful to those who come in contact with it, although its detrimental effects are lessened by shortening the time of exposure to it.[3]

The fear of the pollution from the corpse is seen in New Caledonia in the strict injunction that no one except the grave diggers may handle a corpse. After their duty has been performed, they must stay with the dead body four or five days, fasting and praying and keeping away from their wives. They are also forbidden to shave or cut their hair or to partake of food with their hands.[4]

AUSTRALIA

Among the Dieri of Australia it is the custom of the relatives of the dying man to divide into two groups, one comprising his near relatives, and the other his distant ones. While those of the first group sit close to the dying person, and even after his death throw themselves on the body, those of the other group remain at some distance. Here we see that even a glance

---

[1] Fison, *Tales from Old Fiji*, p. 163.

In Samoa those who attended the deceased were most careful not to handle food and for days were fed by others. (Turner, *Samoa, a Hundred Years and Long Before*, p. 145.)

[2] Fraser, *The Aborigines of New South Wales*, p. 82.

* In Great Fiji the office of the chief's grave digger is hereditary in a certain clan. After the funeral rites are over, he is shut up in a house and painted black from head to foot. When he is forced to leave even for a very short time, he covers himself with a very large cloth and is supposed to be invisible. Food is brought to him after dark by silent messengers who place it within the doorway. Such seclusion may last a long time. (Fison, *Tales from Old Fiji*, p. 167.)

[3] Seligmann, *The Melanesians*, p. 161.

[4] Lambert, *Moeurs et Superstitions des Néo-Calédonians*, pp. 235-239. (Quoted by Frazer, p. 327.)

directed upon the corpse by a distant relative is saturated with danger. According to some, the reason given for this custom is to prevent an intense longing for the deceased, while others say the spirit of the deceased might draw them to itself, and death then would be inevitable.[1]

When one of the now practically extinct Australian Tribe Wiimbaio died, his face was covered with the corner of his rug, because no one could look at the face of a dead person. The body was laid out, rolled in a rug, and tightly corded. The relatives would place their heads on the body and sometimes were even stretched out full length on the corpse.[2]

In Victoria no one cared to touch a dead body with his hand.[3] The grave-diggers at Copper's Creek, New South Wales, smear their bodies with the red and white spots and put pipe clay on their heads.[4]

INDIA

As long as the body of a Hindu remains in the house neither the inmates nor their neighbours can eat, drink, or work. A temple service was entirely suspended until the body of a man who had died not far off had been removed.[5]

Among the Dhānwar, a primitive tribe, the male relatives, when filling the grave, keep their backs toward it to avoid seeing the corpse.[6] Those who go near a corpse while a Teivali is being buried are *ishchiloivichior ichchil*, denoting a condition of impurity.[7]

SIBERIAN AREA

In Kamenshoye some one closes the eyes of the deceased and his face is covered with a fur robe, for it is a sin to look at the face of a dead person.[8]

[1] Howitt, *Native Tribes of South-East Australia*, p. 447.

[2] *Ibid*, p. 451.

[3] Fraser, *The Aborigines of New South Wales*, p. 86.

[4] *Ibid*, p. 82.

[5] Dubois, *Hindu Manners, Customs, and Ceremonies*, p. 179.

[6] Russell, *Tribes and Castes of India*, Vol. II, p. 495.

[7] Rivers, *The Todas*, p. 368.

[8] Jochelson, *The Koryak*, J.N.P.E., Vol. VI (1905), p. 104.

It is a custom among the Reindeer Koryak for one of the nearest relatives of the deceased, mother, husband, or wife, to wipe the face of the departed with wet moss without, however, looking at it.[1] No part of the body of a deceased Chukchee must be seen by those present. It is covered with a heavy skin.[2]

At the funeral obsequies of a Reindeer Chukchee, the " fortifier " or nearest relative of the deceased rips open the body to see if he can ascertain the cause of the death. He does this with a long knife, carefully avoiding touching the body with his hands, notwithstanding that they are protected with mittens or gloves of a peculiar kind.[3]

LACK OF DREAD ATTITUDE TOWARD THE CORPSE AS SUCH.

MELANESIA

When a Sulka dies, his relatives come and sleep beside the corpse.[4] In describing the funeral ceremonies of the Fijians, Wilkes tells us that the female mourners kiss the corpse.[5] A New Guinea native kissed her deceased husband's body every day until the skin dried up.[6]

AUSTRALIA

In Encounter Bay we find that one of the nearest relatives sleeps on the head of a corpse if the deceased has been killed in battle.[7] Among the Dieri when a dead body is about to be disposed of, eight men take the corpse on their heads.[8] In the Boulia district the body is carried by two or three men. It usually is placed crosswise and rests on their shoulders.[9]*

[1] Jochelson, *The Koryak*, *J.N.P.E.*,Vol. VI (1905), p. 110.

[2] Bogoras, *The Chukchee*, *J.N.P.E.*, Vol. VIII (1907), p. 522.

[3] *Ibid.* p. 527.

[4] Frazer, *Belief in Immortality*, Vol. I, p. 399.

[5] Wilkes, *United States Exploring Expedition*, Vol. III, p. 96.

[6] Allen, *Evolution of the Idea of God*, p. 50.

[7] Meyer, "The Aborigines of the Encounter Bay Tribes", in *Native Tribes of South Australia*, p. 199.

[8] Thomas, *The Natives of Australia*, p. 196.

[9] Roth, *Ethnological Studies among the North-West Central Queensland Aborigines*, pp. 163-164.

* At Port Moresby the husband throws himself on the body of his dead wife. (Lawes "Ethnographical Notes on the Mohe, Koitapu, and Koiari," *J.A.I.*, Vol. VIII (1879), p. 371.)

SIMILARITIES

INDIA

At a funeral the Todas touch the dead body with their foreheads.[1] Dubois tells us that a Hindu widow holds the corpse tightly clasped in her arms.[2] At the cremation ceremony the chief mourner kisses the dead body.[3]

---

[1] Rivers *The Todas*, p. 343.
For further discussion of attitude toward the corpse, see sections on " Purification " and " Mourning."
[2] Dubois, *Life and Customs of the Hindus*, Vol. II, p. 353.
[3] *Ibid*, p. 492.
A Hupa grave-digger is under taboo. After the funeral he is required to carry a bough of Douglas spruce over his head " that he may not by any chance glance at the sky or any human being thereby contaminating them." (Goddard, *Life and Culture of the Hupa*, p. 72.)
Among the Maoris we find the attitude toward the corpse most pronounced. Anyone who handled a dead body, or assisted to carry it to the grave, or even touched a dead man's bones was tabooed and had innumerable restrictions imposed upon him. He was not permitted to enter any house nor to come in contact with anything. Not only was he forbidden to touch food with his hands, but the man designated to feed him is likewise subject to restrictions. This feeder presented a picture of the most abject corruption and filth, and degradation of the most appalling nature. (Frazer, *Golden Bough*, Vol. III, pp. 138-139.)
Those who have touched a corpse among the Shuswap of British Columbia sleep with thorn bushes for pillows, and thorn bushes are also placed round their beds. (Boas, *Sixth Report on the Western Tribes of Canada*, p. 91.) For one year among the Thompson River Indians the widow or widower who has come in direct contact with a dead body has a bed made of fir boughs on which sticks of rose bush are placed. (Teit, " The Thompson River Indians of British Columbia ". *J.N.P.E.*, Vol. I (1900), pp. 332-333.) There seems to be a belief that the ghost attaches itself to the thorn. Those who handle a dead body and dig a grave are isolated for four days.
The Salish, British Columbia, hand the corpse to a wutltzĕt or funeral shaman who washes it and prepares it for burial. This official because of his magical power is supposed to be immune to the " bad medicine " of dead bodies. His head is sprinkled with bull-rushes which are regarded as potent in checking the evil influences of corpses. The grave is brushed out by the mystic red fire to drive off the evil influence. (Hill-Tout, " Report on the Ethnology of the StlatlumH of British Columbia," *J.A.I.*, Vol. XXXV (1905), N.S., p. 137.)
Of the Greenlanders it is stated, " If they have happened to touch a corpse, they immediately cast away the clothes they have then on ". (Westermarck, *Development of Moral Ideas*, Vol. II, p. 545, quoting Egede, *History of Greenland*.)
The Eskimos are filled with the greatest awe when touching a dead body. (Boas, " Central Eskimo," *Sixth Annual Report, Bureau of Ethnology* (1888), p. 612.)
" Whosoever is unclean by the dead, both male and female, shall be put out, without the camp shall ye put them ; that they defile not their camps in the midst whereof Yahweh dwells." (*Numbers* v. 2-3.) In reference to the high priest we read : " Neither shall he go to any dead body ". (*Leviticus* xxi. 10.)
In Samoa the men who take hold of the body are paia (sacred) for the time and are forbidden to touch food. They are also fed by others. (Brown, *Melanesians and Polynesians*, p. 402.)

CHAPTER VI

MOURNING

ALMOST as varied as the methods of disposing of the dead are the mourning customs. Only a few illustrations of each mourning observance will be given, just sufficient to keep in line with the general plan of the work.

HAIR

MELANESIA

The widow and children of a deceased Wagawaga native of British New Guinea shave their heads after bathing in the sea.[1] The Fijian Islanders cut their hair and beard after a death has occurred in their midst. Sometimes they make bald only the crown of the head.[2] The widow and widowers of a departed native of the Hood Peninsula in British New Guinea also shave their heads and blacken their bodies.[3] Among the New Caledonians the grave diggers are forbidden to shave or to cut their hair.[4]

Mourners at Windessi of Dutch New Guinea have their hair shorn as a sign of mourning.[5] Among the Lenguas of Paraguay it is a custom for the relatives to cut their hair and the mourning lasts until it is grown again.[6] In Greece the men allow the beard to grow, and in parts of Bulgaria for forty days the men neither shave nor cut their hair.[7] The men in districts of Southern Italy do not shave their beards for one month.[8] The male inhabitants of Malta go out on the seventh day with faces unshaven.[9] Among the negroes of

---

[1] Seligmann, *Melanesians*, p. 611.
[2] Frazer, *Belief in Immortality*, Vol. I, p. 451.
[3] *Ibid*, p. 204.
[4] Lambert, *Moeurs et Superstitions des Néo-Calédonians*, pp. 235-239 (Quoted by Frazer, p. 327).
[5] Frazer, *Belief in Immortality*, Vol. I, p. 320.
[6] Koch, "Zum Ani mus der Südamerikanischen Indianer," *Int. Arch.*, Vol. XIII, Suppl., p. 76.
[7] Hartland, in *Hastings*, Vol. IV, p. 439.
[8] Ramage, *Nooks and By-Ways of Italy*, p. 72.
[9] Busuttil, *Holiday Customs of Malta*, p. 131.

the Gold Coast the relatives may not wash themselves or comb their hair during the funeral ceremony and among both the Ewe and Yoruba-speaking people, shaving marks the termination of the mourning period.[1] Upon the death of a Bakongo chief, all his followers shave their heads as a sign of mourning.[2] In the Tonga Islands the entire population shave their heads upon the death of one of the inhabitants.[3] Spencer mentions the fact that the Todas, the Chippewayans, the Comanches, the Dakotahs, the Mandans, the Tupis, cut their hair after a death.[4] A Greenland widow likewise cuts her hair.[5] Among the Tlingit Indians, as soon as a person dies, his friends cut or singe their hair just below the ears to show respect for the dead.[6]

The widow of a member of the Trobriand community of Northern Massim cuts her hair as one of the outward signs of mourning.[7] At Waima children may cut off a few locks of their hair as a sign of mourning and both male and female adults shave their heads to indicate that one of their kinsmen has died.[8] In the Shortland Group both men and women cut their hair when in mourning.[9]

AUSTRALIA

The relatives and friends of a Barrinyeri native who has departed this life have their hair cut close to their heads and cover themselves with oil and powdered charcoal.[10] Shaving the head with a mussel shell was practised by the men in South Australia and with a fire-stick by the women.[11] In

---

[1] Ellis, *Yoruba-Speaking People*, p. 160,
[2] Word, *Congo Cannibals*, p. 43.
[3] Mariner, *Tonga Islands*, Vol. II, p. 181.
[4] Spencer, *Principles of Sociology*, Vol. I, pp. 166, 167.
[5] *Ibid.*
[6] Swanton, " Social Conditions, Beliefs, and Linguistic Relationships of the Tlingit Indians," *Twenty-sixth Annual Report, Bureau of Ethnology* (1908) p. 429.
[7] Seligmann, *Melanesians*, p. 716.
[8] *Ibid*, p. 276.
[9] Brown, *Melanesians and Polynesians*, p. 216.
[10] Taplin, " The Narrinyeri," in *Native Tribes of South Australia*, p. 20.
[11] Thomas, *The Natives of Australia*, p. 203.
The hair is cropped as a sign of mourning among the Sonmoo and Wollwa Indians of America. (*J.A.I.*, Vol. XXIV (1894-1895), p. 207.) Among the Indians of Guiana it is a custom for the survivors to crop their hair as a sign of mourning. (*Im. Thurn. Indians of Guiana*, p. 224.) Cutting of the hair among the Ainu is imperative upon the death of husband or wife; ordinarily such a custom is unheard of among them. (Batchelor, *The Ainu and Their Folk-Lore*, p. 167.)

many parts of Australia the natives cut off portions of their beards, and singeing these, throw them upon the dead body. Sometimes they cut off the beard of the corpse and burning it, rub themselves and the dead body with the singed portions.[1] We also meet with the idea that the hair of the dead confers the gift of clear sightedness.[2] Thus among the Narringeri it is usual to preserve the hair of a dead man. It is spun into a cord and fastened round the head of a warrior who now sees more clearly, is more active, and can parry with his shield or avoid the spear of his foe.[3]

INDIA

During the ten days period of mourning the Hindus were not allowed to shave. The immediate relatives of the Paharias of the Rajmahal Hills for five days are regarded as unclean and then they shave. On the eleventh day following a death the Bhumijas of Manbhum shave.[4] In Bengal to-day, according to Bose, the son is forbidden to shave from the moment of his father's death to the conclusion of the funeral ceremony.[5] When any one dies among the Kumbi, a great agricultural

---

That hair cutting must have been in vogue among the Israelites is seen in God's injunction to his children to the effect that they should not disfigure themselves in mourning. "Ye shall not cut yourselves, nor make any baldness between your eyes for the dead." (*Deut.* xiv. 1.) Regarding the priests' mourning we read : "They shall not make any baldness upon their heads, neither shall they shave off the corner of their beard ". (*Lev.* xxi. 5.) "For every head shall be bald and every beard clipped, and upon all hands shall be cutting." (*Jer.* xlviii. 37.)

It is interesting to note that a coin of Augustus has been discovered which represents this princeps bearded as a sign of mourning. (Shuckburgh, *Augustus*, facing p. 16.) We also read that after the death of Hephaestion Alexander ordered the manes of the horses to be shorn as a sign of mourning. (Jackson, *Persia, Past and Present*, p. 165.) See *Herodotus*, IX, 24. Among the Greeks the hair was cut as a token of mourning.

We find hair cutting practices by the Wichita in time of mourning, by the Achomawi Indians of California, and the Crow. (Yarrow, *A Study of Mortuary Customs among the North American Indians*, pp. 8, 61, 91.) Although the Dakotas never cut their hair under other circumstances, yet after a death they cut it off even with the neck and the top of the forehead. (Yarrow, *A Study of Mortuary Customs among the North American Indians*, pp. 71-72.)

The Lkungen of Vancouver Island forbid a widow and widower to cut their hair for fear they might gain too much power over the souls and welfare of others. (Hartland, *Ritual and Beliefs*, p. 254.)

[1] Grey, *Expeditions of Discovery in North-West and West Australia*, Vol. II, p. 335.

[2] Curr, *The Australian Race*, Vol. II, p. 249.

[3] Smyth, *The Aborigines of Victoria*, p. 112.

[4] *Statistical Accounts of Bombay*.

[5] Bose, *Hindoos as They Are*, p. 261.

caste, the male mourners shave their heads.[1] The Kurmi mourners likewise shave after a funeral.[2] The same custom is practised by the Dhākar caste whose members are of illegitimate descent.[3] The chief mourner of the Dhīmar caste of fishermen shaves ten days after a death has occurred.[4]

What, we ask ourselves, is the significance of these mourning customs ? Among the most primitive peoples, the hair, because it continually keeps growing, is inseparably connected with life ; indeed, it is the very incarnation of life. Then, too, it could be so easily detached that cutting was a simple expedient to conform to certain emotional values in the life of a tribe. To the primitive mind, the possession of a man's hair is a valid representation of the individual himself and its possession insures mana to the recipient. It is primarily a case of "pars pro toto," being one of the innumerable instances of sympathetic magic. Then, too, there is a belief that spirits attach themselves to hair.

The importance of hair in the life of a savage is by no means restricted to the death-situation alone. Thus at the close of the initiation ceremonies of Ariltha among the Northern Arunta the elder sisters of the boy who has just figured in the ceremony cut off a few locks of his hair which they keep. Among some of the tribes of Central Australia, when a man has his hair cut, which he does periodically, it is incumbent upon him to present it to certain individuals. It is significant to note that in so doing, he always sits facing the direction where the Alcheringa camp of his mother is supposed to be situated, for otherwise a great calamity would befall him.[5] A man's hair always goes to some one who is either Ikuntera or Umbirna to him.[6]*

---

[1] Russell, *Tribes and Castes of India*, Vol. IV, p. 37.
[2] *Ibid*, p. 78.
[3] *Ibid*, Vol. II, p. 479.
[4] *Ibid*, Vol. II, p. 506.

Among the Salish of British Columbia it was the custom for the mortuary shaman to cut the hair of the members of the household. The severed hair was tied up in a little ball and taken into the forest and fastened to the branches of a red fir tree on its eastern side. (Hill-Tout, " Report on the Ethnology of the StlatlumH of British Columbia," *J.A.I.*, Vol. XXXV (1905), p. 138.)

[5] Spencer and Gillen, *Native Tribes of Central Australia*, p. 466.
[6] *Ibid*, p. 465.

* The importance of hair in initiation rites is seen in the Omaha tribe. (Fletcher, *Twenty-seventh Annual Report of the Bureau of Ethnology* (1911), pp. 122-124.)

In Australia we find an exchange of locks for affection. These are worn round the neck and it is considered unlucky to give away or lose such a keepsake. If it chances to be lost the owner of the other lock is asked to undo the exchange by returning it, otherwise the owner of the lock will die.[1] It is esteemed a mark of the greatest confidence if a young girl gives her lover a lock of her hair.[2]

At Cape Grafton there is a firm belief that heavy rains are sure to follow if hair is burnt. We also note a similar belief along the Proserpina River.[3] In the Keppel Islands a human hair string is often tied to the spot where pain is.[4]

Innumerable instances can be cited to show that hair is often used as a charm ; again, it serves the purpose of a curse ; and it is also used in sacrifice. Thus in Victoria hair is burnt as a charm, and if a tribesman is taken ill, it is thought that a member of a hostile tribe has stolen some of his hair.[5] Among the New Caledonians we find that the hair of the deceased is used as an amulet.[6] Sometimes in memory of the dead the Yabim wear a lock of his hair.[7] The Bhils of India shave the heads of their children between the ages of two and five and the sacrifice idea seems to be accentuated here.[8] Oldenberg tells us that in India before the ceremony of the new and full moons, the head of a child was cut into a certain form identified with its particular family.[9] Among the Omaha, each gens had a special hair arrangement.[10] In many areas we find the hair fixed to represent the totem animal. Again, some primitive tribes require a rain arrangement of coiffure after marriage. Thus the Hopi maidens wear their hair in a whorl representing the squash, but after their entrance upon wedded life, they fix it in braids.

The sacrificial idea is often met with in Greek life. Before

[1] Dawson, *Australian Aborigines*, p. 55.

[2] Smyth, *The Aborigines of Victoria*, Vol. I, p. 83.

[3] Roth, "Superstition, Magic, and Medicine," *North Queensland Ethnography, Bulletin No. V*, pp. 10-21.

[4] *Ibid*, p. 37.

[5] Smyth, *The Aborigines of Victoria*, Vol. I, p. 110.

[6] Lambert, *Mœurs et Superstitions des Néo-Calédoniens*, p. 276.

[7] Frazer, *Belief in Immortality*, Vol. I, p. 249.

[8] Crooke, *The Popular Religion and Folk-Lore of North India*, Vol. II, p. 66.

[9] Oldenberg, *Religion des Veda*, pp. 425-429.

[10] Fletcher, *Handbook, American Indians*, Vol, I, p. 525.

marriage, girls frequently dedicated their hair to some patron saint.[1] The particular sanctity which attaches itself to hair is evident in the Samson story and in the tale of the avenger of Baldur, who will not cut his hair until he has killed his enemies. Perhaps the possession of the hair of the deceased which we find coveted in many cases, is supposed to effect a sacramental union with the dead, and for this reason we not only find the hair of the departed preserved as a precious relic, but the locks of the living are often thrown into the grave at the time of the funeral ceremonies.[2]

The head itself is regarded as especially sacred by some primitives. The Greeks identified the head with the rest of life[3] and a modification of this belief is found among the Omaha.[4]

That great significance is attached to the skull, and that, in the mind of the primitive, the possession of one's skull, especially if such belongs to a chief or a person of power, was evidently realized by all Indians.

We find hair left unshorn during the period of a vow, as in the case of Achilles when his father vowed that he would dedicate his son's locks to the River Spercheius if Achilles would return from the war.[5] The idea that uncut hair is associated with a vow is also seen in the Nazarites.[6] Here hair cutting is connected with purification for the Nazarite was regarded as unclean until his vow had been fulfilled. The purification idea is likewise associated with hair cutting in India, for thus the death pollution was removed. It is interesting to note that the Tlingit thought that the locks cut from a corpse were associated with reincarnation. We also hear that it is often imperative for hair to be left uncut during a journey.

Tylor advances the theory that hair cutting was a substitution for the whole person who by this means did not offer himself as a sacrifice for the dead.

[1] *Herodotus*, IV, 34 ; *Paus*, I, 43-44.
[2] For a discussion of hair see article by Gray, "Hair and Nails", *Hasting's Encyclopædia of Religion and Ethics*, Vol. VI, pp. 474-477.
[3] Gruppe, *Myth and Religion Geschichte*, pp. 187-728.
[4] Fletcher, *The Omaha Twenty-seventh Report, Bureau of Ethnology*, (1911), p. 124.
[5] *Iliad*, XXIII, 144, et seqq.
[6] *Numbers* vi. 5.

The general reasons, then, for hair cutting seem to be as follows :

(1) The belief that hair is the reincarnation of life.
(2) Its possession insures mana to the owner.
(3) The belief that spirits attach themselves to the hair.
(4) Hair cutting and its supposed purificatory properties.
(5) Hair cutting is a substitution for the whole person who by this means need not offer himself as a sacrifice to the dead.

LACERATIONS

MELANESIA

In New Caledonia in South Malenesia the nearest relatives of the deceased tear the lobes of their ears and burn their arms and breasts.[1]* It is a custom of the natives of Mafulu and the Fijian Islands to amputate finger joints as a sign of mourning.[2] Thomson tells us that few of the elder natives can be found who have the fingers of both hands intact.[3] This act of cutting off a finger is confined to the relatives of the deceased unless one of the highest chiefs dies. When the little finger is cut off, the fourth finger is said to " cry itself hoarse in vain for its absent mate ". (Droga-droga-wale.[4]) Upon the death of a king of Tonga, one hundred fingers were ordered

---

[1] Lambert, *Mœurs et Superstitions de Néo Calédoniens*, pp. 235-239 (quoted by Frazer, p. 327).

* A similar custom of having the lobes of the ears cut in mourning is practised in the Islands of Torres Straits. Here youths who have been recently initiated and girls who have reached puberty follow this custom. (Cambridge, *Anthropological Expedition to Torres Straits*, Vol. VI, p. 154.) The flaps of ears are also slit by mourners in German New Guinea. (Keysser, " Aus dem Leben der Kaileute ", in *Neuhauss' Deutsch Neu Guinea*, Vol. III, pp. 80-142.)

The Dakotahs not infrequently amputate one or more fingers. (Spencer, *Principles of Sociology*, Vol. I, p. 167.) The Greenlanders sometimes lacerate their bodies. (*Ibid.*)

The widow and married daughter and sister of a deceased Carruas native cut off their finger joints and inflict other wounds. (Hartland, article in *Hastings*, Vol. IV, p. 438.)

And they cried aloud and cut themselves after their manner with knives and lancets, until the blood gushed out upon them. (1 *Kings* xviii. 28.)

After a chief's death in the Sandwich Islands, it is a custom to taboo a spot on the tongue or to cut the ears or to knock out one of the front teeth. (Spencer, *Principles of Sociology*, p. 167.) When a death occurs among the Arapho the women gash themselves across the upper and lower arm and below the knee. (Kroeber, " The Arapho," *Bulletin, American Museum of Natural History*, Vol. XVIII. (1902), p. 16.)

[2] Williamson, *The Mafulu Mountain People of British New Guinea*, p. 247.
[3] Thomson, *The Fijians*, p. 375.
[4] Fison, *Tales from Old Fiji*, p. 168.

to be cut but only sixty were amputated.[1] The aborigines of Vaté or Efat of the New Hebrides wail loudly at the death of a native, and scratch their faces until they are covered with blood.[2]

AUSTRALIA

It is said that nowhere perhaps has the practice of laceration upon the death of an individual been practised more extensively than in Australia. In reference to the tribes of Victoria, we are told that a widow, upon the death of a husband, seizes fire-brands and burns her breast, arms, legs, and thighs. When exhausted she takes the ashes and rubs them into her wounds and then scratches her face until the blood flows.[3] The parents of the deceased in Central Victoria lacerate themselves upon a death, more especially in the case of an only son. Sometimes this self-inflicted punishment continues until death ensues.[4] The Kurnai of South-East Victoria have a custom of cutting and gashing themselves with sharp stones and tomahawks until their heads and bodies are covered with blood. This practice is observed by the relatives of the dead man.[5] When a man meets death in the Mukjara-waint tribe, his kinsmen cut themselves with tomahawks and other instruments for about a week.[6] The mourners among the Kamilaroi, and more especially the women, cut their heads with tomahawks until the blood comes.[7] Laceration of mourners is a common custom among the tribes of Lower Murray and Lower Darling Rivers.[8] Among the Alatunja of the Alice Springs Group it is a custom for the women to dig the sharp ends of yam sticks into the crown of their heads, while the men also lacerate themselves with knives.[9]

At the funeral ceremony of the Kakadu native every one wails and cuts himself freely until the blood flows.[10] Cutting

[1] Turner, *Samoa, a Hundred Years Ago and Long Before*, p. 335.
[2] Williams, *Fiji and the Fijians*, p. 198.
[3] Smyth, *Aborigines of Victoria*, Vol. I, p. 105.
[4] Stanbridge, "Tribes in the Central Part of Victoria", *Transaction of the Ethnological Society of London*, N.S., Vol. I, p. 298.
[5] Howitt, *Native Tribes of South-East Australia*, p. 459.
[6] *Ibid*, p. 453.
[7] *Ibid*, p. 466.
[8] Beveridge, *Journal and Proceedings of the Royal Society of New South Wales*, Vol. XVII (1883), pp. 28-29, quoted by Frazer, p. 155.
[9] Spencer and Gillen, *Native Tribes of Central Australia*, p. 509.
[10] Spencer, *Native Tribes of the Northern Territory of Australia*, p. 241.

as a sign of mourning is resorted to for one week by the Wotjobaluk natives.[1]

Mutilation of the corpse and of the mourners is such a common feature in the areas under consideration, that many reasons occur as to why this practice is almost universal.

Again, we must here accentuate the " dread " attitude on the part of the survivors. The fear of the evil influence of the deceased is sufficient to induce them to resort to every possible expedient to mitigate that influence. Again, we must not lose sight of the fact that their desire is to divert the suspicion of having caused the death by witchcraft. Indeed, the very definite regulations regarding cuttings for the dead which we find emphasized in the Australian area could not be prompted by an expression of sorrow, but rather by the fact that severe punishment would be the outcome if such were neglected. In the Warramunga tribe a woman who does not lacerate herself in accordance with certain prescribed rules can be killed by her brother. By such mutilation the ghost might be convinced that the " sorrow " of the survivor is sincere. The lacerations to the skull of the deceased which are so common seem to have been made with the object of rendering the ghost harmless.

The custom of allowing the blood of the mourners to drip on the corpse into the grave seems to be followed with the ostensible object of establishing a corporal union between the living and the dead. Then, too, this blood is supposed by some primitives to strengthen the deceased who, because of renewed physical strength, is in a condition to undergo reincarnation. In speaking of the aborigines of Australia Smyth says that the object of letting blood drip over a corpse

---

[1] Howitt, *Native Tribes of South-East Australia*, p. 453.

Beckwourth describes a scene which he witnessed among the Crow Indians when the blood was streaming from every part of the bodies of those who were old enough to comprehend the loss. (*Autobiography of James Beckwourth*, p. 269, quoted by Yarrow, *A Study of the Mortuary Customs of the North American Indians*, p. 90.) When describing the mourning for a chief of the Crows, Yarrow tells us that hundreds of fingers were dismembered. We read that the Samoans after death " beat the head with stones until the blood runs ". They call this an offering for the dead. (Turner, *Nineteen Years in Polynesia*, p. 150.) Lacerations were likewise practised among the Dakotas. (Yarrow, p. 72.)

The Roman women who figured in the funeral procession were in the habit of crying aloud, tearing their hair, and lacerating their cheeks. (*Prop.*, III, 13-27.)

is to strengthen the deceased in the grave and to assist him to rise in another country.[1]

Perhaps the purification motive in conjunction with bloodletting is in the mind of the primitive when he lacerates himself until the blood flows, for there is a belief that impure or evil spirits attach themselves to blood. This impurity idea in connection with blood is very common. Farnell tells us that the material substance most generally felt to be impure is blood and nothing is more uncanny to the savage. Since death is one of the great mysteries, together with birth and sexual crisis, physical substances which are associated with them partake of their mystical quality.[2]

A study of the mentality of reactions of primitive man does not justify the conclusion of Hirn that mutilations are practised to get relief from effervescing emotional states, which are caused by the pain or exhaustion which follows a death.[3]

Mutilations following a death are resorted to

(1) In order to render his ghost harmless, thus lessening the fear of the evil influence of the deceased.

(2) To convince the ghost of the sincerity of the mourners.

(3) To establish a corporal union between the living and the dead.

(4) To strengthen the departed.

(5) As an offering.

(6) For purification.

Lacerations, too, are connected with other complexes. Thus in south-eastern New Guinea we find the custom of amputating a joint or joints from the fingers of those individuals who are relatives of a sick person. Brown states that at Iakalova he saw people whose hands had been thus mutilated—one woman who had one or two joints removed from her first, third, and fourth fingers ; even mere children were disfigured.[4] In referring to the aborigines of Sitka, Lisiansky tells us that when a female enters upon womanhood, she must have her lower lip cut.[5]

---

[1] Smyth, *The Aborigines of Victoria*, Vol. II, p. 274.
[2] Farnell, *Evolution of Religion*, pp. 90-95 ; Brinton, *Myths of the New World*, p. 176.
[3] Hirn, *Origins of Art*, p. 66.
[4] Brown, *Melanesians and Polynesians*, p. 394.
[5] Lisiansky, *A Voyage round the World*, p. 243.

REVERSAL OF CUSTOM

MELANESIA

The widows and widowers in the Hood Peninsula blacken their bodies as an indication of mourning.[1] In the Duke of York Island, all the female relatives of a man of prominence blacken their faces for a long time.[2] Fijian mourners would sometimes dress in leaves instead of cloth.[3]

The widow, children, and father of a deceased Trobriand in Northern Massim blacken themselves before they take part in the funeral feast. The widow's mourning costume consists of a long petticoat with a special kind of neck ornament; her legs are covered with leglets and her arms with armlets. The children of the dead man are smeared with black pigment for a month, during which period they wear a special lace. A widower blackens himself and wears mourning in much the same way as a widow does. Among the same tribe when the paramount chief of a district dies, and also at the Trobriands, black mourning pigment should be worn by his subjects except by those of his own clan.[4]

At Gawa the widow and children all wear mourning. The widow blackens herself and is attired in a long petticoat and cross shoulder belts, these articles being made for her by her dead husband's sister, but wears no armlets. The children also blacken themselves and wear cross shoulder belts and armlets. A few days after the death of a woman the husband blackens himself and puts on cross shoulder bands.[5]

At Murua if the deceased is a person of distinction, such as a chief, all the tribe goes into mourning for some months. The mourning consists in blackening the body with charcoal.[6] Three or four days after her husband's death a Wagawaga widow blackens herself all over with a mixture of cocoanut oil, and soot, and puts on a neck ornament, armlets, and a long petticoat. The children wear necklaces, armlets, and leglets, and also blacken themselves. The father adopts mourning similar to that worn by children of the deceased. The mother of the dead man wears a mourning like that adopted by the

---

[1] Frazer, *Belief in Immortality*, Vol. I, p. 204.
[2] Brown, *Melanesians and Polynesians*, p. 390.
[3] Williams, *Fiji and the Fijians*, Vol. I, p. 198.
[4] Seligmann, *Melanesians*, pp. 716-717.
[5] *Ibid*, p. 724.
[6] *Ibid*, p. 727.

widow. Brothers wear one or more armlets and blacken themselves for the funeral feast, while the sisters do not blacken themselves at all, but wear armlets until the first feast, and a mourning necklace until the last. Black is not worn by a mother, but both sexes wear armlets and necklaces until the last funeral feast. A widower blackens himself and dons a neck ornament until the first feast, but wears his fishing-net perineal bandage belt and cane armlets until the last one.[1]

The kinsfolk and friends of a deceased Torres Strait Islander have their faces and bodies smeared with greyish earth and water and ashes are strewn upon their heads.[2] We also hear that the relatives cut off their hair, paint their bodies with white coral mud, plaster their hair with mud, pull off their ear ornaments, and sever the distended loop of the lobe.[3]*

A great number of net collars and armlets, and a long petticoat are worn by Waima widows when in mourning. The widower in addition wears leglets and a special belt. This mourning period usually lasts for one or two years. The other mourners, not including the widow and widower, though they blacken the rest of their bodies, leave the face untouched.[4] At Maewo, in Aurora, one of the New Hebrides, after the sacrifice in honour of the deceased, the mourners smear their bodies and faces with ashes, and wear cords round their necks.[5] In the Shortland group, women throw ashes over their heads at an interment.[6]

AUSTRALIA

Among the Arunta when a man dies, his special Unawa or Unawas smear their faces, hair, and breasts with white pipe clay.[7] The Warramunga women likewise cover themselves

[1] Seligmann, *Melanesians*, pp. 618-619.
[2] Cambridge, *Anthropological Expedition to Torres Straits*, Vol. VI, pp. 138-153-157.
[3] *Ibid*, Vol. V, p. 249.
* We also read in the Bible that when the decree of Ahasuerus had gone forth that all the Jews in Persia were to be exterminated, Mordecai rent his clothes and put on sackcloth with ashes. (*Esther* iv. 1.)
The Dakotas sometimes smear their whole body with a species of white earth as a sign of mourning. (Yarrow, *A Study of the Mortuary Customs among the North American Indians*, pp. 71-72.)
[4] Seligmann, *Melanesians*, pp. 276-277.
[5] Codrington, *Melanesians*, p. 282.
[6] Brown, *Melanesians and Polynesians*, p. 213.
[7] Spencer and Gillen, *Native Tribes of Central Australia*, p. 500.

from head to foot with pipe clay.[1] A widow of a deceased Alatunja of the Alice Springs group paints herself white.[2]

It is a belief among the Kaitish tribe of Central Australia that if a widow does not keep her body covered with ashes from the camp fire during the entire mourning period, the spirit of her deceased husband will kill her and strip all the flesh from her bones.[3]*

The women of the Koombokkaburra plaster their heads with clay and ashes until not a particle of hair is visible, whereas the men blacken their bodies with a mixture of burnt bark and grease.[4] Of the Port Mackay tribes we read that in times of rejoicing they paint themselves red, but during the mourning period a white preparation is used.[5]

In the Boulia district the head is plastered with a sort of gypsum, making the whole hair appear white. This form of mourning is adopted by all in any camp uncontaminated and away from the settlements. The nearest relatives only " colour-grease " themselves down to the waist after the design for males and females.[6] Formerly old women in the Cloncurry district wore gypsum for mourning but now both sexes smear themselves with mud or paint themselves red as far as the waist.[7]*

INDIA

In the funeral procession the Hindus wear the cord over the right shoulder and under the left one, contrary to their usual custom. They likewise cover the head with dust. We also read that they use leaves for plates instead of metal dishes.[8]

---

[1] Spencer and Gillen, *Northern Tribes of Central Australia*, p. 521.

[2] Spencer and Gillen, *Native Tribes of Central Australia*, p. 503.

[3] *Ibid*, p. 507.

* A Uriyas widow who is especially fond of bright colours, in time of mourning wears a white borderless sari of cloth. (Rici, *Occasional Essays on Native South Indian Life*, pp. 56-57.)

For the use of ashes as a symbol of mourning see *Ezekiel* xxvii. 30-31 ; *Revelation* xviii. 19.

[4] Curr, *The Australian Race*, Vol. III, p. 21.

[5] *Ibid*, p. 45.

[6] Roth, *Ethnological Studies among the North-West-Central Queensland Aborigines*, p. 164.

[7] *Ibid*, p. 165.

* The Navajos smear their bodies with tar for a protection from the evil influence which caused the death. (Yarrow, " Mortuary Customs of the North American Indians," *First Report, Bureau of Ethnology* (1881), p. 123.)

[8] Crooke, *Northern India*, p. 218.

SIBERIA

The reindeer which convey the sledge containing the body of the deceased Chukchee to the cremation place as they are being slaughtered, have their reins placed over the right shoulder, the reverse of the customary way.[1]*

ABSTINENCE FROM THE ORDINARY PURSUITS OF LIFE.

INDIA

As before intimated, the Hindus must lead a pure life during the mourning period and must refrain from intercourse with others. The Lohār caste requires abstinence from the ordinary pursuits of life and forbids offerings to deities during this interval.[2] No work is permitted to be done by the chief mourner of the Kurmi caste, while the others under the mourning taboo may work yet they are enjoined to touch no one since they are impure.[3] A Kunbi chief mourner must refrain from sexual intercourse and abstains from ordinary work and all amusements.[4]*

[1] Bogoras, *The Chukchee, J.N.P.E.*, Vol. VII (1907), p. 526.

* In the funeral procession of a Roman the sons had their heads veiled while the daughters went uncovered with dishevelled hair. (*Plut. Quaest. Rom.*, II.) This was, as we know, a reversal of their usual custom. Women in the northern part of Greece left their heads uncovered with their hair hanging and dressed in white contrary to their ordinary habits. The Arapaho, who ordinarily wear their hair long and braided when in mourning, wear it unbound; in addition, they wear old clothing, and refrain from painting themselves which they usually do. (Kroeber, "The Arapaho," *Bull. American Museum Natural History*, Vol. XVIII (1902), p. 17.) The Ainu mourners, when following a corpse, wear their coats inside out and upside down. (Batchelor, *The Ainu and Their Folk-Lore*, p. 106.) The Ngonlango mourners discard their ornaments, wear brown garments and paint different parts of the body with red earth. Furthermore, the widows go out carrying a piece of wood which is supposed to be impregnated with the power of causing death to any one who comes within reach. (Clozel, *Les Coutumes Indigenes de la Cote d'Ivoire*, p. 363.)

Among the Pima Indians the women who are observing mourning are allowed to bring their blankets under the armpits, but not over the shoulders, even in the coldest weather. When the chemise was adopted and blankets went out of use, it was the custom to revert to blankets during the mourning period. (Russell, "The Pima Indians," *Twenty-sixth Annual Report, Bureau of Ethnology*, (1908), p. 195.)

After a death the Central Eskimos mourners do not smoke and keep their hoods on from morning to night while the women do not work. (Boas, "Central Eskimo," *Sixth Annual Report, Bureau of Ethnology* (1888), p. 614.)

[2] Russell, *Tribes and Castes of India*, Vol. IV, p. 125.

[3] *Ibid*, p. 78.

[4] *Ibid*, p. 37.

* Some natives on the Congo district do not sweep a house for one year after a death for fear the dust will injure the ghost. (Bastian, *Der Mensch in der Geschichte*, Vol. II, p. 323.)

Taboos are associated with so many complexes that it is unnecessary to call attention to their prevalence. Among taboos may be mentioned those

The object of seclusion is to get a revelation into the mystery of life. The ceremonial lodge is a sacred symbol and under its protecting shadow the primitive wishes to come into communication with a higher power which can direct his path by giving him the desired insight. When the spell is riveted upon him he comes out uplifted, experiencing pleasurable emotion, and thereby getting consolation and strength to enable him to withstand some of the mysteries and dangers with which he will be compassed, and to obtain important life values. By such mental concentration and fasting he reaches such a state of purity that the spirits can see through him.[1]

Lacerations too figure in complexes other than that of the death-situation. "Near Doenella or Deonhully, a town in Mysore, is a sect or subdivision of the Murressoo Wocal caste and every woman previous to piercing the ears of her eldest daughter preparatory to her being betrothed in marriage must undergo the amputation of the first joints of the third and fourth fingers of her right hand[2]". The origin of this custom is ascribed to a tradition.[3]

Such mourning customs as we have just described seem to be practised.

(1) For protection against any attempts of the departed to wreak vengeance upon the survivors.

---

connected with (1) special religious observances—the Sabbath, various religious festivals, regular periods consecrated to the gods, the appearance of the full moon, the offering of the first fruits, certain totemic animals ; (2) critical periods—birth, sexual crises, marriage, death, drought, famine, sickness. (3) house building, boat construction, agricultural enterprises ; (4) miscellaneous—the end of the old year and the beginning of the new, the commencing of a war period, fishing seasons, avoidance of hurricanes, rain compelling ceremonies, the appearance of certain animals, the ceremony of driving out malevolent spirits, the induction into office of a priest or chief, the departure of a native from one village and the taking up of his residence in another. The object of such taboos is, as Webster points out, both protective and conciliatory.

For discussion of taboo, see Frazer, *Taboo and Perils of the Soul*, Webster, *Rest Days*, Crawley, *The Mystic Rose*, Marett, *Is Magic a Negative Taboo ?*

Other examples of taboo during the mourning period have been treated under Dread of the Spirit and in Part II.

[1] Jones, "The Algonquin Manitou," *J.A.F.L.*, Vol. XVIII (1905), pp. 183-190 ; Radin, "Religion of the North American Indians," *J.A.F.L.*, Vol. XXVII (1914), pp. 335-373.

[2] Thurston, *Castes and Tribes of Southern India*, Vol. V, p. 75 ; quoting Buchanan (Hamilton).

[3] *Ibid*, pp. 76-77.

(2) To distinguish those who are under taboo.
(3) As a safeguard against the evil influence which caused the death.

DIETARY RESTRICTIONS

MELANESIA

If a widow, widower, or other near relative of a deceased native of Mafulu prefers, he may abstain from eating a favourite food of the dead member of his group, instead of wearing the customary mourning necklace.[1] The Massim in South-eastern British New Guinea forbid widows to eat the same kinds of food which their husbands ate during their last illness and this prohibition is strictly enforced until after the last funeral feast.[2] At Maewo, in Aurora, one of the New Hebrides, the very closely related may not eat foods such as yams, bananas and caladium. Only gigantic caladium, bread-fruit, cocoanuts, mallows, and similar products are permitted to be eaten. Never is food which has been planted allowed to them during the mourning period.[3] The Fijians sometimes, because of grief, would not eat fish, fruit, or other pleasant food for months.[4] In New Caledonia in Southern Melanesia, the grave diggers observe a strict fast after the burial ceremony.[5]

Among the Trobriands the widow and widower are not allowed to eat yams for one and a half months after the death of their mates.[6] Certain kinds of yams and bananas are forbidden to widows and widowers at Warma. Wallaby, pig, fish, are also denied to the widow, and the widower avoids shell fish and, although he does not eat yams, he may eat sweet potatoes.[7] Cocoanuts, yams, and bananas from the garden of a dead man are denied to his sons in the Island of Wapuru. If this injunction were not adhered to, the belly and face of the violator of this tribal custom are supposed to swell and death will result. The same prohibition is applied to the dead man's brothers' children.[8] A Koita widow and

[1] Williamson, *The Mafulu Mountain People of British New Guinea*, p. 247.
[2] Seligman, *The Melanesians*, p. 617.
[3] Codrington, *Melanesians*, p. 281.
[4] Williams, *Fiji and the Fijians*, Vol. I, p. 198.
[5] Lambert, *Mœurs et Superstitions des Néo-Calédoniens*, pp. 235-239.
[6] Seligmann, *Melanesians*, p. 717.
[7] *Ibid*, p. 276.
[8] *Ibid*, pp. 730-731.

other relatives of the dead man must abstain from such articles of food as the deceased was especially fond of until after the funeral feast six months later.[1]

Two or three weeks after a Wagawaga funeral, the Gariauna may not eat boiled food but only roast ; they are not permitted to drink water but only hot milk from young cocoanuts and although yams are allowed, they must not eat bananas and sugar cane. Pork is denied to them until after the last of the funeral feasts called banahivi.[2] At Tubetube the cocoanut trees of the dead man which have not been cut down may be eaten by the brothers, sisters, and other relatives of the deceased, but not by his children. A child of the dead man eats no produce grown, nor pigs fattened near the house.[3]

At Tokunu only the cocoanuts of the dead man's settlement become taboo at his death.[4]*

The Monumbo of German New Guinea compel a widower during the mourning period to abstain from certain foods such as fish and sauces.[5] At Windessi, the mourners are forbidden to eat anything cooked in a pot. Sago-porridge which is a staple food of some of the natives of New Guinea is not allowed to be eaten and if rice is taken it must be cooked in a bamboo.[6] In some parts of Geelvink Bay the family of the deceased must refrain from eating the usual food and are compelled to substitute half-baked cakes of sago and other non-desirable foodstuffs, and at the same time they are not allowed to bring their own eatables and drink.[7]

INDIA

Certain customs, consisting of the performance of daily exercises, must be observed by the relatives. Caland tells us that during the period of impurity the Hindoos must lead

---

[1] Seligmann, *Melanesians*, p. 164.

[2] *Ibid*, p. 611.

[3] *Ibid*, p. 614.

[4] *Ibid*, p. 730.

* Or possibly only the cocoa-nuts belonging to members of the dead man's totem in his settlement. (*Ibid*, p. 730n.)

[5] Vormann, "Dorf und Hausanlange dei den Monumbu Deutsch-Neu Guinea," *Anthropos*, Vol. V (1910), p. 412.

[6] Van der Roest, "Vit the leven der bevolking van Windessi," *Tijdschrift voor Indische Taal-Land en Volkenkunde*, Vol. XL (1898), p. 161 et seqq., quoted by Frazer, p. 320.

[7] Gondswaard, *De papoewa's van de Geelvinksbaai*, p. 75, et seqq., quoted by Frazer, p. 314.

a chaste life, and Jolly furthermore says that they must
neither beg, nor study, nor have intercourse with others.
They must refrain from eating meat and consume only the
food that is brought and given as a present.

If any of the Dhanwar tribe dies, food is brought to the
chief mourners for three days.[1] The agricultural caste, the
Kunbi, does not permit the principal mourner to partake
of the betel-leaf.[2] Abstinence from certain foods is required
of the Kurmi caste mourners.[3] The Lohār caste of blacksmiths also forbid the partaking of certain kinds of food.[4]

Fasting and abstinence from certain foods are associated
with various complexes. Thus we find prohibition of food
and drink intimately connected with many religious practices
in primitive, antique, ancient, and modern society.[5] Again,
fasting is observed when astronomical changes occur. Among
such phenomena, placed in the realm of the mysterious and
uncanny, might be mentioned eclipse of the sun, equinoxes,
the periods of the new or full moon, twilight and darkness.[6]

[1] Russell, *Tribes and Castes of India*, Vol. II, p. 496.
[2] *Ibid*, Vol. IV, p. 37.
[3] *Ibid*, Vol. IV, p. 78.
[4] *Ibid*, Vol. IV, p. 125.
In Togoland a Ewe widow is forbidden beans, flesh, fish, palm wine, and
rum. (Seidel, " Krankheit Tod, und Begräbnis bei den Togonegern," *Globus*,
Vol. LXXII (1897), p. 22.) Among the Salish, the widower must abstain
from fresh meat for a period varying with his age. (Hill-Tout, " Report
on the Ethnology of the StlatlumH of British Columbia," *J.A.I.*, Vol. XXXV
(1905), N.S., p. 139.)
In Samoa those who touched the dead were most careful not to handle
food. For days they were fed by others. Baldness and bad health were the
penalties for transgression. (Turner, *Samoa*, p. 145.) No native of Tonga
can touch a dead chief without being tabooed for ten months except chiefs
whose taboo lasts from three to ten months according to the rank of the
deceased. Upon no condition must food be touched with the hands. (Marine,
The Tonga Islands, Vol. II, p. 133n.)
For restrictions in diet, see Westermarck, *Development of Moral Ideas*,
Vol. II, pp. 290-345.
[5] In savage tribes girls and boys at puberty are often requested to fast
or at least not to partake of certain kinds of food. (Boas, *First General Report
on the Indians of British Columbia*, p. 40.) The Hindus fast the last day
before a visit to a sacred shrine as well as the last day of the journey. Before
sacrificing to Isis the Egyptians abstained from food. (Herod, Vol. II p. 40.)
The injunction relative to fasting on the Day of Atonement is familiar to all Old
Testament readers. (*Leviticus* xvi. 29, 31, xxiii. 27, 29, *Numbers* xxix. 7.)
[6] The Hindus at the time of eclipse do not drink nor eat. (Crooke,
Popular Religion of Northern Inda, Vol. I, p. 21.) At such a time the Todas
likewise do not partake of food. (Rivers. *The Todas*, p. 592.) Brâhmanas
who have been received into the fold abstain from food at twilight. (*Laws
of Manu*, Vol. IV, p. 55.) The Brahmins fast at the time of the equinoxes
and of the new or full moon. (Dubois, *Description of the People of India*,
p. 160.) The Snanaimuq Indians do not eat while it is dark. (Bóas, *First
General Report on the Indians of British Columbia*, p. 51.)

Prohibition of certain food is often enjoined upon the young.[1] In many instances women are not allowed to partake of certain articles of diet.[2] Sacred individuals such as shamans and priests are not permitted to eat some designated foods.[3] Among dietary prohibitions animals figure most prominently. Thus we find some animals closely associated with the daily life of the people are not eaten because of their utility.[4] The non-partaking of the totemic animal is very common ; animals supposed to impart detrimental qualities when eaten, are not used for food ; animals are frequently not eaten because of their obnoxious habits, and foreign animals are sometimes not consumed for fear of their harmful influence.

What interests us is why does fasting play such a prominent part in the death-complex ? The object of such privation which first suggests itself is that it would be indiscreet for the survivors to touch food until the deceased is adequately provided for, because of the fear of the return of the dead to his old haunts. This is all the more apparent when we find restrictions of the kind of food in which the dead especially delighted. The importance of this motive appears more clearly when we note that the period of abstinence frequently lasts until after burial or until the departed has reached his permanent future abode. Then, again, the conception that under certain conditions, food defiles, is by no means uncommon. Fasting, too, must be regarded as a purification ceremony ; more particularly if the survivors have come in contact with the dead.

In some of the areas under consideration cooked food is prohibited. As food undergoes transformation when cooked, and as transformations are regarded by primitive man as

---

[1] In south-east Australia the boys of the Wotjobaluk tribe are not permitted to eat kangaroo and padi-melon. (Howitt, *Native Tribes of South-East Australia*, p. 769.)

[2] By some Australian tribes this prohibition is very strict. (Curr, *The Australian Race*. Vol. I, p. 81.) In Mawata the mother is not allowed to eat food which comes out of the sea until her child has cut its first tooth. (Cambridge, *Anthropological Expedition to Torres Straits*, Vol. V, p. 500.) One of the seven principles of the Satnāmi sect of India includes abstinence from spirituous liquor and vegetables, like lentils and tomatoes, whose juice resembles blood. (*Imperial Gazetteer of India*, Vo.l I, p. 428.)

[3] The dairymen of the Todas can partake only of the milk of certain buffaloes. (Rivers, *The Todas*, p. 102.)

[4] In ancient Rome excommunication was the penalty meted out to those who slaughtered an ox (Pliny, *Historia Naturalis*, VIII, 70), and in Athens and in the Poloponneseus, the death penalty was the punishment.

fraught with danger, such a stipulation should not surprise us. The savage realizes that he must not only rid himself of the death pollution, but also prevent any possibility of future contamination. Then, too, because of his contact with death, he must not defile himself even more by preparing his own food. To further fortify himself and his tribesmen he must refrain from the ordinary activities of life.

In frequent instances eating and drinking before others is prohibited. Perhaps this injunction might have been instituted because of the belief that the evil eye of another might contaminate since there is contagion in the look and the deadly influence of one who who has come in contact with death may be thus transmitted.

Another object of fasting after a death may be to acquire supernatural powers, for then the survivors would be able to cope with the many dangers which now beset them, largely because of the extraordinary powers with which ghosts are endowed. Perhaps the desire to get a revelation pertaining to the mysteries with which the mourners are encompassed, may prompt them to resort to fasting ; by such an expedient the longed for objects may be secured.

Food restrictions then seem to be instituted :

(1) For propitiation.
(2) As purifying agencies.
(3) To avoid any possible future defilement.
(4) To prevent danger because of the transformation of un-
    cooked food to cooked food.
(5) Because of the susceptibility of the hands to evil influences
    since they are regarded as carriers of ceremonial un-
    cleanliness.
(6) For the acquisition of supernatural powers.

The meaning of these mourning ceremonies now concerns us. Perhaps the most evident reason for the many restrictions and elaborate ceremonies seems to be the desire for the protection of the survivors against the machinations of the departed spirit who would wreak vengeance upon the living, unless intense sorrow be shown. However, this in itself is not sufficient to explain the entire situation, inasmuch as protection of a more telling character is often resorted to. By the reversal of custom which we find so characteristic of the areas we are describing, the mourners who are thus under

taboo, are distinguished. Thus they serve as a warning to others who refrain from coming in touch with those who have had intimate contact with death. As the mourner is polluted for a certain time after a death and as the garment worn during this taboo period is saturated with contagion and must be discarded after the infection interval is past, a different one from that ordinarily worn is utilized. The evidence is not enough to show that one of the main motives which actuate the survivors to don mourning garb is to deceive the deceased. Although the theory has often been advanced that the object of that garb is to express sympathy for the departed or grief at his loss, yet our investigation warrants no such deduction. Despite the fact that the sympathetic motive does not seem to be in evidence, yet such a custom may incite pity and avert the suspicion of sorcery. Not much credence can be attached to the theory that the mourner is a slave of the dead and must humiliate himself.

The seclusion which we find so characteristic of the mourning ceremonies is by no means identified with the death-complex alone. It is frequently required of girls and boys arriving at the age of maturity. Among the Eskimo, the natives of British Columbia, many Bantu tribes of Africa, the Southern Asiatics, the Melanesians and some of the natives in India, seclusion is demanded of adolescent girls.

CHAPTER VII

ERECTION OF A HUT ON THE GRAVE

MELANESIA

IN the Hood Peninsula we find the custom of erecting a temporary hut over the grave and in it the widower or widow lives alone for three months.[1] From what we know of the attitude in this section toward spirits, since the natives have no belief in good spirits, but in a great number of bad ones, we may conclude that the fear motive in this case is the paramount conception. The Southern Massim build a shelter over the grave.[2]

At Maralug the nearest relative sleeps in a hut erected near the grave.[3] In South-Eastern New Guinea a small roughly built house is erected on the grave with the object of protecting the burial place from the inroads of pigs and dogs and of preventing the rain from washing away the earth which covers the grave.[4]

At Kai in German New Guinea, the widow or widower lives day and night for several weeks in a hovel built directly over the grave.[5] Over a Bakaua grave is erected a rude hut in which the widower remains for some time.[6]

AUSTRALIA

In Widadhari County, New South Wales, friends of the deceased visit a hut erected over the grave. After several months it is pulled down.[7] Smyth also refers to the numbers of huts with thatched roofs erected along the Murrumbidgee and Murray River.[8] We also find thatched huts north of Victoria.[9]

[1] Frazer, *Belief in Immortality*, Vol. I, pp. 203, 204.
[2] Seligman, *Melanesians*, p. 614.
[3] Cambridge, *Anthropological Expedition to Torres Straits*, Vol V, p. 260.
[4] Brown, *Melanesians and Polynesians*, p. 442, quoting Field.
[5] Keysser, "Aus dem Leben der Keileute," in Neuhauss' *Deutsch Nue Guinea*, Vol. III, pp. 83, 84.
[6] Lehner-Bukua, in Neuhauss' *Deutsch Neu Guinea*, Vol. III, p. 430.
[7] Fraser, *The Aborigines of New South Wales*, p. 82.
[8] Smyth, *The Aborigines of Victoria*, p. 99.
[9] Thomas, *The Natives of Australia*, p. 198.

The Herbert River tribes erect a hut on the grave, put a drinking vessel in it, and clear a path from this hut to the water, presumably for the convenience of the ghost. However, as was before intimated, this outward act might be interpreted as a mark of deep devotion, but the subsequent brutal treatment accorded the ghost shows that the fear motive is predominant.[1] When a person died who was highly esteemed among the tribes of the Lower Murray, Lower Darling, and Lower Lachlan Rivers, a hut was erected over the grave and this was sometimes enveloped with a net. Although the motive here is not mentioned, yet the fact that such was done for a tribesman who held a position of honour among the natives, seems to point to the fact that in this case we might have had, if these huts had been kept permanently, as Frazer suggests, an incipient form of ancestor worship.[2] We also find the erection of a hut in an account given of a native burial on the Vasse River in Western Australia.[3] Among the Port Jackson tribes we find the erection over the grave of what might be called a hut.[4]*

DESERTION OF A HOUSE

MELANESIA

The Koita commonly leave a house after death and let it fall into decay, because of their dread of the ghost. Children who play in the neighbourhood of a house thus deserted are supposed to fall sick.[5] In the South-Eastern part of British New Guinea, especially in Tubetube and Wagawaga, we find the custom of abandoning or destroying a house in which a death has occurred, another evidence of the horror which ghosts suggest.[6] In the Island of Florida, after the

---

[1] Howitt, *Native Tribes of South-East Australia*, p. 474.

[2] Frazer, *Belief in Immortality*, Vol. I, p. 151.

[3] Grey, *Journals of Two Expeditions of Discovery*, Vol. II, p. 332.

[4] Howitt, *Native Tribes of South-East Australia*, p. 464.

* Burial places in the vicinity of river banks among the Woolwa Indians are marked by a large thatched shed similar to the lodges inhabited during life. This is built over the place of interment and the whole is kept clear of bush growth. (Wickham, "Notes on the Soumoo or Woolwa Indians," *J.A.I.*, Vol. XXIV (1894-1985), p. 207.)
The Monbutta erect a hut in the forest for the dead and place there some oil and provisions to prevent the spirit from returning to earth for food. (Burrows, *The Land of the Pigmies*, pp. 100, 103.)

[5] Seligmann, *Melanesians*, p. 191.

[6] *Ibid*, p. 631.

death of a chief, everything in his house is left untouched and the house is allowed to fall into ruin.[1] If a Sulka dies suddenly in his house, it is then shut up and deserted, because so intense is the dread of the survivors on account of the harm which his ghost might possibly do.[2] At Waima the day after a man's death many of his effects are broken or damaged and hung beneath the eaves of his house which is usually not again inhabited and is allowed to decay. Likewise, when the vegetables planted by the dead man become ripe they are also hung on the eaves of the house and permitted to rot.[3] In the Duke of York Islands, houses and villages are often abandoned on account of sickness or death and their sides broken in.[4] The Yabim usually abandon a house, however solidly it may be built.[5]

AUSTRALIA

Immediately after a death the Dieri shift their camp.[6] The Warramunga remove every camp a considerable distance from the burial place, since no one desires to come in contact with the spirit of the dead man.[7] The Herbert River tribes likewise shift their camp after a death.[8] As soon as anyone belonging to the Yungman, Nullakun, Mungarai, Karrawa,

---

[1] Frazer, *Belief in Immortality*, Vol. I, p. 349.

[2] Rascher, "Die Sulka, Ein Beitrag zur Ethnographie von Neu-Pommern", *Archiv für Anthropologie*, Vol. XXIX (1904), pp. 214, 216.

[3] Seligmann, *Melanesians*, p. 274.

Beckwourth relates that after a death among the Crows, every lodge lay prostrate. (*Autobiography of James Beckwourth*, p. 269, quoted by Yarrow, p. 90.) It is also said that upon a death, the Dakotas gave the lodge, the tepee, and the family possessions away. (*Ibid*, p. 72.)

The tribes of British Central Africa destroy a house in which a man has died. The mourners shave their heads and bury the hair on the site of the house. (Werner, *Native Tribes of British Central Africa*, pp. 165-167.)

If a Navajo Indian dies in the house, the rafters are pulled down over the remains and the place is usually set on fire. (Mindeleff, "Navajo Houses," *Annual Report, Bureau of Ethnology*, Vol. XVII, p. 487.) Destruction of huts is recorded by Hyades in Deniker of the Fuegians. Westermarck, *Development of Moral Ideas*, Vol. II, p. 536 ; by Butler, *Travels in Assam*, p. 228 ; by Batchelor, *The Ainu of Japan*, p. 130 ; by Fawcett, *Saoras*, p. 50 ; Cunningham, *Uganda*, p. 130.

[4] Brown, *Melanesians and Polynesians*, pp. 397, 403.

[5] Frazer, *Belief in Immortality*, Vol. I, p. 248.

[6] Howitt, *Native Tribes of South-East Australia*, p. 449 ; Gason, *The Dieri*, p. 275.

[7] Spencer and Gillen, *Northern Tribes of Central Australia*, p. 519.

[8] Howitt, *Native Tribes of South-East Australia*, p. 474.

Binbinga, and Willingara tribes dies, the camp is immediately shifted, because it is a belief that the spirit of which they have fear haunts its old camping ground.[1] The aborigines of New South Wales shift their camp after a death has occurred.[2]*

INDIA

Among the Bengal Chakmas, a bamboo post or other part of the dead man's house is burned with him.[3] The Banjaras of Khandesh move their huts after a death.[4] Among the Todas we hear of the burning of a hut at a woman's funeral, which is regarded by Rivers as a survival of the common custom of burning the house of a dead person.[5] Women also lament round huts. The author of *The Todas* raises the question as to whether the hut is supposed to be useful to the deceased in the next world.[6]

On the seventh day after the burial of a male Kudiya, a booth is erected over the grave or place of ceremony.[7]

SIBERIA

After the Chukchee return from their second visit to the burial place, the family move their tent to another place, even though it be only five or six feet away. More especially is this custom observed if the dead one is carried out, as sometimes occurs, through the usual tent entrance.[8] A Chukchee tale, The Sacrifice to the Dead, tells us that after the natives of a village died, a girl, the only inhabitant who was left, in accordance with directions received from her father whose voice she heard, removed with all the herdsmen,

[1] Spencer, *Native Tribes of the Northern Territory of Australia*, p. 254.

[2] Fraser, *Aborigines of New South Wales*, p. 84.

* After a Central Eskimo is buried, the mourners shut themselves up for three days in the hut in which he died, and then leave it forever. (Boas, "Central Eskimo," *Sixth Annual Report, Bureau of Ethnology* (1888), p. 614.)

[3] Crooke, *The Popular Religion and Folk-Lore of North India*, Vol. II, p. 71.

[4] *Ibid*, p. 56.

[5] Rivers, *The Todas*, p. 403.

[6] *Ibid*, pp. 338, 339, 403.

[7] Thurston, *Ethnographic Notes in Southern India*, p. 145.

* The Tartars of Tomsk bury their dead near a forest and commonly erect on every grave a hut of balks. These are sepulchral huts and have the shape of houses. As a consequence their cemeteries have the appearance of villages. (Georgi, *Russia*, Vol. II, p. 70.)

[8] Bogoras, *The Chukchee*, *J.N.P.E.*, Vol. VII (1907), p. 532.

who were occupying the nearby district, from the settlement, and remained away until the snow covered the ground. This they did after slaughtering reindeer and offering them in sacrifice.[1]

The Yahuts let the hut fall into ruins when any one died, thinking that it was the habitation of demons.[2]*

---

[1] Bogoras, *The Chukchee, J.N.P.E.*, Vol. VIII (1913), p. 159.

[2] Tylor, *Primitive Culture*, Vol. II, p. 26.

* The Navajos of New Mexico and Arizona abandon a house when a body is removed hence for burial for they believe that devils come to the place of death. (Yarrow, "Mortuary Customs of the North Amer. Indians," *First Report Bureau of Ethnology* (1879-1880), p. 123.) Among the Arapho, the family of a dead man moves to another site. (Kroeber, "The Arapho," *Bulletin American Museum of Natural History*, Vol. XVIII (1902), p. 17.)

We find desertion of a house after death practised by the Hottentots and the Karens. (Tylor, *Primitive Culture*, Vol. II, p. 26.) The Hottentots move their entire village to some other place. Thurnberg, "Account of the Cape of Good Hope," *Pinkerton's Voyages and Travels*, Vol. XVI, p. 142.

The Bantu usually burn or pull down the hut of an ordinary person, but if a chief dies, the entire kraal is left for a time, and among some tribes it is burnt down. (Hartland, article in *Hastings*, Vol. IV, p. 441.) The reason given by the Ngoni for desertion is not that the ghost always lives there, but there is a possibility of its return to its former haunts, and thus the way is cleared for it. (Elmslie, *Among the Wild Ngoni*, p. 71.) As Hartland suggests, (Vol. IV, p. 441), similar customs are reported for the various tribes of negroes, the North and South American Indians, the Andaman Islanders, the Karens, the Yahuts, the Kamtchadals, the Central Eskimo, etc.

In earlier times, at the death of a Japanese sovereign, the capital was removed to a new site. (Aston, *Shinto*, p. 252.)

A relic of the custom of destroying the house after a death is found in some of the Nicobar Islands, where the supporting post is cut through or so notched, that its removal is necessary. (Ind. Cens. Report, Vol. III (1901), p. 209.) Another possible relic of the abandonment of the house may be found in the modern Roman custom, by which the family, if such can be arranged, leave the house where a death has occurred, and remain away a week. (Hare and Baddeley, *Walks in Rome*, p. 433.)

Hastings is of the opinion that where huts are of little value and easily erected, or where sentimental reasons have not taken great possession of the natives, the house where a death has occurred may be abandoned or an entire new settlement may be chosen. However, from the illustrations cited, we see that even dwelling-places which are well constructed may be deserted, as is seen among the Yabim of German New Guinea.

The Arkansas leave the body in a lodge and burn over it the dwelling of the deceased with its contents. (Brinton, *Myths of the New World*, p. 278.) The Hupa Indians sometimes burn the hut of the deceased either because they fear his return or as a mark of respect. A modern house is vacated for a time at least. (Goddard, *Life and Culture of the Hupa*, p. 73.)

CHAPTER VIII

DESTRUCTION OF PROPERTY

MELANESIA

IN Wagawaga when the relatives return from their purification rites, they cut down three or four of the dead man's cocoanut trees. Both nuts and trees are left to rot, but the mother and sisters of the dead man may use the leaves of these cocoanuts to make petticoats or a basket commonly in use for carrying fish. Cocoanuts are cut down for a woman in the same fashion as for a man.[1] Immediately after the funeral of a deceased Tubetube native the brother of the dead man cuts down two or three of the cocoanut trees belonging to the latter. This might also be done by the son or a sister's child.[2] When an aborigine dies among the Trobriands of Northern Massim, four or five of his cocoanut trees are cut down by his brothers, children, and sisters' children. No restrictions seemed to be in evidence relative to eating these nuts, and the leaves might be used by the women of any clan for baskets or for making petticoats.[3] Although when a paramount chief dies in the Trobriands, no cocoanut trees are destroyed in the village subject to his jurisdiction, yet a number of cocoanuts are cut down in his own village.[4] In the Island of Ysabel cocoanut trees are cut and groves of bananas hacked.[5]

Among the Koita, if a man dies without wife, brothers, sisters, or children, his house is allowed to rot, and later another house will be built on the same site.[6] At Bartle Bay the house is sometimes deserted or destroyed. It is thought that if this were not done, the evil spirits of the dead would come back and thus jeopardize the surviving relatives.[7] It

[1] Seligmann, *Melanesians*, p. 611.
[2] *Ibid*, p. 614.
[3] *Ibid*, p. 716.
[4] *Ibid*, p. 718.
[5] Brown, *Melanesians and Polynesians*, p. 396.
[6] Seligmann, *Melanesians*, p. 89.
[7] *Ibid*, p. 525.

is a custom in Tubetube, for a widower, if he has brother, sisters, or married children, to live with them, in which case his old house will be destroyed soon after he has left it.   If a man should be living in his wife's house at the time of her death, his children would go to live with their maternal uncle or aunt, and the house which the widower leaves may be destroyed or allowed to rot.   If a widow should die childless, the house in which she had lived with her husband would be broken up or perhaps burnt.[1]

In New Caledonia situated in Southern Melanesia, tho houses, nets, and other possessions of the dead are burnt, his plantations are laid waste, and his cocoanut palms destroyed.[2] In the Shortland group, the chief's boats, spears, bows, arrows, tomahawks are broken and destroyed.[3]

It is worth noting that the house in which a married man or woman has died is commonly allowed to rot or is destroyed. Seligmann is of the opinion that the motives which actuate the survivors to do this are prompted by their feeling in regard to intimate association with objects connected with the dead in foreign clans.   Such contact must be avoided whatever the sacrifice.   The identity of the dead man with his former home is so marked that a line of demarcation can hardly be drawn between them, and for this reason we have such an attitude evinced.   In support of this theory Seligmann cites numerous instances to show that even so close a relative as a child dissociates himself from everything which was connected with his father.[4]

AUSTRALIA

The Wogal tribe are very careful about burying everything which belongs to a dead man with him.   Even valuable articles such as spears and nets are included; indeed, a canoe, too, has been sacrificed in this manner and pieces of it placed in the grave.   " Everything belonging to a dead man was put out of sight ".[5] In South Victoria we find that after the grave has been dug, the dead man's property is brought and a sorcerer takes out the contents from two bags.   Small

---

[1] Seligmann, *Melanesians*, p. 632.
[2] Lambert, *Mœurs et Superstitions des Néo-Calédoniens*, pp. 235-239.
[3] Brown, *Melanesians and Polynesians*, p. 217.
[4] Seligmann, *Melanesians*, pp. 13-14-73.
[5] Howitt, *Native Tribes of South East Australia*, pp. 461-462.

pieces of stones for cutting skins, bones for boring holes, and twine are placed in the grave. The bags and rugs of the deceased are torn and also deposited. All the dead man's possessions must accompany him in death.[1] The Jajaurung of the Upper Loddon River inter every piece of inanimate property with the dead man.[2] A similar practice of burying all the property of the deceased is seen among the tribes of the Lower Murray, Lachlan, and Darling Rivers in New South Wales.[3]

All of the implements of a warrior of the Geawegal tribe are interred with his body, also every piece of inanimate property formerly possessed by him. Likewise in the Gringai country the articles belonging to the deceased are buried with him and those present at the interment also contribute something.[4] The Herbert River tribes bury a man with his weapons, his ornaments and everything he had used in life.[5] In the Ngarigo tribes everything belonging to the deceased is interred with him.[6] During the night following a death all the camps are demolished by the Warramunga and are shifted across the creek, the only trace which is left is a small mound called Kaiti piled on the spot where the man has died. The camps are moved a great distance away, because no one is anxious to meet the spirit of the dead man or of the one who perhaps caused the death by evil magic.[7] South of Carpentaria the property of the deceased is usually destroyed by fire; in a few instances it is given to his tribesmen, but never to his children.[8] In West Australia the spear and wommer, or spear-thrower, of the dead man are broken.[9]

[1] Smyth, *The Aborigines of Victoria*, Vol. I, p. 104.
[2] Howitt, *Native Tribes of South East Australia*, p. 441.
[3] Frazer, *Belief in Immortality*, Vol. I, p. 147.
[4] Howitt, *Native Tribes of South East Australia*, p. 464.
[5] *Ibid*, p. 474.   [6] *Ibid*, p. 462.
[7] Spencer and Gillen, *Across Australia*, Vol. II, p. 428.
[8] Thomas, *The Natives of Australia*, p. 200.   [9] *Ibid*, p. 192.
Among the Brazilian Tupinambas " whoever happened to have anything which belonged to the dead man produced it, lest he should come and claim it." (Southey, *History of Brazil*, Vol. I, p. 248.) " As soon as a man dies, the Greenlanders throw out all his former possessions, otherwise they would be polluted." (Cranz, *History of Greenland*, Vol. I, p. 237.) All the clothing, beds, and other articles which are in the same place where an Arapaho dies, are burned, lest the spirit come back; even the sticks that touch the dead body are burned. (Kroeber, "The Arapaho," *Bulletin, American Museum of Natural History*, Vol. XVIII (1902), p. 17.)
In Samoa mats are thrown out of the house of a deceased member of the community and the sides are broken in. (Brown, *Melanesia and Polynesia*, p. 403.)

INDIA

The sacrifice of a goat at the grave of the Vedic Indian
and apparently burned with the body was to permit it to act
as a guide to the deceased in the other world and the slaughter
of a draft-ox enabled the dead to have a means of conveyance
while en route to the regions beyond.[1] Among the Khasis,
before burial, a cock, u'iar krad lynti (literally, " the cock
that scratched the way "), is sacrificed with the idea that
the cock will scratch a path for the spirit in the next world.[2]
After burial a cock is sacrificed so that it can bear the sins of
the departed.[3]*

Dubois states that the sacrifice of a cow at the cremation
of a Hindu was for the purpose of leading the dead by a happy
road to the other world.[4]

Although different motives seem to have actuated the
survivors to destroy or abandon the property of the dead,
yet in the instances cited, the fear attitude is generally most
emphasized. When a Saora was asked the reason for burning
the property of a dead person he replied, " If we do not burn
these things with the body, the kulba (soul) will come back
and ask for them and trouble us ".[5]

In many cases in this connection, we not only find destruction resorted to, but such is invariably followed by other
observances which point to this conception of dread. That
the intention of such a practice is also to supply the needs
of the ghost is evident in some instances ; this would
not account for the burning and absolute destruction of the
property of the deceased, but would seem to apply to those
things which are buried with him.

---

[1] *Av.* XII, 2, 48.

[2] Gurdon, *The Khasis,* p. 132.

[3] *Ibid,* p. 142.

* The Aztecs killed a dog and buried it with the body of a deceased
native. A cotton thread was put round its throat to enable it to lead the dead
over the deep waters en route to the other world. (Nansen, *Eskimo Life,*
p. 238, quoting Tylor, *Primitive Culture,* (1873), p. 472.)

[4] Dubois, *Hindu Manners and Customs,* Vol. II, p. 489.

Among the Hupa Indians money and the dancing regalia of the deceased
are placed in his grave after being broken. They say that the object of such
destruction is to prevent grave robbery. (Goddard, *Life and Culture of the
Hupa,* p. 71.) The natives of Alaska sometimes leave a sledge or household
utensil or weapon, all of which they break, beside the dead body. (Dall,
The Resources of Alaska, p. 383.)

[5] Fawcett, " On the Saoras," *J.A.S.B.,* Vol. I, p. 47.

The fear of pollution, too, has to be considered when pondering the prevalence of the custom of the destruction of the entire property of the deceased and the abandonment of his ordinary dwelling place, but sometimes such destruction is connected with the different ideas as to what constitutes a man's personality. (See subsequent discussion, Part II.) Although some primitives, such as the Kafirs, believe that a man's personality haunts his possessions,[1] yet this conception is not always held.

Although Seligmann is of the opinion that, when the house of a married man or woman is destroyed, the attitude which actuates the survivors to pursue this course is prompted by the feeling of a clan to the dead of another clan, yet this does not seem in itself sufficient to explain the numerous instances of property destruction. True, the home with which the dead has been so identified becomes inseparably linked with his personality, yet in many such cases no mention is made of the destruction of other property just as closely associated with the deceased. As was before intimated, the fear attitude seems to be the paramount consideration, especially since the spirits of the departed are, above all, supposed to return to their old haunts.

It is interesting to note that although the practice of destruction of property is found in the south-eastern part of the Australian Continent, yet it does not appear to be the custom in Central Australia.[2] Frazer here draws a distinction between the central part of the Australian continent where natural conditions are most unfavourable, and as a result the central aborigines have remained in a more primitive state than those on the coast where food and water are more easily obtained. He is of the opinion that such conditions encourage religious development. Again, this advance step is attended by a consequent economic loss.[3] Although we are willing to concede that religious development may often be seen where social progress is apparent, yet we are most reluctant to subscribe to the idea that physical environmental causes alone are responsible. Here we must voice our condemnation of the conception which regards environment as a sole determin-

[1] Kidd, *The Essential Kafir*, p. 83.
[2] Spencer and Gillen, *Native Tribes of Central Australia*, pp. 466-497-538.
[3] Frazer, *Belief in Immortality*, Vol. I, pp. 148-149.

ant in culture. However, much as we are in sympathy with the idea that it is a most important factor in stimulating certain forms of economic and social development, we cannot endorse the idea so widely prevalent, that physical environment determines the particular form of culture.

We may add that our data shows that the sacrifice both of animals and human beings is practised in some of the areas under consideration. The motives which seem to instigate such sacrifices are :

(1) To provide for the wants and comforts of the deceased and thus to prevent " walking ".

(2) The idea that the right of ownership does not cease at death. Here we must consider the different conceptions as to what constitutes man's personality ; that " a man's personality haunts his possessions " after death is a belief of the Kafirs.[1]

(3) The desire of the dead for revenge since death in only exceptionally few instances is supposed to be due to natural causes.

(4) The strengthening of the departed by means of blood.

(5) To afford companionship in the future world.

(6) To guide the way to the realms beyond.

---

[1] Kidd, *The Essential Kafir*, p. 83.

CHAPTER IX

PURIFICATION

THE ritual of purification plays such an important part in the death customs of all peoples, that we cannot afford to lose sight of its potent significance. It is most vital to stress at the outset that the modern conception of cleansing is entirely at variance with that of the primitive or that of the members of ancient society. Our motive is, as Farnell points out, for hygienic or pleasure-giving considerations, connected in some measure with the self-preservation instinct. " No hygienic, or utilitarian, or secular consideration will carry us far into explaining the cathartic code of Leviticus, or the Zend-Avesta, of Buddhism, or the impurity of tabooed animals. These codes are instinct with religious or superstitious beliefs ".[1]

The purity conception of the Hebrews seems to be on the same level with that of the Zarathustrian, Persian, and the Vedic Indian, the purity idea stressed in the law of the pure God, who declares that he would mete out the death penalty to Aaron if he entered the holy place without purification.[2] This idea appears as more material than spiritual and more a ritualistic injunction than an ethical one. Perhaps nowhere else do we find such emphasis laid upon purification as we do in the Vendîdâd, and for this reason the sentiments found in this sacred book have been chosen as the starting point of the subject under discussion.

The general tenor of the purification concept, as seen in the Vendîdâd, is the idea of impurity as a taint or as the " miasma of an evil spirit ".

In the Avesta, the corpse, after drying a year under the light of the sun, at last becomes pure. Here we see that light was regarded as the purest thing in the world. The same

---

[1] Farnell, *Evolution of Religion*, pp. 88-162.
[2] *Lev.* xvi. 2.

instinct which caused an aversion to blood has come to regard light as most potent in removing uncleanliness.

Farnell has called our attention to the fact that the idea of a spontaneous mesmeric power of evil that certain things possess is much in evidence in the Avesta.[1] This plays such an important part in the Vendîdâd, that its significance cannot be overestimated. Most specific is the injunction regarding the burial of the dead.[2] Again, the question of the uncleanliness of the earth caused by defiling the ground with dead matter is most carefully emphasized.[3] We likewise read of penalties assigned for non-observance of the laws regarding the dead bodies.[4] Minute directions are given concerning the purification of a house which has been visited by death,[5] of the cleaning of vessels defiled by the dead.[6] The fire which has come near the deceased must be purified with particular care.[7] Then too, we hear of the management of the sacrificial spoons contaminated with Nasu, the spirit of defilement. Not only is the eating of food which has come in touch with nasu regarded as an abomination, but the bringing of this powerful drug to fire and water is most scathingly denounced.[8] The route along which a corpse has been carried must be purified.[9] Here again, as in India, we perceive the supposed efficacious power of the dog in dispelling contamination. Merely allusion can be made to the significant rôle played by Cerberus in Greek and Latin mythology. The ceremony of the "glance of the dog" is likewise practised after the washing of the dead body to remove the defilement caused by contact with the dead. Jackson says that this ancient custom, dating back to the Avestan period, consists in making a dog bark at a dead body, since its glance was supposed to drive away the Nasu. He goes on to say that there are various explanations of this custom, from the mythical idea of the four-eyed dogs of Yama in the Veda, to the rationalistic theory that this is due to the

[1] Farnell, *Evolution of Religion*, p. 102.
[2] *Vd.*, III, 36-42.
[3] *Vd.*, I, 1-9.
[4] *Vd.*, LX, 10-15.
[5] *Vd.*, VIII, 1-3.
[6] *Vd.*, VIII, 73-75.
[7] *Vd.*, VIII, 73-80.
[8] *Vd.*, IV, 23-24.
[9] *Ibid*, VIII, 14-22.

instinct which the dog has for detecting if any life remains, and it owes its origin to the time when the corpse was devoured by dogs as well as by birds.[1] The part which the dog has played in funeral ceremonies is so significant, that scholars like Bloomfield, Hovelacque, Kuka, have made it a theme for discussion.[2]

The period of uncleanliness resulting from nasu is defined; here, as among other peoples, are varying periods, due to the kind of death.

The statement of Farnell is interesting who says that there is a certain common sense discernible in the distinction between substances on the ground and their greater or less susceptibility to spiritual contagion. Earthen pots have been considered more easily infected than metal ones, and thus need longer purification, whereas liquid substances are more dangerous conductors than dry.[3] "Should the dry mingle with the dry," says Ahura Mazda in conversation with Zarathustra, "how soon all this material earth of mine would be only one Peshôtami", which is another way of saying that the entire earth would thus become permeated with impurity.[4]

MELANESIA

After the funeral of a Wagawaga native, the relatives who have participated in the funeral ceremonies, and also the widow and children of the deceased, go to the sea and bathe.[5] After this ceremony the widow and children shave their heads. After five or ten days the Gariauuna of a deceased Tubetube native bathe in the sea.[6]

In the Hood Peninsula, special precautions are taken by manslayers against the ghosts of their victims. A man who has thus taken a life is regarded as impure until he has undergone certain ceremonies. He must live by himself for several days and must also abstain from every kind of food except toasted bananas. After various performances he solemnly proceeds to the nearest water where he washes himself. The following day at dawn he walks out of his house and calls

---

[1] Jackson, *Persia, Past and Present*, p. 388.
[2] Bloomfield, *Cerberus, The Dog of Hades*; Hovelacque, *Le Chien dans l'Avesta*; Kuka, *The Dog in the Vendîdâd*.
[3] Farnell, *Evolution of Religion*, p. 99.
[4] *Vd.*, VIII, 34.
[5] Seligmann, *Melanesians*, p. 611.
[6] *Ibid*, p. 614.

upon the name of his victim. If there is no response, he concludes that he has frightened the ghost. In addition, fires are kindled and floors beaten with the object of driving away the ghost, if perchance it might be lurking in the vicinity. The purification is completed the next day and for the first time since the death the manslayer is permitted to enter his wife's house.

From the account which Jackson gives of the burial of a young Fijian, we learn that after the conclusion of the ceremony, the father and mother walked away in opposite directions toward a running stream nearby, where they rested and washed themselves ; the narrator of the experience was compelled to do the same.[1] Among this same people, all mourners for a chief who are under burdensome taboos, go to a stream and wash themselves ; after this they catch some animal such as a pig or a turtle, and after wiping their hands on it, the animal becomes sacred to the chief.[2] In the Duke of York Islands the masters of sorcery after uttering imprecations upon the enchanter who has killed a man of distinction, go and bathe.[3]

In the Trobriands of Northern Massim the widow, after the end of her mourning period, goes to the seashore and washes herself.[4] Ten months after a death a widow in the Marshall Bennetts is washed at the seashore by her sisters-in-law ; a widower too undergoes similar treatment at the hands of his wife's sisters.[5]

At Bartle Bay after the mourning period is over, the widow takes off her necklace and washes herself.[6] After the body of a member of the Shortland Islands group is consumed, all the men go to the sea and wash themselves to remove any traces of dust or ashes, thus avoiding misfortune or sickness.[7] After a death the Papuans of the Mimika district of Dutch New Guinea sometimes bathe in a river.[8]

[1] Jackson's Narrative in Capt. Erskine's *Journal of a Cruise among the Islands of the Western Pacific*, pp. 475-477 ; quoted by Frazer, p. 422.
[2] Wilkes, *Narrative of the United States Exploring Expedition*, Vol. III, p. 99.
[3] Brown, *Melanesians and Polynesians*, pp. 387-390.
[4] Seligmann, *Melanesians*, p. 717.
[5] *Ibid*, p. 725.
[6] *Ibid*, p. 628.
[7] Brown, *Melanesians and Polynesians*, p. 215.
[8] Wollaston, *Pygmies and Papuans*, p. 139.

AUSTRALIA

In the Benbinga, Anula, and Mara tribes it is the custom, before the women are released from the silence ban, for the lubras to take small boughs, light them in the fire, and brush themselves with burning twigs.[1]

The Morlil ceremony, following the burial of a Kakadu native, partakes in part, at least, of the nature of a purification ceremony.[2] What may be interpreted as a purification rite consists in the pouring of water followed by the rubbing of charcoal over the bodies of men. The rugs, weapons, nets, and other possessions of a deceased native of New South Wales are hung in a tree and after two months are washed and used by some of his relatives.[3]

INDIA

As the Hindu funeral party proceeds homeward, a purifying ablution is performed by all relatives to the seventh or tenth degree. Clad in one garment, they plunge into still water. Before entering the house in which the body of the deceased has been, they must chew nimba leaves, sip water, and step upon a stone. Herbs are placed upon the fire which is invoked to protect the relatives and likewise water to cleanse the mourners. It is interesting to draw an analogy between the Hindu and Roman ritual of purification which follows the cremation ceremony. In ancient Rome after the ashes had been collected and placed in an urn, the persons were thrice sprinkled with water for purification.[4] The four corners of the house in India are sprinkled with holy water by means of which it is purified. The same kind of ceremony took place among the Romans on the tenth day named " denicales feriae ". Among the Romans, it was the custom for the whole family to undergo an elaborate purification to remove the pollution arising from contact with a corpse. Those who were in the funeral procession were purified by being sprinkled with water and stepping over a stone. The house which contained the dead body was swept with a certain kind of broom.

[1] Spencer and Gillen, *Northern Tribes of Central Australia*, pp. 554-555.
[2] Spencer, *Native Tribes of the Northern Territory of Australia*, p. 242.
[3] Bonney, " On Some Customs of the Aborigines of New South Wales ", *J.A.I.*, Vol. XIII (1884), p. 135.
[4] Virgil, *Aeneid*, VI, 229.

As we have mentioned before, Caland and Jolly state that during the time of impurity the Hindus must not practise certain customs closely associated with their daily life, and must make no personal contacts. To carry out more strictly the purification idea, food restrictions are also enjoined. From our knowledge of Hindu customs, we know that the Hindus are most zealous in complying with purification stipulations. It might be added that the period of impurity is followed by one of cleansing.

Macdonell claims that the period of impurity lasts for three days.[1] According to Caland, the period varies with the degree of relationship and extends from two to twelve days. Jolly supplements this and says that in computing the time of impurity, we have to consider not only the degree of relationship, but the age and sex of the deceased. There is no impurity, he declares, in connection with the corpse of a child who dies before it gets its teeth.[2] The Romans too did not consider any impurity connected with the dead body of a child if he died at a very early age. According to the Hindu conception, the death of a woman makes only her husband and his relatives impure. He states that the impurity period of a father and mother of the higher class is three days, for the lowest class from eleven days to one month.[3]

What seems to be a contradiction regarding the time of impurity seems to be easily explained. Thus in the Grihya-Sutras the impurity lasted either three or eight months. In later times the mourning period lasts longer. According to the Vishnu-Purana, the time of impurity for a Brāhman is ten

---

[1] Macdonell, *History of Sanskrit Literature*, p. 256.

Before a Greek house which contained a corpse there was placed water for persons who had been in the house to purify themselves from death pollution. When Thucydides refers to the purification of Delos he tells us that the Athenians took away all the coffins of the dead and passed a decree that henceforth no one should die or give birth to a child there.

In the Old Testament we read : "Whoever toucheth the dead body of any man and purifieth not himself, defileth the tabernacle of the Lord and his soul shall be cut off from Israel ; because the water of separation was not sprinkled upon him, he shall be unclean." (*Numbers* xix. 11-13.) "And for all the unclean persons they shall take the ashes of a burnt heifer for purification for sin, and running water shall be put into a vessel, and a clean person shall take hysop and dip it into the water, and sprinkle it upon the tent, and upon all the vessels and upon all the persons who were there, and upon him who touched a bone, or one slain, or one dead, or a grave." (*Numbers* xix. 17-18.)

[2] Jolly, *Recht und Sitte*, p. 155.

[3] *Ibid*, p. 155.

days, for a Kshatriya twelve, for a Vaisya fourteen, for a Sudra one month or thirty-one days. The higher the caste, the less the inconvenience.[1]

INDIA

Among the Bodos and Dhimals, the family remain unclean three days, after which they shave, bathe, and are sprinkled with holy water.[2] Thus purified, they prepare for the funeral banquet. The immediate relatives of the Paharias of the Rajmahal Hills are regarded as unclean for five days ; on the sixth day they shave themselves and bathe. We are told that the Bhumijas of Hanbhum do not shave for ten days, but on the eleventh day they shave, bathe, and have a feast.[3] The relatives of the deceased among the Muppan, a hill tribe of Wynaad, Malabar, do no work on the day after the funeral and also partially abstain from food. At a subsequent date they perform a final ceremony and remove every trace of death pollution to assure peace to the departed.[4] In Upper India among the lower Hindu castes the mourners, upon their return from the ceremony, bathe, and at the house door touch a stone, cow dung, iron, fire, and water which have been placed outside the house when the corpse was removed. The Ghasiyas pass their feet through the smoke of burning oil and others rub their feet with oil to drive away the ghost.[5] After the cremation the officiating Brāhman touches fire and bathes to purify himself and to bar the return of the ghost.[6] The relatives of a deceased Kondayamkottai Maravars bathe on the sixteenth day after a death and on the seventeenth the punyagavachanam, or purification, takes place, followed by an oil bath taken by the karma karta, or funeral official.[7] The Kurmi, one of the cultivating castes of India, upon their home-coming after a funeral, chew nīm leaves which are bitter and purifying, and then spit them out,

---

[1] Williams, *Religious Life and Thought in India*, p. 306n.

[2] *J.A.S.B.*, Vol. II, p. 563.

[3] *Statistical Accounts of Bombay.*

[4] Fawcett, "Odikal and Other Customs of the Muppans", *Folk-Lore*, Vol. XXIII (1912), pp. 42-43.

[5] *Bombay Gazetteer*, Vol. VIII, p. 159 ; Crooke, *Popular Religion and Folk-Lore of Northern India*, Vol. II, p. 59.

[6] Crooke, *Popular Religion and Folk-Lore of Northern India*, Vol. II, p. 59.

[7] Fawcett, "The Kondayamkottai Maravars", *J.A.I.*, Vol. XXXIII (1903), p. 64.

thus severing their connection with the corpse.[1] The Lohār,
a caste of blacksmiths, bathe on the eleventh day after a
funeral.[2] After the mourning period all the clothes of a family
of the Dhīmar caste of fishermen are washed and the house
is newly whitewashed.[3]

We read that cow dung was used extensively in purification.
At a funeral of a Bedouin Morocco women scratch their faces
and rub the wounds with cow dung which is thought to be a
purifying agency.[4]

Three days after a funeral the Kurmi collect ashes and
throw salt with the hope that a cow will come and lick up the
salt, which is looked upon by the natives as a purifying agency.
By this means the place and soul would be sanctified.[5]

The Lohār caste of blacksmiths remove with rice the
impurity resulting from contact with a dead body. Seven
persons pass it from hand to hand, and after pounding it,
they make it into a figure representing a human being. With
the words, " Go, become incarnate in some human being,"
they throw the cast into the water. Cakes of rice are placed
seven times on the shoulder of each person who carried the
corpse to remove the impurity.[6]

In some parts of Malabar, on the fifteenth day after a death,
a purificatory ceremony is performed. Oil into which some
gingelly seeds have been put is sprinkled over the persons of
those under pollution. This sprinkling and the bath which
follows it are supposed to remove the death pollution.[7]

Among the Todas, the wursol, or sacred dairyman, loses
his office because of his participation in the funeral rites.
On the day before the new moon following a death, all the
things of the wursol are thrown away and either the old
wursol is reappointed when he must repeat the ordination
requirements, or a new dairyman is named in his stead. The
sacred bell is taken from the stream where it has been placed,

---

[1] Russell, *The Tribes and Castes of India*, Vol. IV, p. 76.

[2] *Ibid*, p. 124.

[3] *Ibid*, Vol. II, p. 506.

[4] Frazer, "On Certain Burial Customs," *J.A.I.*, Vol. XXV (1885-1886),
p. 73.

[5] Russell, *Tribes and Castes of India*, Vol. IV, p. 76.

[6] *Ibid*, p. 124.

[7] Fawcett, "Deaths and Succeeding Ceremonies", *Madras Museum
Report*, Vol. III, Bulletin No. 3 (1901), p. 251.

and is purified by rubbing it with powdered tudr bark and water. The new dairy vessels are also purified.[1]

On the day of the new moon following the second funeral there is a purification ceremony connected with all the places used during the funeral rites. Two of the same clan as the deceased take buffaloes to a spot about one-half mile from the village. This animal is killed and the blood drawn from one side is mixed with earth contained in a basket. Some tribes add tudr bark and the mixture is thrown over the places connected with the two burials. The men who participate in this ceremony then go back to the village, bathe, and partake of food which has been denied them while performing this rite.[2]

Before lifting the bier a handful of rice and water from a jar is thrown outside and a goat is sacrificed. These are regarded by the Khasis as purifying ceremonies.[3] After three days, the family bathe and the clothes and mats in the house are washed. Before this is done they are under taboo and cannot work.[4]

The Nāyars on the fifteenth day after a death perform a purificatory ceremony. A man of the Athikurisi clan officiates. He sprinkles milk and oil in which some gingelly seeds have been put over the persons of those under pollution. This sprinkling and the bath which follows it remove the death pollution.[5] Among the same caste the members of the family wear clothes washed by a Vēlan and before and after bathing assemble for purification by the Nāyar priest who throws on them paddy and rice.[6] On the tenth day after a death, the sons of a deceased member of the Nāyādi caste return home at the end of various other ceremonies, and cow dung mixed with water is sprinkled over them by relatives and poured on the floor of the hut. Thus they are purified.[7] It is a custom among the Nambūtiri Brāhman on the eleventh day after a death for all the members of the family to go through a purifying ceremony.[8] The Mukkuvan corpse bearers

[1] Rivers, *The Todas*, p. 389.
[2] *Ibid*, p. 390.
[3] Gurdon, *The Khasis*, p. 133.
[4] *Ibid*, p. 135.
[5] Thurston, *Castes and Tribes of Southern India*, Vol. V, p, 357.
[6] *Ibid*, p. 361.
[7] *Ibid*, p. 281.
[8] *Ibid*, p. 215.

after anointing themselves bathe in the sea before the burial ceremony. After the interment, the bearers and son of the deceased bathe in the sea. Again, upon returning home they are met by a barber woman who sprinkles them with rice and water. The death pollution lasts for seven days and the son abstains from salt and tamarinds.[1] Among the Tiyans the Pula-kuli, or washing away the pollution, is the final ceremony of putting off the unpleasant consequences of death. Members of the family rub themselves all over with oil and are sprinkled by the barber with cow's milk and gingelly oil after which they bathe.[2]

Among the Hindus the four Brahmins who carry a corpse take the bath of the Ganges. They perform their ablutions and purify themselves of the pollution caused by carrying a corpse.[3] The chief mourner bathes without taking off his clothes, and his head and face are then shaved. Again he bathes to purify himself from the defilement of the barber's touch. After cremation he bathes a third time.[4]

A new king of Tangore made a pilgrimage to a temple a few leagues from his capital. He there took a bath in a sacred tank, thereby purifying himself from all the uncleanliness which he had contracted during the various mourning ceremonies.[5]

SIBERIA

The Chukchee put a twig on the hearth as a purifying sacrifice, thus destroying any unclean influence caused by contact with a dead body.[6] We are told that Siberians get rid of their ghosts by stepping over a fire.[7] It is said that the sled which conveyed the body of a deceased Yukaghir is fumigated over the fire ; likewise a similar fire is made before the tent and all those who have participated in the funeral pass through it before entering the habitation. The Reindeer Chukchee immerse all the iron objects left with a corpse in the

---

[1] Thurston, *Castes and Tribes of Southern India*, Vol. V, p. 116.

[2] *Ibid*, Vol. VII, p. 87.

[4] Dubois, *Hindu Manners and Customs*, Vol. II, p. 493.

[3] *Ibid*, p. 489.

[5] *Ibid*, p. 368.

[6] Bogoras, *The Chukchee*, J.N.P.E., Vol. VII (1907), p. 529.

[7] Meiners, *Geschichte der Religionen*, Vol. II, p. 303.

refuse of the paunches of the slaughtered animals.[1] A man supposed to have perished at sea, but who finally lands, must undergo a purifying ceremony. This Chukchee is girded with a thong, and after a dog has been sacrificed to the sea, he is taken to the family refuse heap where he must wallow in the filth.[2] Yahut grave diggers upon their return from

[1] Bogoras, *The Chukchee*, *J.N.P.E.*, Vol. VII (1907), p. 531.

[2] *Ibid*, p. 536.

Among the Ewe-speaking people purification was not only required of the mourners but of all those who had touched the dead. Contact with a corpse renders a person unclean and he must purify himself by washing from head to foot. (Ellis, *Ewe-Speaking People*, p. 160.) The persons connected with the funeral rites of the Tshi-speaking people proceed immediately after the interment to the nearest well or brook, and sprinkle themselves with water which is the ordinary mode of purification. (Ellis, *Tshi-Speaking People*, p. 241.)

In Samoa, the fifth day of mourning is a day of purification. The inhabitants bathe the face and hands with hot water, and then they are regarded as " clean", and resume the usual time and method of eating. (Turner, *Nineteen Years in Polynesia*, p. 228.) Certain springs in Peru were assigned as places of ablution after the performance of funeral rites. (Payne, *New World*, p. 445 ; Markham, *Rites and Laws of the Incas*, p. 12.) The contagious character of the death pollution is shown by the custom of the Hupa who require every one who has touched a corpse to cover his head until purified " lest the world be spoiled." (Goddard, *Hupa Texts*, p. 224n.)

The Salish of British Columbia hand the corpse to a wultzētca, or funeral shaman, who washes it and prepares it for burial. This official because of his magical power is supposed to be immune to the " bad medicine " of dead bodies. His head is sprinkled with bulrushes which are regarded as potent in checking the evil influences of corpses. The grave is brushed out by a mystic red fire to drive off the evil influence. (Hill-Tout, " Report on the Ethnology of the StlatlumH of British Columbia," *J.A.I.*, Vol. XXXV (1905), p. 137.)

After a death the winter house of a Thompson River Indian was purified with water in which tobacco and juniper had been soaked and fresh fir boughs were spread on the floor each morning. If two or more deaths occurred at the same time or in quick succession, then the house was burned. Most of the household utensils of the deceased as well as the bed on which he died were burned also. (Teit, *J.N.P.E.*, Vol. I, 1900, p. 331.)

Among the Navajos a person touching or carrying a dead body takes off all his clothes and afterwards washes his body with water. (Yarrow, " Mortuary Customs of the North American Indians," *First Report Bureau of Ethnology* (1881), p. 123.)

When describing the burial rites of the Ainu, Batchelor tells us that a tub of water is usually carried to the grave, and after the body has been interred, those who have taken part in the ceremony wash their hands. (Batcheler, *The Ainu and Their Folk-Lore*, p. 558.)

In Tonga the women who are tabooed because of their contact with a dead body remain constantly in the fytoca except when they want food and then they retire to one of the temporary houses. (Mariner, *Tonga Islands*, Vol. I, p. 320.)

In Greenland, as soon as a death occurs, they throw out all the clothes of the deceased, otherwise they would be polluted and their lives would be rendered unfortunate. (Cranz, *History of Greenland*, Vol. I, p. 237.) After a death the mourners must abstain from certain kinds of food and cannot perform their usual tasks, and the clothes worn when they touched the corpse must be thrown away. (*Ibid*, p. 215.)

Immediately after the burial of an Arapaho, the relatives bathe because they have touched a corpse. For several nights they burn cedar leaves with

the cemetery, purify themselves at a fire made of chips from a coffin.

" From the lowest fetish worshipper and half-charlatan wizard to those learned in the ancient philosophy of the Vedas the main business of life is to escape the baneful miasma of

the idea that smoke or smell will keep away the spirit. After the mourning period an old man paints red the faces and hair of the former mourners. This is called cleansing and is done in the morning so that they can be under the influence of the sun all day. (Kroeber, *Bulletin American Museum of Natural History*, Vol. XVIII (1902), p. 17.)

It is a Yao and Wayisa custom to wrap a dead body in mats. Those who perform this office must wash their hands. This is called by Macdonald a ceremonial act and he says that this is entirely different from the idea of uncleanliness after handling a dead body which requires bathing in running water before those who perform this function can associate with their fellow-men. (Macdonald, " East Central African Customs," *J.A.I.*, Vol. XXII, (1893), p. 112.)

Among the Bulgarians it is obligatory for those who have participated in the general rites to wash upon their return home. Running water is supposed to be especially efficacious inasmuch as it is supposed to carry objects to another world. (Murgoci, *Customs Connected with Death and Burial among the Roumanians*, pp. 97-101.)

A man of the Motu Tribe, New Guinea, was tabooed for three days after handling a corpse. Usually he touched no food with his hand for three days, and bathed at the expiration of this time. (Lawes, " Ethnological Notes on the Motu, Koitapu, and Koiari Tribes of New Guinea," *J.A.I.*, Vol. VIII (1879), p. 370.)

The Thompson River Indians bathe in a stream during their four days' seclusion because they touched a dead body. (Teit, " The Thompson Indians of British Columbia," *J.N.P.E.*, Vol. XIV (1900), pp. 331-332.) The widows and widowers of the Shuswap of British Columbia are forbidden to touch their own head and body. They must sweat all night in the lodges which they construct for the purpose and bathe regularly, after which they rub their bodies with spruce. (Boas, *Sixth Report on the Western Tribes of Canada*, p. 91.)

Among the Salish it is not unusual for a young widower to seclude himself in a forest for one year after the death of his wife and purify himself from death defilement. To accomplish this, he would construct himself a sweat house or hot bath by the side of a stream and expel the " bad medicine " of his dead wife from his body by repeated sweatings and hot baths. The young widow too had to undergo many ceremonial washings, the object of which was to make her long-lived and innocuous to her second husband. (Hill-Tout, " Report of the Ethnology of the StlatlumH of British Columbia," *J.A.I.*, Vol. XXXV, (1905), N.S., p. 139.)

One who has been associated with a corpse is regarded by the Japanese as a source of ceremonial uncleanliness. If purification is not resorted to, then such an individual can bring misfortune upon himself and others. (Hildburgh, " Notes on Some Japanese Methods of Personal Purification after a Funeral," *Man*, Vol. XVIII (1918), p, 92.) The ordinary form of purification for a person returning from a funeral is the throwing of salt upon him by some one who had no connection with the obsequies ; the threshold of the house and the room where the corpse rested are also subject to similar treatment. (*Ibid*, p. 93.) However, such salt throwing is not necessary if the person thus defiled through connection with a corpse first goes to a tea house. Chinese travellers to Japan say that in times far remote there prevailed a practice, when the funeral was over, for the whole family of the deceased to go into the water and wash. (Aston, " Japanese Mythology," *F.L.*, Vol. X (1899), p. 302.)

ceremonial impurity by washing in sacred rivers or by spells that bring good luck ".[1]   A way to drive away the spirit was to plunge into a stream to drown, or at least to wash off, the ghost.[2]

Summing up the evidence, the following seem to be the forms of purification practised in the Melanesian, Australian, Indian, and Siberian areas.

(1) Bathing.

(2) Use of fire.

(3) Hair cutting.

(4) Painting the body with mud and charcoal.

(5) Changing the usual garments.

(6) Abstinence from the ordinary pursuits of life.

(7) Non-indulgence in the usual food-stuffs.

(8) Refraining from sexual intercourse.

(9) Confinement in a lodge.

(10) Destruction of a house and the possessions of the dead.

(11) No contact with deity.

(12) Brushing with twigs.

(13) Chewing nimbus leaves.

(14) Carrying out the corpse through an exit other than of the ordinary one.

(15) The glance of a dog.

A Mohammedan renders himself impure by touching a dead body.   Both washing and praying are efficacious, the Mohammedan supposes, in purifying a polluted person.   If no water is available, the hands are rubbed with earth or sand.   (Georgi, *Russia*, Vol. II, pp. 50-51.)

An interesting purification ceremony is participated in by the Hupa Indians after a death.   As soon as the body is disposed of, the grave-digger and the household retire to a sweat house where they enter naked.   A hired priest repeats a formula of purification delivered over a basket of medicine. The medicine is then put into basket bowls and applied to the persons to be purified.   The grave-digger rubs the palms of his hands and the soles of his feet because they have handled a corpse and trodden on the grave.   When this is completed all go to a river and wash again with the medicine.   After this they plunge in and bathe.   This finished, they go to the *xonta*.   The grave-digger now goes through special observances.   He sits in silence near a fire with a cane of tsēlitso (ceanothus integerrimus) in his hand.   He takes his food apart from the rest and each night goes to the grave carrying over his head a bough of Douglas spruce so as not to glance at the sky or any one, thereby contaminating them.   After various other ceremonies, his clothes and dishes are hid on the fourth day and then are thrown into the river.   Even the coals are buried.   Finally all those who have been under taboo are washed again with the medicine and again they bathe.   (Goddard, *Life and Culture of the Hupa*, pp. 72-73.)

[1] Shotwell, *Religious Revolution*, p. 12.

[2] Frazer, "On Certain Burial Customs Illustrative of the Primitive Theory of the Soul," *J.A.I.*, Vol. XV (1885-1886), p. 78.

(16) The use of cow dung and salt.
(17) Wallowing in the dirt.
(18) Blood-letting.
(19) The use of rice, oil.
(20) The sacrifice of certain animals.

Because the very thought of a ghost haunts the mind of primitive man and since he is cognizant of the evil influence which may radiate from it, he must purify himself from the awful contagion brought about even through the most remote contact with a corpse. It is not surprising then that we find numerous forms of purification such as hair cutting, fasting, the use of water, fire, ashes, charcoal, salt, anointing with mud and paint, wallowing in the refuse, the look of a dog, abstention from sexual intercourse, the practice of certain religious customs such as retirement to a sweat lodge, employed to eradicate the uncleanliness which comes from a dead body.

The question which concerns us is why are such expedients resorted to. Reference has already been made to the use of water in religious ceremonies. As the body is cleansed from physical pollution, so the soul likewise is purified.[1] Crooke calls our attention to the fact that rivers and springs are believed to flow under the agency of an indwelling spirit, generally kindly by nature. Thus bathing brings the sinner and the polluted individual in communion with this spirit, and makes him clean.[2] Mud and paint are perhaps so often used because of their liquid properties. Liquids are supposed to absorb impurities quickly and thus to attract the contagion to themselves.[3] Surely savage man must not only have noticed the practical uses of fire, but also its potency in removing dampness which to the primitive is permeated with impurity. Again, sprinkling the body with ashes, brushing the survivors with burning twigs, and rubbing with charcoal since they may be said to be the by-product of fire, would be found as forms of purification. Then, too, we are concerned with the fact, that in the dietary restrictions imposed upon the survivors during the taboo period following a death, some

---

[1] Crooke, *Popular Religion and Folk-Lore of Northern India*, Vol. I, p. 37
[2] Crooke, *Natives of Northern India*, p. 227.
For water as a purifying agency see Scheftelowitz, " Die Sündentilgung durch Wasser," *Archiv Religionswissenschaft*, Vol. XVII (1914), pp. 353-412.
[3] Farnell, *Evolution of Religion*, p. 100.

foods are permitted to be eaten while others are forbidden. Perhaps an explanation of this is found in certain inherent qualities which different foods possess for enticing ghosts. Thus we saw that mourners often sleep on thorn pillows, or thorn bushes are placed about, because of the propensity of ghosts to attach themselves to them; and the same may be said of blood-letting, since the idea is very common among primitives that impure and evil spirits attach themselves to blood. This study endorses Marett's conception that pure, unadulterated sympathy is not in itself sufficient to account for taboo.[1] As intimated before, in the case of death, the sympathetic element seems reduced almost to a minimum. However, not only terror is centred in the religious taboo but a feeling of awe also enters,[2] although in the death-situation itself the fear motive appears far more accentuated than any other.

---

[1] Marett, *The Threshold of Religion*, p. 93.
[2] *Ibid*, p. 113.

CHAPTER X

THE POTENT POWER OF THE NAME

MELANESIA

IN South-Eastern British New Guinea the dread of the spirits of the deceased is manifested by the avoidance of the use of their names. If common objects have the same name as the dead, then these words are dropped from the language as long as the community remembers the deceased, and new names are substituted.[1] However, when the natives of the Aroma district in British New Guinea begin to plant their gardens, they take a bunch of sugar-cane and bananas, and standing in the middle of the garden, call over the names of the dead members of the family saying : " There is your food, your bananas and sugar-cane ; let our food grow well, and let it be plentiful ".[2] After a funeral in Lepers' Island, a meal is prepared, and the chief mourner takes a piece of the fowl and yam and calls upon the name of some person of the place who has died, saying : " This is for you." He repeats this until he has called all those in the district whose death is remembered.[3]

A Papuo-Melanesian will fight if the name of his dead father or paternal uncle is mentioned in his presence, but will betray no emotionalism if some remote dead relative of his father's clan is named.[4]

When any one dies in the Shortland group, all the members of the family change their names.[5] At Dobu the name of the dead must not be mentioned in the hearing of friends. If the deceased bore the name of a fish, a tree, or a flower, some other name for the objects must be substituted.[6] At

---

[1] Seligmann, *The Melanesians*, pp. 629-631.
[2] Frazer, *Belief in Immortality*, Vol. I, p. 201.
[3] Codrington, *Melanesians*, p. 284.
[4] Seligmann, *Melanesians*, p. 14.
[5] Brown, *Melanesians and Polynesians*, p. 207.
[6] *Ibid*, p. 399.

Murua we find the avoidance of mentioning the name of the dead.[1]

In Northern Massim in British New Guinea, although the names of the dead are not stringently avoided, yet there is a certain delicacy about mentioning them. The term of relationship is used rather than the exact name. But the names of certain near relatives of the deceased are not used for some time after a death.[2]

AUSTRALIA

We are told that one of the customs most strictly enforced among the natives of Australia is the injunction never to mention the name of a deceased person, whether male or female,—to transgress this prohibition would be looked upon as a serious infraction of their sacred traditions.[3] Although, as Spencer and Gillen point out,[4] it is usually supposed that the name of the deceased is never mentioned, yet this prohibition is not absolute in the tribes of the northern and central Australian area. The degrees of silence which are observed during the mourning period depend upon the relationship between the living and the dead. During this time which occupies from twelve to eighteen months no one must mention the name of the deceased only except when absolutely necessary and then in a whisper for fear of disturbing the Ulthana, or spirit of the deceased. If this ghost form hears his name, he is of the opinion that the mourning is not sincere, otherwise his relatives would be too much grieved to refer to him by name. He then decides to annoy the survivors as an indication that their conduct has been distasteful to him.

The individuals who are the Okilia, Oknia, Mia, Ungaraitcha, Uwinna or Mura of the dead man or woman may never mention his or her name, nor may they go near the grave when once the ceremony of the Urpmilchima has been performed. Those who are the Allira, Itia, Umbirna, Umba,

---

[1] Seligmann, *Melanesians*, p. 731.
[2] *Ibid*, p. 720.
It is interesting to note that there is ample evidence which shows that at Mabuiag there is no taboo on the names of the dead. (Cambridge, *Anthropological Expedition to Torres Straits*, Vol. V, p. 281.)
[3] Grey, *Journal of Two Expeditions of Discovery in North West and West Australia*, Vol. II, pp. 232-257.
[4] Spencer and Gillen, *Northern Tribes of Central Australia*, p. 526n.

Unkulla, Unawa, Kuntera, Chimmia, or Arunga may, after the mourning period is over, speak of the dead or mention his name, without bringing upon them the indignation of the Ulthana. So great is the dread connected with disturbing the Ulthana that no camp will be pitched near a grave for at least two years.

The Gammona of the deceased must not only never mention his name, but cannot be present when the burial takes place, nor are they permitted to participate in the marriage ceremony which is conducted at the grave. If by any accident the name of the deceased is called in camp, the Gammona will immediately rattle his boomerang to prevent the conversation from being heard.[1]

The silence injunction is also found among the Warramunga. Here we find it enforced sometimes for two years by widows, mothers, and mothers-in-law, although when a man dies no woman may ever again mention his name. This prohibition does not apply so strictly to men as the name may be mentioned by the two sub-classes to which wife's father and wife's brother belong.[2]

If a Kaiabara native dies, his tribes people never mention his name, but call him Wurponum, "the dead".[3] When a Kurnai was once spoken to about a friend who had recently died, he manifested some uneasiness as he looked around, and said: "Do not do that, he might kill me".[4] In Victoria we find the belief that reference to the name of a dead member of a group might excite the malignity of the spirit of the departed.[5] The dead man's name is never mentioned in North-West Australia after burial, for if this were done, the ghost of the deceased would return to camp and frighten the survivors.[6] Among the Narrinyeri the name of the dead is not to be mentioned until his body has decayed lest a lack of sorrow would seem to be inferred by the careless use of his name. A native wishes the deceased

---

[1] Spencer and Gillen, *Northern Tribes of Central Australia*, pp. 498-499.
[2] *Ibid*, pp. 525-526.
[3] Howitt, *Native Tribes of South East Australia*, p. 469.
[4] Howitt, "On Some Australian Beliefs," *J.A.I.*, Vol. XIII (1884), p. 191 ; *Native Tribes of South-East Australia*, p. 469.
[5] Stanbridge, "On the Aborigines of Victoria," *Transactions of the Ethnographic Society of London*, N.S., Vol. I (1861), p. 299.
[6] Clement, "Ethnographical Notes on the West Australian Aborigines," *Internationales Archiv für Ethnographie*, Vol. XVI (1904), p. 9.

to think that the mourners cannot speak or think of his name without weeping.[1]

It seems to be a universal custom among the Dieri, the Kurnai, the Ngarigo, the Theddora, the Kulm, the Kamilaroi, the Wiradjuri to speak with reluctance of the dead. However, it is significant to note that this restriction applies to the living as well, since a knowledge of the personal name would enable an enemy to "catch" its owner by evil magic. But we must bear in mind that this reticence concerning the name of the dead is prompted by fear of the spirit of the deceased. Many instances are cited by Howitt which testify to this dread attitude.[2] After a death the Dieri always shift their camp, and never mention or refer to the deceased.[3] The name of a family of the Chepara tribe is dropped for several months after a death. The males are addressed as Warkumbul, the females as Waimungun, which implies that one of their kindred has died.[4] The Wakelbura cannot bear to hear the name of the dead mentioned, and a violation of this taboo would cause serious quarrels and perhaps bloodshed.[5] The name of a deceased Wiradjuri is never used, and if any one else has the same name, he is obliged to drop it and take another.[6]

Among some tribes of North Australia, the name of the deceased is not mentioned, and he or she is referred to as "the old man" or "the old woman". If perchance, any one should mention the name of the departed member of his tribe, he says : "Dead, do not say his name". "Why do you do that ? It is bad talk". If a lubra mentions it, any son or brother of the dead man may strike her.[7]

The Jajaurung, the Geawe-gal, and the tribes about Maryborough do not mention the name of the dead.[8] In the Watchan-die tribe a dead man's name is not mentioned, for by uttering such a name a survivor places himself in the power

[1] Taplin, "The Narrinyeri," in *Native Tribes of South Australia*, p. 19.
[2] Howitt, *Native Tribes of South East Australia*, pp. 440-447.
[3] *Ibid*, p. 449.
[4] *Ibid*, p. 469.
[5] *Ibid*, p. 474.
[6] *Ibid*, p. 466.
[7] Spencer, *Native Tribes of the Northern Territory of Australia*, p. 246.
[8] Howitt, *Native Tribes of South East Australia*, pp. 440-441.

of malign spirits, who are provoked by the mention of such
a name.[1]

Dawson tells us that personal names are rarely perpetuated
and it is believed that any one adopting the name of a deceased
person will not live long. When a dead man or woman is
referred to, it is by the general name of " dead person ", but
when the mourning period is over, they may be spoken of by
name but only with the greatest possible reluctance. If
during the interval of mourning the deceased must be mentioned by strangers, the allusion is always in whispers.
Not only is the name of the dead forbidden but also the names
of all his near relatives are taboo during the mourning period.
These are called by general terms and to call them by their
own names is considered an insult to the deceased. A similar
law is enforced concerning animals and things for which the
dead has been called. No reference can be made to the
animal, place, or thing during the interval of mourning by the
tribe of the departed because it recalls the memory of the
dead.[2] Curr and Fraser too stress the fact that the names
of the dead are not mentioned.[3]

The natives of Adelaide and Encounter Bay feel great
repugnance when they speak of a person who has lately died
and especially avoid mentioning his name. Temporary
names are given to the people who have the same name as
the deceased.[4]

Not until several months after a death, when the corpse is
completely decayed, is the name of the dead allowed to be
mentioned. This explains certainly in part why we often
find so many names for the same being. If, for instance,
a man has a name signifying water, the whole tribe must,
for a considerable time after his death, use some other word
to express water.[5] The natives of Cooper's Creek also refrain
from mentioning the dead man's name.[6] In the Boulia district

[1] Oldfield, "The Aborigines of Victoria", *Transactions of the Ethnological
Society*, Vol. III (1865), p. 238.

[2] Dawson, *Australian Aborigines*, p. 42.

[3] Curr, *The Australian Race*, Vol. I, p. 338 ; Fraser, *The Aborigines of
New South Wales*, p. 82.

[4] Wyatt, *Some Accounts of the Manners and Superstitions of the Adelaide
and Encounter Bay Aborigines*, p. 165.

[5] Meyer, *The Aborigines of Encounter Bay*, p. 199.

[6] Smyth, *The Aborigines of Victoria*, Vol. I, p. 120.

the personal individual name of the deceased is never mentioned again.[1]*

Although among some people such as the Mallanpara (scrub blacks) of the Tully River, we do not find absolute prohibition of the name of the deceased, yet such an individual is alluded to in whispers.[2]

HINDU

The name of the dying must be given by those who perform the ceremonies connected with the last moments of death's victim.[3]*   The Khasis call upon the name of the dead three times to make sure that death has occurred.[4]

---

[1] Roth, *Ethnological Studies Among the North-West-Central Queensland Aborigines*, p. 164.

* Spencer in quoting Dove says of the Tasmanians : "They fear pronouncing a name by which a deceased friend was known, as if his shade might be offended". (Spencer, *Principles of Sociology*, Vol. I, p. 246.)

[2] Roth, "Superstition, Magic, and Medicine", *North Queensland Ethnography*, Bulletin No. 5, p. 20.

[3] Caland, *Albindische Todten Gebraucher*, p. 9.

* The Yoruba-Speaking People call upon the name of the deceased three times and urge him to depart. (Ellis, *Yoruba-Speaking People*, p. 160.) The name of the deceased is likewise called loudly by the Fijians and Banks Islanders but with a different object.   They hope by this means that the soul may hear and come back. (Spencer, *Principles of Sociology*, Vol. I, p. 155.)   Morgan states that the Iroquois call upon the name of the dead before burial. (Morgan, *League of the Iroquois*, Vol. I, p. 175n.)

[4] Gurdon, *The Khasis*, p. 142.

The Hindus have a prohibition which prevents a wife addressing a husband by his name. (Risley, *The People of India*, p. 81.)

Among nearly all tribes occasionally a name would be discarded after a severe sickness or other misfortune, and among eastern tribes such an action required the consent of the clan.   Names were likewise lent as a mark of particular favour or friendship, either for a limited time or for life. (Farrand, *Basis of American History*, pp. 203-204.)

The name of the dead as well as similar sounds are tabooed among the Bantu tribes.   This practice would necessarily occasion a change in the vocabulary of the natives. (Hartland, article in *Hastings*, Vol. IV, p. 442.)

A king at his death becomes sacred in the islands of Nossi-Bé and Mayotte near Madagascar, and no one in the locality dare henceforth utter his name. (Hartland, article in *Hastings*, Vol. IV, p. 441.)

The Mosquito Indians of Central America avoid mentioning the name of the dead. (Yarrow, *Study of Mortuary Customs among North American Indians*, p. 106.)   The Karok of California regard the mere mention of a dead man's name as the highest crime. (*Ibid*, quoting Powers, *Contrib. to North American Ethnology*, Vol. II, p. 58.)   The Tolawa of North California were also forbidden to mention the name of the dead. (Yarrow, p. 105.)

Among the Salish of British Columbia the name of the dead is not uttered. This, as Hill-Tout suggests, is done not so much out of regard to the feelings of surviving relatives, but because of the mystical connection between names and their owners.   The utterance of the name of a dead person disturbs his spirit and entices it to its former haunts.   Thus we see that such a procedure as calling upon the deceased by name would be inimical to both the departed

It is interesting to note that with all Hindus two names are given to children, one secret and used only for ceremonial purposes, and the other for ordinary use ; for sorcery can be practised if the real name is known.[1]

SIBERIA

When a mother dies among the Chukchee, the name of her youngest and dearest child is changed so that her ghost may not have communication with this survivor.[2]

In the areas under consideration the avoidance of the name of an individual is not identified solely with death. We hear that in some tribes the name of the male is given up forever at the ceremony which introduces him into manhood and the Bangerang have almost forgotten the names which the males bore in infancy.[3] At different parts of Queensland, changes in name may not only take place upon the death of

---

and the living. (Hill-Tout, " Report on the Ethnology of the StlatlumH of British Columbia ", *J.A.I.*, Vol. XXXV (1905), N.S., p. 138.)

The names of the dead are never mentioned among the Iroquois until the mourning period is over. (Morgan, *The League of the Iroquois*, Vol. I, p. 175.) Teit states that the Thompson River Indians do not mention the name of the dead. (Teit, " The Thompson Indians of British Columbia ", *J.N.P.E.*, Vol. I (1900), p. 332.)

In South America among the Abipones and Lenguas, when a man dies, his family and neighbours change their names. (Southey, *History of Brazil*, Vol. III, p. 394, quoted by Tylor, *Early History of Mankind*, p. 127.)

It is a Jewish superstition that a man's destiny may be changed by giving him a different name. (Tylor, *Early History of Mankind*, p. 128, quoting Eisenmenger.)

In referring to the natives of America, Brinton says : " Savages have an awful horror of death ; they thought that to meet it without flinching was the highest proof of courage. Everything connected with the deceased was in many tribes shunned with supernatural terror ; his name was not mentioned, his property was left untouched, all references to him were sedulously avoided ". (Brinton, *Myths of the New World*, p. 278.)

To the Greenlanders the name is of great importance. They believe that the characteristics of a dead person are transferred to that individual who is named for him. If two people have the same name, and one of them dies, then the survivor must change his name. Moreover, if the deceased has the name of an animal, object, or abstract idea, then the word designating such objects or ideas must not be used. In Eastern Greenland the natives are afraid to speak their own names. When a mother is asked her child's name, she replies that she could not tell and the father declares that he has forgotten it. (Nansen, *Eskimo Life*, pp. 230-231.)

Among the Hupa Indians the name of the deceased cannot be spoken without offence and such an insult must be avenged. (Goddard, *Life and Culture of the Hupa*, pp. 73-74.)

[1] Clodd, " What's in a Name," *F.L.*, Vol. I (1890), p. 273.

[2] Enderli, " Zwei Jahre bei den Tschuktschen und Korjaken ", Peter-mann's, *Mitteilungen*, Vol. XLIX (1903), p. 257.

[3] Curr, *The Australian Race*, Vol. I, p. 46.

one of the tribal members, but at initiation, upon the occurrence of some important event happening to a member of a community, on the discovery of the control of some charm, upon recovery from sickness, and upon the advance of old age.[1]* In many Australian tribes we find the belief that the life of an enemy may be taken by the use of his name in incantations.[2]

Indeed, name taboos and change of name are so numerous in all primitive communities that we must stress the great importance of the name.† Even the influence of physical environment causes a change of name as is seen among the Kwakiutl Indians whose nobles have winter and summer names.[3] Frequently the names of sacred persons and kings are tabooed. Dennett has shown that in Africa there is a distinct correlation between the name of a chief and the being or god whom he represents.[4] It is very common to find that the personal name is not pronounced and Tylor sees in this a parallel with the use of secret names.[5] In New Britain there are prohibitions against calling by names certain relatives such as mother-in-law, brother-in-law, and others. A native will never speak of these by their names.[6] A taboo on the name of relatives by marriage is found in the Western Islands of the Torres Straits Settlements. A person subject to such a taboo is likewise prevented from uttering the name of a relative if it should be the name of an object.[7]

Judging from the wide prevalence of the avoidance of the name of the dead, we feel inclined to believe that this is one of the chief devices employed to prevent the return of the departed to the realms of the living. Roth says that in those cases where he was able to ascertain why the name of the dead is not pronounced, in Queensland, he always met with the same response—the spiritual representation or ghost might

---

[1] Roth, " Superstition, Magic and Medicine," *North Queensland Ethnography*, Bulletin No. 5, p. 20.

* The Land Dyaks often change the names of children especially if they are sickly : " There being an idea that they will deceive the inimical spirits by following this practice ". (Spencer, *Principles of Sociology*, Vol. I, p. 245.)

[2] Curr, *The Australian Race*, Vol. I, p. 46.

† For some tabooed names, see Batchelor, *The Ainu and Their Folk-Lore*, pp. 242-253.

[3] Frazer, *Golden Bough*, Vol. III, p. 386.

[4] Dennett, *At the Back of a Black Man's Mind*, p. 100.

[5] Tylor, *Early History of Mankind*, p. 142.

[6] Brown, *Melanesians and Polynesians*, p. 275.

[7] Cambridge, *Anthropological Expedition to Torres Straits*, Vol. VI, p. 250.

return and do harm to the living.[1] The evidence cannot support the idea that avoidance of the name of the dead is a sign of regard for the deceased.

Foucart emphasizes the fact that the name of a person is his soul and that the name is controlled by pronunciation.[2] Since sound is a manifestation of life, the sound uttered by an animate being is a junction of that life. Because it is perceived by the ears and the touch and the eyes, the primitive thinks of it as a force, the vibrations of which stand for life.[3] The power of the name with its intrinsic characteristics is associated with this idea of voice, whose alluring and fascinating qualities are identified with many forms of magical activity.[4]

That a belief exists in the material virtue and substance of the written word is seen in the Mohammedan idea that if the ink is washed from the paper containing a verse of the Koran, such a drink if swallowed will be most efficacious. A Chinese physician when he does not chance to have the drug he requires for his patient, will write the prescription on a piece of paper, and after burning it, will let the sick man swallow the ashes.[5]

The Hindus think that by the continued repetition of the Gayatri, or sacred prayer to the sun, virtue may be acquired and that the prayer is personified as a goddess.[6] The enunciation of the holy syllable, Aum or Om, will produce significant results. How familiar to us is the injunction: "Thou shalt not take the name of the Lord thy God in vain". That the force of the law exists in the sound and not in the sense is emphasized in the non-desirability of translating the sacred books, for then their holy character is lost.[7] Not only must

[1] Roth, " Superstition, Magic, and Medicine," *North Queensland Ethnology* Bulletin No. 5, p. 20.

[2] Foucart, article " Primitive Name", Hasting's *Encyclopedia of Religion and Ethics*, Vol. IX, pp. 130-136; Conybeare, *Myth, Magic, and Morals*, pp. 235-250.

[3] *Ibid*, p. 135.

[4] Combarien, *La Musique de la Magie*, p. 125.
The Goajiro Indians of Columbia consider the mentioning of a dead man's name a serious offence, often punishable by death. (Westermarck, *Development of Moral Ideas*, Vol. II, p. 546.) The Indians of Washington Territory even change their own names upon the death of a relative. (*Ibid*, p. 545.)

[5] Tylor, *Early History of Mankind*, p. 128, quoting Davis.

[6] Russell, *Tribes and Castes of India*, Vol. I, p. 108.

[7] *Ibid*, pp. 108-109.

the original tongue be used but the exact words are necessary if the desired results are to be the outcome.   In relating the story of a man whose neighbour cut his vines, Gaius states the facts most specifically and clearly.   Although in all other respects the law was on his side, yet because he said vines for trees, he lost his case.[1]

When a Hindu mother fears that her child is going to die, she sometimes gives it some obnoxious name such as dirt or rubbish to deceive the evil spirit who wishes to carry away her offspring.   He will then not think it worth while to steal her child.[2]*   By the savage names are regarded as a concrete, not as an abstract, representation.

There seems then to be no doubt that among primitive people as in ancient religions, a man's name is equivalent to his personality.   As we have seen, it is a belief among savages that to know one's name is to have power over him.   Perhaps this is an explanation of the fact that every Egyptian had two names, one by which his companions knew him, and the other known to the higher powers in the spiritual world.[3]   The same may be said of the Nāmakarana, the Indian rite of naming a child when two names are given, one for common use, another a secret name known to the parents only.[4]   If we go back to the earliest forms of Egyptian religion, we find the doctrine that " The man who has learned and can pronounce the divine words revealed through God of Thought, and Mind, would be elevated to the God, and be blended with him as one and inseparable ".   To refer to the Biblical narrative : " In the beginning was the word, and the word was with God, and God was the Word ".[5]

---

[1] Fustel de Coulanges, *La Cité Antique*, p. 225.
[2] Russell, *Tribes and Castes of India*, Vol. I, p. 108.
* The Tonquin give young children horrid names to frighten the demons from them. (Richard, " Tonquin", in *Pinkerton*, Vol. IX, p. 734.)
[3] Conybeare, *Myth, Magic, and Morals*, p. 236.
[4] Barnett, *Antiquities of India*, pp. 138-139.
[5] *John* I. 1.
As a Roman breathes his last, the relatives who had gathered around, loudly called upon his name.   The recall of the dead to life by uttering his name three times, and if there were no answer to make sure of death, is a custom which is still in use at the death-bed of a pope ; the lamentation for the dead takes place when there is no longer any doubt that death has snatched its victim. (Harper's *Dictionary of Greek and Roman Antiquities*, p. 698.)   The mourners called repeatedly the names of the dead with loud cries and exclamations, such as " vale." (Obid, *Met.*, X, 62 ; Ovid, *Fasti*, IV, 852 ; Lucan, *Phars.*, II, 22.)

Authors even write, says Conybeare,[1] when enumerating a population, that there are so many names in a city, " In that hour there was a great earthquake, and the tenth part of the city fell ; and there were killed in the earthquake names of men seven thousand."[2]

A prayer which depends upon the use of a name of power is often analogous to a spell or magical incantation. Such expressions as " Hallowed be thy name ",[3] " They that know thy name put their trust in thee ",[4] are too well known to elicit further comment.

---

[1] Conybeare, *Myth, Magic, and Morals,* p. 235.
[2] *Revelation* XI. 13.
[3] *Matthew* VI. 9.
[4] *Psalms* IX. 10.

CHAPTER XI

FEASTS

At Wagawaga about two to four weeks after a death the family of the deceased, including his father and widow, prepare the first of a series of feasts called banahivi. These banahivi succeed one another at intervals of one to two months. After a particular feast, usually the third, a taboo is put on all the cocoanuts of the dead man's hamlet. The last banahivi ten or twelve months after the first is similar to the first but larger. Two to three weeks after the burial of a native of Tubetube, the first of the feasts called kane-kapu takes place. It is not clear whether in every case more than one such feast is held, and Seligmann suggests that probably the number is regulated by the amount of food and quantity of pigs available, although in every case a feast is given usually about ten months after a death and upon this occasion the widow dispenses with her mourning.[1]

A mourning feast is held at Bartle Bay a month or two after a death. Here, too, we note a number of such feasts called banivi followed by a big feast named torela. The widow discards her food taboos after the last banivi, but does not eat pig until the torela.[2]

Feasts for the dead are also held in the Mekeo tribes of British New Guinea where those of the Ufuapie group have certain definite functions.[3] Among the Koita on the first or second day following a burial, a feast (bowa) is held. On the fourth day, a much more important feast (venedari) takes place. Although there are no cooking and fire taboos imposed upon the widow, yet she must abstain from such articles of food as the dead man especially cared for, until after the feast called ita, which takes place some six months later.

---

[1] Seligmann, *Melanesians*, pp. 620-624.
[2] *Ibid*, pp. 626-629.
[3] *Ibid*, pp. 350-363.

At this feast the widow leaves off her mourning, and the ceremony connected with its removal is the most important part of the ita celebration.[1]

At some of the villages in the northern Massim the shades are thought of as visiting a feast called kaiwos womilamala, which appears to be held ten or more months after a death has occurred. The importance of this feast is that on kadawaga food is especially cooked for the spirits of the dead, and that this is left for them over night, and the next morning is found to have entirely or partly disappeared. No definite time is assigned for this feast, for it is supposed that the spirits will be aware when a sufficient quantity of food has been gathered. In speaking of the natives of New Britain, Brown tells us that the spirits of the dead eat the spirit of the food but they do not consume it materially.[2]

In Florida, after the funeral of a chief or of one who is much esteemed, a feast is held. At this feast a bit of food is thrown into the fire for the deceased with the words : " This is for you ".[3] When a death feast is held in the San Cristoval Islands a morsel of food is thrown upon the fire as the dead man's share. At burial feasts the image of a great man is put up in a canoe house before which food is placed.[4] On the fifth day after the funeral of a Santa Cruz Islander a feast commemorates the end of the burial ceremonies.[5] A series of feasts follow the funeral rites in the Banks Islands. These meals are regarded as the most important phase of those ceremonies held to commemorate the dead. The number of such feasts and the length of time during which they are repeated vary in the different islands, and depend upon the estimation in which the deceased is held.[6]

At Aurora, one of the New Hebrides, the relatives of the dead man celebrate a death feast the fifth or tenth day after the demise of one of their number. The ghosts call this the great feast of the man who died and carry away the tamani of the offering until the hundredth day.[7] Among the Fijians a

---

[1] Seligmann, *Melanesians*, pp. 162-166.
[2] Brown, *Melanesians and Polynesians*, p. 193.
[3] Codrington, *Melanesians*, p. 255.
[4] *Ibid*, p. 262.
[5] *Ibid*, pp. 263-264.
[6] *Ibid*, pp. 271.
[7] *Ibid*, pp. 282-283.

feast is held on the fourth day. Others follow on the tenth, thirtieth, fortieth, and hundredth days.[1] After the funeral of a native of Leper's Island, pigs and five fowls are killed, and the fowls are roasted over a fire. When the meal is prepared, the chief mourner takes a piece of fowl and of yam and calls the name of some person of the place who has died, saying : " This is for you ". This he continues to do until he has addressed all those deceased members of the community and has given each some fowl and yam. He and the assembled mourners eat what remains. This performance is celebrated on the fifth and the tenth days following a death. The tenth day is an occasion for a special feast with a large assemblage and a similar feast is held on the fiftieth day. Every fifth day also there is a death meal until the hundredth is reached. On this day for every great man there will be a hundred ovens and this is a remarkable occasion.[2] At Agara, Pentecost, after burial a fire is lighted for the death meal and as in Leper's Island, feasts are held until the hundred days' cycle is completed.[3] In Saa, after the lapse of a considerable interval, there is a great funeral feast at which the bones are removed to the common burial ground.

It is recorded that among some tribes in Northern Melanesia they offer food to their departed kinsfolk for a long time after death until all the funeral feasts are over.[*]

INDIAN AREA

One of the most interesting subjects with which the Grihya-Sutras deal is the worship of the Manes. In the Rig-Veda the good dead return with Yama to the sacrifice to enjoy the soma and viands prepared for them and their descendants. Thus we see the belief in the necessity of having a son if joy is to be secured in the hereafter. The Pindapitri-yajna, the

---

[1] Rougier, "Maladies et Medicines à Fiji autrefois et aujourd'hui", *Anthropos*, Vol. II (1907), p. 74.

[2] Codrington, *Melanesians*, p. 284.

[3] *Ibid*, p. 287.

[*] In North America it is a common belief that the souls remain near the bodies until the feast of the dead. After such a ceremony they are now free to go to the land of spirits, situated in the regions of the setting sun. (Yarrow, *Study of Mortuary Customs among the North American Indians*, pp. 94-95, quoting Rind, *Red River Exploring Expedition*, Vol. II (1860), p. 164.) We also find the belief that while the survivors partake of the visible material, the ghost feeds upon the spirit which dwells in the food.

gift of cakes to departed ancestors, consists of an offering to
Soma and to Fire, and is still performed to-day in some parts
of India.[1] The fathers are invoked to receive their share.
Then follows an address to the fathers in reference to the six
seasons of the year. The worshipper looks at his wife and
exclaims : " You have made no domestic men, we have
brought these gifts to you according to our power ". Then
offering a thread, wool, and hair, he says : " Fathers, this is
your apparel, wear it ". The wife then eats a cake with the
desire to have a child, and calls : " Fathers, let a male be born
to me this season. Do you protect the child in this womb
from all sickness ". It is the religious belief of the Hindus
that only descendants may offer sacrifices to deceased ancestors.
Since extinction of family is naturally much concerned about
dying without male descendants, the birth or adoption of
a son is a ceremony which cannot be divorced from his
religion.[2]

The Sraddha ceremony then, based upon the necessity of
feeding the dead, must be repeated at frequent intervals.
The rites are discontinued after a year or two when it is assumed
that the soul has reached its final resting place. At each
successive death in the family the sainted dead are remembered
and are invited to attend the funeral feast when their souls
are refreshed by periodical feeding. However, the desire to
feed the soul is not the only motive which prompts the celebration of the Sraddha rites. Other reasons for this ceremony
are even of more vital importance. One is for the purpose
of embodying the soul of the deceased after cremation, or to
release the body so as to convey the soul away, or raising it
from the regions of the atmosphere, where he would otherwise
have to roam for an indefinite period among evil spirits.
Manu states that the performance of the Sraddha by a son
or nearest male relative is necessary to deliver a father from
a kind of hell called Put, and that the spirits of the departed
are sustained by the offered food. Monier-Williams has given
such a detailed treatment of the worship of " Brahmanized
Hindu " men, that further narrative is unnecessary here.[3]
The spirits of departed ancestors attend upon the Brahmans

[1] Dutt, *History of India*, Vol. I, pp. 165-166.
[2] *Ibid*, Vol. I, p. 166.
[3] Williams, *Brahmanism and Hinduism*, p. 278.

invited to the ceremony of the Sraddha "hovering round them like pure spirits, and sitting by them when they are seated ".[1] Williams has also compiled an interesting list of departed relatives supposed to benefit from the Sraddha rites.[2]* "Verily there are Deaths in all the worlds, and were he not to offer oblations to them, Death would get hold of him in every world ".[3]

Crooke says that the Ghasiyas of Mirzapur, about the most savage of the Dravidian tribes, feed the brotherhood at the door of the cook house, and spread ashes and flour a cubit square on the ground.[4] They light a lamp there and cover both the square and the light with a basket. Then the son of the dead man goes a little distance from where the corpse has been carried out, and calls out his name two or three times. He then invites him to come to the celebration which his ancestors have prepared, and requests him to partake of the offerings. The same author cites the ritual of the Kharwārs who worship the spirits of the dead in the month of Sawan. At the same house-fire the master of the house offers one or two black fowls and some cakes, and makes a burnt offering with butter and molasses. He then calls out : "Whatever ghosts of the holy dead or evil spirits may be in my family, accept this offering, and keep the house free from trouble ". The same customs are characteristic of other Dravidian tribes. The Kurus and the Sonas worship their dead relatives in February, the eldest son offering goats to his deceased ancestors, a ceremony analogous to the Sraddha of the Hindus.[5] In this same connection Monier-Williams

[1] The pum-savana, a rite to obtain male off-spring is performed in the second, third, and fourth month of pregnancy. (Barnett, *Antiquities of India*, p. 137.)

[2] Williams, *Hinduism*, p. 67.

* In Rome it was necessary to have a son who could perform the sacrifices to ancestors. Not only did the head of the family officiate at such ceremonies, but it was also incumbent upon him to appoint a successor. If he had no son, then adoption was resorted to after the permission of the priest had been secured. Upon no condition was such consent given if the male to be adopted was the only representative of his family. If there was an inheritance, provision for the traditional crifice had precedence over all other claims. (Carter, *The Religion of Numa*, ρ. 16.) The shades clamor for their rightful due, the sacrifice at the grave and such they could accept only at the hands of their descendants. (Carter, *Religious Life of Ancient Rome*, p. 12.)

[3] *Catapatha Brâhmana*, Vol. I.

[4] Crooke, *Popular Religion and Folk-Lore of India*, Vol. I, p. 176.

[5] *Indian Antiquary*, Vol. I, pt. 4.

has described funeral ceremonies which he witnessed on the Black Bay of Bombay and also at Benares and Faya.[1]

SIBERIAN AREA

After the body is cremated, the Gilyaks sit round and partake of the flesh of dogs which are to accompany the deceased.[2] The Yahuts kill horses and cattle at the death feast so that the dead can ride them to his future home.[3] At the funeral of a Reindeer Koryak, reindeer are slaughtered to enable the dead to have them in the next world. The meat is then eaten by relatives and neighbours who assemble at the funeral.[4] Even from a radius of fifty miles guests are represented at the funeral feast of a Reindeer Chukchee. Just to what extent a portion of the sacrifice can be regarded as a sacramental meal in the sense that divine virtue passes over to the eaters, is a matter of conjecture. Each member of the party brings an offering which usually takes the form of meat, marrow, a tobacco leaf, or something similar. After a part of these have been presented to the corpse, the remainder of the food is spread on stones near the dead body. Those present then partake of this feast which is regarded as a meat offering by the deceased. On the second day after the funeral the grave is again visited and upon the return of the party there is another feast.[5]

Although the anthropologist is inclined to look upon so-called " survivals " with caution, yet it seems very fitting at this stage of our discussion to introduce a somewhat detailed description of the Roman Manes celebrations, days so full of meaning to the citizens of Italy and so identified with the life of the community.

The " Dies Parentales " which began February thirteenth and ended the twenty-first or twenty-second of the same month, were not days of terror, but times for the performance of a duty, a general holiday when the dead were propitiated. Nothing was to be feared from the dead provided the living under the supervision of the state and its pontifices performed their duty to their departed kinsmen. The relation between

---

[1] Williams, *Brahmanism or Hinduism*, p. 308.
[2] *A.R.W.*, Vol. VIII, p. 473.
[3] *R.H.R.*, Vol. XLVI, p. 208.
[4] Jochelson, *The Koryak, J.N.P.E.*, Vol. VI (1905), p. 111.
[5] Bogoras, *The Chukchee, J.N.P.E.*, Vol. VII (1907), pp. 530-531.

the dead and their surviving relatives was looked upon as a
jus sacrum. The abode of the deceased tribesmen was
without the limits of the city and in no way did they manifest
a malevolent spirit toward the living.[1]

The Parentalia were a yearly renewal of the burial rite.
As sacra privata they took place upon the death of a deceased
member of the family. Upon such an occasion the family
would proceed to the grave bringing offerings of water, milk,
honey, oil, and the blood of black victims, and decking the
tomb with flowers.[2] Furthermore they would recite once
again the solemn greeting " salve sancte parens ", to partake
of a meal with the dead, and to appeal to them to confer
all things needful upon the survivors. That the heir was
expected to continue the observance is expressed most
specifically, " Jamque dies ni fallor, adest, quem semper
acerbum semper honoratum sic di voluistis, habebo ".[3]
During the Dies Parentalia temples were closed, marriages
were forbidden, and the magistrates appeared without insignia.[4]
February, then, with its Parentalia, is conspicuous for its
performance of expiatory rites.

Fowler points out the fact that Aeneas, when he is cele-
brating the funeral games in honour of his father, is represented
for the first time as the father of a family, discharging the
duties necessary for the perpetuation and prosperity of that
family with gravitas combined with cheerfulness, and his
pietas has taken a definite, practical, Roman turn.[5]

Another offering to the Manes, other than that referred to,
took place the ninth day after burial in accordance with
the Greek custom. On the steps of the grave monument a
simple meal of milk, honey, oil, and the blood of sacrificed
animals was offered. These sacrifices were repeated by
relatives on the anniversary of the birth and death of the
deceased.

In this connection we may add that among the Greeks it
was the custom for the feast in honour of the dead to be given
at the house of the nearest relative.[6] Celebrations were

[1] Fowler, *Roman Festivals*, p. 307.
[2] Virgil, " Purpureosque jacet flores," *Aeneid*, V, 79 ; *Juv.*, V., 84.
[3] Virgil, *Aeneid*, V, 49 ; cf. Cic. *De Legg*, II, 48.
[4] *Fasti*, Vol. II, p. 615, et seqq.
[5] Fowler, *Religious Experience of the Roman People*, p. 418.
[6] Lucian, *de Luctu*, 24 ; *Demosth. De Cor.*, 321-355.

common on the third, ninth, and thirtieth days after the funeral.[1] The rites on the thirtieth day included a representation of the funeral feast.[2] Again it was the custom to bring offerings on certain days of the year.[3] Offerings were likewise supposed to have been made on the birthday of the deceased,[4] and these consisted for the most part of wine, oil, and milk.[5]

The Romans guarded zealously an opening called mundus which they represented as a shallow pit at the bottom of which was a large stone. Only on memorial days did the pit open so that the people might bring offerings to an appropriate place.[6]

This was looked upon as marking the union of the upper with the lower world. Although the primitive regards the spirits of departed ancestors as permeated with malevolent influence, and thus capable of harming the survivors, there is no evidence that the Romans held such a conception. The reception accorded ghosts was most royal and spontaneous, and they seem to regard the dead as spirits desirous of returning to their former homes, but this inclination was limited to certain specific days in the civic calendar. Naturally a certain anxiety in regard to these spirits was experienced by the Romans, but this does not partake of the dread attitude which the primitive manifests.

This anxiety phase is expressed at the celebration of the Lemuria in May when the head of the house could get rid of the ghosts by spitting out black beans and saying : " With these I redeem me and mine ". This he repeats nine times without looking round, whereupon the ghosts come and gather the beans unseen. After this, he nine times calls : " Manes exite paterni ". Then he looks about and the ghosts have disappeared.

Very interesting is the arrangement for making offerings to the dead. To facilitate the pouring of libations directly upon the cinerary urns, these were connected with the surface by means of tubes. An instance is recorded of a lead pipe

[1] *Poll.*, VIII, 146.
[2] *Poll.*, I, 66 ; III, 102.
[3] Plato, *De Leg.*, IV, 717.
[4] Cf. Diog. Laert, X, 18.
[5] Aesch. *Pers.*, 609.
[6] Ovid, *Fast.*, IV, 821 ; Plut. *Rom.*, 10.

running from above into an opening made for it in the top
of a lead case enclosing an urn. Often the connection was
made by round tiles. Among collections of Roman antiquities we find square blocks of stone with a depression in the
centre where the block is pierced by several holes. Along
the edge on the upper surface runs an inscription bearing
the name of the deceased. Through the holes in the centre
the bereaved relatives might, at the Parentalia, pour offerings which reached the urn placed beneath the surface of the
ground. Here we see that pagan antiquity, as well as the
primitive, could not dissociate the spirit of the dead from
the place of interment. Ancestor worship was in a large
degree the product of local associations.*

In Egypt we find sumptuous rituals performed at the
tomb. A few portions of such ceremonies are preserved in
the Pyramid Texts. These show that the usual calendar
of feasts of the living was celebrated for the king.[1] Evidently
the observances consisted chiefly in the presentation of
plentiful food, clothing, and other necessary equipment.
One hundred and seventy-eight formulas and utterances
forming about one-twentieth of the bulk of the Pyramid
Texts, contain the words spoken by the royal mortuary
priests in offering food, drink, clothing, ointment, perfume.[2]

" The strangely potent bread and beer which the priest
offers the dead, not only makes him a ' soul ' and makes him
' prepared ', but it also gives him ' power ' and makes him a
' mighty ' one ".[3] This " power " was intended to control
the body of the deceased and to guide its actions, otherwise,
the body would be helpless.[4] Again this power was to assist
him against the many hostile spirits he would encounter in
the land beyond. Finally, this force gave the deceased power
over the other powers within him for the priests addressed
him thus : " Thou hast power over the other powers that are
in thee ".[5]

* In Rome the food was for the dead only. It was considered a great
impiety for the survivors to partake of the offering. The Roman tomb also
had its " culina," a kind of kitchen only for the use of the dead. If neglected,
the dead became noxious spirits, but if revered, tutelary deities. Those who
brought nourishment were loved by the departed.

[1] *Pyr.*, p. 2117.
[2] Breasted, *Development of Religion and Thought in Ancient Egypt*, p. 78.
[3] *Pyr.*, § 859 ;   Breasted, *Ibid*, p. 60.
[4] *Ibid*, § 2096.
[5] *Ibid*, § 2011.

The Persians too had numerous funeral feasts and anniversaries for departed ones. These generally took place on the tenth day following a death, upon the return of the same day each month, and festivals were held the tenth or eighteenth day at the end of the Parsi year. These bear a close analogy to the celebration of All Saints' Day.

In reference to Asa we read the following in the *Old Testament*: "And they buried him in his own sepulchre which he made in the City of David, and they laid him in a bed which was filled with sweet odours and divers kinds of spices; and they made a very great burning for him".[1] We read in Jeremiah: "Neither shall men break bread for them in mourning to comfort them for the dead; neither shall men give them the cup of consolation to drink for father and mother".[2]

Upon the death of an Ainu a large cup of food or a cake of millet and water are placed by the head of the corpse. The dead man is invited to partake of this offering with the words: "This is a good-bye feast made especially for you". After this food remains by the corpse for a time, it is taken and reverently distributed among the relatives. Millet cakes are brought to the hut and distributed to all present. Before any one drinks he offers two or three drops to the spirit of the dead. As soon as the burial services are concluded the remnants of food are collected and carried to be reverently divided among the nearest relatives.[3] The Ainu mourners then return to their hut; the men eat, drink, and get helplessly intoxicated.[4]

The Veddas, after making an offering to the dead, consume it. The natives of Nicobar Islands feast at the grave the day after the funeral.[5] After a death the Patagonians feast on horse-flesh and indulge in drink-bouts; this is renewed every month. Finally after celebrations extending over a period of three years, no more feasts are held.[6] Relatives and friends of a deceased Araucanian sit round the corpse and weep.

[1] II *Chronicles* XVI. 14.
[2] *Jeremiah* XVI. 7.
[3] Batchelor, *The Ainu and Their Folk-Lore*, p. 556.
[4] *Ibid*, p. 559.
[5] Svoboda, "Die Bewohner des Nikobaren Archipels", *Int. Arch.*, Vol. VI (1893), p. 25.
[6] Koch, "Zum Animismus der Südamerikanischen Indianer", *Int. Arch.*, Vol. XIII (1900), suppl., p. 103.

Others bring food and drink of which all partake.[1] When a Buryat shaman dies, a funeral feast is held at the place of cremation. This is repeated on the third day when the bones are deposited.[2]

The Ojibwas sit in a circle at the head of a grave and partake of the offerings of meat, soup, and firewater which they present to the deceased.[3] Among the Tlingit of British Columbia the body of a deceased native is carried out by the members of his wife's class, while those of his own class give them a feast. Before this takes place, the name of the dead is pronounced and at the same time a little food is put into the fire for him.[4]*

Similar instances might be multiplied indefinitely to show the general prevalence of funeral feasts in widely scattered areas and among peoples of all phases of culture.

Again we ask the oft repeated question : " What are the objects of such an institution as death feasts ? " Is there any specific motive which actuates people of so widely scattered areas and so many cultural levels, to emphasize funeral meals to such an extent ?

Undoubtedly, many reasons may have prompted primitives and those of a more advanced civilization to resort to such an expedient. An examination of the evidence seems to point to the conclusion that in nearly every instance, the dead is actually supposed to partake of the food offered. The many explicit references stipulating that " This food is for you ", seem to imply this definite conception. Certainly the Sraddha ceremony, whatever else it may include, was based upon the necessity of feeding the dead. The conception so often held among primitives that existence in the future world is merely a continuance of the life here would naturally lead to such a materialistic point of view. Thus in Melanesia where this idea is so strangely emphasized, we find innumerable feasts in honour of the dead—far more, as far as the investigation

[1] Koch, " Zum Animismus der Südamerikanischen Indianer ", *Int. Arch.* Vol. XIII (1900), supple., p. 105.

[2] Mikailovski, *Shamanism in Siberia and European Russia, J.A.I.*, Vol. XXIV, p. 135.

[3] Hartland, article in *Hastings*, Vol. IV, p. 435.

[4] Swanton, " The Tlingit Indians ", *Twenty-sixth Annual Report, Bureau, of Ethnology* (1904-1905), p. 431.

* All property given or destroyed at a Tlingit death feast is dedicated to some dead person who is supposed to receive its spiritual counterpart. (*Ibid*, p. 431.)

goes, than in any other area of like extent. But in the Australian area, there is no evidence to the effect that life in the other world is identical or similar to existence here. The only view which they seem to hold is that the dead go to a spirit land, but we have no account of their life in these realms. Their ideas of reincarnation seem to have been so definitely established, especially in Central Australia, that in all probability they are so much impregnated with this idea and its identification with local centres that existence in the spirit land would receive little contemplation and consideration. However, we must bear in mind that the burying of implements and other paraphernalia seems to point to the fact, although we never find it so expressed, that after death they expect to continue some sort of existence, perhaps somewhat in keeping with their life in this world.

Although the desire to feed the dead was perhaps the original intention of those entrusted with the celebration of the death feasts, yet we must not lose sight of the various other causes for such rites. In many instances the desire to secure rest or happiness for the departed member of a community seems to account for the desire of the tribesmen to carry out these elaborate rites. Thus if the Sraddha is not performed, the survivors think that the deceased would roam among the evil spirits and that he would be destined to a kind of hell called Put. The Hindus likewise sacrificed a draught-ox to facilitate the journey of the deceased to the other world and to minister to his wants there. The Yahuts kill horses and cattle at the death feast, so that the dead can ride them to the distant realms and also for the purpose of contributing to his comfort. The Melanesians of Aurora are impressed with the idea that if they do not kill many pigs, the dead man will have no proper existence, but will hang on tangled creepers. Although the feasts in Banks Islands are distinctively commemorative, yet they are not devoid of the purpose of benefiting the dead.[1] It is thought that the ghost is gratified at the remembrance shown him, and honoured by the performance of this duty.

Again, the desire that the funeral feast should be a benefit to the ghost is seen in the Egyptian idea that by means of

[1] Codrington, *Melanesians*, p. 271.

such a rite, the departed spirit acquires power and becomes a "mighty one". Without such power the dead would be helpless in combating the many hostile spirits that he would encounter on his journey to the nether world. Likewise at Saa in the Melanesian area, the power of the shades fades away if no sacrificial food is offered them, and as a result they turn into ant's nests. Among the Romans we find the benefit conception stressed when we read : " I pray that thy divine names may keep thee in place and watch over thee ". At the Roman Parentalia the relatives went to the place of burial to see " that all went well with the dead ".

In many areas the desire for a descendant is one of the principal motives which are responsible for the funeral feast. This attitude is especially in evidence in the higher cultural areas, such as in the Hindu, Egyptian, and Roman civilizations. Allusion has already been made to the Pindapitri-yajna, the gift of cakes to departed ancestors performed with the ostensible desire of having children. " Fathers, let a male be born to me this season ". The belief of the Hindus that only living descendants may offer sacrifices further corroborates this point of view and makes the ceremony partake of a religious character. If such rites would not be performed, extinction of family would be the inevitable outcome.

The ritualistic character of the meal must also be stressed. That the food was probably looked upon as representing the flesh of the deceased is perhaps shown by the use of certain specific foods at the death feast, and Abbé Dubois tells us that at the funeral of a chief of Tangore, the bones remaining after the cremation were ground and cooked with rice and this mixture was eaten by twelve Brahmans, who by this expiatory act, transferred the sins of the deceased to their own persons. Is not the same idea always accentuated in the sacrificial meal of the Church ?

Then selfish motives often instigate the celebration of the funeral feast. Propitiation is necessary, for unless the dead are sufficiently revered, their spirits might return to the earth and bring havoc upon the survivors. Although, as was before intimated, the Romans did not manifest the dread attitude toward spirits so characteristic of the primitive,

yet the nature of the Lemuria celebration points to the fact that their presence is not especially desirable. We also hear in some parts of Melanesia of the propitiation of sea ghosts by casting a fragment of food to them upon the waves, if on the return from a fishing trip, the canoe occupant falls ill.[1]

The desire to partake of a meal with the dead may be one of the incentives which prompt the funeral feast celebration. It is most difficult to determine how far friendly association of the living with the dead is determined by both of them partaking of the meal. Not only is common participation in the meal a characteristic of almost all areas, but it is a belief of Aurora natives of the New Hebrides group, Melanesia, that the ghosts of all departed ancestors come back for such a feast.[2] One of the objects of the Parentalia was to partake of a meal with the dead. In Rome especially we find the idea emphasized that the feasts held in honour of the dead effected a communion of the upper with the lower world. Just to what extent a portion of the sacrifice can be regarded as a sacramental meal in the sense that divine virtue passes over to the eaters, is a matter of conjecture.

The argument advanced by Jevons[3] that feasts are the spontaneous expression of natural affection, cannot be verified by the facts. That the living solace themselves in their grief and satisfy something of their sense of loss by affecting commemoration, seems to figure so insignificantly in the considerations which actuate funeral feast celebrations, that there is no justification for regarding this motive as prominent; indeed, in many instances it seems eliminated entirely. Sometimes the feast seems to have no underlying motive than the desire to give merely a farewell banquet to the deceased.

When the tendency comes to consider motives for emotional conduct, explanations are introduced which have no connection with the origin of the actions. Action seems to come first, and the reasons which are supposed to prompt us to the performance of certain customs and ceremonies appear as a later development. It is with this idea in mind that we must consider the various motives which have entered into

[1] Codrington, *Melanesians*, p. 259.
[2] *Ibid*, p. 283.
[3] Jevons, *History of Religion*, p. 96.

our discussion of funeral feasts and anniversary celebrations commemorated in honour of the dead.

The following motives then seem to figure in feasts for the dead :

(1) The desire to feed the dead.
(2) The securing of rest or happiness for the departed.
(3) The wish to obtain descendants.
(4) The desire to take a meal with the dead and thus to establish a closer union.
(5) The propitiation of the spirit of the departed.

CHAPTER XII

LIFE AFTER DEATH

LAND OF THE DEAD

MELANESIA

As usual, the land of the dead of the Wagawaga resembles the land of the living, except that it is day there when it is night on the world. Tumudurere, a mythical being, receives the ghosts on their arrival in the spirit land, and directs them how to make their gardens.[1] The Motu, a tribe of fishermen and potters of British New Guinea, believe that the spirits of the dead dwell in a happy land where former friends meet and no hunger is ever experienced. They carry on the same activities to which they were accustomed when in this world. These spirits are subjected to a most peculiar ceremony when they arrive in the realms of the blest. They are laid over a slow fire with the object of causing the grossness of the body to disappear, and thus they become light as it behoves spirits to be.[2] The Koita' or Koitapu, who live side by side with the Motu, believe that the human spirit leaves the body and goes to live with other ghosts on a mountain called Idu. Here again, the life they lead is very similar to that they have lived on earth. Their entire elimination of moral values is what interests us, for they make no distinction between the righteous and the wicked; all fare alike with the exception of those who have had no holes bored in their noses during life and those guilty of a few other social infractions. However, these ghosts do not live forever; gradually they grow weaker and weaker and finally they die a second death, never to revive. Although the residence of ghosts is on a mountain called Idu, yet they often return to their natives villages to haunt the survivors.[3]

[1] Seligmann, *Melanesians*, p. 655.
[2] Lawes, " Ethnological Notes on the Motu, Koitapu, or Koiari Tribes of New Guinea ", *J.A.I.*, Vol. VIII (1879), pp. 370-371.
[3] Seligmann, *The Melanesians*, pp. 189-192.

The natives of Tubetube conceive of a spirit land where eternal youth prevails. Old men and women renew their youth in this blissful realm where there is no sickness, no bad spirits, no death. Marriages continue, and births do not cease. The usual activities of life such as house building, canoe construction, agriculture, continue as hitherto. It is of interest to note that fighting and stealing are unknown, and here we see inaugurated a universal brotherhood. The natives of Kiwai call the land of the dead Adiri or Woibu. The first individual to go there and show the way to others was Sido, a popular hero, round whose name many tales are centred. Here we might draw an analogy between Sido and Yama, the God of the Dead among the Hindus, who, too, first spied out the path to the other world and directed his successors.

Adiri is located somewhere to the far west and here, too, we see an elimination of moral values, for the fate of the good and bad is the same in this distant land.[1] The tribes of the Hood Peninsula believe that at death the ghosts join their ancestors in a subterranean region dotted with gardens, houses, and other conveniences.

So, too, for the Duke of York Islanders of Northern Melanesia, life in the other world is very much the same as that experienced while on earth. The rich continue to be rich; the poor remain poor. The only idea which we get of moral retribution is the fact that the ghosts of the miserly will be punished by being knocked against the projecting roots of chestnut trees. Then, too, punishments will be meted out to those who have been guilty of infringements of social etiquette.[2]

The Central Melanesians are universally of the opinion that the soul survives the death of the body and goes to some more or less distant region where the spirits of all the dead congregate and live for an indefinite time although some are supposed to die a second death and thus to end their existence together. In Western Melanesia, the inhabitants of the Solomon Islands identify certain islands as the abode of the

---

[1] Landtman, "Wanderings of the Dead in the Folk-Lore of the Kiwai-speaking Papuans', Festskrift tillägnad Edvard Westmarck, pp. 59-66; quoted by Frazer, pp. 210-213.

[2] Brown, *Melanesians and Polynesians*, p. 195.

dead, but the Eastern Melanesians conceive of it as a subterranean region called Panoi. The natives of Saa, one of the
Solomon Islands, think of the life of the other world in all
respects as identical with that in this, except the ghosts of
children live in one island and the ghosts of grown-up people
in another.[1] The exact location of Panoi cannot be ascertained,
but there as elsewhere this land resembles that of the living,
although everything seems unreal ; the ghosts occupy their
entire time talking, singing, and dancing. No marriages take
place but men and women live together. Here we perceive
different realms for those who die different kinds of deaths.
In this region also we find the belief that the ghosts die a
second death. Two kingdoms are spoken of, each called Panoi,
the one located above the other. After the second death in
the upper realm they rise again from the dead in the other
region and here they do not experience another death, but
are converted into white ants' nests.[2] It is of great interest
to learn that there is a distinction between the fate of the
good and the fate of the bad in the other world.[3]

The ghosts of such Florida natives as have been buried with
appropriate ceremonies depart to Betindalo which seems
to be located in the south-eastern part of Guadalcanar. Nevertheless, the souls of the departed may also come to earth
where they dance and shout and partake of the sacrifice
offered to them.[4]

The Torres Straits Islanders conceive of the land of the
dead as a mythical island in the far west ; the Western
Islanders call it kibu, which means " sundown ", and the
Eastern Islanders, Boigu.[5] The New Caledonians are among
those who have no conception of ethical value in regard to the
land of their dead. Good and bad alike go to a very beautiful
and productive country at the bottom of the sea, to the
north-east of the Island of Pott. " No night, no illness, no
death, no old age, not even ' boredom ' are known in these
blessed realms ". These spirits too may visit earth when
they so desire.[6]

[1] Codrington, *Melanesians*, p. 260.
[2] *Ibid*, pp. 260-277.
[3] *Ibid*, p. 274.
[4] *Ibid*, p. 255.
[5] Cambridge, *Anthropological Expedition to Torres Straits*, Vol. V, p. 355 ;
Vol. VI, p. 252.
[6] Lambert, *Mœurs et Superstitions des Néo-Calédoniens*, pp. 13-16.

The North Melanesians are unable to give the exact situation of the land of the dead. All that they know about its location is that it is far distant. As we have seen elsewhere, we find different compartments for those who have died various deaths, and we also see that life in the realms of the dead is very similar to that on this world. However, in the Duke of York Islands, when a soul has done penance, it is supposed to enter the body of some animal.[1]

The soul of a deceased native of Lepers' Island makes its way along the mountain path to Manaro to a lake which fills the crater of the island. The newcomers who are received by Nggaleva, the master of the realms of the dead, must pass by a pig before they can reach their final destination. In Lolomboctogitogi, where the dead congregate, are trees and houses. Here they are supposed to live a free and empty life, free from pain and sickness.[2] The abode of the dead of the inhabitants of Araga, Pentecost, is Bonoi. A town is located here where are houses, trees, sweet-smelling plants, and shrubs with coloured leaves, but no gardens, because there is no work. The ghost upon his arrival is weak at first and rests before he commences to move about. A dance greets all newcomers when they enter. In this final resting place of the dead we see different realms for those who have experienced various kinds of death.[3]

In Nitus there is a belief that the dead are changed into devils and go to Alu first, then to the heights of Gieta on Bougainville, and after they have sojourned here some time they direct their steps to the volcano Bagama and to Balbi Mountain. These devils are placed in two categories : the Sakesali, or bad ones who rob children, bring storms and sickness, and steal souls, and the Koriti, good ghosts or devils who are the guardians of seafarers, children, houses, and canoes.[4]

AUSTRALIA

The Narrinyeri think that the spirits of the dead go up to the sky and that they also roam about the earth. The

[1] Brown, *Melanesians and Polynesians*, p. 195.
[2] Codrington, *Melanesians*, pp. 285-286.
[3] *Ibid*, pp. 287-288.
[4] Haddon, " Review of Ribbe's Zwei Jahre unter den Kannbalen der Salomo-Inseln ", *F.L.*, Vol. (1905), pp. 115-116.

Buandik who are their neighbours believe that there are two spirits in mankind ; at death one goes into the sea and returns as a white man ; the other goes to the region of the clouds.[1] The Theddora conceive of another land beyond the sky ; and the Ngarigo, who live next to them, think that the spirit of a dead person goes up to the sky where it is met by one of the old Ngarigo men, who takes care of it.[2] The belief that souls of the dead go to the sky is also shared by the Dieri, the Kurnai, and the Kulin tribes.[3] The Kulin imagine that the spirits of the dead ascend to heaven by the rays of the sun.[4] The Wailwun natives of New South Wales used to bury their dead in hollow trees and when the body was dropped into place the mourners uttered a sound like the rush of the wind which was supposed to represent the upward flight of the soul to the sky.[5] The Narrinyeri believe that the ghost ascends to heaven in the flame.[6] In this connection we might mention the H'ndu conception, that if at the cremation the smoke went directly upward, the deceased would reach heaven.

Such beliefs, as Howitt suggests, are characteristic of a large number of tribes of the eastern part of the continent. He refers to the account of Collins who says that though some think they go either on or beyond the great water, yet the larger number believe they go to the clouds.[7]

INDIAN AREA

Yama, the God of the Dead, was " the first to spy out the path to the other world ".[8] Although we cannot trace the original conception of this so-called " first mortal ", yet in the Rig-Veda he is undoubtedly the King of the Dead and the kind and merciful monarch of the happy world where the righteous find enjoyment after death.[9] We find his character much changed in the Puranas. Here he is called the " Child of the Sun ", and is pictured as the stern avenger of

---

[1] Howitt, *Native Tribes of South East Australia*, p. 434.
[2] *Ibid*, p. 437.
[3] *Ibid*, pp. 434, 436-438.
[4] *Ibid*, p. 438.
[5] Ridley, *Kamilaroi*, p. 160.
[6] Taplin, "The Narrinyeri", *Native Tribes of South Australia*, p. 19.
[7] Howitt, *Native Tribes of South-East Australia*, p. 438.
[8] *Rv.*, X. 14, 1.
[9] *Rv.*, X., 14, 7.

sin, and the King of Death or Hell. Not yet in the Rig-
Veda, as in the Atharva-Veda of later mythology (as Macdonell
suggests), was Yama a God of Death.[1] However, concerning
the position held by Yama in early Vedic times, Hopkins
claims that even in the Rig-Veda he is regarded as a god,
though called " King ".[2] So near did Yama stand to the
dead, that " to go on Yama's path " is always interpreted
as " to go on the path of death ".[3] Even in one passage
Yama is regarded by Hopkins as identified with death.[4] In
the Atharva-Veda it is said that Death is the lord of men,
Yama of the Manes.[5] The significant point is that whereas
in the later epic period the other nature gods pass into an
inactive or negative state, Yama still holds sovereignty.

Yama's abode is where the dead heroes congregate.[6] The
fathers who died in ages past are looked after by him as he
sits drinking with the gods beneath a fair tree.[7] The place
is not specifically located, but since Yama's abode in the sky
is supposed to be identical with the sun in several passages,
the conception is that the dead entered the realms of the sun
where Yama received them. " My home is there where are
the sun's rays " ; the dead shall go to Yama to the fathers,
the seers that guard the sun.[8]

Although the Vedic Indian takes an optimistic view concerning his future state in paradise, yet his real desire is
expressed in Vedic literature innumerable times. " May
we live our hundred autumns, surrounded by lusty sons " !
Many charms are resorted to with the object of securing the
allotted hundred years.[9] It is significant to note that the
dead have left all imperfections behind them—no lame or
crooked of limb ; the weak no longer pay tribute to the
strong. Notwithstanding this, we are in hearty accord with
the sentiment of Bloomfield, who says, in reference to the
Vedic situation, " Say or do what you will, death always
remains uncanny ".[10] Do we not hear of the foot-snare of

[1] Macdonell, *History of Sanskrit Literature*, p. 117.
[2] Hopkins, *Religions of India*, p. 128 ; X., 14, 1, 11.
[3] *Rv.*, I, 38, 5.
[4] *Rv.*, I, 116, 2.
[5] *Av.*, V, 24, 13-14.
[6] *Rv.*, I, 35, 6 ; X, 64, 3.
[7] *Rv.*, X, 135, 1-7.
[8] *Rv.*, I, 105, 9 ; X, 154, 4-5.
[9] Bloomfield, *Atharva-Veda*, p. 62, et seqq.
[10] Bloomfield, *Religion of the Veda*, p. 251.

Yama ? The prospect of paradise is indeed marred by the conception of hell. An idea of retribution is detected from the start, for to Yama's abode only the good are assigned. It was a common belief that the things sacrificed and given to the priests wait in the highest heaven for the faithful. But what a different fate awaits the oppressors of the Brahmans! They sit in a pool of blood chewing hair.[1] "The tears which did roll from the eyes of the oppressed lamenting Brahmana, these very ones, Oh oppressor of Brahmans, the gods did assign to thee as thy share of water". In an early version of hell the sage Bhrigu observes some yellow men who are being cut up by other men who cry : "So they have done to us in the yonder world, so we do to them in return in this world".[2] The Hindu is always perturbed about the thought of a possible death in the other world. One text pictures a limited immortality of one hundred years. Since there is an end of our good deeds death anew must be inevitable. "There is only one Death in the other world, even Hunger".[3] In the Brahmana we read of many rites to insure permanent immortality.[4] The sacrifice to departed ancestors has also this end in view. Bloomfield says that although this death "anew" is a characteristic idea, it is not as yet transmigration of souls. "As long as its scene is located entirely in the other world, and as long as it is thought possible to avoid or cure it by the ordinary expedients of sacrifice, so long the essential character of this belief is not present".[5]

Macdonell agrees with Bloomfield in his conception that there is no indication in the Rig-Veda, or even in the later Vedas of the transmigration of souls, although this belief was firmly established in the sixth century B.C. when Buddhism arose.[6] However, he states that one passage in the Rig-Veda in which the soul is spoken of as departing to the water and the plants may contain the germs of this theory. The optimistic Vedic Indian, unlike his descendants of much later years, seems to have been little concerned with the nether

---

[1] *Atharva-Veda*, 5, 19, 3 and 13.
[2] Catapatha, *Brâhmana*, 11, 16, 1.
[3] Catapatha, *Brâhmana*, 5, 2.
[4] Taittirîya, *Brâhmana*, 3, 2, 8, 5.
[5] Bloomfield, *Religion of the Veda*, p. 253.
[6] Macdonell, *History of Sanskrit Literature*, p. 115.

world. Most of his ideas about existence after death are found in the funeral hymns of the last book. Here we have a suggestion that the real personality is immortal, whereas the body only is destroyed. The soul is not only separated from the body after death, but even during unconsciousness.[1]

Clothed in a glorious body, the virtuous sit by the side of Yama in the abode of light and sparkling waters.[2] Here they enjoy untold bliss under the name of " Fathers ".[3] But before they are thus enrolled the son of a dead man is generally conceived of as first becoming a " Preta " or unhoused ghost, which is approached with appropriate oblations, otherwise the spirit would return and disquiet the relatives.[4] Before the expiration of one year this ghost is admitted to the Manes by a rite which makes him their " Sapinda " (united by a funeral cake).[5] After the lapse of one year or more another elaborate ceremony (pitrimedha) takes place in connection with the erection of a monument when the bones are taken out of the urn and buried in a suitable place. After three years this spirit loses its identity and is named no more at the sacrifice, becoming simply one of the " Fathers ". It is said that the departed Fathers could assume a mortal form. Seven kinds of Manes are enumerated.[6] Brahma is identified with the Father-God in connection with the Manes ; all worship him including Siva and Vishnu. " Kings and sinners " with the Manes are found in Yama's house as well as those who die at the solstice. The old belief was that the stars are the souls of the departed.

Although the Atharva-Veda shows a belief in future punishment, the most, Macdonell says, that can be gathered from the Rig-Vedic literature is the idea that non-believers are consigned to underground darkness after death.[7] So scanty is our evidence upon this subject that Roth conceived the total destruction of the wicked to be the belief of the very early Hindus,[8]* but their ideas about future punishment so developed,

[1] *Rv.*, X, 58.
[2] Dutt, *History of India*, Vol. I, p. 73.
[3] *Rv.*, I, 35, 1-7.
[4] Hopkins, *India Old and New*, p. 102.
[5] Macdonell, *History of Sanskrit Literature*, p. 257.
[6] Hopkins, *Religions of India*, p. 365.
[7] Macdonell, *History of Sanskrit Literature*, p. 117.
[8] Roth, *J.A.O.S.*, Vol. III, pp. 329-347.
* Many scholars think that in the Rig-Veda there is no hint of extinction as Roth would have us believe. *Vedic Index*, Vol. II (1900), p. 176.

as we have before intimated, that we are surprised to find
an intricate system of hells in post-Vedic times. It is significant to note that in the Brahmanas, the resting places of the
Gods and Fathers are entirely distinct, for the " heavenly
world " is contrasted with that of " the Fathers ". Such is
the honour of death that Yama becomes in due time the
Hindu Pluto, God of Hell and Judge of the wicked.[1]

The doctrine of the Transmigration of Souls is explained
in the Brihadaranyaka Upanishad. " The Self after having
thrown off this body and having dispelled all ignorance, and
after making another approach to another body, draws itself
together toward it ".[2] This doctrine was to the Hindu what
the doctrine of resurrection was to the Christians ; while the
Christians believe that our souls will live in another sphere,
the Hindu believes that they have lived in another sphere
and will continue to do so after death. Here we see an
important phase of the Indian religion ; good acts have
their proper reward and only by true knowledge can the Hindu
expect to be united to the Universal Spirit. Dutt said that
" There is nothing more sublime in the literature of the
ancient Hindus than the passages in which they record their
hope and faith that the disembodied soul, purified of all stains
and all sins, will at last be received in the Universal Soul,
even as light mingles with light ". From the Brihadaranyaka
Upanishad we read : " He therefore that knows, after having
become quiet, subdued, patient, and collected, sees self in
Self, sees all in Self ".[3] Evil does not overcome him : he
burns all the evil. Free from evil, free from spots, he becomes
a true Brahman and enters the Brahma world.*

SIBERIA

The deceased among the Chukchee live in several places.
One way to get to the lower world is by opening a hole in the
ground and pulling out a stopper. Another way for the dead
to ascend to heaven is to follow the smoke of his funeral pyre.

---

[1] Bloomfield, *The Religion of the Veda*, p. 145.
[2] Dutt, *History of India*, Vol. I, p. 179.
[3] *Ibid*, p. 181.
* It is interesting to compare this belief with that of the Assyrians and
Babylonians who do not believe in a " paradise " for privileged persons nor
any distinction between the good and the bad—all, things and subjects,
virtuous and wicked, go to Aralu. (Jastrow, *The Religion of Assyria and
Babylonia*, p. 578.)

This is the reason given for burning dead bodies. Different realms are assigned to those who meet with various deaths, and while some of the dead are in the upper worlds, the usual habitation for the dead is underground where the life they live is very similar to that on earth. So complicated are the roads, that unless the forefathers and relatives of the deceased would come to meet him upon his entrance to the lower world, he would be unable to find his way, The realm of the dead is very extensive and the houses are round tents without seams, and the reindeer herds are numerous.[1]

The Koryak have a double conception of the realm of the dead which they call the country of shadows. When the soul rises to the Supreme Being, the deceased and his other soul, or his shadow, depart into the world of shadows, as the underground abode for the dead is called. Here, as among the Chukchee, we find the entrance guarded by dogs. The mode of life too is identical to that of the living.* Relatives live in the same house and each new-comer joins his family. Immediately, after the dead reach the lower world, the road leading from earth to it seems to close.[2]

REINCARNATION

MELANESIA

The natives of New Caledonia in Southern Melanesia identify white men with the spirits of the dead, and they give this belief as the reason for their wish to kill strangers.[3] The Torres Straits natives believe that " immediately after death they are changed into white people or Europeans " and as such pass the second and final period of their existence.[4] At Darnley Island, the Prince of Wales Islands, and Cape York the word for ghost and white man is the same.[5] The Cape York natives received several of the English officers

---

[1] Bogoras, *The Chukchee, J.N.P.E.*, Vol. VII (1907), pp. 333-336.

* The Babylonians and Assyrians believed that the life in the realm of the dead is similar to that in this world with one exception. The future life is one of inactivity, everything is in a state of decay and neglect. The dead are depicted as weak and suffer from hunger, their only food being dust and clay. (Jastrow, *The Religion of Babylon and Assyria*, p. 568.) The Hebrews, too, believed that the dead were weak and inactive, but at the same time they were looked upon as divine.

[2] Jochelson, *The Koryak, J.N.P.E.*, Vol. VI (1905), pp. 102-103.

[3] Turner, *Samoa, A Hundred Years Ago and Before*, p. 342.

[4] Cambridge, *Anthropological Expedition to Torres Straits*, Vol. V, p. 354, quoting Macgillivray.

[5] *Ibid*, p. 355.

as ghosts of departed friends.[1] In Nukahavi, one of tne Marquesas Islands, every one is persuaded that the soul of a grandfather is transmitted into the body of his grandchildren.[2]

A similar belief is found in Vanua-levu, the second largest island of the Fiji Group. In this island the child is considered as more closely related to his grandfather than to its father, because kinship is reckoned through the mother. Fison calls our attention to the fact that where exogamy prevails with female descent, a child regularly belongs to the exogamous class of its grandfather and not of its father. Thus it is that he is looked upon as more closely related to his grandfather than his father.[3]

In Northern Melanesia we find the belief that if the soul has done appropriate penance it takes possession of the body of some animal.[4] Numerous instances of transformation of people into animals are found in Torres Straits. Such transformation is sometimes temporary but usually it is final and the former human beings remain as animals.[5] The Mafulu, who live among the mountains at the head of the St. Joseph River, suppose that ghosts go to the tops of mountains and then become either a glimmering light on the ground or a kind of fungus found only on the mountains.[6] The natives of Koita believe that although the sua (souls) on Idu have gardens, houses, and wives, and live for an unknown period, longer than their earthly existence, yet they finally weaken and cease to exist.[7]

Among the Mafulu people of British New Guinea, Williamson could find no idea of reincarnation, nor trace of a belief in any future state except that the ghost sometimes apparently becomes a plant.[8]

At Aurora, one of the New Hebrides group, women speak of a child as nunu or echo of some dead person. This is not the metempsychosis idea that the soul of the dead returns to the new-born child; indeed, the connection is so close

---

[1] Cambridge, *Anthropological Expedition to Torres Straits, Vol. V, p.* 354, quoting Macgillivray.
[2] Lisiansky, *A Voyage Round the World,* p. 89.
[3] Fison, *Tales from Old Fiji,* pp. 168-169.
[4] Brown, *Melanesians and Polynesians,* p. 195.
[5] Cambridge, *Anthropological Expedition to Torres Straits,* Vol. V, p. 354.
[6] Williamson, *The Mafulu Mountain People of British New Guinea,* p. 267.
[7] Seligmann, *Melanesians,* p. 190.
[8] Williamson, *The Mafulu Mountain People of British New Guinea,* p. 267.

that the natives believe that the infant takes the place of the deceased.[1]

The Yabim believe that the souls of the dead transmigrate into the bodies of animals such as crocodiles and fabulous pigs.[2]

The inhabitants of Ayambori, New Guinea, believe that the soul of a dead man returns to his eldest son, and that of a dead woman to her eldest daughter. The natives of Windessi believe that when a woman dies both her spirits depart to the lower world where they are clothed with flesh and bones and live forever, but when a man dies only one of his spirits gets to the underworld, the other may transmigrate into a living man, or in rare cases, to a living woman.[3]

Some of the natives of German New Guinea think that the spirits of the dead transmigrate into animals and prolong their life in the bodies of the lower creatures.[4] In the village of Simbaug the ghosts may pass into the dead bodies of crocodiles and mythical pigs.[5]

AUSTRALIA

The ideas of the Central Australians are clear and definite in regard to reincarnation. They imagine that the spirits of the dead haunt their native land, and that certain landscape features are especially conducive and attract such spirits. These souls of the departed are awaiting a propitious moment when they can be born as infants. With this idea in view they are constantly on the lookout for any woman whom they may see, whether she be virgin or matron, married or unmarried. Any woman may give birth if one of these lurking spirits enter her, although they show their preference for plump females.[6] The Central Australians also think that the spirits of all the dead return to the very spots where they entered into their mother's womb, and there they remain until re-born into the world. As the people believe

---

[1] Codrington, "Social Regulations in Melanesia", *J.A.I.*, Vol. XVIII (1888-1889), p. 311.
[2] Vetter, *Komm herüber und hilf uns !* Vol. III, p. 21, et seqq. ; quoted by Frazer, p. 245.
[3] Frazer, *Belief in Immortality*, pp. 315-322.
[4] Stolz, " De Ungebung von Kap König Wilhelm," in Neuhauss' *Deutsch Neu Guinea*, Vol. III, p. 259.
[5] Vetter, *Komm herüber und hilfuns*, Vol. III, p. 21, quoted by Frazer, p. 245.
[6] Frazer, *Belief in Immortality*, Vol. I, p. 93.

that they will come to live again as infants, they adopt all measures which they believe will facilitate re-birth.[1]* Among the Australian tribe of Marup we find the conception that the natives after death become white men.[2]   The Kamilaroi call a white man Wunda (ghost), and believe him to be black come to life again.   The Kaiabara also think that the white men are blacks returned after death.   The old men about Maryborough declared at their first sight of white men " That is all right, they are the Muthara (ghosts) come back from the island ".   They recognized such men as relatives, gave them names and showed numerous courtesies to them. Near Moreton Bay, " Makoron " and " Mudhere " signify ghost, and each of these words is applied to white men.   In Queensland, in the vicinity of Mackay, a man's spirit is called " Meeglo " and the whites are conceived of as the spirits of their forefathers.   Likewise the Namoi, and Barwan blacks also call the white man " Wunda ".   Howitt recounts an experience which happened to him.   When in 1862 he was in Cooper's Creek, he was often addressed by the natives with the words :   " Pirri-wirri-kutchi ", which means wandering ghost.[3]

A belief exists among the New Bedford natives that the spirits of the dead are sometimes reincarnated in white people. The natives of Port Lincoln think that white people are the incorporated souls of their forefathers.[4]

We have seen that this belief is not only characteristic of this area, but of widely separated parts of Australia.   This, as Frazer suggests, has been of service to white people who have been cast among blacks, for because of this idea, an hospitable welcome has been accorded them.   Thus, Buckley was found by some of the Wudthaurung tribe carrying a piece of broken spear, which he had taken from the grave of one of their tribesmen.   They regarded him as the dead man risen from the grave, gave him the name of the deceased,

---

[1] Frazer, *Belief in Immortality*, Vol. I, p. 161.

* It is a common occurrence when children die young to take measures to secure their return.   (Hartland, *Primitive Paternity*, Vol. I, pp. 226-229.) The Romans buried children under the eaves of their houses.   (Pliny, VII, 15.) In this connection see Dietrich, *Mutter Erde*.

[2] Howitt, *Native Tribes of South-East Australia*, p. 443.

[3] *Ibid*, pp. 445-446.

[4] Schürmann, " The Port Lincoln Tribe ", in *Native Tribes of South Australia*, p. 235.

and the relatives of the departed member of the tribe adopted
him.[1] Another instance is recorded of a Mr. Naseby who
lived in the Kamilaroi country for fifty years. The marks
of cupping which appeared on his back were looked upon by
the natives as the marks of initiation which Australian youths
were accustomed to receive, and they insisted that he was
one of them.[2] Sir George Grey was caressed by an Australian
woman who thought that he was her son come back to this
world again.[3] Other stories could be cited which emphasize
this same belief.

Frazer believes that the reincarnation idea is universal
among the Central Australian tribes[4] and introduces an
interesting conception which Roth found common among the
natives of Queensland.[5] The natives of Pennefather River,
Queensland, believe that a person's spirit undergoes a number
of reincarnations and in the interval between two of them
it resides in the haunts of a mythical creature who puts mud
babies into their bodies. Frazer furthermore points out[6]
that a curious feature of their belief is that in addition to the
spirit called " choi " which lies in a disembodied state between
two reincarnations, every person is the possessor of a different
kind of spirit called " ngai ". At death the ngai spirit does
not go into a bush for the purpose of reincarnation, but
it finds its way immediately into the children of the deceased
who before their father's death had no ngai spirit. Although
the choi spirit never leaves a man during life, the ngai spirit
may depart at intervals. When a woman dies, her ngai spirit
does not go to her children, but to her sisters, one after the
other ; and when the sisters are no more this spirit disappears
for all time among the mangroves.[7]

The Central Australians, from the centre northwards to the
Gulf of Carpentaria, believe that the souls of the dead survive
and are afterward re-born as infants.[8] Frazer says that this

[1] Frazer, *Belief in Immortality*, Vol. I, p. 131.
[2] Howitt, *Native Tribes of South East Australia*, p. 445.
[3] Spencer, *Principles of Sociology*, Vol. I, p. 172.
[4] Frazer, *Belief in Immortality*, Vol. I, pp. 127-129.
[5] Roth, " Superstition, Magic and Medicine,", *North Queensland Ethnography*, Bulletin No. 5, p. 18.
[6] Frazer, *Belief in Immortality*, Vol. I, p. 129.
[7] Roth, " Superstition, Magic and Medicine", *North Queensland Ethnography*, Bulletin No. 5, p. 18.
[8] Frazer, *Belief in Immortality*, Vol. I, p. 92.

is the universal belief with a single exception. According to their conception, every living person is the reincarnation of a dead individual who lived on earth before. The exception noted[1] is that of the Gnanji who eat their dead enemies, and perhaps their dead friends.[2] Although these aborigines deny that women have spirits which live after death, yet the spirit of a dead man is supposed to be born in a woman at some time in the future.[3]

The Warramunga removed every camp to a distance from where one of the natives died, since no one desired to come in contact with the spirit—ungwulan—of the dead man which would be hovering in the vicinity, or with the spirit of the man who had brought about the death by evil magic, as it would in all likelihood come to visit the spot in the form of an animal.[4]

Among the Narrinyeri we find the absence of a belief in the reincarnation of the dead and they think that the dead live above in the sky.[5] However, the Narrinyeri are not alone in this belief, for the Dieri, the Buandik, the Kurnai, and the Kulin have the same conception.[6]

The tribes of South Australia and from the Murray to the main range, believe that every totem clan has its own spirit land where the dead go. Afterward they are re-born in human shape.[7]

The natives of New South Wales believe that the souls pass into other bodies and that the spirit of the deceased still lives in another state, and for this reason they inter the dead with all his effects.[8]

The Arunta conceive the spirit of a dead person to be about the size of a grain of sand. As soon as death occurs, the spirit goes to the abode where they congregate and remains there until ready for reincarnation when it becomes a male and female alternately.[9] Among the Arunta Ilpirra of Finke River, the souls of new born infants are held to come from trees which are probably those into which the dead man has passed, especially since in many sections we find the

[1] Frazer, *Belief in Immortality*, Vol. I, p. 92.
[2] Spencer and Gillen, *Northern Tribes of Central Australia*, p. 545.
[3] *Ibid*, p. 546.   [4] *Ibid*, p. 519.
[5] Frazer, *Belief in Immortality*, Vol. I, p. 135.
[6] Howitt, *Native Tribes of South-East Australia*, pp. 434-436-438.
[7] Hartland, *Primitive Paternity*, Vol. I, pp. 241-242.
[8] Fraser, *The Aborigines of New South Wales*, p. 83.
[9] Thomas, *The Natives of Australia*, p. 195.

belief that the dead had their abode in trees. The Dieri, too, think that souls assume the form of trees.[1] In Western Australia, Salvado says that a small bird with a cheerful note was the form which a dead man assumed.[2]* The natives of the northern districts of Queensland when they wish to speak of the earliest period usually refers to it as " when the animals and birds were all black fellows ".[3]

The Narrinyeri believe the dead become stars.[4]†

Among all people, irrespective of degree of culture or race affiliation, we find significance attached to the idea of life after death ; indeed, not only are many of the ceremonies connected with the death-situation performed to insure a blissful state in the hereafter, but other ritualistic acts not concerned directly with death and burial rites have the same idea in view. Although conceptions of the future world and the life there are much at variance, and are usually hazy and indefinite, yet it is the desire of the living to resort to every expedient to guarantee peaceful existence after death.[5]

[1] Gason, " The Dieyeri ", *Native Tribes of South Australia*, p. 280.

[2] The Powhatans of North America also have the belief that the souls of the dead became wood birds. (Brinton, *Myths of the Old World* (1905), p. 124.)

* The Aztecs and various other nations thought that all good people as a reward of merit were metamorphosed into birds. (*Ibid*, pp. 124-125.) The Babylonians and Assyrians, too, believed that the dead assumed the form of birds. (Jastrow, *The Religion of the Assyrians and Babylonians*, p. 568.) In the songs of the Russian People we read of the dead assuming the forms of birds. The Little Russians believe that the dead are often transformed into pigs and crows. In Volhynia the natives believe that children come back to this world under the semblance of swallows and small birds. (Ralston, *Songs of the Russian People*, pp. 118-334.) Some of the Pima Indians believe that the soul passes into the body of an owl. (Russell, " The Pima Indian," *Twenty-sixth Annual Report Bureau of Ethnology* (1905-1906), p. 252.) The natives think that after death Mohaves become spirits ; after dying again, they become owls, the second time they turn into a different kind of owl, the third time into another kind, and finally into water-beetles. (*Ibid*, p. 252na.)

[3] Roth, " Superstition, Magic and Medicine," *North Queensland Ethnography*, Bulletin No. 5, p. 15.

[4] Frazer, *Belief in Immortality*, Vol. I, p. 134.

† The Greenlanders, too, have a similar belief. (Nansen, *Eskimo Life*, p. 235.)

[5] This study does not lead us to an endorsement of Leuba's view that the savage is not concerned with his own fate after death. (Leuba, *The Belief in God and Immortality*, pp. 63-78.) Although we agree that primitive man makes the present his chief interest and lives principally in the world of to-day, yet he certainly thinks of life after death. Even the Chukchee, who represent an exceedingly simple form of culture and social organization, take infinitive pains long before death to provide suitable funeral equipment. True, the belief in immortality gains no adherents among primitive man and belongs to a much higher culture ; yet the problem of life after death interests him and in many instances he provides for the means of meeting this situation.

12

So firmly is the conception fixed among people that the life to come is a continuation of the experience here, that in many primitive tribes we find a son killing a father before the age of decrepitude sets in to prevent the parent reaching the future world in a weakened or debilitated state. In many cases there is supposed to be complete resuscitation of the body and sometimes of the mental faculties.*

Not always does primitive man conceive of death as a transition stage whereby he passes from one state of life to another, as Rivers supposes.[1] Although we see from the concrete instances cited in this study that he often dies in that land where he sojourns after death, yet we too find the belief that he never dies. In very many cases we do perceive that to primitive man existence after death is real, but in the Solomon Islands there is a belief that everything seems "unreal", dancing and singing are indulged in the entire time, and there are no marriages. Again, in New Caledonia the natives think that there is no night, no illness, no old age, not even boredom in the regions beyond the grave ; and to the inhabitants of Leper's Island, life after death is an "empty" existence characterized by freedom from pain and sickness and with no work to do. The natives of Tubetube believe that in the other world there is no sickness, no death, no bad spirits, no fighting, no stealing, and eternal youth prevails.[2]

About Port Moresby in British New Guinea we find the belief that ghosts hunt, fish, plant, and are just like live men with the exception that they have no noses. They never suffer hunger.[3]

In discussing the primitive conception of death, Lévy-Bruhl thinks that to the savage it is merely an event in his life and places it in the same category as birth, initiation rites, and all the ceremonies which identify the individual with

* The Assyrians and Babylonians after death believed that those who go to Aralû or the land of the dead, sorrowful and neglected, would continue thus. (Jastrow, *The Religion of Assyria and Babylonia*, p. 568.) The Hebrews like the Babylonians, believed that the condition of the individual at the time of death was the index of the kind of life in store for him in Sheol. Even deformities follow the individual to the grave. (*Ibid*, p. 607.)

[1] Rivers, "The Primitive Conception of Death," *Hibbert Journal*, Vol. X (1911-1912), p. 406 ; see Van Gennep, *Les Rites de Passage*.

[2] Seligmann, *Melanesians*, pp. 189-192.

[3] Chambers, *Pioneering in New Guinea*, pp. 168-170, quoted by Frazer, p. 192.

group life. So strong is the bond of social participation established between the tribesman and his group, that after all the
rites encumbent upon him are performed, not even death
can sever this union. Even after he departs from the world
of the living, he continues to prolong his existence as a member
of his former community, at the same time participating in
all of its activities.[1]

Our investigation leads us to disagree in large part with the
deductions of Lévy-Bruhl. Without question, the ghost has
certainly not the same standing as had the individual for whom
it stands. Because of the mystery in which he is shrouded
he is sometimes elevated to the rank of a superior being who
performs the functions of a guardian spirit, at others he is
degraded to the status of a formidable and despised individual
whose main concern is to bring vengeance upon the survivors
because his connection with them has been cut off. If this
union were the same as before, why, we ask, is the sudden
manifestation of dread and horror at the merest possibility
of a return of the dead ? Although in many areas life after
death is depicted the same as existence here, yet, as we have
seen, this is not invariably so, and ofttimes we find a mode
of life entirely at variance with the existence on this earth,
thus excluding participation in the forms of activities here.*

True, one of the objects of funeral feasts and anniversary
celebrations is to allow the dead to partake of a meal with
the living, but the ostensible object of such a meal seems to
be to establish a bond of union between the living and the

---

[1] Lévy-Bruhl, *Les Fonctions Mentales des Sociétés Inférieures*, pp. 352-421.

* Among some of the many instances which might be cited, in addition
to those already given, to show that life in the future world is different from
the existence on this earth, may be mentioned :

1. The belief of the Hebrews and Babylonians that life in the future world
is characterized by great inactivity ; everything is in a state of neglect or
decay, a marked contrast to life here. The dead are depicted as weak or
suffering from hunger. (Jastrow, *Religion of the Assyrians or Babylonians*,
pp. 568-607.)

2. The idea of the Hupa Indians who think that the spirits of the dead
are fed upon spoiled salmon and everything is gloomy, dark, and damp ;
brawls and fights are common. (Goddard, *Life and Customs of the Hupa*,
p. 74.)

3. The conception of the Samoans that the realm for common people is
gloomy or dismal, a decided contrast to life here. (Brown, *Melanesians and
Polynesians*, p. 222.)

4. The belief of the Pima Indians who go to the opposite extreme and
think that in the future world all is rejoicing and gladness.

dead.   Again if this bond is riveted with such links of adamant, what need of such a ceremonial ?

In most cases the dead are treated as having far more power than before death.   They often become affiliated with a different or alien order of beings and as a consequence are subjects of the most rigid taboo.[1] Since they may now be classed as powers, we find an attitude of the most pronounced religious awe directed toward them.

The immortality idea of the soul, as we understand it, is unknown among savages, and even the Egyptians, with their advanced civilization and elaborate mortuary equipment, had no belief in the imperishability of the soul ; in fact, it is incorrect to speak of their "ideas of immortality".[2] Before mention has been made that in the Melanesian area we find the belief that ghosts do not live forever ; indeed, some spirits are supposed to die a second or final death.   Vedic literature tells us of a limited immortality of one hundred years.

In a previous part of this study, when discussing the significance of burial, we saw that it was a most common practice for both primitives and those of a very high cultural level to take unusual precautions to recover a dead body. We found that it was a Roman custom to erect an empty tomb to the deceased if his body could not be procured.   As was pointed out, not only did fear actuate the survivors lest the ghost of the disgruntled dead might return to harass the living, but one of the objects in recovering the corpse, especially in Egypt, was that it might be embalmed and thus preserved ; otherwise, the man might lose the prospect of life beyond the grave.[3] It was the duty of the son to arrange the material equipment of his father for the future life, this idea being presented in the Osiris myth as the duty of Horus to Osiris.[4] The conflicting beliefs which we find among so many peoples should occasion us no surprise.   In various tribes we note the idea stressed that the dead continue to live in or near the tribe, and at the same time depart to a far distant and peaceful region.

---

[1] Ames, *Psychology of Religious Experience*, p. 68.

[2] Breasted, *Development of Religion and Thought in Ancient Egypt*, p. 61.

[3] *B.A.R.*, Vol. I, pp. 362-374.

[4] Breasted, *Development of Religion and Thought in Ancient Egypt*, p. 63.

No people certainly have developed a more prominent idea of the hereafter than the ancient Egyptians. Breasted suggests that conditions of soil and climate have resulted in an unusual preservation of the human body.[1] This remarkable state of preservation in which the Egyptian found his dead ancestors certainly must have been a potent factor in making him ponder future existence. But the significance of environment in influencing ideas about future life is by no means peculiar to these ancient people, for in different areas we find that primitive beliefs relating to life beyond the grave are associated with conditions of physical environment. This is exactly what we would expect, especially when we perceive the idea emphasized that life in the next world is a replica of existence in this.

In many tribes the deceased cannot become a ghost or a soul, or what you will, of his own accord ; he must be assisted by his surviving relatives and friends. For this or other reasons, we find innumerable offerings presented, or frequently abstinence from those foods in which the dead especially delighted in life. Thus among the ancient Egyptians, the bread and beer which the priest offers the dead, not only make him " prepared ", but give him power to become a " mighty one ".[2]

It is interesting to note that in Australia we find a belief that the spirit is met by one of the old Ngarigo men who take care of it. This brings to our mind the conception of a guardian spirit so characteristic of many Indian areas of North America, and also of Australia. Thus the Gournditch-mara of Australia believe that the spirit of a deceased father or grandfather visits his male descendants in dreams and shows him charms against witchcraft.[3] The dead are invoked by the Vedic Indian ; " and Fathers, may the sky-people grant us life ".[4] The Nayadis of Malabar offer prayers to those who have died for protection against snake-bites and the attacks of animals.[5] The function of such a spirit is, as its

---

[1] Breasted, *Development of Religion and Thought in Ancient Egypt*, p. 49 ; see Eliott Smith, *History of Mummification in Egypt*, proceedings of the *Royal Phil. Soc.*, Glasgow, (1910).

[2] *Pyr.*, p. 859.

[3] Fison and Howitt, *Kamilaroi and Kurmai*, p. 278.

[4] *Rv.*, X, 57, 5.

[5] Iyer, "Nayadis of Malabar ", in *Madras Government Museum's Bulletin*, Vol. IV (1900), p. 72.

name implies, to protect its possessor.[1] A protecting genius,
the " ka," is likewise found in ancient Egypt. The ka expels
all the evil that is before Pepi (the dead king) and removes
all the evil that is behind Pepi.[2] But the chief function of this
spirit is to direct the individual in the life hereafter, although
his protecting power begins at his birth.[3] It is in the future
world that the ka lives almost entirely, and the oldest
inscriptions announce the death of a man by saying that he has
gone to his ka.[4] However, in North America, where we find
the guardian spirit idea so extensively developed, we perceive
that this genius performs his mission during the lifetime of the
individual. To us it is significant that the ka was originally
the possession of kings only, each of whom lived under the
protection of his individual genius. Very gradually the ka
became the universal property of all classes.[5] Here again, as
in primitive society, we have a conception based upon rank.

The malevolence of ghosts seems even to be more pronounced than their function as guardian spirits. As intimated
before, this dread attitude manifested most markedly to those
who were nearest and dearest to the departed is one of those
seemingly paradoxical attitudes of primitive man. Thus the
Australians believe that the dead are malevolent for a long
time after death,[6] and that this ill-will increases with the
degree of relationship.[7]

[1] Among examples of guardian spirits found in primitive life may be
mentioned the head of each house of the Amazulu who is worshipped by his
children because they say : " He will treat us the same way now he is dead."
(Westermarck, *Development of Moral Ideas*, Vol. II, p. 529.) The head of the
family among the West African Slave Coast tribes is regarded as their protector
and often as the guardian of the entire community. (Ellis, *Ewe-Speaking
People*, p. 104.) The departed ancestors among the Czechs who look after
the fields of the survivors and aid them in hunting and fishing ; (Ralston,
Songs of the Russian People, p. 121), the departed relatives of the Veddahs
of Ceylon who are prayed to as " sympathetic and kindred, though higher
powers than man, to direct him to a life pleasing to the gods through which
he may gain their protection or favour." (Westermarck, *Development of
Moral Ideas*, Vol. II, p. 529.) The Mpongwe teach the child " to look up to its
parent not only as its earthly protector, but as a friend in the spirit land."
(*Ibid.*)
[2] *Pyr*, p. 908.
[3] Breasted, *Development of Religion and Thought in Ancient Egypt*,
pp. 52-54.
[4] *B.A.R.*, Vol. I, pp. 187-253.
[5] Steindorff, *Zeitschrift für aegypt. Sprache*, pp. 48-151, quoted by
Breasted, p. 55.
[6] Fraser, *Aborigines of New South Wales*, p. 80.
[7] Curr, *The Australian Race*, Vol. I, p. 87.
Even a mother may become an enemy to her own child as seen in the
Votyak conception that such a parent, as soon as she dies, is an agency for

We also note that even the " good " become very wicked after death. The diwars or genii loci, the spirits of good men, Brahmans, or village heroes of the North-Western Provinces of India, manage, when they become objects of worship, to be generally considered very malicious devils.

Our investigation emphatically supports the point of view of Westermarck as against Jevons and Grant Allen who hold that strangers only are the targets for the machinations of evil spirits.[1] Although, as we have seen, the guardian spirit plays a rôle, yet this is most insignificant when compared with the overwhelmingly malicious influence of the spirits of those who have departed this life.

Tylor has correctly stated that the principle of ancestor worship is not difficult to understand since the dead keep up the religion of the living world. The deceased ancestor simply goes on protecting his own family, at the same time receiving service from them. Thus the dead chief watches over his own tribe, and, as in times past, assists friends and torments enemies, rewarding what, according to his conception, is right, and meting out punishment for wrong.[2]

Spencer, too, has given much consideration to the worship of the dead. However, he has overstepped the bounds in his enthusiasm to stress his point that all forms of religion are derived from worship of the dead, inasmuch as in some of the areas we are considering, we find no ancestor cult, but a significant development of the forms of worship. Spirits are not derived from ghosts, as Spencer would have us believe, but are entirely distinct from them.

The principal theories relating to survival after death can merely be touched upon here.[3] Among them we might allude to the vegetation and insect metamorphosis conception, the

---

evil to her offspring. (Westermarck, *Development of Moral Ideas*, Vol. II, pp. 533-534.) The spirits of parents and children, sisters and brothers in Tahir " seem to have been regarded as a sort of demon ". (Ellis, *Polynesian Researches*, Vol. I, pp. 334-335.) The Ainu of Japan attribute calamities for which there is no apparent reason, to the machinations of a dead wife, mother, grandmother, or especially to a mother-in-law. (Westermarck, *Development of Moral Ideas*, Vol. II, p. 534.) The Maoris think that " the nearest and most beloved relatives were supposed to have their natures changed by death, and to become malignant even toward those they formerly loved." (*Ibid*, p. 533.)

[1] Jevons *Introduction to the History of Religion*, p. 53 ; Allen, *Evolution of the Idea of God*, p. 347.

[2] Tylor, *Primitive Culture*, Vol. II, p. 113.

[3] Leuba, *The Belief in God and Immortality*, pp. 65-81.

rising and setting sun, and the waxing and waning moon in conjunction with life after death, the reflection and echo theory, and the instinct idea. Feuerbach's theory is that the origin of the ghost is the idea of the living as it remains in the memory of those who knew the dead.[1]

After careful investigation, it may be said that the doctrine of transmigration or reincarnation is found among many primitive tribes. As we have suggested, many different theories have been advanced, most of which appear untenable, but it seems evident that the resemblance existing between children and their ancestors must have contributed much to the idea that the souls of the departed are re-born in their successors.

---

[1] Feuerbach, *Gedanken uber Todt und Unsterblickheit,* p. 273. For other conceptions see Part II.

CHAPTER XIII

CONCLUSION

WHEN we examine the evidence, we see a considerable similarity both in customs and beliefs, and an almost universal agreement in some elements, such as the conceptions connected with the disposal of the body, of the general attitude toward the corpse, of the dread of the spirit of the deceased, of the necessity of observing mourning ceremonies, of the practice of commemorating the dead by feasts at which some portion of the food is offered them, and the belief in the continued existence of the soul. Our object now is to analyse some of these elements, and see why certain phases of the death-situation are brought into prominence at the expense of others. Before we have voiced the sentiment that, although ours is not a search for ultimate origins, yet this does not make us eliminate psychological considerations from our discussion.

Our attention has been directed to the universal pandemonium which centres round the dead body. Not only is it to be shunned by the survivors, but the contagion from it is alarming. Perhaps the reasons which may account for such an attitude may be (1) that the dead body as such incites this antipathy, (2) because of its connection with the disembodied spirit, (3) because it is regarded as the carrier of death, (4) because of the relation between the living and the dead. This relation which we regard of vital importance is responsible for the shock which the living must experience when they become aware that the deceased, who has been so near and dear to them, cannot speak, or move, or become a participant in those activities with which he has been ordinarily associated. This spontaneous reaction on the part of the survivors brings with it a change from a positive to an indifferent or negative attitude toward the corpse, and positive customs become a thing of the past for the same being or are eliminated

entirely. A different action which is associated with the shock is now the outcome, and, as a result, all the values are affected. Then the actions of the survivors become standardized since they are no longer charged. In all probability, the attitude toward the corpse which we find in so many areas is primarily caused by the shock of death followed by the break-up of kinship bonds and social relations.

When Rivers claims that preservation in the house of the body of the deceased which we often find practised in parts of Melanesia, and burial in the open which too is a method of disposal of the dead in this area, must represent the blending of two strata of immigrant people because of the conflicting conception implied in their different attitudes toward the dead body, he advances an argument which has no justification as far as the facts in Melanesia or other areas are concerned. Nor does he attempt to prove this point of view. If he wishes to account for such an attitude by diffusion, he must use proof to demonstrate his hypothesis inasmuch as mere assumption is not enough.

In Australia we find various methods of the disposal of the dead, including cannibalism, earth-burial, cremation, or sub-aerial exposure. Some of the natives who practise cannibalism resort to this expedient, not as we might suppose from greedy motives, but since by so doing they think that they are honouring the dead. The abhorrent attitude usually identified with a dead body does not prevent these natives from devouring the flesh of the deceased.

The same may be said of preservation in the house. Although the dread attitude toward the dead might be most pronounced, yet this would not hinder such preservation. Often in this discussion we shall have to make use of our contention that the same characteristic which causes an object to be regarded as sacred, may cause it to be looked upon as unclean ; the identical reason which makes some esteem fire as the purest thing in the world, may lead others to regard it as an abomination, as is seen in the attitude of the Persians toward cremation, and the same argument might be advanced in connection with preservation in the house or field burial. Then, too, as we understand it, preservation in the house in Melanesia is usually associated with rank, and this would cause another element to enter into the complex.

The Wagogo of East Africa also keep the corpse of a man of rank in the house, and in Gilbert Islands the body of a king or warrior is often preserved on the crossbeams of his hut.[1]

Again, in different areas, we find many instances where children are buried directly before the door of the hut to facilitate re-birth, and in the Aaru Archipelago they are not buried, but hung 'in the house over their parents' bed ; the ancient Italians buried children under the eaves of their house, and even to-day the Russian peasant places the still-born child under the floor. These illustrations demonstrate the fact that age considerations, too, determine the method of preservation in the house.

Oldenberg dismisses as unnecessary the question as to the priority of cremation or earth burial in the Rig-Vedic times. This idea is in accord with our point of view, for it is significant that the most advanced nations, as well as the most primitive tribes, practise cremation. While we would expect exposure of the body to be associated with people representing the lowest stratum of culture, yet we find such a method practised by the Persians whose civilization is decidedly in advance of the most savage tribes. May we not add that in Rome burial and cremation existed side by side ? As is shown by our evidence, methods of disposal in Rome and in Rig-Vedic times were dependent upon age and sex distinctions. This is another factor which must not be overlooked.

Investigation shows that preservation in the house is usually found in a rude condition of society and that it is abandoned in favour of permanent burial as civilization advances. A native tradition in Tahiti tells of a time when the dead were placed on a kind of stage in the house where they had lived, but later special houses were built for them.[2] It is evident that such a method as preservation in the house must have proved intolerable.

In North India we find earth-burial identified with the menial castes, whereas in some of the wildest tribes the corpse is flung into a ravine or some cleft in the rocks.[3]

We must stress the fact that not all apparent similarities are comparable. Thus in Australia we find different motives

[1] *International Archeology*, Vol. II, p. 43.
[2] Hartland, article in *Hastings*, Vol. IV, p. 422.
[3] Crooke, *Popular Religion and Folk-Lore of Northern India*, pp. 215-216.

for killing the old, such as to prevent the possibility of ill-treatment should they fall into the hands of the enemy, their inability to cope with a perilous journey, and the danger of becoming a burden to the tribe, while in the Siberian area the desire is to allow the deceased to go to the land beyond with his faculties and physical condition unimpaired by old age.

Similarities are not as easily ascertainable as some methodologists, such as Graebner, would have us believe, since they are often associated with the most intricate complexes.

Such practice as killing the aged as is found in Australia cannot be compared with the Siberian custom without taking into consideration the general cultural setting, for an ethnic unit classified independently is highly artificial. Historical relationship is not sufficient in itself to make the comparison. If the psychological factor is not examined in trying to account for a cultural phenomenon, then we would at all times be comparing similarities not comparable at all. Again, it is not only necessary to consider the psychological setting for a custom, but the psychological sources for its origin. However, the close connection between the historical and the psychological methods cannot be overlooked, notwithstanding the tendency of some investigators of cultural phenomena to regard such methods as diametrically opposed to each other. " Historical analysis will furnish the data referring to the growth of ideas among different people ; and a comparison of the processes of their growth will give us a knowledge of the laws which govern the evolution and selection of ideas ".[1]*

---

[1] Boas, "The Mythology of the Bella Coola Indians ", *J.N.P.E.*, Vol. I, p. 127.

* This is exactly what we would expect, for resemblances, in cultural complexes, have been noted long since by ethnologists and sociologists. Although parallelisms of a certain kind have occurred, yet this is not one of those parallelisms of any degree of complexity or for integral historical processes. (See Goldenweiser, " Principle of Limited Possibilities ", *J.A.F.L.*, Vol. XXVI (1913), p. 281.)

CHAPTER XIV

CONCLUSION (*continued*)

As we survey our concrete material we are at first struck by what at first glance appears as a general similarity between cultures especially in regard to particular phases of the death-situation. Thus we find almost identical stories accounting for the origin of death among peoples so far apart, and representing such different cultural levels, that diffusion of culture does not seem at all probable. However, such tales although prevalent in some areas, yet are completely absent in others. This leads us to emphasize the deduction that not all things which are plausible actually develop. Cultures are not consistent and logical developments. This is why psychological interpretations of specific cultural features are wont to be so hazardous, yet, in certain instances, sufficiently plausible psychological assumptions may be made and are, perhaps, worth venturing.

It is evident that the many features usually associated with the death-situation also occur in other complexes. A comparative study shows that the horror with which the dead body is regarded is not only associated with a corpse, but with any thing or event which is identified with the mystical, the uncanny, the awful. This is especially demonstrated in connection with taboo. Not only do we find innumerable taboos enforced as an outcome of the death-situation, but they are equally common in connection with every phase of human endeavour. The primitive adopts numerous precautions to rid himself of that contagious power which is supposed to permeate the things looked upon as polluted and sacred. Here we voice a strong objection to Durkheim's theory that infection is characteristic of the sacred only which makes it a specifically religious phenomenon. The sacred is not inherent in the object, but projected into it.[1] In the primitive

[1] Goldenweiser, "Spirit Mana and the Religious Thrill", *Journal of Philosophy, Psychology, and Scientific Methods*, Vol. XII (1915), p. 635.

consciousness what is dangerous because polluted, and what is dangerous because sacred, are not sharply differentiated. Because of this infectious character, the sacred pilgrims who make a tour to the tomb of Mecca discard their clothes, which become the property of the shrine ; the visitor to a Mohammedan mosque is requested to take off his shoes ; God's injunction to Moses, as he approached the burning bush, " Draw not hither, put off thy shoes from off thy feet, for thou art on holy ground " ;[1] has become proverbial. Holiness and cleanliness arise from taboo and are identical with it. Among the Syrians any one who touched a dove was considered unclean for a day ; the Canonical books defiled the hands by rendering them unclean. Farnell has called our attention to the fact that the term " sacer " has a double meaning, " holy " and " accursed " ; from the same Greek root, " $\alpha\gamma$ " comes a word meaning " holiness " and one meaning "pollution". "The power of radiating dangerous influence supposed to attach itself to the holy man, the polluted man, and the polluted thing, brought them originally under the same dim concept ".[2]

To illustrate our point further,—abstinence from food as well as avoidance of the ordinary pursuits and occupations of life is characteristic of many situations. Thus we perceive that food restrictions as well as feasts are not connected primarily with the death-complex, but with initiation ceremonies, with the period indicating the change from girlhood to womanhood, with pregnancy, in fact, with all phases of activity regarded as most vital and potent in the life of a community. The same consideration which prompts hair cutting as a sign of mourning, may induce one to regard such cutting as especially noxious : the motive which brings water into requisition for purification ceremonies may forbid its use ; the identical reason which causes some people to regard an object or ceremonial as sacred, may influence others to deem it as profane ; while abstinence from food may be looked upon as a necessary accompaniment of mourning, feasts may be classed in that category of rites desirable for propitiation. The silence injunction though so common in many areas, in connection with mourning rites, is not identified with the

---

[1] *Exodus* iii. 5.
[2] Farnell, *Evolution of Religion*, p. 97.

death-complex alone. The evidence presented shows that silence taboos or the prohibition of speaking to certain definite relatives, both blood and fictitious, is common to many areas. Abstinence and acquiescence naturally seem to be the best and surest way of avoiding danger. However, the suspension of ordinary activities is certainly commonest after a death. We have seen that this passivity phase may affect at times not only a family but an entire community, and then, too, the period of inactivity differs greatly, such variation being sometimes due to the sanctity or esteem in which the deceased was held, to the relationship between the living and the dead, to the sex of the deceased individual, and to various local causes.

Abstinence from the ordinary activities of life is seen upon numerous occasions, such as in the " Sweat Lodge " experience of the Indian, who renounces the usual activities of daily existence, and retires to a hut to become so pure that the spirits may look through him ; on various holy days, such as the Atonement Day of the Hebrews, where prohibition of food and of the ordinary occupations is most emphatically enjoined, on the Israelitish Sabbath, when the direst results would befall one who dares violate the strict taboos associated with the sacred day, with eclipses of the moon, when the usual business is suspended, and with numerous other situations. When Westermarck tries to account for the inactivity which follows a death as due to a natural condition of sorrow, or assumes that the mourner may be in a delicate condition requiring rest, he cannot have a grasp of the real situation.[1] Although the sorrow motive may occasionally figure in the complex, yet its rôle is so unimportant that we may eliminate it entirely when considering the specific phase of the problem. What might at first glance be interpreted as a mark of sorrow, certainly assumes an entirely different aspect when carefully investigated. Taboo is entwined with social and political institutions ; it is significant to note that everything sacred seems to be taboo, but not *vice versa*, and that the belief may not be imposed, but spontaneous. Thus the death taboo seems primarily to be a result of the terror and bewilderment caused by the entrance of death into the circle.

While the specific mourning rites concerning attire and

[1] Westermarck, *Origin and Development of Moral Ideas*, Vol. II, p. 283.

complete reversal of custom form an integral part of the death-complex in all the areas we are considering, yet in a few isolated instances we have found a marked indifference to mourning regulations. In regard to mourning garb as well as to the observance of taboos, we find that these weigh much more heavily upon women than upon men. Indeed, the rôle of woman in the entire death-situation is so conspicuous, that we ponder the reason. When we consider that her connection with life must be recognized by the primitive, it is not surprising to find her connection with death of equal significance. This is especially true when we realize that the savage for the most part conceives of life after death as a re-birth, a renewal of the kind of existence he had in this world. Thus woman would figure prominently in the death-rites. Then again, the necessity of vigilance expected from men, their part in securing provision and protecting the community from the attacks of wild animals and foes, may be adduced as another reason for the exemption of the male element from many mourning taboos.

Numerous instances have been cited to show that lacerations play an important rôle in the mourning ceremonies of primitive tribes. Here again the practice is not confined to the death-complex. Thus in the Worgait tribe we have noted the custom of cutting women's backs during initiation ceremonies, while among the Larakia the women practise the custom of mutilating their index finger of the left hand by removing the terminal joint. This practice has nothing to do with initiation, and the natives have no idea what it means.[1]

Dancing rites, too, are identified with many complexes, and are indeed a very common ceremonial form of expression. Here too a special ceremony may be associated with a certain event, as in the case of the Ghost Dance where the resurrection idea is brought out prominently. Perhaps such a conception may have been the outcome of contact with the whites, although in other areas the same idea figures largely in native myths.

The same argument advanced as a possible solution of why reversal of custom plays such a significant part in the mourning customs of primitives, may also account for the presence of buffoons, and those who mimic the mannerisms of the

---

[1] Spencer, *Native Tribes of the Northern Territory of Australia*, p. 10.

deceased. Here, again, deviation from the common is most desirable. Though this may be true, we are not insensible to the fact that the object of many dances in which mimicry figures so largely, is to drive away the dead or the evil spirit to whose influence the death is due. The savage thinks that the performer not merely represents the departed member of his group, but in reality is the one who just departed from their midst. By such means, a stronger bond of union is established between the living and the dead.

Then, again, the object of such imitation might be to gain the power of the dead. King is of the opinion that these ceremonies imitative of animals produce the belief that the performer is the reincarnation of the spiritual representative.[1] Again, this conception is connected with phases of life other than those relating to the death-complex. Thus in the dance of the Intichiuma the performers believe that they are the animals whose multiplication they desire, whose cries and actions they imitate. The ceremony itself thus adds flame to the belief and produces a marked effect upon the social consciousness. We may also mention in this connection the Sacred-Bundle rites of the Blackfoot and the shrine performance of the Hidatsa which are mimetic animal dances, some of the performers imitating the buffalo who have for their object the luring of game. Likewise in the Mosquito and Fly Dances the actors impersonate mosquitoes.

The Central Eskimos have an annual festival which is supposed to bring about the home-sending of the deity protecting sea mammals, and masked performers who impersonate this divinity take a conspicuous part in this rite.[2] In the ceremony of the fish totem among the Arunta, the actor feigns to be a fish.[3] The Arunta also have a ceremony of the witchetty grub totem, in which the actor wriggles and flaps his arms in imitation of the fluttering of the insect when it leaves its chrysalis. The participant is supposed to represent a celebrated ancestor of the witchetty grub totem.[4] A ceremony is practised

---

[1] King, *Development of Religion*, p. 76.
[2] Boas, *The Central Eskimo, Sixth Annual Report, Bureau American Ethnology*, pp. 583-609; "The Eskimo of Baffin Land and Hudson Bay". *Bulletin American Museum Natural History*, Vol. XV (1901), p. 119 et seqq., p. 489 et seqq.
[3] Spencer and Gillen, *Northern Tribes of Central Australia*, pp. 199-204.
[4] *Ibid*, p. 179.

among the Arunta in which the actor represents the emu. Both the decoration and the aimless walking of the performer are characteristic of this bird.[1]

Clownish activities figure in the potlatch ceremony of the North-Western Coast the object of which ceremony is to secure social prestige.[2] In the performances of the South-West Indians, of the North-West group of the Ojibwa ceremonials, perhaps of the Iroquois festivals, and the Plains Sun Dance, the religious features are coupled with the buffoonery element. The comic element is likewise present in the Inviting-In-Feast of the Alaskan Eskimo.[3] It should not escape our notice that all the ceremonies are collective, not individual undertakings.

---

[1] Spencer and Gillen, *Native Tribes of Northern Australia*, pp. 343-358.
[2] Boas, "The Social Organization and Secret Society of the Kwakiutl Indians", *Report, United States National Museum* (1895), pp. 311-737.
[3] Hawkes, "The Inviting-In-Feast of the Alaskan Eskimo", *Geological Survey of Canada, Memoir,* Vol. XLV, p. 12.

PART II

DIFFERENCES

(*Note.*—Since several of the illustrations given come under different categories, we have thought it best to introduce them again under each classification.)

CHAPTER XV

DISPOSAL OF THE DEAD

RANK DIFFERENCES

MELANESIA

AT Saa, the burial of common people is extremely simple ; an inferior person is buried immediately ; an ordinary man is buried the day after his death. However, men of rank are not buried for two days. Women sit around the corpse and wail and gather to get a last glimpse at the deceased and to partake of the funeral feast. If a very great man dies, or a man much beloved by his son, the body is hung up in the son's house either in a canoe or enclosed in the figure of a sword fish, and we likewise note that favourite children have the same treatment accorded them.[1]

We find that burial is not the universal method of disposing of the body at Saa, for the corpse of a chief or lesser man may be thrown into the sea, either at the request of the deceased or to save trouble.

For a man who has no significant position his friends throw yams and other food upon the roof of the dead man's house in his memory ; whereas if a chief dies, they "ngoli-ta'a", fence round a plot of ground, and place his canoe, his bowls, and weapons there ; his friends add their own tributes in his honour, and decorate the fence with leaves and flowers.[2]

In Savo the bodies of commoners are thrown into the sea, while those of chiefs are interred.[3] We find that in Malikolo the body is either interred or exposed on a platform until it decays, when the bones are buried. A chief is interred, but his skull is dug up later, and put in a special house called the " House of the Chiefs ".[4]

In Ambrym we find interment in the house. Here we find the skull, jawbones, and ribs disinterred and five months

[1] Codrington, *The Melanesians*, p. 261.
[2] *Ibid*, p. 263.
[3] Rivers, *History of Melanesian Society*, Vol. II, p. 277.
[4] Leggatt, *Report Australian Association*, Vol. IV (1892), p. 700 ; " Hagen et Pineau ", *Rev. a' Ethnog.*, Vol. VII (1889), p. 332.

later these are put under the root of a hollow tree. The body of an important man is kept in the house in a drum or canoe, whereas the body of a chief is kept in the house in a framework under which a slow fire is lighted, and in some villages is placed on a high platform.[1]

Bodies are usually thrown into the sea in Aneityum, but the highest chiefs are interred with the head above the ground for the purpose of taking the skull and placing it in a sacred grove.[2] It is the custom in San Cristoval to cast the bodies of common people into the sea, while chiefs are buried and some possession of the deceased such as a tooth or a skull is preserved in a shrine in the village.[3] The bodies of important persons are placed on wooden platforms surrounded by palisades and are so kept until only the bones remain.[4]

Burial is usual in Ysabel, but the body of a chief is interred with the head near the surface and a fire is kept burning under it with the object that soon the skull might be removed and placed in the house.[5]

We also find different methods of disposal of the body in Shortland Islands. While the bodies of ordinary people are interred or thrown into the sea, the chiefs and the wives of chiefs are burnt.[6]

The Mafulu bury their common people in shallow graves in the village, but the corpses of chiefs, their wives, and other members of the family are not buried in graves, but laid in rude coffins which are deposited in the fork of a kind of fig tree.[7] The Fijians not only considered rank differences when disposing of the dead, but also even when crossing the ferry en route to the other world, the social status of the deceased was of great concern to them. The classes had definite assignments in the boats which were to convey them to the life beyond the grave. At one end were the hierarchy of the chiefs, at the other end were the commoners.[8] Generally the Banks' Islanders buried their dead in the forest not far from the village; however, if the deceased were a great man

[1] Lamb, *Saints and Savages*, p. 118.
[2] Brown, *Melanesians, Polynesians*, p. 396.
[3] Codrington, *Melanesians*, p. 258.
[4] Rivers, *History of Melanesian Society*, Vol. II, p. 267.
[5] Codrington, *Melanesians*, p. 267.
[6] Wheeler, *Archiv für Religionwissenschaft*, Vol. XVII (1914), p. 64.
[7] Williamson, *The Mafulu Mountain People of British New Guinea*, p. 259.
[8] Thomson, *The Fijians*, p. 121.

or died an unusual death, he was sometimes interred in the village near the gamal (men's clubhouse). In Motlav the corpses of great men were decorated with their finery and placed in an open space in the centre of the village and cocoanuts and other fruit were placed beside the body. Proper deference would be then accorded him, since it was known that he was a great man.[1]

At the funeral of a king of Ulivou of East Fiji five of his wives and daughters were strangled.[2]

Wives are often strangled or buried alive at the funeral of their husbands in Fiji. This is supposed to be the only way by which they can reach the blissful realms, and she who meets death with the great mark of devotedness will become a favourite wife in the abode of spirits. The women who are thus put to death to accompany the spirits of their husband are laid at the bottom of the grave for the dead man to lie upon. Fison tells us that the widow must follow her husband ; it would be " abominable " for her to do otherwise. At least some woman must go with the dead man to wait upon him.[3] Sometimes a man's mother was strangled as well as his wife. Although wives are sacrificed at a husband's death, husbands are not sacrificed at the death of their wives.[4]

Among the Sulka in New Britain we find it a custom, if the deceased is a rich man, for his wife or wives to be sometimes killed.[5] A case is remembered at Saa where the wife of a dead chief asked that she might follow her husband and was strangled accordingly. At Maewo a woman has often requested to be buried with her husband or beloved child.[6] The wife and child of a dead Bugota chief were dragged to the grave and strangled.[7]

[1] Codrington, *Melanesians*, pp. 267-278.
[2] Wilkes, *United States Exploring Expedition*, Vol. III, p. 96.
Frazer, *Belief in Immortality*, Vol. I, p. 425.
When Ra Nbith, the pride of the Samoans, was lost at sea, seventeen of his wives were destroyed. After the news of the massacre of the Namena people at Viwa in 1839, eighty women were strangled to accompany the spirits of their deceased husbands. (Williams, *Fiji and the Fijians*, Vol. I, p. 200.)
[3] Fison, *Tales from Old Fiji*, p. 168.
[4] Frazer, *Belief in Immortality*, Vol. I, p. 425.
[5] *Ibid*, p. 399.
[6] Codrington, *Melanesians*, p. 289.
[7] *Ibid*, p. 257n.
Either on the day of the death or burial, the chief widow of a Tonga Island native is strangled (Mariner, *Tonga Island*, Vol. II, p. 181).

In German New Guinea the widow at her own request is sometimes strangled and buried with her husband in the same grave so that her soul may accompany his on its passage to the other world. In doing this she is often actuated by selfish motives, for by thus sacrificing herself, she thinks that she will be no worse off than she was in this world, since she will have the same husband. However, she is not encouraged to make the sacrifice, but if she insists, the survivors consent, for fear that the ghost of the departed will be chagrined if they are determined to keep her with them.[1]*

Moreover, men likewise were killed among the Fijians to follow their masters to the far country. The confidential companion of a chief was supposed to accompany his master when he died.† If he did not volunteer to do so, he could not retain his influence in the tribe. When Mbithi, a Mathuata chief of high rank, died in 1840, not only his wife, but five men with their wives were strangled to make a floor for the deceased.[2] Slaves are sometimes put to death at the cremation of their master.[3]

In the Island of Ysabel a case is recorded that when a certain chief died, his wife and child were strangled and their bodies were placed in the grave.[4]

AUSTRALIA

A case is recorded among the Bennillong, of South-East Australia, when a woman died, her infant at her breast was

---

[1] Keysser, " Aus dem Leben der Kaileute ", in Neuhauss *Deutsch Neu Guinea*, Vol. III, pp. 82-83, 143.

* In speaking of the Hottentots, Thurnberg tells us that if a woman dies in childbed or soon after, the child is buried with its mother since there is no nurse to look after the child. (Thurnberg, " Account of the Cape of Good Hope ", in Pinkerton's *Voyages and Travels*, Vol. XVI, p. 142.)

† Among the Natchez Indians when a chief died, one or several of his wives and his highest officers were knocked on the head and buried with him. In the province of Guataro there was great rivalry for the privilege of being slain for by this means those slain could find a way to the paradise of the departed chief. (Brinton, *Myths of the Old World*, p. 280.)
Burrows relates that when a high chief dies, five women, selected from his widows are strangled outside of a new hut built on the banks of a stream. (Burrows, *The Land of the Pigmies*, p. 104.)

[2] Williams, *Fiji and the Fijians*, Vol. I, p. 194.

[3] Wilkes, *United States Exploring Expedition*, Vol. III, p. 97.

[4] Brown, *Melanesians and Polynesians*, p. 396, quoting Penny, *Ten Years in Melanesia*.

placed alive in the grave with her ;[1] a similar case is reported among the Port Jackson tribes.[2]

It is significant to note the different modes of burial accorded by the Unmatjera and Kaitish tribes of Central Australia to different classes of persons. Frequently the same tribe disposes of various classes of people in different ways, both by burning and by burying. Among the Victoria tribes we note a distinction in the method of disposal between people of common rank and chiefs. When a person of common rank dies, the body is immediately bound with the knees upon the chest and tied up with an acacia bark cord in an opossum rug. But as soon as a chief dies, the bones of the lower part of the leg and forearm are extracted, cleaned with a flint knife and placed in a basket ; the body is tied with a bark cord, with the knees to the face and wrapped in an opossum rug.[3] At Dungog venerable men and men of distinction were buried with much ceremony, but ordinary members and females were disposed of in a perfunctory way.[4]

When one of the old headmen, or men of note, or fathers of strong families, died, they were buried in what might be called their cemeteries.[5]

INDIA

The Pauariyas of Chota Nagpur bury their dead, except the bodies of their priests, which are carried on a cot into the forest covered with leaves and branches and kept there. The natives declare that if they were placed in the village cemetery, their ghosts would become very troublesome.[6]

ORIENTATION AFFECTED BY RANK DISTINCTION

In Tenimber and Timor-Laut we find two directions of orientation ; eastward for chiefs and celebrated members of the community and westward for commoners.[7]

---

[1] Howitt, *Native Tribes of South-East Australia*, p. 464.
[2] *Ibid*, p. 464.
[3] *Ibid*, p. 455 ; Dawson, *Australian Aborigines*, p. 63.
[4] *Ibid*, p. 464.
[5] *Ibid*, p. 451.
[6] Crooke, *Popular Belief and Religion of Northern India*, Vol. II, p. 64.
[7] Perry, " Orientation of the Dead in Indonesia ", *J.A.I.* (1914), p. 284, quoting Riedel, p. 306.

Whereas in Samoa, Tonga, and Tikopia in Polynesia the bodies of all are interred, in many other places this mode of disposing of the body is used for

MELANESIA

The bodies of men are interred in the men's house among the Barriai while those of the women in their dwelling house, and in each case the house of the living continues to be used by the living as before.[1]

At Murna the women of the same clan who put the body in the grave exhume the bones of the dead.[2]

AUSTRALIA

At Dungog venerable men and women of distinction were buried with much ceremony, but ordinary members and females were disposed of in a perfunctory way.[3] A male

---

those not of high rank. In some places, such as in Tikopia burial takes place either in a house or in a structure representing a house, while in Tonga and Samoa the bodies of chiefs are interred in stone vaults. Again, in Samoa, where a process of mummification is resorted to, the body is preserved above ground, and the bones may be finally interred, or preserved in a house, or removed to a secret cavern ; sometimes it is the skull only which is thus kept. But, as Rivers remarks, nearly everywhere, the bodies of chiefs are interred above the ground. Sometimes in Samoa and Rarotonga, interment is delayed with chiefs many days, during which time the body is exposed, and in Samoa the body of a dead chief may be carried round the places which he frequented during life. (Rivers, *History of Melanesian Society*, Vol. II, p. 269.)

At Tahiti the bodies of chiefs are preserved, and their skulls removed, but the bodies of commoners are interred in a sitting position (Ellis, *Polynesian Researches*, Vol. I, p. 519) ; in the Marquesas, only the bodies of the rich and influential are preserved. (Baessler, *Neue Sudsee-Bilder*, p. 225) ; the bodies of chiefs are placed on platforms in the Paumotu Islands (Meinicke, *Die Inseln d. stielen Ozeans*, Vol. II, p. 218). Interment in a contracted position is general in the Hawaiian Islands, but the bones of a king are disinterred, preserved and deified (Malo, *Old Hawaiian Antiquities*, pp. 132-192). In Anaiteum, Savo, the Islands of Bougainville Straits, and many parts of the Polynesia, only the bodies of commoners are thrown into the sea. (Rivers, *History of Melanesian Society*, Vol. II, pp. 270-271.)

In the Island of Keisar, one of the Moluccas, the dead of rank were buried under a great nanu tree in an open square ; the forefathers are supposed to sleep here and it is regarded as a sacred place. (Riedel, *Die Stuiken Kroesharige Rassen*, pp. 422.)

Among the Bantu of West Africa, chiefs and medicine-men such as Bantu monarchs and Buriat shamans are frequently buried in a grove or thicket which is afterward shunned as sacred. We also hear that chiefs on the Island of Rotuma are buried on the hilltops. (Gardiner, " The Natives of Rotuma ", *J.A.I.*, Vol. XXVII (1898), pp. 431-432.)

The Angoni of British Central Africa burn the corpses of chiefs but the bodies of commoners are buried in caves. (Rattray, *Some Folk-lore Stories and Songs in Chinyanja*, pp. 99-101, 182 ; quoted by Frazer, p. 162.)

The Tlingit Indians of Alaska burn the bodies of their common dead on a pyre, but place their deceased shamans in coffins. (de Pauly, " Description Ethnographique des Peuples de la Russia ", *Peuples de l' Amerique Russe*, p. 13.)

[1] Rivers, *History of Melanesian Society*, Vol. II, p. 529.
[2] Seligmann, *Melanesians*, p. 728.
[3] Howitt, *Native Tribes of South-East Australia*, p. 464.

among the Wollaroi was not buried until the flesh left the bones, but a female was buried at once.[1]

In the Warramunga tribe, who usually place their dead in trees first and in the earth later, we find it a custom for the mother of the deceased and the women who are in the relation of tribal motherhood to the dead, to go from time to time to the tree until the flesh entirely disappears from the bones. The putrid juices which drip from the dead fall upon their bodies into which they rub them as a sign of sorrow. As the ghost is supposed to haunt the tree to see if his widows are sincere in their grief, this ceremony seems to be performed with the ostensible object of appeasing the ghost.[2]

The deceased males of the Boyne River tribe are buried in the ground, but the remains of the females are put in the trunks of trees.[3] Sometimes in the Goulburn tribes the old women are burnt immediately without any ceremony, but the same custom is not carried out with the old men.[4] So too among the Belyando River tribe, when a man dies the women cry out and cut themselves but when a woman departs this life, she is burnt at once without ceremony.[5]

It is a custom in the Wonkomarra tribe for the women to bury the dead.[6] The natives of Victoria raise a tumulus for a young girl; otherwise the body is placed in an ordinary grave.[7] In New South Wales we read of one kind of stone to mark the grave of a man, another to designate that of a woman.[8] The natives of the Fitzroy River leave the corpse of a woman exposed in an open trench.[9] North of the Arunta we hear of the custom that burial in the earth is preceded by a longer or shorter sojourn in a tree, except in the case of old women, for the tribes say that it is not worth while to trouble about them.[10]

INDIA

The Coorgs bury the bodies of women and boys under sixteen, but cremate the bodies of men.[11]

---

[1] Howitt, *Native Tribes of South-East Australia*, p. 464.
[2] Spencer and Gillen, *Northern Tribes of Central Australia*, p. 530.
[3] Curr, *The Australian Race*, Vol. III, p. 123.
[4] *Ibid*, p. 22.   [5] *Ibid*, p. 29.   [6] *Ibid*, p. 38.
[7] Smyth, *The Aborigines of Victoria*, Vol. I, p. 108.
[8] Thomas, *The Natives of Australia*, p. 199.
[9] *Ibid*., p. 199   [10] *Ibid*, p. 193.
[11] Thurston, *Ethnological Notes in Southern India*, p. 205.

The Todas have two funeral places, one for males, another for females. However, among some natives there may be more than one interment place for each sex, others have a special place for boys who have not passed through the ear-piercing ceremony.[1] We also find specially appointed days for the burial of males and females. Usually Sunday, Tuesday, and Thursday are the days allotted to men, and Thursday and Saturday for females.[2] At the funeral of a woman no earth is thrown, as at the burial of a man, but a ceremony is performed which is said to correspond to it.[3]

The Khasis place the bones of males in one bed and those of females in another.[4]

AGE DIFFERENCES

AUSTRALIA

The Unmatjera and Kaitish Tribes of Central Australia draw a sharp distinction between young children and very old men and women in the disposal of their dead. When the aged die their bodies are at once buried in the ground, but the bodies of children are placed in wooden troughs and then deposited on platforms of boughs arranged in the branches of trees.[5] The Ghanji of North Australia bury younger men and women on tree platforms, but older people are placed directly on the ground. We hear that in Port Jackson young people were buried, but those who had passed middle age were burned.[6] Among the Jajaurung, persons of mature life, especially old men and medicine-men, were buried with much ceremony.[7]*

---

[1] Rivers, *The Todas*, p. 338.

The Blackfoot Indian places the body of men high in trees beyond the reach of wolves whereas the bodies of women or children are put in the underbrush or jungle. (Yarrow, *Introduction to the Study of Mortuary Customs among the North American Indians*, p. 67.)

[2] Rivers, *The Todas*, p. 341.

[3] *Ibid*, p. 347.

[4] Gurdon, *The Khasis*, p. 141.

In describing the funeral customs of the aborigines of Alaska Dall states that women are not usually burned because of the scarcity of wood. (Dall, *Resources of Alaska*, p. 382.)

[5] Frazer, *The Belief in Immortality*, Vol. I, p. 161.

[6] Howitt, *Native Tribes of South-East Australia*, p. 463.

[7] *Ibid*, p. 458.

* The Eskimo bury their young in the direction of the rising sun; they place the aged in the opposite direction; half-grown children are interred with their feet to the south-east, young men and women with their feet to the south, and the middle-aged with their feet to the south-west. (Boas, "Central Eskimo," *Sixth Annual Report Bureau of Ethnology* (1888), p. 613.)

If a male among the Wollaroi died, the body was burned after the flesh left the bones ; a female was buried at once, and a child was placed in a tree.[1]

Dawson tells us that the bodies of children under four years of age who have died a natural death are kept for a day and a night and are then interred without ceremony.[2] In referring to the tribes inhabiting the district from the Murray River to Lacepede Bay, Curr says that children who died in infancy were sometimes burned, but are now always buried.[3] It seems that the conception was held that children who had not reached the age of four or five years had no souls and as a consequence no future life awaited them.[4] In the western part of Victoria the native thinks that children under five have no spirits, but every person over this age has not only a soul spirit, but also another spirit of visible form. For it a fire is kept burning all night.[5]

In reference to the tribes of Encounter Bay we are told that aged persons are not treated with the same ceremony as younger ones and are buried immediately after death.[6] Still-born children are burned and if a child dies a natural death, it is sometimes carried by the mother or grandmother for about a year and then put on a tree and later the bones are buried.[7]

When a young man dies in Frazer Island (Great Sandy Island, Queensland) the survivors first skin him, then cut off his flesh, and finally extract the marrow from his bones. The skin, flesh, and marrow are distributed among his relatives and are carried about to ward off evil. But when the old and " stale " die, their bodies are placed on the boughs of trees.[8]

INDIAN AREA

From the Grihya-Sutras we learn that children who died under the age of two were buried, but that older people were cremated.[9]

---

[1] Howitt, *Native Tribes of South-East Australia*, p. 467.
[2] Dawson, *Australian Aborigines*, p. 63.
[3] Curr, *The Australian Race*, Vol. II, p. 248.
[4] Dawson, *Australian Aborigines*, pp. 50-51.
[5] Fraser, *The Aborigines of New South Wales*, p. 85.
[6] Meyer, *The Aborigines of Encounter Bay*, p. 200.
[7] *Ibid*, p. 198.
[8] Smyth, *The Aborigines of Victoria*, Vol. I, p. 121.
[9] *The Grihya-Sutras*, trans. by Oldenberg, *Sacred Books of the East*, Vol. XXIX, pt. 1, p. 355.

Among the Malayālis of Malabar men and women are burned but the bodies of children under two are buried as are those of all who have died of certain contagious diseases.[1]

The Nāyars, Kadupattans, and other castes of Cochin, practise a similar custom.[2] The Bhotias of the Himalayas bury all children who have not their permanent teeth, but they cremate all other people.[3] The Komars bury their young but burn their old.[*]

SIBERIA

In alluding to the Koibales, Georgi states that some Siberian tribes formerly buried adults but placed the corpses of children on trees.[4]

CEREMONIES CONNECTED WITH CLAN SPIRIT

MELANESIA

It is most interesting to note that in the Solomon Islands the disposal of the bones is connected with features of great importance in relation to totemism. When the bones are thrown into the water (which is more frequently the case) this is done at places called " keno ", each lake or clan having its own keno. Here is the belief that the bones are swallowed by fish, by animals, or by mysterious beings. We are told that in some instances the animals which become the receptacles for the bones are included in the list of totems of the latu included in Mr. Wheeler's list, and in each case the dead is looked upon as the " fabin " of the animal or other being.

---

[1] Thurston, *Ethnographic Notes in South India*, p. 207.
[2] Iyer, *The Cochin Tribes and Castes*, Vol. II, pp. 91-112, 157, 360-362, 378.
[3] Sherring, *Western Tibet and the British Borderland*, p. 123.
[*] In the Andaman Islands infants are buried within their encampment, whereas others are buried in distant and secluded spots. (Man, " Aboriginal Inhabitants of the Andaman Islands ", *J.A.I.*, Vol. XII (1885), p. 144.) At Karawge and Nkole in the neighbourhood of Victoria Nyanza in Central Africa children are buried in huts and adults usually in cultivated fields. (Kollmann, *The Victoria Nyanza*, p. 63.)
[4] Bose, " Chkattisgar ", *J.A.S.B.*, Vol. LIX, pt. 1, p. 29.
The Kois or Koyis of the Godāvari district bury bodies of children and young men and women. If a child dies within a month of its birth it is buried near the house so that the water, falling from the eaves, may reach the grave, thereby insuring another child to the parents. With the exception of the instances just cited, corpses are usually burned. (Thurston, *Ethnographic Notes in Southern India*, p. 155.) Among the Hurons there are special ceremonies for small children who die under two months of age. They are not placed in sepulchres of bark raised on stakes but are buried in the road with the object of facilitating rebirth in the womb of a woman who passes such a spot. (Thomas, " Burial Mounds in the Northern Sections of the U.S.", *Fifth Annual Report Bureau of Ethnology* (1887), p. 111.)

This is all the more significant when we consider that " fabin " is a term of relationship reciprocal to " tete " and " tua ", terms for grandparent, and also for the totem. Likewise the " keno " is supposed to be the bathing place of the " nunu " or soul of the deceased. Although when a chief is buried, a clan may have a special locality not called " keno ", yet it seems to be an equivalent.[1]

The places called " paga " connected with sub-groups of the moieties of New Ireland are supposed to be the abode of the ghosts. Rivers suggests that these are places where the bodies of the dead were thrown into the rivers or ponds, just as it seems to have happened in the Shortland Islands. Furthermore, he goes on to say, here we may have a relic of the mode of disposal the same as existed in the Shortland Islands before cremation. If the sub-groups of the moieties of New Ireland have arisen through the mechanism which the author supposes to have been in vogue in other parts of Melanesia, they should have been totemic. It is possible, Rivers thinks, that in the streams or ponds connected with these sub-groups, we have evidence of such a totemic character of the ritual of death as is still present in the Shortland Islands.[2]

At Kwaiawata the body of a man who dies away from his own village must be brought to his native hamlet by his sisters' children, and the corpse is placed in the grave by the mother-in-law of the deceased and his sisters' husbands.[3] We find it a custom in Murua for the body to be placed in the grave by women representing other clans than that to which the dead man belonged.[4]

At Tubetube the grave is dug by the dead man's sisters' sons. Four of these should officiate, but if this is not possible, any men of the same totem may perform this function. The totem relationship here determines the office.[5] In Bartle Bay the grave is dug by the Gariauna who may be the varina (brothers and cousins) or aü (sisters' children) assisted by the dead man's kimta mates, or if this cannot be arranged, by any member of the clan.[6]

[1] Thurnwald, *Forschungen auf den Salomo-Inseln und dem Bismarck Archip.* (1912), Vol. III, p. 27.

[2] Rivers, *History of Melanesian Society*, Vol. II, p. 531.

[3] Seligmann, *Melanesians*, p. 725.

[4] *Ibid*, p. 728.   [5] *Ibid*, p. 612.   [6] *Ibid*, pp. 615-616.

After the death of a paramount chief in the Trobriands, the bones of the arms, legs, and sometimes the ribs are distributed to the people of all the totems, except that of the dead man. Each village chief over whose district the deceased ruled receives one bone, provided that he does not belong to the dead man's totem.[1]

When a native of Torres Straits Island dies, the office of looking after the body belongs to the brothers-in-law of the deceased. These individuals were always of a different totem from the deceased. If the dead person was a man, the " mariget " or " ghosthand ", as these officials were called, were his wife's brothers, and hence had the same totem as the deceased man's wife, which because of the practice of exogamy among them, was always different from the totem of her husband. If the deceased was a woman, the " mariget " were her husband's brothers who had his totem which could not correspond with hers. The ceremony which followed the duties connected with the corpse is very interesting. The relatives and friends were then informed of the death, and in pantomime they imitated the animal which had been the totem of the deceased. If the crocodile was the totem of the dead man, they mimicked the awkward waddling of this animal ; if a snake, they imitated its movements.[2]

Manner of Disposal Affected by Clan Spirit

Australia

In the Unmatjera and Kaitish tribes we find that they do not bury in trees any young man who has violated tribal law by taking as wife a woman of a clan not coming under the exogamy relation. The guilty one in this case is buried in the ground.[3]

Orientation Identified with Clan Affiliation

Melanesia

The people of the Wotjo nation bury their dead with the head in a certain direction which is determined by his class

[1] Seligmann, *Melanesians*, p. 718.
[2] Frazer, *Belief in Immortality*, Vol. I, p. 177 ; Cambridge, *Anthropological Expedition to Torres Straits*, Vol. V, p. 248.
[3] Spencer and Gillen, *Northern Tribes of Central Australia*, v. 512.

and totem.   It is interesting to note that the several directions
are all fixed with reference to the rising sun.*

At Bartle Bay the dead are orientated with their heads
pointing from where the totem clan of the deceased is said to
have originated.[1]

INDIA

The Khasis bury their dead and then deposit the ashes in
small cairns.   They are then removed to large bone reposi-
tories of which one is the property of every branch of the clan.
Later the contents are removed at certain definite intervals
after the adjustment of all disputes between members of a
clan, where the remains finally rest.[2]

BURIAL CUSTOMS AFFECTED BY PHRATRY RELATIONS

MELANESIA

In the Banks' Islands it is the duty of the members of the
other Veve, or of the other side of the house, to dig the grave.[3]*

Immediately after the death of one of the representatives
of the Binbinga tribe, the body is dissected by men who
belong to the opposite side of the tribe.   If, for instance,
a Tjurulum man dies, the body is dismembered by Tjuanaku,
Tjulantjuka, Paliarinji, and Pungarinji men.   These then
partake of a meal which consists of parts of the body of the
deceased.   Almost the same custom prevails among the Mara
and Anula tribes, only those who take part in the feast are
members of both moieties of the tribe.[4]

---

* The direction in which the deceased is buried in Augkola, Indonesia,
depends upon the marga or exogamous clan to which the dead man belongs.
In the case of the marga siregar the body is placed with the head to the west
and with a marga harahap the head is directed to the east.   (Kruijt, *Animisme*,
p. 371.)

At Ofnet we find orientation identified with clan affiliation.   Here bodies
have been found orientated toward the setting sun, such a position being
definitely determined by the clan and totem.

[1] Seligmann, *Melanesians*, p. 616.
[2] Gurdon, *The Khasis*, p. 140.
[3] Codrington, *Melanesians*, p. 267.
* Among the Iroquois the members of one phratry bury those of another
phratry.   The same is true of the phratries of the north-west coast.   The
Tlinget of British Columbia are divided into two marrying groups with descent
exclusively through the women.   When a man dies his body is carried out by
members of his wife's class and the members of his own class give them a
feast.   (Swanton, "The Tlingit Indians", *Twenty-sixth Annual Report,
Bureau of Ethnology* (1905-1906), p. 430.)
[4] Spencer and Gillen, *Northern Tribes of Central Australia*, p. 548.

AUSTRALIA

We find it a custom among the Dieri for those who belong to the group consisting of the distant relatives, or who are in this way connected with a certain phratry, to dig the grave ; but if none of that group is present, then a Ngaperi-waka (father's brother or male Pirrauru) digs it with the idea that he may be useful to the dead.[1]

INDIA

At the burial of a Toda the men of one division take part in the earth-throwing ceremony connected with the inter-ment of a member of the other division.[2]

BURIAL CUSTOMS AFFECTED BY KINSHIP

AUSTRALIA

The Dieri practice, cited above, not only comes within the category of phratry, but can also be classified under the head of kinship. The desire to be of service to the departed is the motive which prompts a near-relative to prepare the grave.*

We find it a custom among the Unmatjera and Kaitish that after the flesh has disappeared from the bones, a kinsman of the deceased, in reality a younger brother, climbs up the tree, secures the bones, and hands them to a female relative.[3]

BURIAL IN ACCORDANCE WITH CLASS AND SUB-CLASS

AUSTRALIA

When one of the Wakellura died his body was placed on a frame, lying on bark and covered with branches, all of which must be of a tree of the same class or sub-class as that to which the deceased belonged. Thus, if he were a Banbe, then the wood, bark, and branches must be of the broad-leaved box tree which belonged also to the Banbe sub-class. Men of the Malera class, which includes both Banbe and Kurgilla, would build the stage and cover the dead body. Howitt calls our

---

[1] Howitt, *Native Tribes of South-East Australia*, p. 447.

[2] Rivers, *The Todas*, p. 346.

* Each family or clan among many people has its own burial place. This was a custom among the ancient Greeks (Rhode, I, 229) as well as among the ancient Hebrews ; indeed, it is still practised in the Holy Land.

This we might say is a natural and common outgrowth of the kinship feeling and we would expect to find it especially where group and family solidarity prevails extensively.

[3] Spencer and Gillen, *Northern Tribes of Central Australia*, pp. 506-508.

attention to the fact that in this tribe the two class names divide the whole universe between them.[1]

Ceremonies Connected with the Local Group

Melanesia

Among the Roro-speaking tribes the men of the local group dig a shallow grave in which the corpse is placed, usually with its head turned toward the rising sun.[2]

Traditional Tales

A Connection Between the Land of the Dead and the Orientation of the Dead

The Kei Islanders inter their dead toward the north. The body is placed with the head to the south and the feet toward the north so that when rising, the deceased will face the land of the dead.[3]

In Savoe the dead are buried in a sitting position toward the west and the land of their dead is also in this direction.[4]

The Karo-Batak, before burial, place the corpse on a stool facing toward the west and they also look upon the land of their origin as in the west.[5]

The Tenggerese of Bantam place their dead toward a certain holy mountain. Perry shows that the land of their dead would be situated on this mount.[6]

It has been said that the To-Radja place the land of the dead in the west and orient their dead toward the west. Here, a peculiar circumstance greets us, for tradition assigns the north as the direction of their place of origin, and in this case we do not have, as in other instances, a correlation between the land of the dead, the orientation of the dead, and the original land of the race.

---

[1] Howitt, *Native Tribes of South-East Australia,* p. 471.

At the funeral of an Iroquois tribesman, the moiety complementary to that of the deceased participates in the ceremony. (Lowie, " Social Organization ", *A.J.S.*, Vol. XX, 1914, p. 85.)

[2] Seligmann, *Melanesians*, p. 274.

[3] " Perry's Orientation of the Dead in Indonesia ", *J.A.I.* (1914), p. 283.

[4] Riedel, *Revue Coloniale Internationale* (1885), p. 309.

[5] Kruijt, *Het Animisme in den Indischen Archipel.*, p. 371.

[6] Perry, " Orientation of the Dead in Indonesia ", *J.A.I.* (1914), p. 286.

MELANESIA

In the Port Lincoln tribe we find the head of the deceased placed in the grave to the westward, from the notion that departed souls reside on an island situated eastward.[*][1]

In describing a death which he witnessed in West Australia, Grey tells us that the face was turned due east and great precaution was taken to see that the grave should extend due east and west.[2]

A CONNECTION EXISTS BETWEEN THE MYTHS OF ORIGIN AND THE LAND OF THE DEAD

The To-Bada houses are built in a north-south direction. As one enters a To-Bada house, he faces north, the direction from whence he has come and in which direction the inhabitants place the land of the dead. It is also significant to note that the Minahassers build their houses with reference to the land of their origin.[3] The Pangin of the Ella district believe that the land of their dead is in the east and they also think that they originated from this direction.[4]

AUSTRALIA

In Central Australia we find burial in a sitting position, with knees doubled up against the chin. The deceased is interred in a mound depression which faces the dead man's or woman's camping ground in the Alcheringa, that is the spot which he or she has inhabited when in spirit form.[5] The graves of the Alatunja of the Alice Springs Group are always heaped up on one side or have a slight depression facing toward the place where the Alcheringa, the mythical ancestor of the deceased lived, and where the spiritual double of the man has continued to live.[6]

---

[*] However, some say that the island is to the west.

[1] Smyth, *The Aborigines of Victoria*, p. 115 ; Schürmann, *The Aborigines of Port Lincoln*, Vol. I, p. 234.

[2] Grey, *Expeditions of Discovery in Northwest and West Australia*, Vol. II, p. 327.

[3] Perry, "Orientation of the Dead in Indonesia", *J.A.I.*, (1914), p. 290.

[4] *Ibid*, p. 288.

[5] Spencer and Gillen, *Native Tribes of Central Australia*, p. 497.

[6] *Ibid*, p. 508.

A Connection Exists Between the Myths of Origin and the Disposal of the Dead

We find that some of the clans of the Old Kuki of Manipur believe that their ancestors came out of the ground.[1] The Purum claim descent from Tonring and Tonshu who came from the ground and the ancestors of the Kohlen sprang out of the Khurpui.[2] These people and the natives of Keisar, whose first ancestor is represented as emanating from Mount Wahkuleren,[3] inter their dead in the same manner. In Beloe where the first ancestor of the inhabitants of Fialarang originated from Mount Lekaan we likewise find burial in the ground practised. In these instances we see that the belief in origin from the ground is connected with the idea of a return to the ground.[4]

In Indonesia we also note that associated with interment are certain myths which represent the first man as coming out of the earth by means of a cave. Some of the old Kuki of Manipur claim that their first ancestor originally made his appearance from a cave while the other clans declare that he originated from the ground. As several peoples in Indonesia practise cave burial, the question arises, as Perry suggests, as to whether there is not some connection between cave burial and interment, both being means of ushering the dead into the lower world.[5]

It must be obvious that cave burial, whether in natural or artificial recesses, can be carried out in rocky or mountainous areas and then only when the geological formation is adapted to such method of disposal.

Stone Disposal

In some parts of Indonesia a correspondence exists between the myths of origin which connect the first ancestor with stones,

---

[1] Perry, "Myths of Origin and Homes of the Dead in Indonesia", *F.L.*, Vol. XXVI (1915), p. 147.

[2] Shakespeare, *The Lushei Kuki Clans*, pp. 151-164, quoted.

[3] Riedel, *Slink en Kroeshaarige Rassen*, pp. 401-420.

[4] Perry, "Myths of Origin and Homes of the Dead in Indonesia", *F.L.*, Vol. XXVI (1915), p. 148.

We find the dead buried in a sitting position among the Omaha, orientated toward the east. This is the direction in which they are supposed to have come. (Fletcher, "The Omaha," *Bulletin Twenty-seventh Annual Report Bureau of Ethnology* (1911), p. 592.)

[5] Perry, "Myths of Origin and Homes of the Dead in Indonesia", *F.L.*, Vol. XXVI (1915), p. 149.

and the disposal of the dead. The Kabin Naga place their dead in a cave hollowed out in the side of a hill. They likewise have a practice of interring their dead in flat ground with a stone placed on the grave, or else an upright stone is erected. In the case where the dead are buried in a cave the opening is filled up with stones.[1] The Tangkhul Naga bury their dead and place stones on the mound.[2] In the instances cited we find a correlation between the myths of origin and the manner of disposal. The myth which connects the first ancestor of the race with stones occurs in different parts of Minahassa. Lumimunt, the oldest goddess, created Kareima, the first woman out of a rock.[3]

A Connection Exists Between the Myths of Origin and the Orientation of the Dead

The Mentawi Islanders of Indonesia place the dead body on a platform facing east. It is interesting to note that there exists among these people a tradition of migration from the neighbouring coast of Sumatra which is from the east.[4] The Hajong division of the Kachari of Assam orient their dead toward the south and they are supposed to have come from the south.[5] The Khasi place their deceased on the pyre facing east, the body orientated in an east-west direction with the head at the west end. Tradition represents them as coming from the east.[6]

A Connection Exists between the Myths of Origin and the Land of the Dead, and the Orientation of the Dead

In Babar-Archipelago of Indonesia the land of the forefathers and of the dead, and the orientation of the dead is in the west.[7]

---

[1] M'Culloch, *Account of the Valley of Munnipore*, p. 52 ; *Gov't. India, Foreign Department*, p. 107, quoted by Frazer.

[2] Pettigrew Kathikasham, *J.A.S.*, Straits Branch, N. Series, Vol. IV, p. 37, et seqq., quoted by Frazer.

[3] Hickson, *A Naturalist in Celebes*, pp. 240-241.

[4] Perry, "The Orientation of the Dead in Indonesia", *J.A.I.*, Vol. XLIV (1914), p. 288.

[5] *Assam Census Report* (1881), p. 71 ; Endle, *The Kacharis*, p. 87.

[6] Gurdon, *The Khasis*, p. 10.

The significance of the myths of origin is by no means confined to the death situation. Thus the Bada possess two images, one male and one female ; both face north, the direction of the land of their origin. (Perry, " Orientation of the Dead in Indonesia," *J.A.I.*, Vol. XLIV (1914), p. 292.)

[7] Riedel, *Slink en Kroeshaarige Rassen*, p. 275.

Among the Leti-Moa-Lakor Group we find that the orientation and the land of the dead and the land of the forefathers
are eastward.[1]   At Beloe the graves are dug in the direction
of the land of the dead and in the direction of those places
where the first chiefs procured their wives.   Here the land
of the ancestors is in the same direction as the land of the
dead.   Although, as Perry suggests,[2] the body does   not
actually face the land of the dead, there is no doubt as to the
intention of the survivors.[3]   In this case we not only see
a connection between the location of the original home of the
natives and the realms of the dead, but their social status-
rank is likewise taken into account.

The Kom Clan of the Kuki of Manipur inter their dead on
the south side of the village and the land of the dead is likewise
in the south, and it is also from this direction that they suppose
themselves to have originated.   Here as in many other
instances the aim seems to be to send the deceased back to
the land whence he first came.[4]

The Badoej of Bantam orient their dead to the south and
think that the land of the dead is in this same direction.   The
Badoej are looked upon as Soendaneeze who came from the
south before accepting Islam as their religion.[5]

A Connection between the Myths Relating to Totemic Ancestors and Tree Burial

Australia

In the course of a conversation, Unkurta, a jew-lizard, asked
Qualpa (a long-tailed rat totem), "What do you do when
another man dies", and he replied, "I do not bury him, I
throw him away anywhere along the ground".   Then Unkurta
said that it was not good to throw him away like that, but
that if he felt real sorry he ought to bury him in a tree, and
said, "Tell your sons to put you up in a tree when you are
dead, and tell them to teach other men to do the same ".[6]

---

[1] Perry, " Orientation of the Dead in Indonesia ", *J.A.I.* (1914), p. 287.
[2] *Ibid*, pp. 287-288.   [3] Kruigt, *Animisme*, p. 345.
[4] Shakespeare, *The Lushei Clans*, p. 150 ; Brown, *Account of Munnipore*,
pp. 136-137.
[5] Kruijt, *Animisme*, pp. 373-374.'
[6] Spencer and Gillen, *Northern Tribes of Central Australia*, pp. 400-401.
    The forefather of the Wamakonde, the man from the bush, gave his
children the command to bury their dead upright in memory of the mother
of their race who was cut out of wood and awoke to life when stood upright.
(This tale is the tribal legend of the Makonde.) (Weule, *Native Life in East
Africa*, p. 259.)

DIFFERENCES

DEPENDENT UPON THE KIND OF DEATH

MELANESIA

The corpses of those who died a sudden death among the Sulka are not buried, but are wrapped up with leaves and placed in a scaffold in the house which is then shut up and deserted.[1]

AUSTRALIA

Among the Maranoa tribe of South-East Australia it is the custom of the relatives of a young man who has died a violent death to carry about his body instead of burying it. The reason assigned for this practice is that he had died before his time and as a consequence could not rest in his grave. Such a body is tied in a sheet of bark which is painted or decorated with emu feathers.[2*]

Among some of the Victorian tribes we find the custom of eating the bodies of relatives of either sex. But it is important to bear in mind that this is only done in cases where the person has been killed by violence. The natives declare that the body was eaten as a sign of respect for the dead.[3] In the Ovens River district of Victoria, the body of a man killed by accident receives special attention.[4]

---

[1] Rascher, "Die Sulka, ein Beitrag zur Ethnographie, New Pommern", *Archiv für Anthropologie*, Vol. XXIX (1904), p. 216.

[2] Howitt, *Tribes of South-East Australia*, p. 468.

[*] The Chukchausi Indians of Caledonia burned those who died a violent death or were bitten by snakes, but buried others. (Powers, *Tribes of Caledonia*, p. 383.)

[3] Howitt, *Tribes of South-East Australia*, pp. 457-458.

[4] Thomas, *The Natives of Australia*, p. 199.

Orientation among the Route clan of the Kuki, of Manipur, is connected with the kind of death. Persons who had died an ordinary death are buried toward the west. Women who have died during partus and children who died before one year of age are buried toward the east of the village. Those who have died an accidental death are orientated toward the south of the village. (Perry, " Orientation of the Dead of Indonesia," *J.A.I.*, Vol. XLIV (1914), p. 289.) The Galelareeze of Halmahera direct the bodies of those who have died a natural death toward the west, and those who have died an unnatural death toward the east. (Perry, *Ibid*, p. 286.)

The Dayaks of South-east Borneo do not bury those who have died by accident. (Grabowsky, "Der Tod, das Begräbnis, das Tiwah oder Todtenfest," *Int. Arch.*, Vol. II, p. 181.) The Caddoes of North America do not bury the warrior slain in battle.

The Choctaws of North America place their dead on scaffolds but bury at once those who have commited suicide. The Hurons do not place the slain on raised platforms as is their usual custom. (Thomas, " Burial Mounds of the Northern Sections of the United States," *Fifth Annual Report of the Bureau of Ethnology* (1887), p. 111.) The Samoans erect a different platform for the

INDIA

The bodies of those who die of contagious diseases are not buried, but are carried into the forest and are kept there, covered with leaves and branches. Death in such a case is looked upon as due to the act of one of the deities who govern plagues.[1]

Usually the Gonds bury their dead, but "those who die in their beds" are burned as the Hindus.[2] The Kurmi deny the ordinary funeral rites to those who have met their death by hanging or drowning, or through snake-bite. These individuals are merely burned without the ceremonies performed subsequent to cremation and necessary to secure salvation to the soul. Adults who have died of smallpox or leprosy are buried.[3]

Among the Khasis those who die of cholera or smallpox or of any infectious or contagious disease are first buried but later their bodies are dug up and burned, whereas the usual custom is to burn the body without the preliminary process of burial.[4]

We read that a man of the Latooka, slain in battle, remains unburied on the field.[5] At Uilong a man killed in war is buried outside the village opposite to that of the enemies who inflict the fatal wound.

The Hindus of the Punjab believe that if a mother dies thirteen days within her delivery, she will return in the form of a malignant spirit and torment her family. To prevent this some of the natives drive nails through her head and eyes.[6]

---

body of a man killed in fighting from that of a man killed from any other cause. (Brown, *Melanesians and Polynesians*, p. 142.)

Among the aborigines of Sitka, we find it a custom to burn the bodies of those who lose their life in war, with the exception of the head. This is preserved in a separate box other than that in which the ashes and bones are placed. (Lisiansky, *A Voyage Round the World*, p. 241.)

[1] Crooke, *Popular Religion and Folk-Lore of Northern India*, Vol. II, p. 64.

[2] *Indian Antiquary*, Vol. I. p. 349.

[3] Russell, *Tribes and Castes of India*, Vol. IV, p. 73.

[4] Gurdon, *The Khasis*, p. 137.

[5] Smyth, *The Aborigines of Victoria*, Vol. I, p. 122; Hodson, *The Naga Tribes of Manipur*.

[6] Rose, "Hindu Birth Observances in the Punjab", *J.A.I.*, Vol. XXXVII (1907), pp. 225-226.

The ghosts of women who die in childbed are especially feared. See Frazer, *Psyche's Task*, pp. 64-65.

SIBERIA

The bodies of those among the Chukchee who have died from syphilis must not be burned lest the fire should be contaminated.[1] The manner of death often determines the rites to be performed because it determines the fate of the deceased in the other world.*

INFLUENCED BY MORAL CONSIDERATIONS

MELANESIA

The Sulkas do not bury in the house, as is their usual custom, persons who at their death left few relatives, or did evil in their life, or were murdered outside the village. Such bodies are placed on rocks or on scaffolds in the forest or are buried on the spot where they met their death.[2] Frazer adds that probably such ghosts are regarded with contempt or fear, and thus their bodies are interred at some distance from the village.[3]

AUSTRALIA

In Victoria when a man is killed in a fight the tribesmen inquire whether the slain one was sulky or sullen. If violent or mad or vicious, that is, if he pursued his enemy with malignity and not in the calm manner of a man seeking victory merely, but rather with blood-thirstiness, he would not be deserving of a decent burial. He would be left to mutilation and decay where he fell. If, again, he were the aggressor, and death were the outcome, burial rites would not be performed. However, if the deceased acted in self-defence,

[1] Bogoras, *The Chukchee*, *J.N.P.E.*, Vol. VII (1907), p. 523.

* The books of the pontiffs forbade burial to those who put an end to their lives by hanging. (Granger, *The Worship of the Romans*, p. 66.) Such were left tossing between death and life since the good spirits of the upper air refused to receive them. (*Ibid.*)

Among the Tuski of Alaska those who die a natural death are carried out through a hole cut in the back of the hut or yarang. This opening is immediately closed so that the dead man cannot find his way back. (Dall, *Alaska and its Resources*, p. 382.) In Germany and the Highlands of Scotland the bodies of suicides are carried out through a special opening, not by means of the ordinary doorway. (Roscoe, *The Baganda*, p. 20.)

In Travancore the spirits of men who have died a violent death by drowning or hanging are supposed to become demons wandering about intent upon inflicting injury. To prevent this the heels of the deceased are cut. (Frazer, *Psyche's Task*, p. 63.)

[2] Rascher, "Die Sulka, ein Beitrag Zur Ethnographie Neu Pommern", *Archiv für Anthropologie*, Vol. XXIX (1904), p. 214.

[3] Frazer, *Belief in Immortality*, Vol. I, pp. 399-400.

burial would be accorded him and his body and bones would be placed in a hollow tree.[1]

A CONNECTION BETWEEN THE METHOD OF BURIAL AND THE WORSHIP OF THE SUN

MELANESIA

The only place where the upright position is recorded in another part of Melanesia, other than in New Ireland, is in the Island of Ureparapara, though Rivers suggests it may also be present at the southern end of Malaita. Burial in this position points to the association of the cult of the sun with this practice.[2] This cult, the author supposes, is embodied in the religious ritual of the people who practice this form of burial, and he declares that it is a remarkable fact that the Duke of York Islands, where the upright position also occurs, is especially the home of the Duk-duk, which embodies a sun cult. Rivers claims that interaction brought about such a conception and he says evidence can be adduced to show that the cult of the sun was not a part of the general culture of the Kava-people, but was brought into Melanesia by a distinct and relatively late migration who placed their dead in the upright position. We should expect, he says, to find such a

[1] Smyth, *The Aborigines of Victoria*, Vol. I, p. 108.

In some parts of Central America men of high standing who had committed a crime were exposed. (Preuss, *Die Begräbnisarten des Amerikaner und Nordostasiaten*, p. 301, quoted by Frazer.) Among the people of Greenland it is the custom for the body of a malefactor to be dismembered and the legs to be scattered. (Rink, *Tales and Traditions of the Eskimo*, p. 64.)

Although the Hidatsa usually place their dead on scaffolds, yet they bury in the earth those who quarrel and kill one another because the Lord of Life is displeased with such conduct. The object of such burial is to prevent the body from being seen. The Crows who have no fear of death likewise are filled with horror at the thought of being buried in the ground. (Dorsey, *A Study of Siouan Cults*, p. 176, quoting Maximilian, *Travels in North America*, pp 404-405.)

In speaking of the aborigines of Alaska, Dall tells us that the bodies of good men were burned or rather broiled with oil, moss, and driftwood, whereas the corpses of bad men were simply exposed to rot. (Dall, *Resources of Alaska*, p. 382.) When any man died the Eskimo of Bering Strait formerly cut the sinews of his arms and legs "in order to prevent the shade from returning to the body and causing it to walk at night as a ghoul". (Nelson, "The Eskimo about Bering Strait", *Eighteenth Annual Report, Bureau of Ethnology* (1899), p. 423.)

The Herero of South Africa think that the ghosts of bad people appear and are just as mischievous as they were in life ; they rob, steal, seduce women and girls. To prevent this the Herero used to cut through the backbone of the corpse, tie it in a bunch, and sew it in an ox-hide. (Brincker, *Character, Sitten, und Gebräuche speciell der Bantu Deutsch Südwestafrikas ;* quoted by Frazer in *Psyche's Task*, p. 64.)

[2] Rivers, *History of Melanesian Society*, Vol. II, p. 531.

method of burial in the Society or Marquesas Islands, as well as in New Britain, and the adjacent islands, where the sun cult is practised, but as yet there is no evidence.

DISPOSAL OF THE BONES RELATED TO ANIMAL BELIEFS
MELANESIA

In Melanesia we find features of great significance in connection with animal beliefs. When the bones are thrown into the water at places called keno, it is believed that they are swallowed by fishes or animals. In some cases the animals which become the receptacles of the bones are included among the totems of the clan. The keno is also regarded as the nunu or soul of the dead man. The bone ceremony seems to have been instituted for the acquisition of the mana of the dead man by the possession of his bones. The flesh is taken off the bones as soon as possible so that the soul can be free to go to the land of the dead.*

CONNECTED WITH SOCIAL INFRACTIONS
INDIA

The Kurmi, a cultivating caste, bury children whose ears have not been bored.[1]

CONNECTED WITH THE REPUTATION OF THE DECEASED
AUSTRALIA

If the departed tribesman were a great hunter or an esteemed counsellor, or if he had performed unusual feats, the sorcerer would make a significant speech at the burial.[2]

CONNECTED WITH DIVINATION
INDIA

In Tibet the priest settles the method of disposal. The place, the day, the hour, all depend on astrological combinations known only to him.[3]

ASSOCIATED WITH ETHICAL CONSIDERATIONS

Persons who left few relatives, or did evil or who were murdered outside the village were not buried in the house but were deposited on rocks or scaffold.[4]

---

* Also considered on pages 206 and 207.
[1] Russell, *Tribes and Castes of India*, Vol. IV, p. 73.
[2] Smyth, *The Aborigines of Victoria*, Vol. I, p. 106.
[3] Williams, *Buddhism*, p. 365.
[4] Rascher, "Die Sulka", *Archiv für Anthropologie*, Vol. XXIX (1904), pp. 214-216.

CEREMONIES CONNECTED WITH SOCIAL STATUS

MELANESIA

Among the Koita a tobi is made for a married man, a married woman, and an unmarried male if an adult, but not for an unmarried girl or child.[1]

AUSTRALIA

In the Ovens River district of Victoria, the bodies of married people are burned, whereas others are buried.[2]

INDIA

In different Indian castes or tribes it is the custom to bury the bodies of the unmarried but to burn the bodies of the married.[3] The Kondayamkottai Maravars bury the unmarried but cremate the married.[4]

Among the Kurmi we find that poor families who cannot afford firewood are buried.[5] In Northern India the bodies of all low caste representatives are sometimes buried face downward to prevent the escape of the evil spirit.[6]

In Tibet and Mongolia corpses of the lowly, especially of the poor, are often exposed in fields, deserts, mountains, rocks, lonely ravines and sometimes in open places.[7]

Great ascetics (Sannyasis) and holy men (Samahus) are generally buried, and their tombs are called Samadhis.[8]

METHOD OF BURIAL INFLUENCED BY ENVIRONMENTAL CONDITIONS

AUSTRALIA

In the northern districts of the Kaimlarai country the burial was sometimes in soft ground. If there was no soft ground in the locality the body was placed in a hollow tree.[9]

[1] Seligmann, *Melanesians*, p. 161.
[2] Thomas, *The Natives of Australia*, p. 199.
[3] Fawcett, "The Kondayamkottai Maravars, a Dravidian Tribe of Tinnevelly, Southern India", *J.A.I.*, Vol. XXXIII (1903), p. 64 ; Thurston, *Castes and Tribes of S. India*, Vol. IV, p. 226, Vol. VI, p. 244.
[4] Fawcett, "The Kondayamkottai Maravars", *J.A.I.*, Vol. XXXIII (1903), p. 64.
[5] Russell, *Tribes and Castes of India*, Vol. IV, p. 73.
[6] Crooke, *Popular Religion of Northern India*, Vol. I, p. 269.
The Tlinkets threw the bodies of slaves into the sea. (Westermarck, Vol. II, p. 527, note 9.) The Law of the Twelve Tables prohibited the embalming of slaves. (Lex Duodecim Tabularum, X, 6.)
[7] Williams, *Brahmanism*, p. 369.
[8] Williams, *Hinduism*, p. 65n.
[9] Howitt, *Native Tribes of South East Australia*, p. 466.

The Umbaia Tribe do not bury their dead, like their neighbours, in trees, but put them on the ground, a practice which is due to the fact that over a large area of the country inhabited by this tribe there are no trees.[1]

It is very evident that environmental conditions influence the method of disposal of the body, whether such takes the form of earth, tree, cave or sea burial, or exposure to wild beasts, or cremation. Naturally environmental conditions figure in many complexes.

SIBERIA

Although we find cremation and exposure in the wilderness both resorted to amongst the Chukchee, yet exposure may be said to be their fundamental burial, such being encouraged by environmental conditions, due to the lack of fuel. On the contrary, the Koryak, living more to the south where there is an abundance of fuel, have adopted exclusively cremation. The Koryak in whose country there is dearth of fuel throw their dead into the sea from some steep rock.[2]

Here underground burial is difficult, because of climate conditions. Again, we find that only among the Kerk division (Koryak) possibly owing to the absence of forests, the dead are not cremated, but sunk into the sea.[3]

AFFECTED BY THE PHYSICAL CONDITION OF THE DECEASED
AUSTRALIA

Among the tribes inhabiting the district from the Murray River to Lacepede Bay, we find that the bodies of youths and adults in the prime of life are dried, whereas a different method of preparing the body for burial is seen in the case of others not in this category.[4] In Frazer Island, Queensland, old men, old women, and young women who are not fat are rolled in their rugs and buried.[5]

When a man is killed or dies in the vigor of manhood his nearest relatives summon all their friends to a feast. The body is skinned and then devoured amidst the wailing of women and the chanting of men.[6]

[1] Spencer and Gillen, *Northern Tribes of Central Australia*, p. 545.
[2] Bogoras, *The Chukchee*, J.N.P.E., Vol. VII, 2-3 (1907), p. 523.
[3] Jochelson, *The Koryak*, J.N.P.E., Vol. VI, 1 (1905), p. 104.
[4] Curr, *The Australian Race*, Vol. II, p. 248.
[5] Smyth, *The Aborigines of Victoria*, Vol. I, p. 121.
[6] *Memoirs of the Queensland Museum*, Vol. I (1915), p. 22.

Orientation of the Dead Correlated with their Original Home

Australia

Among the Arunta we find the custom that the body is buried with the face looking toward the place from which the spirit of the deceased was supposed to have come originally.[1]

Connected with the Birthplace of the Deceased

Australia

In Western Australia we are told that " dying persons, especially those dying from old age, generally express an earnest desire to be taken to their birth-place that they may die and be buried there. Parents will point out the spot where they were born so that when they become old and infirm, their children may know where they wish their bodies to be disposed of."[2]

Burial Dependent upon the Exigencies of the Occasion

Among the Wurunjerri we find that the body is burned if there is no time to dig a grave.[3] Likewise it is a custom of the natives of the Victorian tribes, if time is lacking for digging a grave, to place the body on a bier and to remove it a mile or two.[4]

Manner of Digging the Grave Dependent upon the Conception of the Resting Place of the Deceased

Australia

The Theddora of South-East Australia believe that the dead do not always remain in the grave but at times come out. Thus their graves are dug in cylindrical pits with a side chamber in which the dead body is placed, surrounded by pieces of wood. This arrangement is for the purpose of providing for egress if such is ever desired by the deceased.[5] Among the Ngarigo we find graves made like a well with a side chamber ; again, they were constructed by digging out a cavity just as we find among the Theddora.[6]

---

[1] Thomas, *The Native Tribes of Australia*, p. 193.
[2] Dawson, *Australian Aborigines*, p. 62.
[3] Howitt, *Native Tribes of South-East Australia*, p. 444.
[4] *Ibid*, p. 455.
[5] *Ibid*, p. 460.
[6] *Ibid*, p. 462.

AFFECTED BY THE LOCATION OF THE REALMS OF THE DEAD

MELANESIA

The practice of placing the dead in canoes and throwing them into the sea is associated with the belief that the home of the dead may be reached by water.[1] Although this may be true in certain specific instances, yet we have numerous other cases where the realms of the dead are to be reached by a passage across a large body of water, and where there is no such practice resorted to as placing the dead in canoes or of throwing the dead bodies into the sea.

---

[1] Rivers, *History of Melanesian Society*, Vol. II, p. 550.

CHAPTER XVI

MOURNING

AFFECTED BY RANK

MELANESIA

IN the Fiji Islands we find mourning for a king lasting from ten to twenty days. On these days the entire population fasted until evening and the coast for miles was tabooed. We note abstinence of the people from fish and fruits.[1] The mutilation of finger joints among the Fijians when in mourning is confined to the relatives of the deceased unless he is one of the highest chiefs.[2]

Persons who handle the corpse of a Fijian are forbidden to touch anything for a long time after a death has occurred. This period varies with the rank of the deceased. When great chiefs die, this restriction lasts from two to ten months; upon the demise of a petty chief it does not exceed one month, and when a commoner dies, a four days' taboo is considered sufficient.[3] A whole village will mourn for a chief of Waima and perhaps for an influential man from six to ten days by abstaining from fishing, hunting, and pot-making, and by doing as little gardening as possible.[4]

After the death of a man of some rank in Aurora, New Hebrides, his mother, or wives, or sisters throw ashes over their heads and backs. Men may walk about, but female mourners cannot go into the open and their faces may not be seen. They remain indoors and stay in the dark covered with a large mat reaching to the ground. For one hundred days the widow goes to weep at the grave morning and afternoon. The large mats which the women don remain on their heads as a sign of mourning. They likewise abstain from certain food.[5]

---

[1] Williams, *Fiji and the Fijians*, pp. 197-198.
[2] Frazer, *Belief in Immortality*, Vol. I, p. 451.
[3] *Ibid*, p. 450.
[4] Seligmann, *Melanesians*, p. 275.
[5] Codrington, *Melanesians*, p. 281.

The Fijian female mourners burn their skin into blisters by applying lighted rolls of bark cloth. In the Gazelle Peninsula women with blackened faces sleep on the grave for weeks.[1] If the deceased is a great chief, his corpse is almost covered with shell money and placed in a canoe which is put in a small house. The nearest female relatives are led to the house and under no consideration whatever are they allowed to depart from the hut until nothing but a skeleton remains. Then a solemn funeral takes place.[2] When a man of note is buried in the Duke of York Island the women make fires that the ghost might warm himself at them, and the female relatives blacken their faces for a long time.[3]

Affected by Sex

Melanesia

At Bartle Bay in British New Guinea a widow is forbidden to eat the same kind of food which her husband took during his last illness.[4] When a death takes place among the Roro-speaking tribes of British New Guinea, the female relatives lacerate their arms, legs, skulls, faces, and other parts of the body with shells. This they continue to do until the blood streams and they fall down exhausted.[5]

Australia

Among the Warramunga the women take very active part in the mourning. Here the hair of widows is cut and their bodies are covered with white pipe clay. During the mourning period they live in a small wurley apart from other camps.[6] In Australia, it is especially the women, and most conspicuously the widows, who mutilate themselves by cutting and laceration of the flesh.[7] We are told that upon the death of her husband a widow will seize fire brands and burn her breast and other parts of her body. A certain delight seems to be centred in this self-inflicted torture. Not content with

---

[1] Parkinson, *Dreissig Jahre in der Sudsee*, p. 78.
[2] Frazer, *Belief in Immortality*, Vol. I, p. 398.
[3] *Ibid*, p. 403.
[4] Seligmann, *Melanesians*, p. 617.
[5] Jouet, *La Société des Missionaires du Sacré Coeur Vicariats Apostoliques de la Mélanésie et de la Micronésie*, p. 30 ; quoted by Frazer, p. 197.
[6] Spencer and Gillen, *Northern Tribes of Central Australia*, p. 521.
[7] Frazer, *Belief in Immortality*, Vol. I, p. 154.

this burning, she takes the ashes in her hands, rubs them into her wounds and scratches her face until the blood appears.[1] Among the Kamilaroi, the mourners, and especially the women, cut their heads with tomahawks and allow the blood to dry.[2] The women of the Boulia district of Queensland scratch their thighs with stones or bits of glass. However, the men of the neighbouring section likewise make deeper lacerations on their thighs. The men and women of the Arunta tribes also disfigure themselves after a death. It is a custom among the Arunta for the female relatives of the deceased to cut their own and each other's heads so severely with clubs and digging sticks until blood streams from them on the grave.[3] Although men figure in many of the laceration ceremonies so characteristic of the Australian natives, yet the women take by far the more conspicuous part in such proceedings. Thus among some tribes of Victoria although both males and females disfigure themselves, it is especially the women, and above all the widows, who inflict severe injuries upon themselves when in mourning.[4] When we read of a burial on the Murray River, we learn that " around the bier were many women relatives of the deceased, wailing and lamenting bitterly, and lacerating their thighs, backs, and breasts with shells or flint until the blood flowed copiously from the gashes ".[5]

The men of the Binbinga tribe who belong to the opposite phratry from the deceased participate in a meal which consists of parts of his body, but no woman is permitted to do so, for females are not allowed to touch human flesh.[6]

In Melville Island the mother of the dead man, smeared with ochre, takes a prominent part in the dancing ceremonies connected with burial rites.[7] After the preliminary dance a large fire is lighted and two old men, who are tribal fathers of the dead man, go to it and singe the hair off their arms

[1] Smyth, *Aborigines of Victoria*, Vol. I, p. 105.

[2] Howitt, *Native Tribes of South-East Australia*, p. 466.

[3] Spencer and Gillen, *Native Tribes of Central Australia*, pp. 507-510.

[4] Stanbridge, " Tribes in the Central Part of Victoria ", *Transactions of the Ethnological Society of London, N.S.*, Vol. I (1861), p. 298.

[5] Eyre, *Journals of Expeditions of Discovery into Central Australia*, Vol. II, p. 347.

[6] Spencer and Gillen, *Northern Tribes of Central Australia*, p. 548.

[7] Spencer, *Native Tribes of the Northern Territory of Australia*, p. 233.

and legs. If they neglect to do so, it is believed that they will be seriously ill.[1] The mourning decorations of the women are likewise different from those of the men.[2]

In South Australia we find that after a death men shave their heads with mussel shells, whereas women use fire sticks for the same purpose.[3]

The natives of the Boulia district in colouring themselves for mourning use different patterns for males and females.[4]

Although the natives of Victoria resort to great mourning for a young man, such taking the form of lacerations, yet they indulge in very little weeping when a woman or old man dies.[5] In speaking of the aborigines of Australia, Oldfield says that for the death of a female, none, neither male nor female, mourn.[6] Bonney tells us that most of the women in New South Wales wear mourning.[7]

INDIA (SEX AND RANK)

In former times the Kataharayan, a fishing people on the Malabar Coast, intermitted their fishing three days after the death of a prince of Malabar.[8] When the parents of rich and respectable men die in Tibet, the children refrain from participating in marriage ceremonies and all festivities and undertake no lengthy journeys. Upon the death of the Dalai Lama or of the Tashi Lama, all work is suspended for seven days, public offices are closed, and markets are not held. The people likewise refrain from amusements and love-making. The women are forbidden to wear jewelry for thirty days, and neither men nor women put on new clothes. Here we see universal mourning observed for high officials.[9]

According to the Vishnu-Purana the time of impurity of a Brahman is ten days, for a Kshatriya twelve, for a Vaisya

---

[1] Spencer, *Native Tribes of the Northern Territory of Australia*, p. 233.

[2] *Ibid*, p. 234.

[3] Thomas, *The Natives of Australia*, p. 203.

[4] Roth, *Ethnological Studies among the North-West Central Queensland Aborigines*, p. 164.

[5] Smyth, *The Aborigines of Victoria*, p. 121.

Oldfield, " The Aborigines of Australia ", *Transactions of the Ethnographical Society*, Vol. III (1865), p. 248.

[7] Bonney, " On Some Customs of the Aborigines of New South Wales " *J.A.I.*, Vol. XIII (1883-1884), p. 135.

[8] Iyer, *The Cochin Tribes and Castes*, Vol. I, p. 265.

[9] Das, *Journey to Lhasa and Central Tibet*, p. 256.

fourteen, for a Sutra one month or thirty-one days. The higher the caste, the less the inconvenience.[1]

INDIA

When anyone dies among the Kunbi, a great agricultural caste, the male mourners shave their heads.[2] The Kurmi male mourners likewise shave after a funeral.[3] The same custom is practised by the Dhākar, a small caste whose members are of illegitimate descent.[4] The chief mourner of the Dhīmar caste of fishermen shaves ten days after a death has occurred.[5]

Dubois states that the Hindu widow is in mourning till her death. Her head is shorn once a month, she is not allowed to chew betel, she is permitted no jewels (except one plain ornament), no coloured clothes, only white ones, no marks can be placed on her forehead, no saffron on her face and body. She can partake of no amusements and is not supposed to attend family festivities for her presence is looked upon as an evil omen.[6] However, for the chief mourner, the mourning lasts only for one year.[7]

SIBERIA

Among the Koryaks the designs on a woman's funeral coat are less complicated and the embroidery is not as elaborate as that of a man's. A woman's funeral garment is made of reindeer skins with the hair inside it, whereas that of a man is of the skins of white fawns.[8]

AUSTRALIA

The widows of the Warramunga, living on Termant's Creek, are sometimes not allowed to speak for as long a period as

---

[1] Williams, *Religious Life and Thought in India*, p. 306.

The Natchez mourned for the common dead for three days, while those who fell in battle were honoured with more protracted and grievous lamentation. (Jones, *Antiquities of the South Indians*, p. 105, quoted by Yarrow, *Introduction to the Mortuary Customs of the North American Indians*, p. 77.)

After a sacred chief's death in Samoa, the whole of the lagoon was taboo. There could be no boating nor fishing. (Brown, *Melanesians and Polynesians*, p. 281.)

[2] Russell, *Tribes and Castes of India*, Vol. IV, p. 37.

[3] *Ibid*, p. 78.   [4] *Ibid*, Vol. II, p. 479.   [5] *Ibid*, Vol. II, p. 506.

[6] Dubois, *Hindu Manners and Customs*, Vol. II, p. 356.

[7] *Ibid*, p. 495.

[8] Jochelson, *The Koryak, J.N.P.E.*, Vol. VI (1905), p. 105.

twelve months, during which time their only way of communication is by means of a gesture language.[1]

At the Urpmilchima, or final mourning ceremony, as it is conducted at the Alice Springs group, and when the Chimurilia is complete, no words are spoken, and the only sound is the wailing of the women.[2] The women of the Wakelbura tribe also cut themselves with stone knives and at times with broken glass.[3]

The silence injunction among the Warramunga falls to the lot of the women, who are placed under a strict ban of silence for an interval of one year or even two years. This is participated in by the wife, mother, sister, daughter-in-law. It is a common thing to find the greater number of women in any camp refraining from speaking. With widows, mothers, and mothers-in-law this ban extends over the whole period of mourning, and even at the close of this period the women wish to remain silent and persist in using the gesture language in which they are adepts.[4] Amongst the Gnanji the mother and wives of the dead man are under the silence ban until the final burial ceremonies are concluded.[5]

Although no woman of the Central Australian tribes may mention the name of the deceased, the restriction on males is not so absolute.

[1] Spencer and Gillen, *Native Tribes of Central Australia*, pp. 500-502.
[2] *Ibid*, p. 505.
[3] Howitt, *Native Tribes of South-East Australia*, p. 471.
[4] Spencer and Gillen, *Northern Tribes of Central Australia*, p. 525.
[5] *Ibid*, p. 547.
In South America, as in many other places, women especially were made to bear the burden of mourning regulations. The widows of the deceased members of the Matse tribe of Ewhe were compelled to remain in the dark part of the hut, had to sit on stone instead of a stove, were forced to be attired in clothing similar to that in which a corpse was to be buried, must sleep on the mat upon which the deceased lay, could not appear on the main street of the village, and during the mourning period they could talk to no one. Besides the above, various other restrictions were imposed upon them. Among the Mbayas and Guaycuru the women and slaves were forbidden to speak for three or four months. (Hartland, article in *Hasting's*, Vol. IV, p. 438.) Whereas in Malta the women were secluded for forty days, the men went out on the seventh day. (Bussuttil, *Holiday Customs in Malta*, p. 131; quoted by Hartland, article in *Hasting's*, Vol. IV, p. 439.) The female relatives of the Duke of York Islanders smear their faces with black for a long time after the death of one of the members of their tribe. (Brown, *Melanesians and Polynesians*, p. 390.)
Although the silence injunction is invariably connected with women, yet an instance is cited where men as well as women observe this custom. Among the Lkungen of Vancouver Island, widows and widowers are not allowed to speak for two days after a burial. After this period they may speak a little. (Hartland, *Ritual and Belief*, p. 254.)

It is interesting to observe that the silence ban is by no means identified with the death-situation alone. Thus it is very frequently imposed upon youths at the time of their initiation. We hear of the ban of silence as a prominent feature of the initiation of youths among the Arunta. After a native has become identified as a member of the Unmatjera tribe we hear of his release from the silence restriction which has been imposed upon him.[1] At the ceremony of the Engwara the silence ban is likewise removed.[2] In the initiation ceremonies of the Warramunga[3] and Binbinga tribes, it also figures.[4] It is a custom of the Umbaia tribe to impose the silence restriction upon strangers.[5]

When describing the death customs of the aborigines of Victoria, Smyth tells us that when a woman or child dies, none but the bereaved exhibit sorrow.[6]

DEPENDENT UPON AGE

AUSTRALIA

During the performance of the Morlil, a ceremony practised among the Kakadu tribe, little cakes, made out of lily seeds, are eaten by the older men only, and the younger men are not permitted to eat them.[7] Furthermore, the older women would paint themselves all over with yellow ochre or mud, and wear the special form of bracelet called kundama on both arms, and the younger girls would paint themselves with red ochre.[8] Nobody paints his body for mourning if a young child dies in North-West Central Queensland.[9]

.   .   .   .   .

With the StatlumH of British Columbia the mourning period varied with age ; the younger the man, the longer the abstinence. Elder people might eat fresh salmon as soon as the first

---

[1] Spencer and Gillen, *Northern Tribes of Central Australia*, p. 344.
[2] *Ibid*, p. 383.   [3] *Ibid*, pp. 352-353, 363.
[4] *Ibid*, p. 369.   [5] *Ibid*, p. 221.
[6] Smyth, *The Aborigines of Victoria*, Vol. I, p. 99.
Among the Eskimo of Baffin Land and Hudson Bay we find that when a person who conveys a dead body to its place of burial returns home, he must remain there for three days and nights. The male relatives may leave the house for a short time, but the women must remain within. (Boas, *Bulletin of the American Museum of Natural History*, Vol. XV (1907), p. 144.)
[7] Spencer, *Native Tribes of the Northern Territory of Australia*, p. 244.
[8] *Ibid*, p. 244.
[9] Roth, *Ethnological Studies among the North-West Coast Queensland Aborigines*, p. 164.

salmon run was over and the fish had arrived in numbers and
there was no danger of their being driven away. Salmon
was supposed to be peculiarly susceptible to the influence of
dead bodies.[1]

RELATIONSHIP

AUSTRALIA

When one of the Dieri is dying, his relatives separate into
two groups, those more closely related to him which include
the Ngaperi, Ngata-mura, Noa, and those of the Kami and
Kadi who are closely connected with the deceased, and a
second group which comprises the Ngandri, the Ngatani,
Kaku, Kaka, Tidnari, Buyulu, Neyi, Ngatata, to whom may
be added the Kami, Kadi if not too distantly related to the
dying man.

Although those of the first group sit close to the dying
person, and even after death throw themselves upon the body,
those of the second group remain at some distance away and
are most careful to avoid looking at the face of the deceased.[2]

The distant relatives of the Dieri upon the occasion of a
death, and also those of the Kami and Kadi, if not of too
remote tribal relation, paint themselves with karku (red ochre)
mixed with tuna (gypsum). The Ngaperi, the Ngata-mura,
and Noa, with the closer related Kami and Kadi, paint themselves with tuna only.[3]

DEPENDENT UPON LOCAL CLAN AFFILIATION

MELANESIA

When a Ufuapie woman of Mekeo marries, she goes to live
in her husband's village, but when she dies she is carried back
to her own village. Her husband's village mourns only until
the removal takes place. Mourning customs such as ceremonial taboos and refraining from dancing are observed not
only in the dead woman's clan, but in all the clans of the
village.[4]

All the subjects of a deceased paramount chief of the
Trobriands and the natives at Kitava, except those belonging

[1] Hill-Tout, "Report on the Ethnology of the StatlumH of British
Columbia", *J.A.I.*, Vol. XXXV, p. 139.
[2] Howitt, *Native Tribes of South-East Australia*, p. 447.
[3] *Ibid.*
[4] Seligmann, *Melanesians*, pp. 358-359.

to his own clan, wear black mourning pigment. The same custom is in vogue when a village chief dies, and his paramount chief goes into mourning for him if the dead man is not of his own totem.[1]

CONNECTED WITH CLAN SPIRIT

AUSTRALIA

A man of the Arunta tribe of Central Australia is compelled to cut himself when in mourning for his father-in-law. Otherwise his wife may be given to another man to satisfy the chagrin of the offended ghost.[2] Spencer and Gillen describe a death in the Warramunga tribe when a man of the Tjunguri class died. The men who gashed their sides upon this occasion stood to him in one or the other of the following relationships ; grandfather on the mother's side, mother's brother, brother of the dead man's wife, her mother's brother.[3]

When a man of any particular class of the Warramunga tribe dies, only the men who stand in a particular relationship to him must cut themselves. Among this tribe the lacerations are performed by those who stand to the deceased in the tribal relationship of grandfather on the mother's side, mother's brothers, or brothers-in-law, brothers of the mother of his wife, and wife's brothers. The tribal fathers cut their whiskers off and others also cut their hair closely and smear their scalps with pipe-clay.[4]

In the Urabunna tribe the hair is cut from the head of the dead by a man who stands in the relationship of Kupuka (younger brother) to the deceased. During the mourning ceremonies, survivors who stand in certain tribal relationships also cut their own hair and this is mixed with that of the dead man and woven into a girdle to which the special name of tata is given. This is worn only during the avenging expedition. No man of one moiety is permitted to see the hair of a man of another moiety while it is being made into this girdle. Spencer and Gillen call our attention to the fact that in the Urabunna we meet with a custom not practised elsewhere. If a man's actual elder sister dies, his hair is cut off after her decease, and mixed with hers to form the girdle.

[1] Seligmann, *Melanesians*, p. 718.
[2] Spencer and Gillen, *Native Tribes of Central Australia*, p. 500.
[3] Spencer and Gillen, *Northern Tribes of Central Australia*, pp. 516-522.
[4] Spencer and Gillen, *Across Australia*, Vol. II, pp. 428-429.

This, they claim, may be associated with the idea of the alternation of sexes at successive reincarnations, since this custom seems to place the woman on the same level as the man. Among the Warramunga, the whiskers of the deceased are cut immediately after death by the dead man's son, who presents them to a man who is either the actual or the tribal husband of the daughter of the dead man's sister, and upon whom it is incumbent to avenge the death.[1]

---

[1] Spencer and Gillen, *Northern Tribes of Central Australia*, pp. 543-544.

CHAPTER XVII

TABOOS

CONNECTED WITH SEX

AUSTRALIA

AMONG the Arunta, the Urabunna, the Kaitish, the Warramunga, the Tjingilla, the Binbinga, the hair which is cut off the deceased and made in waist-girdles, tana, chantimmi, and sent on the avenging expedition, is sacred and is never allowed to be seen by women and children. The only occasions when hair is ever destroyed are those on which it is cut off as a symbol of mourning and then it is immediately burnt.[1]

No woman is allowed to participate in the cannibal feast in the Gulf of Carpentaria region.[2]*

INDIA

Among the Kondayamkottai Maravars when there is no son to perform the funeral ceremonies, the husband acts as official funeral director, but a woman never participates in this rite.[3]†

SIBERIA

The Reindeer Chukchee forbid any kind of woman's work with needle and scraper during the performance of the funeral

---

[1] Spencer and Gillen, *Northern Tribes of Central Australia*, p. 604.

[2] Thomas, *The Natives of Australia*, p. 196.

* In a group of small islands in the western extremity of Dutch New Guinea the women are forbidden to set food for the dead in shrines, for if so, they would be childless.

Among the Nandi of East Africa upon the death of a married woman the youngest daughter wears her garment inside out while the other relatives put rope on their ornaments and shave their heads. When unmarried people die, the female relatives cover their ornaments with rope, while the male relatives shave their heads. (Hollis, *The Nandi*, pp. 71-74.)

[3] Fawcett, "The Kondayamkottai Maravars", *J.A.I.*, Vol. XXXIII (1903), p. 64.

† It is not the custom of the females of the Andaman Islands to attend a funeral although they do their part in preparing the body for burial. (Man, "Aboriginal Inhabitants of the Andaman Islands", *J.A.I.*, Vol. XXII (1885), p. 144.)

ceremony.[1]* In Kamenskoye, no woman goes in the funeral procession.[2]

DEPENDENT UPON RELATIONSHIP[3]

MELANESIA

At Tubetube, in British New Guinea, the children of the deceased may not eat any cocoanuts from their father's trees, nor even from any trees grown in his hamlet, nor of any garden produce grown in its vicinity. Likewise they must abstain from all the pork of pigs fattened in their deceased parents' village. However, these restrictions do not include the brothers, sisters, and other relatives of the departed. The relatives who have taken part in the burial remain at the grave five or six days. They are not allowed to drink water, but are permitted a little heated cocoanut milk. They are allowed to eat only a little yam and other vegetable food.[4]

In the Mekeo district of British New Guinea a widower forfeits all civil rights. He is an outcast in the true sense of the term. He is not allowed to go in public, he cannot cultivate his garden, and is forbidden to fish or hunt except at night.[5]

AUSTRALIA

Among the Warramunga the silence ban is imposed upon those who stand in a certain relationship, either actual or tribal, to the deceased.[6]

---

[1] Bogoras, *Memoirs in American Museum of Natural History*, Vol. XI, p. 521.

* The inhabitants of the villages of Baffin Land and Hudson Strait are not allowed to go hunting for one day, and the women must refrain from all work whatever. (Boas, *Bulletin American Museum of Natural History*, Vol. XV, 1907, p. 121.)
The Eskimo women are forbidden to comb their hair, to wash their faces, to dry their boots or stockings. (*Ibid.*)

[2] Jochelson, *The Koryak*, J.N.P.E., Vol. VI (1905), p. 111.

[3] Inasmuch as varying degrees of mourning in connection with the degree of blood relationship are so common in primitive, antique, and modern society only a few of such instances have been cited. The nature of mourning observances are of varying intensity, from the most exacting restrictions placed upon widows and widowers, to the trifling taboos imposed upon the most distant relatives.

[4] Seligmann, *Melanesians*, p. 613 et seq.

[5] Guis, "Les Canaques: Mort-Deuil," *Mission Catholiques*, Vol. XXXIX (1902), p. 208.

[6] Spencer and Gillen, *Northern Tribes of Central Australia*, p. 525.

DEPENDENT UPON PHRATRY RELATIONS

AUSTRALIA

Among the Arunta, the individuals who are identified with certain phratry groups may never mention the name of the deceased, nor may they go near the grave until after the ceremony of the Urpmilchima has been performed. Those who belong to another phratry group, when the time of mourning is over, speak of the dead and mention his name without fear of offending the Ulthana, or the man's spirit in ghost form. The Gammona of the dead man are not only prohibited from mentioning his name, but they are not permitted to attend the burial ceremonies, nor the subsequent marriage ceremony conducted at the grave.[1]

CONNECTED WITH SUB-CLASS

AUSTRALIA

In Central Australia, the name of the deceased may be mentioned by the men of the two sub-classes to which the wife's father or the wife's brother of the dead man belonged.[2]

DEPENDENT UPON THE SOCIAL STATUS

INDIA

The time of impurity for a Brahman is ten days, for a Kshatriya twelve, and for a Sutra one month or thirty-one days. Among the Lodi, an agricultural caste, the impurity period for the higher clans is twelve days and for the lower sub-castes three days.[3] The Dhimar, a caste of fishermen, mourn only one day for children whose ears are not pierced, but for others, ten days.[4]

---

[1] Spencer and Gillen, *Native Tribes of Central Australia*, pp. 499-500.
[2] *Ibid*, p. 526.
[3] Russell, *Tribes and Castes of India*, Vol. IV, p. 118.
[4] *Ibid*, Vol. II, p. 506.

CHAPTER XVIII

WOMAN'S CONNECTION WITH FUNERAL RITES

MELANESIA

AT Saa, the women sit around the corpse and wait.[1]* In the Banks Islands women are hired to wait about the corpse.[2] At Ureparapara the women also wait at the ceremony for driving away the ghost.[3] The women of Gaua, in Santa Maria, watch the corpse until nothing but skin and bones are left.[4]

When a chief named Gorai died in the Shortland Islands, the women performed the funeral dance round the pyre until the body was cremated.[5]

However, at the elaborate funeral dance performed by the Western Islanders on the Island of Pulu, no woman or uninitiated man might witness the operation of making the head-dresses or masques, nor could any woman impersonate the dead, which rôle was always acted by the men.[6]†

During the entire time the body is kept in the house of a deceased Trobriand Islander of Northern Massim, the women indulge in almost continuous wailing, while men manifest their grief by pressing their noses and sniffing.[7]

Among the natives of Murua we find that burial is the duty of the women ; they construct a trench near the village and here they place their dead. Women respectfully exhume the

---

[1] Codrington, *Melanesians*, p. 261.

* Roman women who were in the funeral procession were in the habit of crying aloud, tearing their hair, and lacerating their cheeks. (Prop. III, 13, 27.)

[2] Codrington, *Melanesians*, p. 267.

[3] *Ibid*, p. 270.

[4] *Ibid*, p. 268.

[5] Cambridge, *Anthropological Expedition to Torres Straits*, Vol. V, pp. 252-256.

[6] Brown, *Melanesians and Polynesians*, p. 213.

† At one time in Rome there was a scruple about admitting women to the sacred rites. (Fowler, *Religious Experiences of the Romans*, p. 30.)

[7] Seligmann, *Melanesians*, pp. 715-716.

bones of the deceased and give them to the nearest relatives of the dead man.[1]*

At the celebration given in honour of the dead among the Mafulu Mountain People of British New Guinea, women stay with the dying, and after the death has been announced the incoming women, but not the men, arrive smeared with mud.[2] Each woman, after seeing the body, comes out and sits on the platform of the house or on the ground; after the women cease wailing they commence a funeral song in which all members of the female sex join.[3]

AUSTRALIA

At the ceremony following the final preparation of the body for burial, the men perform certain totemic ceremonies.[4] The second part of the Mortil, a ceremony connected with the burial of a native of the Kakadu tribe, is performed mainly by the women.[5]

For some days after a death the women of Cooper Creek indulge in an occasional lamentation, but the men never give utterance to grief.[6] Although only the women participate in the wailing, yet they are not allowed to come near the corpse immediately after the simple ceremony following a death.[7]

In the Adelaide tribe the grave is dug with women's sticks.[8]

At Encounter Bay we find that the ground upon which a man died is dug up by his wives or the women related to him, occasionally assisted by the men.[9] In Western Australia the mother and other women form a group about the dying one, and weeping, scratch their cheeks, foreheads and noses with their nails. Further lamentation is indulged in by

[1] Seligmann, *Melanesians*, pp. 727-728.

* The Wichita usually employ women to bury the dead. (Yarrow, *Mortuary Customs of the North American Indians*, p. 8.) In Samoa, emblaming is done exclusively by women. (Turner, *Nineteen Years in Polynesia*, p. 231.)

[2] Williamson, *The Mafulu Mountain People of British New Guinea*, pp. 243-244.

[3] *Ibid*, p. 259.

The Iroquois dance for the dead, known as Ohé wä, must be performed by women only. (Morgan, *League of the Iroquois*, p. 287.)

[4] Spencer, *Native Tribes of the Northern Territory of Australia*, p. 252.

[5] *Ibid*, pp. 244-245.

[6] Smyth, *The Aborigines of Victoria*, Vol. I, p. 119.

[7] *Ibid*, p. 101.

[8] Thomas, *The Natives of Australia*, p. 197.

[9] Wyatt, *Some Account of the Manners and Superstitions of the Adelaide and Encounter Bay Aboriginal Tribes*, p. 164.

women who subsequently join those congregated about the dying man. Members of the female sex also wail at the grave.[1]*

INDIA

No woman joins the funeral of an orthodox Hindu.[2]

When a person dies among the Dards, women assemble, weep, and tell the virtues of the departed. After accompanying the funeral procession for about fifty yards, they return to the house to continue their lamentations.[3] Among the Kondayamkottai Maravars no obsequies are ever performed by women.[4] The Todas purify the places connected with a funeral only when a male dies.[5]

There has been much interesting discussion among scholars of Indian history concerning suttee, or widow-burning, not so much in reference to the ceremony itself, but as to the time it was first practised in India.

As far as we can see the Rig-Veda does not contemplate the rite of suttee anywhere.[6] A stanza in the last funeral hymn requests the widow to rise from the pyre and take the hand of her new husband, presumably a brother of the deceased.[7] From the Rig-Veda we learn that the wife occupies a position of greater honour in the household than before, Hopkins says the fact that in the funeral obsequies of the Rig-Veda the widow lies down beside the body of the deceased husband, is in itself sufficient evidence that this custom was merely a survival, and was no longer practised in the Rig-Vedic period. We find the suttee alluded to in the Atharva-Veda, the Mahabharata, the Ramayana, and mentioned in later Sanskrit literature as belonging to the classic period. The sources used by Diodoros Sikelos place its existence as early

---

[1] Grey, *Expeditions of Discovery in Northwest and West Australia*, Vol. II, p. 320.

* We read in *Jeremiah*, " Call for the wailing women that they may come, and let them make haste and take up a wailing for us."

Among the Yoruba-speaking people the conventional mourning is the duty of the women of the household, who utter loud lamentations while the men are feasting. (Ellis, *The Yoruba-Speaking People*, p. 157.)

[2] Crooke, *The Natives of Northern India*, p. 217.

[3] *Indian Antiquary*, Vol. I, p. 13.

[4] Fawcett, "Kondayamkottai Maravars", *J.A.I.*, Vol. XXXIII (1903), p. 64.

[5] Rivers, *The Todas*, p. 390.

[6] Hoernle and Stark, *History of India*, p. 10.

[7] *Rv.* X, 18.

as the fourth century B.C.[1] Hopkins is of the opinion that the
burning of widows begins rather late in India, and was at
first probably confined to the pet wife of royal persons, the
widow being sacrificed as the body of her husband was
cremated. Dubois does not see any reason for its origin,
but his general view would be in accord with that later held
by Hopkins, that it perhaps originated in the noble caste of
the Rajas. The very fact that the law book of Vishnu
advocates the practice of suttee and its preference for female
ancestors, causes the author of the *Religions of India* to place
this manual among the later books.[2] Again, referring to the
Epic Mārkandeya Purana, and noting its new traits, we read
" The sacrifice of widows is recognized in the case of wives of
kings as a means of securing bliss for a woman ".[3] Although
the practice of suttee seems to have been on the decline in the
Vedic period, yet it appears to have been usual among the
warrior class.

Suttee, or widow-burning, is derived from the Sanskrit
" sati ", a true wife. This title of honour was applied to a
wife whose devotion to her husband caused her to sacrifice
herself on the funeral pyre. Her religion was to serve her
husband and to die, if worthy of the honour, at the funeral
pyre.[4] Nickolaos Damaskenos, a Greek historian, who wrote
toward the close of the first century B.C., says in his *Paradoxical Customs*, that when the Hindus die there is a great
rivalry among the wives, each striving to be burnt at the pyre
of her husband, and many others refer to the same fact.
Although this custom among Hindu women does not seem
to have been compulsory, yet the life of the widow was rendered
intolerable if she refused to submit to this trying ordeal.
In support of this theory we might cite the experience of Ibn
Batutu, who visited Hindustan in 1325 A.D. Notwithstanding that this deals with a period very much later than the one
we have under consideration, yet it seems to throw decided
light upon the early rite of suttee. " A woman burning
herself with her husband is not considered an absolute
necessity, but it is encouraged."[5] By this means her family

[1] Dutt, *History of India*, Vol. IX, p. 98.
[2] Hopkins, *The Religions of India*, p. 441.
[3] *Ibid*, p. 369.
[4] Dutt, *History of India*, Vol. IX, p. 76.
[5] *Ibid*, p. 76.

become ennobled. If she refuses to be a participant in the ceremony, she is ever afterward compelled to clothe herself coarsely and remain among her relatives. Abraham Roger, a Dutch missionary to India in the first half of the seventeenth century, corroborates this evidence. Those who survive, he tells us, have their hair shorn, they may eat no betel, they may never marry again, nor wear any jewelry. If after undertaking the duty of a sati the widow recedes, she incurs the penalty of defilement, but she may be purified by observing the feast of the Prájápatya.[1] We have a very interesting account of suttee from the Persian treatise *Dabistan*. "When a woman becomes a suttee the Almighty pardons all the sins committed by wife or husband, and they remain a long time in paradise, nay, even if her husband were in hell, the wife by this means draws him from thence." Moreover, the suttee in a future birth returns not to the female state, but she who becomes not a suttee is never emancipated from it.[2]

SIBERIA

Two small, rough wooden carvings of female figures, one with a child on her back, and the other with two children, one on her back, and the other at her breast, were obtained by Bogoras of two Koryak women. These women claim that the figures represent their female ancestor who was buried or was left dead with her child in her house. The myths likewise inform us that such a form of disposing of the dead was in existence in former times.[3]

---

[1] Colebrooke, *Life and Essays*, Vol. II, p. 137.
[2] Dutt, *History of India*, Vol. IX, p. 80.
[3] Jochelson, *The Koryak*, *J.N.P.E.*, Vol. VI (1905), p. 114.
    Among the old Peruvians, a dead prince's wives would hang themselves to be of service to the deceased in the next world, and many of his attendants would be buried in his fields or favourite haunts, so that his soul on its way through these places might take their souls along for future service. The Peruvians say that their reason for sacrificing property to the dead was that "they have seen, or thought they saw, those who had long been dead walking adorned with the things which were buried with them and accompanied by their wives who had been buried alive". (Ciezade Leon, p. 161 ; Rivers and Tschndi, *Peruvian Antiquities*, pp. 186-200 ; quoted by Tylor, *Primitive Culture*, Vol. I, p. 488.)
    At the funerals of chiefs in the Florida and Carolina Islands, all male relatives and wives were slain. (Yarrow, *An Introduction to the Mortuary Customs of the North American Indians*, p. 73.) We find it a common custom among the old north-west Indians to bury with the dead a living slave, a practice which is common in Mexico, South America, and Africa. (*Ibid*, p. 87.)

After the body of a deceased Chukchee has been disposed of, the two oldest women must meet the funeral cortege.[1]*

The instances cited show that the custom of immolating females at the funerals of their husbands, or of sacrificing children at the death of their mothers, was by no means uncommon in the Hindu, Siberian, Melanesian, and Australian areas, and further investigation shows that such a rite is identified with other peoples and localities. If we examine the motive which prompted such a practice, we will find that the survivors accentuate their desire to provide for the comfort and dignity of the deceased in the other world. Furthermore, it is evident that this sacrifice reaches its greatest extent at the funeral of a king or chief. Not only is this especially true of the Hindu area, but it is also characteristic of other countries. It is interesting to note that the custom of burying alive with the corpse is recalled by Cæsar and Mela of the Gauls,[2] and also we hear of it as identified with the Thracians.[3] This certainly is not incompatible with the idea we have advanced that the more sacred the individual, the greater is the amount of pollution and evil which he is supposed to radiate. At first sight this seeming mark of affection may appear to be contradictory to the theory which we have before suggested in reference to the dread attitude toward the ghosts of the dead. But even here, too, we see a desire to propitiate the spirit of the departed who otherwise might make it most uncomfortable for the survivors. However, we are fully aware that other motives might have actuated the friends and relatives of the deceased. Thus in some areas, such as Australia and Siberia, the reason for the immolation of the child might have been occasioned by the scarcity of the food supply, and the inability to provide for the young one without the assistance of the mother; then, too, the babe might afford its parent some comfort, and thus there would be less need for propitiation. What is of special interest is the desire so often expressed by the women to accompany their husbands. This in many instances was influenced by purely materialistic considerations,

[1] Bogoras, *The Chukchee*, *J.N.P.E.*, Vol. VII, 2-3 (1907), p. 528.
* It is interesting to note the importance of women in the mythology of the American Indian. (Brinton, *Myths of the New World*, pp. 178-180.)
[2] Cæsar, Bell. Gall., VI, 19 ; Mela., III, 2.
[3] Mela., II, 2.

inasmuch as we read that such a wife was regarded as being ennobled and often women were willing to undergo the ceremony, believing that if they did so, their present state of happiness would continue in the world of the dead, and their husbands would still be in a position to acquiesce to many of their wishes. When we consider the social status of the Hindu woman perhaps no stronger appeal could have been made than the reward that she was no longer to enter the female state, but by performing the practice of suttee, in the next reincarnation, hers would be the fate of a male.

CHAPTER XIX

TOTEMIC CONCEPTIONS

RITES CONNECTED WITH TOTEMISM

MELANESIA

RIVERS tells us that important totemic features in connection with burial are found in the Shortland Islands. Bones of the dead are thrown into places called keno, each clan having its own keno. It is believed that the bones are swallowed by fishes, animals, or mysterious beings. Sometimes the animals are included in Mr. Wheeler's list of totems of the clan, at other times they may be classed in the same category, for " in each case the dead person is regarded as the ' fabin ' of the animal or other being ". Fabin is a term of relationship reciprocal to tete and tua, terms for grandparents, and also for the totem. The keno is looked upon as the nanu or soul of the dead man.[1]

AUSTRALIA

The Wotjobaluk, of what is now the Wimmera district of Victoria, have every totem connected with a certain point of the compass. A man is buried with his head toward the point of the compass appropriate to his totem.[2]

When a death occurs among the Wanduman and Mudburra natives the totemic plant or animal may not be eaten until after the performance of a ceremony which takes place three or four weeks after the final placing of the bones in the tree grave. When this is performed, two or three old Kadugo (fathers, fathers' brothers) and Tababa (fathers' fathers) go into the bush and secure some of the totemic plant or animal of the dead man.[3]

If a man of any totemic group dies among the Tjutju, his animal and plant is taboo to all members of his totemic

---

[1] Rivers, *History of Melanesian Society*, Vol. II, p. 268.
[2] Howitt, *Native Tribes of South-East Australia*, p. 453,
[3] Spencer, *Native Tribes of the Northern Territory of Australia*, p. 250.

group until after the performance of a ceremony called Orkan.[1]

In the Mungarai tribe, at the ceremony following the final preparation of the bones for burial, the men perform the totemic ceremony, accompanied by the clanging of boomerangs. The lurkun (bough coffin) is decorated with the design of the man's own totem. The ceremonies are those which belong to the totemic group of his own sub-class and the one associated with it.[2]

A year after a burial it is customary among the Binbinga to place the bones of the deceased in a coffin decorated with the dead man's totem. The men, who have retired to a special camp where the coffin decorated with the designs of the dead man's totem is set up, all night sing and perform corroborees referring to the totem of their departed tribesman.[3]

In the course of conversation, Unkurta (a jew lizard) asked Qualpa (a long-tailed rat totem), " What do you do when another man dies " ? He replied, " I do not bury him, I throw him anywhere along the ground ". Then Unkurta said it was not good to throw him away like that, but if he felt real sorry, he ought to bury him in a tree, and said, " Tell your sons to put you up in a tree when you are dead, and tell them to teach other men to do the same ".[4]*

Among the Arunta we find the belief that the souls of the dead of the plum-tree totem congregate at a certain place in the mulga scrub, and in the Warramunga tribe the spirits of deceased persons who had black snakes for their totems haunt certain gum trees. The same belief is found in other tribes of Central Australia.[5]

Thus we have seen the following totemic considerations :

(1) A connection between the myths relating to totemic ancestors and tree-burial.

(2) Life after death associated with totemic clan.

---

[1] Spencer, *Native Tribes of the Northern Territory of Australia*, p. 198.

[2] *Ibid*, p. 252.

[3] Spencer, *Across Australia*, Vol. II, pp. 475-476.

[4] Spencer, *Native Tribes of the Northern Territory of Australia*, see " Burial and Mourning Ceremonies ", Chapter VI, pp. 228-262.

* Also discussed on page 215.

[5] Spencer and Gillen, *Northern Tribes of Central Australia*, p. 147.

(3) Burial in certain directions determined by the class and totem.

(4) Taboo of the totemic plant or animal of the dead man until after the final tree-burial.

(5) Coffin decorations—the totem of the deceased.

(6) In life after death, the clannishness of certain ghosts is due to their totemic connections.

CHAPTER XX

DESTRUCTION OF PROPERTY

DIFFERENT CONCEPTIONS AS TO WHAT CONSTITUTES A MAN'S PERSONALITY

MELANESIA

IN Florida we find that after a man's death his fruit trees are cut down. This practice is prompted by respect and affection, not with any notion that these things will be of service to him in the world of the ghosts. He partook of them when alive, and as he will never eat again, no one else shall.[1] The cocoanut and bread-fruit trees of a dead man are cut down in Saa by his friends, such an act being prompted by kindly motives. They deny that such things follow a man after his death.[2] When a Sulka dies his plantation is laid waste and his young fruit trees are cut down ; but the ripe fruits are given to the living. His pigs are slaughtered, and his weapons are broken.[3] On the death of one of the natives of Mabniag, one of the Western Islands, the mourners went to the gardens of the deceased, slashed the taro, threw down the cocoanuts, pulled up the sweet potatoes, and destroyed the bananas. This, they said, was done " for the sake of the dead man, and it was like ' good bye ' ".[4] Immediately after the funeral of a native of Tubetube in British New Guinea, a brother of the deceased cuts down two or three of the dead man's cocoanut trees.[5] At Wagawaga several of the cocoanut trees belonging to the deceased are cut down, and both nuts and trees are allowed to rot on the ground.[6]

Perhaps different motives may have originally prompted the survivors to destroy the property of a deceased member of their community. Doubtless selfish as well as unselfish

---

[1] Codrington, *Melanesians*, p. 255.
[2] *Ibid*, p. 263.
[3] Frazer, *Belief in Immortality*, Vol. I, p. 399.
[4] Cambridge, *Anthropological Expedition to Torres Straits*, Vol. V, p. 250.
[5] Seligmann, *Melanesians of British New Guinea*, p. 613.
[6] *Ibid*, p. 611.

considerations entered into this ceremony. Thus we have seen the almost universal tendency to propitiate the spirit of the departed, lest it shall return and be chagrined at some lack of courtesy on the part of the living relatives and friends. As a result, every device was resorted to to gain the goodwill of the deceased, for otherwise the living would stand in constant dread of being haunted by the spirits of the dead. When the property of the deceased was buried with him, this was done not merely to give his possessions over to the dead, but it was also regarded as a benefit to the community. Then, too, the destruction of his personal property might have been influenced by the fact that his relatives would thus be freed from the death pollution. The view of Frazer who attributes the destruction of property to the conception that such an act supplies the needs of the ghost, and that custom is practised because of the overpowering dread of the corpse experienced by the living,[1] does not apply to all cases. Such a motive certainly does not account for the destruction of fruit trees. Again, the evidence does not warrant the conclusion of McGee,[2] when describing the death customs of the Sioux who states that the more strictly personal property was destroyed at the death of the owner. Nor does his statement of the theory of some who claim that the purpose of such a ceremony was to avoid disputes about ownership, seem at all possible. Farrand, too,[3] seems to disregard the cycle of participation when he claims that there can be little doubt that the custom of destroying property arose in America as in other regions, from the desire to provide for the deceased in the next world.

The cycle of participation certainly must be taken into consideration and here we have to bear in mind the different conceptions as to what constitutes a man's personality. Here we see the importance of the cycle of participation which extends beyond the individual to the things most closely associated with him. On the Melanesian Island of Bougainville, a man's work and its produce are regarded as the supreme manifestation of his personality, inextricably

---

[1] Frazer, *Belief in Immortality*, Vol. I, p. 147.
[2] McGee, "The Sioux Indians", *Fifteenth Annual Report, Bureau of Ethnology* (1897), p. 178.
[3] Farrand, *Basis of American History*, pp. 140-141.

linked with his authority. The same view certainly must have been current elsewhere. This would seem to explain the destruction of crops and fruit trees. Without doubt, the things most constantly associated with the dead in his lifetime, especially his garments and personal possessions, are so saturated with his personality that they are regarded as primarily identified with the deceased.

CHAPTER XXI

LIFE AFTER DEATH

INFLUENCED BY RANK

MELANESIA

IT is a belief among the Fijians that the soul of a famous chief might, after death, enter some young man and stimulate him to perform deeds of valour. Such persons are looked upon with great respect, many privileges are accorded them, and their opinions are revered.[1]

In Mota, one of the Banks Islands, cocoanuts, yams, and other foods are placed beside the dead body so that the deceased can give a list of these offerings to the ghosts in Panoi who make inquiries about his rank. In this way, treatment becoming his station would be accorded him. At Gana the carcasses of pigs are placed at the grave to impress the ghosts of the spirit land and thus to insure a pleasing welcome to the deceased.[2]*

REINCARNATION IDEA INFLUENCED BY SEX CONSIDERATIONS

AUSTRALIA

It is a belief of the natives of Pennefather River, Queensland, that upon the death of a man the ngai spirit goes at once to his children, both boys and girls; when a woman dies, her ngai spirit does not go into her children but into her sisters, and when there are no more sisters left, it is destroyed entirely.[3] The Gnanji deny that women have spirits which survive after death, but that the spirit of man is thought to

---

[1] Wilkes, *United States Exploring Expedition*, Vol. III, p. 8511.
[2] Codrington, *Melanesians*, pp. 263-270.
* The Tonga doctrine limits immortality to chiefs, matabooles, mooas. (Williams, *Fiji and the Fijians*, Vol. I, p. 241.)
    In Samoa there is a belief that chiefs go to a realm where everything is in a state of elysium whereas the common people go to a place where life is dismal and mournful. (Brown, *Melanesians and Polynesians*, pp. 221-222.)
[3] Roth, "Superstition, Magic and Medicine", *North Queensland Ethnography*, Bulletin No. 5, p. 18.

be re-born in a woman at some future time.[1] Frazer says that why immortality should be denied to women and reserved for men in this instance, is not manifest, especially since all other Central Australian tribes appear to admit equal rights for men and women, in the life after death.[2]

A dead man among the Gnanji is called Kurti and his spirit Moidna. Here they have a strange belief, not found elsewhere by Spencer and Gillen, that while each man has a Moidna, the woman has no spirit at all, and with her, death ends all. But the spirit of the dead man visits his ancestral camping ground, and undergoes reincarnation after the rains have fallen and washed the bones.[3]

INDIA

It is a belief in Bengal and other parts of India that still-born children are apt to return to their parents in the next pregnancy.[4]

The Todas believe that Amnodr is their future home where they lead the same kind of existence as on this earth, with the exception that their legs wear down. When these are worn down as far as the knees, On sends them back to this world as other men.[5]

One of the rewards that is supposed to befall a suttee is that she will not be re-born into the female state ; but she who becomes not a suttee is never emancipated from it.[6]

The Kunbi caste believe that the dead pass into crows ; perhaps such an idea is conceived of because of the longevity of this bird.[7]*

SIBERIA

The Koryak believe that before a child is born, the Supreme Being sends into the womb of its mother the soul of some deceased relative.[8] A great part of the Chukchee names

---

[1] Spencer and Gillen, *Native Tribes of Central Australia*, p. 546.
[2] Frazer, *Belief in Immortality*, Vol. I, p. 93.
[3] Spencer and Gillen, *Northern Tribes of Central Australia*, p. 546.
[4] Crooke, *Popular Religion and Folk-Lore of Northern India*, Vol. II, p. 67.
[5] Rivers, *Todas*, p. 398.
[6] Dutt, *History of India*, Vol. IX, p. 80.
[7] Russell, *Tribes and Castes of India*, Vol. IV, p. 37.
* The Samoans believe that the body of a drowned man is supposed to become a porpoise. (Turner, *Samoa, A Hundred Years and Long Before*, p. 150.)
[8] Jochelson, *The Koryak, J.N.P.E.*, Vol. VI (1905), p. 100.

have reference to the return of the deceased from another world. These names indicate most clearly re-birth of souls.[1]

DEPENDENT UPON AGE

MELANESIA

The Mafulu are of the opinion that ghosts become, according to their age, either a shimmering light on the ground or a species of fungus found only upon the mountains.[2]

DIFFERENT REALMS ASSOCIATED WITH TOTEMIC CLAN

AUSTRALIA

The clannishness of the ghosts of Central Australia is most apparent. Invariably we find the members of a special totemic clan congregated in one place. The souls of the Arunta dead of the plum-tree totem assemble at a certain stone in the mulga scrub and the spirits of the dead among the Warramunga who are identified with the black snake totem gather about particular gum trees.[*] This applies to every totem, even if it is a hawk, a fly, a bee, a bat, the moon, the sun. Each individual is identified with the totem which had been his during his lifetime. However, this exclusiveness is not characteristic of the Urabunna tribe, for their ghosts associate with the individuals of other totems. But we do find even here that a group of granite rocks represents people of the pigeon-totem.[3]

DIFFERENT REALMS DETERMINED BY THE SOCIAL STATUS

MELANESIA

The fate of a married Fijian ghost, whose wives have not been murdered, is depicted as beset with dangers.[4] However, nothing could be worse than the punishment meted out to bachelor ghosts. A terrible being called the Great Woman, who is concealed in a shady spot, lies in wait to seize him, and if he escapes this awful creature, it is only to fall into the hands of a much more terrible monster, Nangganangga, from whom no escape seems possible. This dreadful goblin is ever on his guard to snatch the souls of bachelors and so wary is he that no unmarried Fijian ghost is said to have reached the blessed realms.[5]

[1] Bogoras, *The Chukchee, J.N.P.E.*, Vol. VII, p. 514.
[2] Williamson, *The Mafulu Mountain People of British New Guinea*, p. 267.
[*] Also considered on page 246.
[3] Spencer and Gillen, *Northern Tribes of Central Australia*, p. 147.
[4] Williams, *Fiji and the Fijians*, Vol. I, p. 244.   [5] *Ibid.*

At the entrance to the happy isles where the departed spirits of the Gazelle Peninsula in New Britain dwell, is a watchman who asks three questions to every ghost who attempts to enter. "Who are you ? Where do you come from ? How much shell money did you leave behind " ? The future fate of the ghost is supposed to hang upon his answers. If he has left much money, the way to the blissful realms is open to him and here he joins other happy souls eating and smoking and partaking of other worldly delights. But if he is financially embarrassed, he is denied admittance to this paradise, and is sent home where he lives like a wild beast. Ofttimes, because of such treatment, he will harass the survivors. However, such a soul is not entirely bereft of hope, for if some one takes compassion upon him by giving him a feast and distributing money among the guests, he is permitted to enter the happy realms.[1]*

Among some of the tribes of New Britain we find the belief that there is a special Hades (Iakupia or Yakup) for poor people. This also was the realm to which those were assigned who had no shell money distributed at burial.[2]

SIBERIA

Deceased women among the Chukchee who have no husbands go to a world of their own. Here they catch reindeer with nooses and nets as they attempt to make their way across Pebbly River. This world which is situated in the lower portion of the sky is much less important than the first upper world.[3]

DIFFERENT REALMS DEPENDENT UPON THE KIND OF DEATH

MELANESIA

The natives of Eastern Melanesia who inhabit Torres Islands, the Banks Islands, and New Hebrides, do not allow their ghosts to mix indiscriminately. Those who die violent

[1] Kleintitschen, *Die Küstenbewohner der Gazellehalbinsel*, p. 225 et seqq., quoted by Frazer, p. 406.

* The Karens believe that the souls of those who die a natural death and are buried according to the designated method of procedure go to a beautiful country where they live as they have in the past, while the ghosts of those who are unburied will wander about on the earth and visit the survivors (Westermarck, *Development of Moral Ideas*, Vol. II, p. 522.)

[2] Brown, *Melanesians and Polynesians*, p. 398.

[3] Bogoras, *The Chukchee, J.N.P.E.*, Vol. VII (1907), p. 335.

deaths have special reservations, another place is allotted
to those who are shot, yet another to those who are clubbed,
and a fourth is assigned to those who meet death by witchcraft.[1]* We learn that the ghosts of those who have been
shot keep rattling the arrows which caused their death. In
Pentecost Island those who die of coughs congregate in one
place ; murderers likewise have special places assigned to
them.[2]

In speaking of the natives of New Britain, Brown tells us
that those who have died from sickness are in one place ;
those who have been killed by sling or tomahawk are in another ;
those who have been eaten are all hanging up ; those who
have been killed by witchcraft or any other cause go to other
places.[3]

The ghosts of the slain Fijians, yaloni-moku, are supposed
to haunt the spot where they met their fate and here they
bewail their unhappy lot.[4]

SIBERIA

The Siberians believe that the Aurora Borealis is the place
of abode for those who die a sudden or a violent death ; the
whitish spots are for those who died from contagious diseases,
the dark spots for those strangled by the spirits of nervous
disease, and the red ones for those stabbed with a knife.[5]
According to the belief of the Gilyak of the Amour country,
the souls of those who have died a violent death, including
suicides, ascend directly to heaven, while those who die a
normal death remain on earth or descend underground.[6]
The Chukchee conceive the Aurora Borealis to be represented
by several parallel bands ; in the region of the uppermost
band are the genuine dead, or those who have died an ordinary

---

[1] Codrington, *Melanesians*, p. 276.

* The Central Eskimos conceive of three heavens. Those who die by
violence go to the lowest ; those who die by disease go to Sedna's house first,
and after their restoration to health they go to the second heaven, while those
who died by drowning go to the third. (Boas, " Central Eskimo ", *Sixth
Annual Report Bureau of Ethnology* (1888), p. 615.)

[2] Codrington, *Melanesians*, p. 288.

[3] *Ibid*, pp. 192-194.

[4] Fison, *Tales from Old Fiji*, p. 164.

[5] Bogoras, *The Chukchee, J.N.P.E.*, Vol. VII (1907), p. 334.

[6] Schrenck, *Reisenemd Forschungen in Amour-Lande*, Vol. III,
p. 560. Quoted by Bogoras, *The Chukchee, J.N.P.E.*, Vol. VII (1907),
p. 334.

death ; the second band contains the kele dead ; while the third is for those who have been strangled.[1]

DIFFERENT REALMS FOR THE DEAD INFLUENCED BY CERTAIN ETHICAL CONSIDERATIONS

MELANESIA

The natives of Motlav, one of the Banks Islands, think that Panoi is a good place open only to the souls of the righteous. They believe that the souls of murderers, sorcerers, liars, and adulterers are denied admittance to the happy land. The bad ghosts congregate in a bad place where they live in misery ; they are pitiable, restless, homeless, they eat the worst food, they eat men's souls and haunt graves. But what a contrast is presented in Panoi ! Here peace and harmony are characteristic of the life of the good who frequent this realm.[2] At Mota, another one of the Banks Islands, the orator who conducts the funeral ceremonies speaks candidly in reference to the character of the deceased. If he were a bad man, he says : " Poor ghost, will you be able to enter Panoi ? I think not ".[3]

AUSTRALIA

The Cape River tribes believe that when a black fellow, whose actions in life have been what they esteem good, dies he ascends to Boorala (the Creator, " good "), where he lives, as he did on earth.[4]*

---

[1] Bogoras, *The Chukchee, J.N.P.E.*, Vol. VII (1907), p. 334.
Among the Hidatsa we find separate realms for those who commit suicide. (Mathews, " Ethnology and Philology of the Hidatsa Indians," *United States Geographical Survey of Territory*, p. 409, quoted by Yarrow, p. 104.)
In speaking of the religious beliefs of the Central Eskimo, Turner tells that the natives think that those who met their death by violence, from starvation, and women who had died in childbed, go to the region above the earth, where though not altogether in want, yet they lack many of the luxuries enjoyed by those in the lower region. (Turner, " Ethnology of the Ungava District, Hudson Bay Territory ", *Eleventh Annual Report Bureau of Ethnology* (1894), p. 193.) Nansen narrates how some of the Eskimos believe that women who die in childbed, men who are drowned at sea, and whale fishers go to the lovely land under the earth as a compensation for the hardships they have experienced in this world. (Nansen, *Eskimo Life*, p. 235.)
[2] Codrington, *Melanesians*, p. 274.
[3] *Ibid*, p. 268.
[4] Howitt, *Native Tribes of South East Australia*, p. 504.
* The Minnetaree Indians disposed of their dead in accordance with their moral character. Bad and quarrelsome men they buried in the earth, that the Master of Light might not see them ; but the bodies of good men they built on scaffolds so that the Master of Light could look upon them. (Prinz zu Wied, *Reise in das Innere Nord-America*, Vol. II, p. 235.)

Among the aborigines of Australia we find the belief that the shade of a good person walks about for three days and though it appears to people, it holds no communication with them. Should it be seen and named by any one during these three days, it instantly disappears and goes to a beautiful country above the clouds abounding with kangaroo and other game where life will be enjoyed forever. Friends meet and recognize each other, but no marriage takes place as the bodies have been left on earth. But a different fate is destined for the wicked. These shades wander miserably about for one year after death frightening people and then they descend to Ummekulleen, never to return.[1]

The Gournditch-mara believe that those who are good go to a " good and bright place ".[2]

South of the Gulf of Carpentaria there is a belief that the spirit goes up to the sky by the Southern Cross which is a ladder reaching the Milky Way, along which it travels to Yalang. Here are plenty of game and water but only the good spirits can get water.[3]

The Wathi-Wathi of the Lower Murray think that the spirit starts for the sky as soon as it leaves the body. Two parallel roads are en route to the sky, one dirty, kept by good spirits, and the other presided over by bad spirits, clean, who hope by this means to entice the deceased. On both of these roads is a deep pit, from which flames rise, but a good spirit with a single bound can clear it.[4]

The Narrinyeri believe that the dead go to some place in the west where their god resides. In passing to this region they perceive below them a great fire. While the bad are in danger of being burned, the good get safe to Nurunderi.[5]

Dawson tells us that the aborigines of Australia believe that Muuruup, the bad spirit, lives under the ground in a place called Ummekulleen, from which no human being has ever returned to tell about its nature. However, we meet with a belief that there is nothing but fire there and that the souls of bad people get neither meat nor drink and are dreadfully

[1] Dawson, *Australian Aborigines*, p. 51.
[2] Fison and Howitt, *Kamilaroi and Kurnai*, p. 278.
[3] Thomas, *The Natives of Australia*, p. 204.
[4] *Ibid.*
[5] Taplin, *The South Australian Aborigines*, p. 38.

tossed about by a number of evil spirits under the guidance of Muuruup.[1]*

INDIA

The Kurmi, a cultivating caste of India, think that the soul is judged before Yama. The length of time it remains chained to a pillar of flame is in proportion to the sins of the deceased.[2]

In the Rig-Veda hints of punishment awaiting evil doers are not in evidence,[3] but in the Atharva-Veda[4] and the Brāhmanas[5] good and evil are said to produce hell or happiness.

SIBERIA

The deceased among the Chukchee who were unkind to dogs are attacked by them as they enter the lower realms.[6] The entrance to the country of the shadows of the Koryak is guarded by dogs and if a person beat dogs during his life he is refused admittance. However, what seems at first sight an ethical conception may be interpreted differently when we hear that these dog guardians are open to bribery. Fish fins are put into the mittens of the deceased to accomplish this purpose.[7]

The Chukchee provide no dead man with reindeer taken from another's herd, with strange clothes, nor with anything stolen or obtained unlawfully, for in the underground world all such things would be seized by the family of the individual to whom they belonged.[8]

[1] Dawson, *Australian Aborigines*, pp. 50-51.

* The Mat-lóal draw a distinction between the treatment which the good and bad receive. Whereas the good Indian goes to the happy region southward in the great ocean, the bad one transmigrates into a grizzly bear, the personification of sin. (Powers, *Contributions to North American Ethnology*, Vol. II, quoted by Yarrow, p. 106.)

[2] Russell, *Tribes and Castes of India*, Vol. IV, p. 80.

[3] *Rv.*, II, 29, 6; III, 20, 8.

[4] *Av.*, II, 14, 3; V, 19, 3.

[5] *Catapatha Brahmana*, XI, 6, 1.

[6] Bogoras, *The Chukchee, J.N.P.E.*, Vol. VII (1907), p. 335.

[7] Jochelson, *The Koryak, J.N.P.E.*, Vol. VI, p. 103.

[8] Bogoras, *The Chukchee, J.N.P.E.*, Vol. VII (1907), p. 336.

The natives of Alaska think that good men go up to the realms of the air whereas bad men go down in the earth. (Dall, *Resources of Alaska*, p. 383.) The Yurok of California believe that the dead must cross a very long pole which bridges a chasm in a mysterious region. The length of time a fire which guides the spirit to the other world far away is left burning at the grave depends upon the character of the deceased. A righteous soul reaches its destination sooner than a wicked one. (Powers, *Contributions to North American Ethnology* (1877), Vol. II, p. 58.) Bessels of the Polavis expedition said there was a similar belief among the Eskimo. (Yarrow, *Mortuary*

DEPENDENT UPON THE PHYSICAL CONDITION OF THE DECEASED

MELANESIA

In Normandy Islands we find the belief that no one who had sores could reach the place where happy people live in Bwebweso.[1]

IDEA OF THE PLACE OF SOJOURN AFTER DEATH INFLUENCED
BY RELIGIOUS PRACTICES

HINDU

Among the Hindus we find the conception that the dead entered the realms of the sun. We read that if the smoke which consumed the dead body was carried straight upward the dead gained Heaven ; if not, he remained on earth. In the Puranas, Yama, the God of the Dead who is assumed to have been the first to " spy out the path to the other world ", is called " Child of the Sun ". Yama's abode is where the dead heroes congregate. The fathers who died in ages past are looked after by him as he sits drinking with the gods underneath a fair tree.[2] The place is not definitely located, but since Yama's habitation in the sky is supposed to be identical with the sun, in several passages, the prevailing conception is that the dead entered the realm of the sun where Yama received them. " My home is there where are the sun's rays ". " The dead shall go to Yama to the fathers, the seers that guard the sun ".[3]

If we glance at the religious ideas of the Hindus, we shall see the prominence of the worship of the personified forces of nature, and of special significance in this connection is the importance of the sun in their pantheon of gods. Here we think we have a definite connection between the Hindu

---

Customs of the North American Indians, p. 103.) When a deceased member of the Hidatsa community arrives at the " village of the dead," his valour, self-denial, and ambition receive their reward, for in all places the same treatment is accorded him. In these regions we find the same attitude as in the land of the living ; " the brave man is honoured and the coward despised." (Mathews, " Ethnology and Philology of the Hidatsa Indians ", *United States Geological Survey of Territory* (1877), p. 409). The Chippewas think that in the land of souls all receive treatment according to their merits ; the good suffer no pain, they have no duties and dance and sing and feed upon mushrooms. The wicked are haunted by visions of those whom they wronged and the ghosts of such ill-treated ones take vengeance upon their former oppressors. (Long's *Expedition*, Vol. II (1824), p. 158, quoted by Yarrow, p. 105.)

[1] Brown, *Melanesians and Polynesians*, p. 400.
[2] *Av.* I, 35, 6 ; X, 64, 3 ; X, 1, 9.
[3] *Av.* I, 109, 9 ; X, 154, 4-5.

conception of the place of sojourn after death and their
worship of the personified forces of nature.*

CONNECTED WITH SOCIAL INFRACTIONS

MELANESIA

Among the Fijians the ghosts of men who committed no
murder in their lives are punished by being forced to pound
muck with clubs.   Those who had not their ears bored while
on earth are compelled to wander in Hades carrying on their
shoulders one of the logs of wood, on which bark cloth is beaten
out with mallets, and are ridiculed by all who see them.
Women wh ohave not been tattooed in their lifetime are pursued
by female ghosts who continually scratch and lacerate them
with shells or scrape the flesh from the bones and bake it into
bread for the gods.   Those who have caused the gods to be
displeased are placed on their faces and transformed into
taro beds.[1]   The Koita think that if any person were so
unfortunate as to be buried without having a hole bored in his
nose, since this is a custom practised in life, he would have to
wander in the other world with a creature like a slow-worm.[2]
The Motu, a tribe of fishermen and potters, who live in and
about Port Moresby in British New Guinea, cannot enter the
blessed realms without bored noses.   These people bore holes
in their noses and insert ornaments in the openings.   This
is done to children of about six years and the operation is
supposed to facilitate the passage of the spirit to the happy
land.   If such a ceremony were neglected, the ghost would
be compelled to sojourn in a bad land called Tageani with
little food and no betel-nuts.[3]   Before the natives of Araga,

* The form of the Egyptian pyramid was determined by the religion of
the Egyptians since the pyramidal form was sacred to the Sun-god.   Breasted
has brought to our notice that the king was buried under the very symbol of
the Sun-god which stood in the Holy of Holies in the Sun Temple at Heliopolis,
a symbol which from the day of his creation by the gods, he took in the form
of a phoenix, and when the gigantic heights of the pyramid towered above the
king's tomb it was the loftiest object which greeted the Sun-god.   Furthermore, he says, that entirely in keeping with their interpretation of the
significance of the pyramid form is its subsequent mortuary use.   A large
number of stone pyramids have been found in the cemeteries of later times
and the inscriptions over these represent the deceased addressing a hymn to
the Sun-god.   (Breasted, *Development of Religion and Thought in Ancient
Egypt*, pp. 72-73.)

[1] Williams, *Fiji and the Fijians*, Vol. I, p. 247.

[2] Frazer, *Belief in Immortality*, Vol. I, pp. 194-195.

[3] Lawes, " Ethnological Notes on the Motu, Koitapu, or Koiari Tribes
of New Guinea ", *J.A.I.*, Vol. VIII (1879), p. 370.

Pentecost, reach Banoi, the land of the dead, they must pass a sea. A shark which is lurking below a tree from which the souls jump, bites off the noses of those who have not killed pigs in accordance with the customs of the island.[1]

The natives of Aurora believe that at the mouth of the hollow which leads to Banoi, the land of the dead, a huge pig stands ready to devour all those who in their lifetime have not planted the *emba,* pandanus, from which mats are made. Here also a ghost who has not had his ears pierced is not allowed to drink water. Those ghosts who in their lifetime have not joined the Suqe hang like flying foxes upon the trees.[2]

INDIA

If a member of the Kurmi caste spills salt, after death he must gather in Pātā (hell) each grain with his eyelids.[3]

PLACE OF SOJOURN AFTER DEATH AFFECTED BY ENVIRONMENTAL CONDITIONS

MELANESIA

Connected with a belief in an underground Hades we find the presence of volcanic activity. Thus in Southern Melanesia, where the belief in an underground world is conspicuous, there are many evidences of volcanic activity. Likewise we find the same belief farther north, in Santa Cruz, Savo, Bougainville. Again, this correlation holds good for Polynesia, because in the Samoan Islands it is the belief that the dead go to an underground world through an entrance on the active volcanic island of Savaii, and the belief in an underground realm is also present in New Zealand where we find evidence of volcanic activity. Furthermore, in such islands as Tahiti where there are no volcanoes, a conception in regard to an underground world is either absent or exceedingly vague.[4]

Lolomboetogitogi is the abode of the dead for the natives of Lepers' Island and descent to it is by a volcanic vent near the lake. Beside the lake on the further side, which no man has ever been known to reach, is a volcanic vent which sends up clouds of steam. Men go up to the nearer side of the lake

---

[1] Codrington, *Melanesians,* p. 287.
[2] *Ibid,* p. 280.
[3] Russell, *Tribes and Castes of India,* Vol. IV, p. 80.
[4] Rivers, *History of Melanesian Society,* Vol. II, p. 263.

and climb a tree which overlooks it ; they then cry aloud to Nggalevu, the spirit in the land of the dead, who receives the newcomers, to give indication that he is there, and a column of steam goes up.[1] The natives of Santa Cruz in the Solomon Islands also imagine that the ghosts of the dead go to the ground volcano Tamami where they are burnt in the crater or remain in the fiery region.[2]

Each tribe among the Fijians filled in the details of the mythical land to agree with its own geographical position.[3]

LOCATION OF LAND OF THE DEAD DEPENDENT UPON ECONOMIC CONDITIONS

MELANESIA

Some of the natives of the Gazelle Peninsula in New Britain think that the home of the spirits is in Nakanei, where they procure their shell money. Others are of the opinion that it is in the islands near Cape Takes.[4]

AFFECTED BY METHOD OF DISPOSAL OF THE BODY

INDIA

The Kurmi caste believe that the deceased will go to heaven if the body is thrown into the water.[5]*

RITES AFFECTED BY TRADITION

SIBERIA

The practice of the Koryak and the Chukchee to prevent the return of the ghost is identical with the episodes in the tales of the " Magic Flight ". The imitation of the action of the magpie of the world of the dead, performed at the funeral of a Koryak child, with the ostensible object of informing the deceased that she was passing into another world and must not again return to her former haunts, the strewing

---

[1] Codrington, *Melanesians*, pp. 285-286.
[2] *Ibid*, p. 264.
[3] Frazer, *Belief in Immortality*, Vol. I, p. 462.
[4] Kleintitschen, *Die Küstenbewohner der Gazellehalbinsel*, p. 225 et seq., quoted by Frazer, p. 406.
[5] Russell, *The Tribes and Castes of India*, Vol. IV, p. 73.
* The Tlinkets have an idea that the bodies of those who are cremated will be warm and comfortable in the other world, but others will suffer from the cold. " Burn my body ! Burn me ! " pleaded a dying Tlinket ; " I fear the cold. Why should I go shivering through all the ages and distances of the next world ? " (Pelvoff, *Report on the Population, Industries and Resources of Alaska*, Tenth census of the U.S., p. 175.)

of twigs about the pyre which represented a dense forest, the drawing of a line across which the mourners jump, might be mentioned in this connection. Then, too, among the Chukchee we find other customs accentuated such as are characteristic of the "Magic Flight" tale. A cup and a bunch of grass are hidden separately with the idea that one will transform itself into a sea and the other into a forest. By such devices the hero and the heroine escape in the Magical Flight from the ogre.[1]*

TRANSMIGRATION DEPENDENT UPON EXPLOITS

The natives of Encounter Bay believe that animals were originally men who performed great prodigies and at last transformed themselves into different animals.[2]

---

[1] Jochelson, *The Koryak, J.N.P.E.*, Vol. VI (1905), p. 112 ; Bogoras, *The Chukchee, J.N.P.E.*, Vol. VII (1907), p. 528.

* Also discussed on page 71.

[2] Meyer, *The Aborigines of Encounter Bay Tribe*, p. 202.

CHAPTER XXII

CULT OF THE DEAD

AFFECTED BY RANK

MELANESIA

THE ghost of a distinguished man is worshipped and is looked upon as very potent in its influence since it retains the powers which belonged to it in life, but the ghosts of insignificant persons are regarded with the same indifference as before.[1] While the ghosts of the powerful are worshipped, those of ordinary people are disregarded and are not identified with the ghosts which are worshipped.[2] It is significant to note that the great people who are buried on land turn into land ghosts, and the commoners who are sunk into the sea become sea ghosts. In Florida, two days after the death of a chief or of any person who was much esteemed, the relatives and friends assemble and hold a funeral feast.[3]

At Bogota in the Island of Ysabel, a chief is buried with his head near the surface, and a fire is kept burning over the grave so that the skull may be taken up and preserved in the house of his successor. The deceased now becomes a tindadho to be worshipped.[4] The preservation of the skulls and bones of chiefs, their wives, and other members of their families at Mafulu in British New Guinea and the dipping of them into the blood of pigs at great festivals every fifteen or twenty years is regarded by Frazer as a device for propitiating the ghost of the person to whom the bones formerly belonged.[5]

AUSTRALIA

When the deceased is a person of great importance, the Dieri place food for many days on the grave and in winter they kindle a fire so that the ghost may warm himself.[6]

[1] Codrington, *Melanesians*, pp. 253-254.
[2] *Ibid*, p. 254.
[3] *Ibid*, p. 255.
[4] *Ibid*, p. 257.
[5] Frazer, *Belief in Immortality*, Vol. I, p. 200.
[6] Howitt, *Native Tribes of South-East Australia*, p. 448.

(*Note.*—Many illustrations pertaining to the " Cult of the Dead " have already been given under the heads of " Feasts " and " Life after Death ", and are not repeated here.)

MELANESIA

In San Cristoval and Florida when public sacrifices are offered to ghosts, boys or men are permitted to be present, but no women.[1]

At Lakona in Santa Maria the death feast lasts only five days for a woman and six for a man.[2]

At Saa it is believed that no woman's ghost can have a lio'a (power) ; it is nothing more than akalo, a mere departed soul.[3]

AUSTRALIA

The New Hollanders believe that most of the Ingnas are the malign spirits of departed black men who have been denied burial rites but there are no female Ingnas. According to the interpretation of Oldfield, this shows the low estimation in which the female is held by the Australian aborigines, and as a consequence females have no souls.[4]

INDIA

Great respect was shown to the memory of such Tottiya women who observed the custom of suttee. Small tombs were erected in their honour on the high road and at these oblations were offered once a year to the Manes of deceased heroines.[5]

Dubois tells us that those who practised suttee were deified. Vows are made and prayers addressed to them and their intercession is sought in times of sickness and death. Women who have been courageous enough to suffer death in this way are numbered among the divinities. Crowds of devotees come to offer them sacrifice and to invoke their protection.[6]

FUTURE LIFE INFLUENCED BY AGE

AUSTRALIA

It is a belief of some tribes of Western Victoria that children under four or five years have no souls, no future life, and are not worshipped.[7]

[1] Codrington, *Melanesians*, p. 288.
[2] *Ibid*, p. 273.
[3] *Ibid*, p. 262.
[4] Oldfield, "The Aborigines of Australia", *Transactions of the Ethnological Society*, N.S., Vol. III (1865), p. 237.
[5] Thurston, *Castes and Tribes of India*, Vol. VII, p. 195.
[6] Dubois, *Hindu Manners, Customs and Ceremonies*, p. 367.
[7] Dawson, *Australian Aborigines*, p. 51.

Religious Conceptions Dependent upon the Kind of Death

Melanesia

In British New Guinea the ghosts of women who die in childbed, people who hang themselves, those who are devoured by crocodiles, and men beheaded in battle are especially dreaded.[1]

The natives of Northern Melanesia draw a line of demarcation between offerings to the soul of a man who died a natural death and offerings to the soul of a man who has been killed in a fight. Although they place the former in a living tree, they leave the latter on a dead tree.[2]

The Yabims of Dutch New Guinea fear ghosts, especial y those of slain men.[3]

India

Among the Khasis, if a man dies by a sword before the body can be burnt, a black hen must be sacrificed to Ka Tyrut, the goddess of Death, a goat is offered to U Syngkai Bamon, and a sow to Ka Ramshandi, both evil deities. The same ceremony is gone through for a murdered man. Similar pujus are offered with the exception of the sacrifice to U Syngkai, when one is drowned or killed by wild animals.[4]

The Muduwans do not propitiate the spirits of those killed by accident or dying a violent death.[5]

Religious Beliefs Associated with Character

Australia

The Narrinyeri dread particularly the ghosts of men of a domineering and revengeful disposition, and worship them.[6]

Influenced by Sub-Class Considerations

Among the Binbinga tribe, the breaking of the silence ban of the women is followed by a ceremony, the object of which is to brush them with burning twigs. Before this takes place, the lubras send the supply to the men and it is

---

[1] Landtman, *Wanderings of the Dead in the Folk-Lore of the Kiwai-Speaking Papuans, Festskrift tillagnad*, Westermarck, pp. 59-66.
[2] Frazer, *Belief in Immortality*, Vol. I, p. 397.
[3] Frazer, *Psyche's Task*, p. 63.
[4] Gurdon, *The Khasis*, p. 136.
[5] Thurston, *Tribes and Castes of India*, Vol. V, p. 96.
[6] Taplin, "The Narrinyeri," *Native Tribes of South Australia*, p. 19.

given to certain ones of their number such distribution depending upon the sub-class to which the deceased belonged.[1]

RITES CONNECTED WITH PHRATRY AND KINSHIP RELATIONS

MELANESIA

In Lepers' Island we find it a custom on the hundredth day after a death for all the people to assemble in the middle of the village; a man of waivung division to which the deceased does not belong, one near to him by male descent, mounts a tree and calls the names of the deceased one after another.[2]

INFLUENCED BY RELIGIOUS IDEAS

MELANESIA

In the Solomon Islands the worship of ghosts is influenced by the natives' concept of mana.[3] The ghost which is worshipped is the spirit of a man who in his lifetime had mana in him, whereas the souls of common men are " nobodies ", either before or after death. The impersonal power, which permeated the individual before death, is still characteristic of his ghost after death, and is even more pronounced. Since this force is supposed to be active after death, someone will claim special acquaintance with the ghost. If this power manifests itself, then the deceased is regarded as worthy of receiving offerings, of being invoked ; if not, he is disregarded for all time.[4]

It is interesting to note that in the Solomon Islands supernatural power and mana may be acquired through ghosts. If a man is a grown warrior, it is not because of certain brave and desirable characteristics which are innate in him ; it is because he is inspired by the ghost of a dead warrior. All other virtues are attributable to the same source.[5] Thus only the ghosts of important people are worshipped while the ghosts of ordinary people are feared and no worship is accorded them. Likewise the ghosts of those who have recently died are regarded as more powerful than those who have passed away at some remote period.[6]

[1] Spencer and Gillen, *Northern Tribes of Central Australia*, p. 554.
[2] Codrington, *Melanesians*, p. 285.
[3] *Ibid*, p. 125.
[4] *Ibid*,
[5] *Ibid*, pp. 120, 253-254.
[6] *Ibid*, p. 258.

CHAPTER XXIII

CONCLUSION

In considering the question of the disposal of the dead, we find that far more motives prompting various methods of burial enter into this complex, than in any other phase of the death-situation. Perhaps these may account for the numerous ways of disposing of a dead body found among all peoples, including those of widely scattered areas and representing every possible degree of culture and environment. The main consideration which seems to have actuated different ways of burial in the same tribe, embracing not only the manner of the disposal of the dead, but also certain definite ceremonials connected with the death ritual, is the rank of the individual. This is most strikingly emphasized in all the areas in which we are specifically interested, with the possible exception of the Siberian one, and here we find that although the unburied body of an ordinary man fills the Yahut with horror, even nature becoming especially turbulent, and violent winds and mysterious noises are everywhere heard, yet when a shaman dies, these manifestations assume tremendous proportions.[1] Naturally we would not expect to find rank differences in connection with burial stressed among the Siberian natives, for here the social organization has the family for its unit, and no line of demarcation is drawn between the social status of individuals, with the possible exception of the shaman, who has more power than an ordinary member of the community. Since the investigation shows that customs are so entwined with the cultural and social setting, we would not look for any other result. Again, as we would expect, the more aristocratic the society, the more stress is laid upon the burial of the higher class, whereas in a democratic society rank considerations would be almost eliminated, or certainly relegated to the background. It is here as it is with taboo—

---

[1] *R.H.R.*, Vol. XLVI, p. 211.

the higher the rank of the individual, the greater is the sanctity associated with him, and thus every expedient must be resorted to, not only to render him homage, but to propitiate his departed spirit.

It is significant that we find methods of burial correlated with kinship, sub-class, class, clan, phratry and tribe affiliations. Here we see that every phase of social organization characteristic of our areas is represented in the disposal of the dead. Again, the very close identification of conduct and rites with the social structure is in evidence ; indeed, the correlation is so marked in many instances, that it is impossible to divorce a rite or ceremony from its cultural setting ; considered in any other light it becomes absolutely meaningless. Not only do we find various units in the social organization represented, but the status of the individual, too, comes in for recognition. An examination of the data makes it evident that few are the cases of virginity and likewise bachelors are almost unknown among primitives. In the Australian area especially we find such a condition unheard of ; as a result, the status of the individual receives no consideration, whereas among the Siberians and Melanesians we find dire penalties meted out to the ghosts of the unmarried. In addition to continuing their woeful unmarried state in the future realms, severe punishments are inflicted upon them.

Sex differences too figure very prominently in the ceremonies connected with burial. Especially is this seen when the body is being disposed of as well as in the mourning stipulations, including questions of attire, silence injunctions, seclusion impositions, and other taboos. Then too this consideration enters, although in a less prominent degree, in what has already been characterized as the cult of the dead, in funeral rites not coming under the category of mourning observances, and in ideas concerning future life, embracing reincarnation theories. As was intimated before, various psychological reasons may be advanced to account for woman's prominence in death-rites. The idea that woman belongs to the weaker sex is " merged into the concept of woman as a mysterious person ; she is more or less a potential witch ".[1] But once more it must be noted that this sex differentiation is

---

[1] Crawley, *The Mystic Rose*, p. 206.

not a special characteristic of the ritual concerned with the dead. Not only are sex differences reflected in the daily materialistic life of the people, and in various forms of economic activity, but in religious observances and many secret societies, in initiation rites and governmental activities, in questions of descent and inheritance, in the domain of art; indeed the line of demarcation is drawn most definitely in every form of social, political, and religious activity.

That certain specific occupations and activities should be assigned to man and others to woman in the death-complex, then, occasions us no surprise, for an examination of various primitive areas shows that whereas hunting is always the work of man, gathering produce falls to the lot of woman. Since this is so, we would expect inventions which are identified with hunting ascribed to men, and those correlated with household activities attributed to women. We find that those occupations which require slowness of movement depend upon the female sex, while those entailing rapidity belong to males. Whenever the food is stationary the work is done by the woman, and this explains why garden culture is always in her hands. The same holds good in the other occupations. Among the Iroquois, for instance, the art work of the women is confined to embroidered plant and flower decorations, and that of the men to animal representations on wampum and wood carvings. If we find this division of labour in different phases in the economic life of the primitive, we certainly would expect to find it emphasized in the death-situation.

The primitive seems to be concerned with the problem of life after death, if we may judge from the prominence which this attitude assumes in the death-complex. In many instances the kind of death determines the disposal of the body, the nature of life after death, the kind of offerings to be made to the deceased, and various ceremonials of a ritualistic character.

Naturally we would expect myths to exert a most appreciable influence upon many specific phases in connection with death such as the disposal of the body, the origin of death and life after death. Therefore, we are not surprised to find conceptions concerning the manner of burial, the orientation of the dead, the birthplace of the deceased, the reasons for

the origin of death inextricably connected with myths accounting for these customs. The question to be considered is whether the myth or the custom is primary or secondary. Here we must stress the point of view that customs seem to be in evidence first, and the tale itself and also as the reasons given in myths accounting for certain actions or ceremonies appear as a later development. Thus in the Banks Island and Lepers' Island and numerous other similar tales dealing with the origin of death, the reasons accounting for such a phenomenon are detached, so to speak, from the rest of the narrative, and create the impression that they are artificially interposed. When the tendency arises to explain motives, or conventional conduct, secondary explanations are given which may have no connection with the historical source of the actions. Although many of the tales cited are introduced specifically to explain the death-situation, yet many may be put to a different use, such as those dealing with the waning and waxing of the moon. Clothed as these myths are in the garb of human experience, the cosmic consideration, as well as the observation of nature, figures in their composition. The fundamental idea is the same although the incidents differ.[1]

It is hardly necessary to add that myths are associated with every form of human endeavour ; they seem to be a natural means of accounting for all phases of life, both material and spiritual.

Despite the fact that we find definite references to show us that frequently the ethical conceptions of the primitive are at variance from ours, an examination of the motives which seem to influence some savages reveals the fact that these are prompted by a moral attitude such as we would expect of a member of a more advanced civilization. Thus, in some instances, such as in the disposal of the body and the kind of life after death which the deceased is supposed to follow, we find certain clearly defined ethical considerations. Even in those cases where the conception is not in accord with our ideas, we feel perfectly justified in classing these attitudes under the category of the moral, for, from the point of view of the savage, they undoubtedly are so ; however their

[1] Boas, " The Development of Folk-Tales and Myths ", *The Scientific Monthly*, Vol. III (1916), pp. 335-343.

ideas of right and wrong may differ from our conception of these attributes.

Although our concept of the sacredness of human life and the equality of people is very different from the primitive idea, yet feelings of sympathy and pity, of filial and paternal love, enter both. However, our conduct and that of the primitive are different in reference to social units. The individuals of other groups are not looked upon by the savage as " human beings " and this attitude develops into a deep-seated feeling between members of one tribe and outsiders. This would account, not only in large measure for the great difference in ethical behaviour among primitives and ourselves, but would help to explain various phases of the ethical problem. Thus in Siberia, as well as in other areas, we find the belief that a person continues his existence in the same state in which he died. Because of their intense desire to perpetuate their existence as a whole people, a son will kill his aged father frequently at his own request before the period of decline sets in ; whereas the desire of individuals of advanced modern society is to protect their parents, the wish of the members of some primitive communities is to kill them, thereby not only affording comfort to the deceased, but insuring a continuance of group solidarity. The relation between instinctive feeling and social ethics is constant throughout the whole range of mankind. These concepts are dependent upon the type of society, and thus we frequently find various ethical considerations regulated by social rank and hemmed in by social customs. The connection between class interests and the wider ethical relations of mankind is always apparent.

Naturally ethical concepts are not confined to the death-complex alone, since, because of their very nature, they cannot be divorced from the social, political, material, or spiritual questions which confront a community.

Although age differences enter into the death-complex, yet the rôle they play is very insignificant, as they are chiefly reflected in but two aspects of the complex, namely, the disposal of the dead, and life after death ; however, in a few instances they are apparent also in mourning rites.

This age difference is concerned mainly with the method of the disposal of the body. In early Roman and Vedic times

the bodies of adults were cremated and those of children buried. Again, many cases are cited where children are buried near their mothers' huts, in the closest possible proximity to their dwelling-places. This method seems to have been instituted with the object of facilitating re-birth, and naturally this would apply to children rather than to those of maturer age. The spirits of the very young and decrepit are looked upon as less dangerous in their noxious influence than those in the prime of life, and the feeling of dread usually associated with dead bodies appears in such cases reduced to a minimum.

The question too would suggest itself as to why, in the regions specified, burial was resorted to for young children instead of cremation which was the usual mode of disposal in these areas.

A glance into the manner of disposal of the dead body makes it evident that cremation is more often practised than any other method. This makes us ponder the reason. To so many primitives, cremation appears as a far more efficacious means of getting rid of the dead than either burial, exposure, or preservation. Burning is not only supposed to destroy the dead body most effectively and thus to prevent the possible return of the ghost, but cremation is regarded as a purifying agency, and likewise prevents hostile tribes and wild animals from getting possession of the corpse. Among the Hindus, for instance, the idea is expressed that if the smoke goes directly upward, the deceased will reach the happy realms. The same conception is found among the Koryak, but in the case of children, the primitive must have looked upon their spirits as insignificant and not worthy of the usual method of procedure which perhaps entails more effort. This is especially true in regard to the Hindu ceremonial. Again, primitive man must have regarded the ghosts of young children and the very old as non-capable of inflicting injury ; particularly since existence in the other world was often looked upon as a continuance of life here, a decrepit individual could not inflict much harm upon the survivors, and the ghosts of children certainly could not have been placed in the category of the powerful.

Environmental conditions also figure in the discussion, but they, too, occupy a most unimportant place when compared

with the frequency with which other elements in the death-situation occur. Thus they often determine the kind of burial and play a part relative to the nature and location of the realms to which the dead are assigned ; but their significance is reduced to a minimum ; indeed, it is evident that only the exigencies of the occasion force the environmental issue to enter the complex. It is only natural for a primitive who lives in a volcanic neighbourhood to associate the location of the realms of the dead and their mysterious atmosphere, with such a phenomenon which must appear to them as unknowable and unfathomable as volcanic activity.

If environment is a basic determinant in culture, as is so often claimed, why, we ask, do we find so few of the elements of our complex associated with environmental considerations ? A comparative study reveals the fact that environmental issues assume no more important rôle in other complexes than they do in the death-situation. This examination then of concrete data makes us take issue with the theories of Ratzel, Semple, Huntington, Myres, and others, who seem to regard environment as a categorical determinant in culture. Although we are cognizant of the potency of environmental considerations as factors, yet we are not willing to endorse the drastic utterances of Huntington in his *Pulse of Asia* who holds that geography is at the foundation of history.

Again, religious concepts are not prominently identified with burial rites. Outside of a few in connection with the disposal of the body and those identified with sun worship, the prominence of the mana concept in Melanesia with its appreciable influence upon the cult of the dead, religious practices in connection with the place of sojourn of the dead, and a few insignificant allusions, religious beliefs as such are hardly in evidence in the death-complex. What might possibly be interpreted as a religious attitude, although with the faintest degree of probability, are certain animal beliefs at places called keno which affect the manner of disposal of the dead, and certain totemic considerations which can hardly be classed as coming under the category of the religious. The claim may be made by some that, since ideas of the future world play such an important rôle in our subject, decided religious attitudes should enter largely into our

problem. That this argument is erroneous and cannot be verified, is evident from concrete material.

Since the dread attitude toward the corpse is overwhelmingly manifest, it is only natural that means should be taken to propitiate the departed spirit; indeed, propitiation of the ghost is inseparably linked with all phases of the death-complex.

When we speak of religion we are inclined to consider emotional states only, but the primitive not only permits the emotional to enter his make-up, but also a will-power figures prominently in the object which he fears. Although fear itself is not a religious feeling, yet when it is looked upon as an evidence of will-power in the thing feared, it becomes permeated with the religious. Because of this conception, a protective charm must be adopted. Such a charm must be looked upon as directed against contamination, or as an amulet which has a certain inherent will-power of religious significance. Again, the characteristic form in which this will-power manifests itself is in motion—motion often in the sense of change. Now, a change of the most decided nature has been caused by the death-situation; the same individual who before has figured in the midst of the activities of life, is now a passive agent. To meet this novel situation, some charm must be brought into play or some device adopted to gain control over this will-power, or to assure the departed spirit that nothing shall be overlooked to gain its goodwill. The compulsion tendency perhaps may manifest itself on the part of the survivors, as is evident from the many instances we have cited where means are employed to prevent the return of the spirit of the deceased. Then a friendly attitude is often displayed, such a tendency often taking the form of service to the departed tribesmen. This may in part account for the many offerings which we find so closely associated with the death ritual. Mere friendliness is often substituted for service and thus a more intimate connection is established between the living and the dead. The mind of the primitive is constantly confronted by things which he does not understand, and when these refer to significant phases of his life, his emotions are stirred to their depths. Such is eminently the case in the death-situation. At the contemplation of death the savage is plunged into a state

of intense excitement ; perplexed, he asks the question, "What is it that has happened here " ? Hence we have the beginning of a certain kind of rational experience.

We have stated that this attitude toward the corpse which we have attempted to characterize is not only identified with the dead body, but with anything which is peculiarly strange and mysterious. Thus thunder and lightning and other phenomena of nature are regarded as potent influences in the life of a primitive and are conceived of as the manifestations of a will-power which ought to be propitiated. Even the sight of a snake causes a natural revulsion toward this reptile, and if we look into the customs of savages, we will find the snake identified with many religious practices.

In line, then, with our argument, we are not surprised to find not only every expedient resorted to by the survivors to win favourable recognition from the dead spirit, but specific mourning customs instituted in which taboos are most conspicuous, and in time an elaborate cult of the dead is established including feasts and offerings. The ideas of future life, then, which form part of the death-complex flow naturally from the peculiar character of the death-situation.

CHAPTER XXIV

CONCLUSION (*continued*)

WE are now in a position to ask ourselves whether the method we have used is justifiable, and if the results of the investigation are valid if applied to general death customs. Can the deductions, formulated upon the basis of an intensive study of four areas about which trustworthy information exists and with some heterogeneous material introduced from promiscuous sections, representing people of various nationalities and degrees of culture, be extended into a generalization concerning the death customs of the world? The similarities found in different areas point to a uniform line of development, and would, we claim, appear in others. The differences show most markedly an association of death customs with other social and cultural aspects, and it is feasible to assume that differences manifest local influences and would in many cases be a direct reflex of the cultural setting. We have seen how various phases of culture react upon the death-situation.

The death-complex receives its colouring from death itself, from the fact that death always and constantly occurs, from certain psychological considerations, and from the cultural background. This study has been an investigation of these influences and causes which determine similarities and differences, and an attempt has been made to show how, in a definite number of instances, customs which seem to have no psychological connection with the death-complex become identified with it. Then, too, although many features of the death-situation are often inextricably bound up with the cultural or historical setting, yet psychological reactions may bring about similarities of ideas without considering the cultural background. Certain specific stimuli may explain similarities in the reaction of the mind. Granted that this be so, the opportunity is opened up for interpretations through independent development. Our deductions make us take

issue with Hocart, who claims that if ethnology is to become a science it must postulate that the same cause cannot produce different results. As customs are often represented as due to certain instinctive tendencies, we would then expect that a definite custom would appear whenever the same psychological setting is in evidence. However, the assumption is not in accord with the facts of the death-situation. Although we perceive that mourning customs seem to be universally practised and appear to be prompted by many of the same considerations, yet we have found instances in which they are not in evidence. Notwithstanding that the general attitude toward a dead body causes most zealous precautions to be taken in regard to the disposal of a corpse, yet among the Yerkla-mining the body of a deceased member of a community is entirely neglected. Thus concrete evidence shows that the same fact may develop along divergent lines.

Our conclusions show that it is unscientific to assert dogmatically a single origin for a practice of like character found in so many areas. In other specific instances outside of the death-situation very definite concrete evidence shows that different traits based upon common tendencies follow divergent lines, each independent of the other. From this it would seem that we have no authority to speak of a uniform line of development which carries mankind from one stage to another. Perhaps the certain kinds of parallel sequence which we find marking the advance of cultural development in all parts of the world are due not so much to historical causes as to psychological ones ; indeed, our analysis of the elements of the death-complex argues for the validity of this conception.*

To the scientist it must seem uncritical to adopt the method of the English classical ethnologists who have stressed independent development at the exclusion of all other theories, and that of Græbner[1] and Foy who claim that all cultural

---

* While all culture is acquired, yet there must be certain dominant instincts which participate in cultural settings ; but to explain the facts of culture it is necessary to know the history of the case, for neither mental attributes nor biological characteristics are of significance in attempting to account for the origin of specific cultural traits. Individual psychological and biological methods may be applied to explain the problems connected with man's innate nature, but when general cultural considerations are involved, the historical relations of the people must be examined, as well as the social psychological aspects.

[1] Græbner does not theoretically deny the psychological point of view but he does not apply it.

similarities are due to diffusion. In considering diffusion it is not only necessary to assume spread, but to show how these features which enter a culture from without are changed by contact with a new cultural setting. When certain features are once in a culture they become connected with the death-situation, and as a consequence, they became permeated with the flavour of this complex ; assimilation may be immediate or not, such depending upon the nature of the two cultures. The elements need not enter the complex in the same order. The order of sequence may be determined by the general culture of the group and by various external influences. Although some of the special phases may have been prevalent in the group, yet others which present marked variation may be drawn in. The acceptance of these external traits would depend upon the culture of the recipient group.

The rôle of the unconscious element in culture is so pronounced that we must consider its vital significance when dealing with the death-situation problem. To this Durkheim and Lévy-Bruhl have not given due importance when discussing primitive mentality. Many of the ideas connected with the death-complex, especially those savouring of the fundamental religious stamp, must have sprung into being without any conscious effort on the part of the participants. Our own experiences convince us that the practices to which we are most addicted are those which are very automatic and require no conscious effort.

The question as to whether the death-complex is an organic unit, and if so, what combination of definite features always appears, or whether certain elements can be regarded as component parts of this situation alone or not identified with other complexes, has been considered. The object has been to show that the similar elements of this psycho-historical problem have been determined by certain inherent psychic features, but that the different elements which we find associated do not always spring from the same psyche.

Although we have drawn from many particular features not included within the category of the death-situation as such, and which may at first appear as irrelevant, yet a critical examination shows that these "foreign elements" have not been indifferently or spasmodically received ;

indeed, that a heterogeneous compound should be found is exactly what would be expected.

We have endeavoured to show that the data collected, representing primary features and heterogeneous elements, are historical accretions moulded into a quasi-organic unit.[1] Naturally, different degrees of assimilation occur, apart from any special explanation. Ours is a criticism against the tendency of those who offer direct psychological explanation of the death-complex.

In this investigation we have used the mechanism of the modern ethnologist who uses various methods for interpreting hypotheses. Thus our position represents a compromise between the evolutionary point of view as voiced by Spencer and Tylor and other exponents of the classical school in stressing the general lines of psychic development, and those extremists who do not see their way clear of divorcing the elements of any one complex from its cultural background. The application of results such as those emanating from a study of the death-situation upon general ethnological theory is most significant. This study shows that no one method can be used exclusively to analyse any cultural complex.

The investigation shows that the content of the specific features is dependent upon rank, sex, age, social organization, status, environmental, moral, religious differences, and myth conceptions, the location of the realms of the dead, the physical condition of the deceased, totemic considerations, and the kind of life after death. However, other differences figure, even of a less pronounced character than those enumerated, especially in regard to the persistence with which they enter the complex. Sometimes it is true that they are introduced merely as one special phase, such as in the disposal of the body, or into the question of life after death, or they may enter in connection with a general custom. Among these we might mention the belief that the disposal of the dead is correlated with the conception of the resting place of the deceased and the location of the realms of the dead. An examination of the beliefs connected with life after death shows us that in addition to those already specified in our analysis we have seen that in Egypt the restoration of the

[1] Goldenweiser, "Principle of Limited Possibilities", *J.A.F.L.*, Vol. XXVI (1913), p. 288.

body is dependent upon the Egyptian's concept of the Ba and in the Plains area resurrection is determined by death on the war-path and membership in the Medicine Dance. Then, too, in regard to life after death, we note that punishments in the future world are directly traceable to social infractions. Again, we are not surprised to find reincarnation beliefs, such as the conception that the soul continues to exist in the form the person had at the time of death, the idea that the soul will be born in another individual of the same family, the conception that the soul will enter the bodies of animals, the belief that shadows continue our human pursuits.

What appears as especially interesting in the death-situation, are the conceptions as to what constitutes a man's personality. These ideas are primarily identified with the practices concerning the destruction of property as well as with the motives which perhaps actuate such an attitude.

Although it is evident that the only particular set of features which are practically always associated with the dead body are the propitiation of the spirit of the deceased which takes various forms, the significance ascribed to burial, and the ideas about future life, yet of these features neither can claim precedence as a basic trait. However, we can see that certain elements become firmly established not only in primitive society, but in modern communities. That the association between the various phases of the death-situation is most intimate, cannot be denied. As has been frequently emphasized, many of the phenomena are definitely connected with every phase of the social, political, ceremonial activity, and cannot be studied independently of the context. Indeed no dependable and scientific interpretation of the death problem in a culture can be given without considering its social condition and historical development. Not only are various death ceremonies directly correlated with definite forms of social and political organization, but the identification of certain cultural features with the religious and ritualistic activities of the people invites the emergence of specific social values.

Concrete evidence shows that the death-situation may be looked upon as a variable compound, differing not only in many features, but with prominent elements. True, some features show far greater persistence than others, nor are all

of the same emotional value. But no features, excepting those specified above, appear invariable ; again, features highly accentuated in some areas are of secondary importance in others, while in still other areas they may be absent altogether.

As far as the investigation goes, the only elements which are exclusively characteristic of the death-situation are mourning customs as such, and the ideas in regard to life after death ; even in mourning customs the reversal of the ordinary way of doing things, so often inseparably connected with this phase, has a parallel in other complexes, although we assume that the motive which may prompt such a reversal, the development of the custom, as well as the nature of the results ascribed to its operation, are of a totally different character. For instance, among the Kwakiutl, the clown who certainly represents an attitude identified with reversal of custom, is regarded by Professor Boas as having evolved from the warrior class, and we maintain that his presence cannot be connected with the same considerations which inspire reversal of customs in mourning ceremonies. Again, Rivers mentions two clans that seem to take delight in doing things contrary to the ordinary modes of life of other tribes in their proximity.[1] Among other examples of reversal of custom, we might mention the use by the Tlingit of " backward speech ". This also seems to be an element of the clownishness so characteristic of the Plains Area.

In practically every phase of the death-complex we have seen that many features connected with it are by no means identified with this situation alone ; nor is it an integral datum, everywhere essentially alike. Indeed, rejecting the view of the complex as an organic unit, we must rather consider that genetically it is a more or less adventitious conglomerate of heterogeneous elements of culture, the specific

---

[1] Rivers, *History of Melanesian Society*, Vol. I, p. 23.
In Nota Island of the Banks Group, the Talvatavat and Gatava divisions of one of the two moieties are called veve Kwakwae, " eccentric divisions ". Their behaviour is different from that of the members of the other groups, the following being instances of their eccentricity : It is usual to begin a meal with yam or bread and fruit, which may be followed by eating pig or the leaves of a kind of hebescus called taape, the meal being finished with the pudding called lot, but the veve Kwakwae eat in the reverse order. Further, when they have difficulty in drawing up a canoe, they will hack off the outrigger, so that when they start again, they have to make a new outrigger from " unseasoned timber ".

content of the complex being in each special case traceable to specific historic and sociological determinants. Without doubt, there is unity in the death-complex of any given group, but this is not due to the genetic relationship of the various elements of the complex, but to the associations formed between such features through the operation of sociological and psychological factors.

BIBLIOGRAPHY[1]

[1] Only the more important publications bearing upon the subject dealt with in this volume are cited in the Bibliography.

ALEXANDER, SIR JAMES : *An Expedition of Discovery into the Interior of of Africa.* Philadelphia, 1838. Vol. I.

ALLEN, GRANT : *The Evolution of the Idea of God.* London, 1903.

AMES, EDWARD S. *Psychology of Religious Experience.* Boston, 1910.

ASTON, W. G. : " Japanese Mythology ", *Folk-Lore.* London, 1899. Vol. X, pp. 294-323.

AUST, EMIL : " Die Religion der Römer ", *Darstellungen der aus dem Gebiete christlichen Religion geschichte.* Münster, 1899. XIII Band, pp. 1-268.

BAESSLER, ARTHUR : *Neue Südsee-Bilder,* Berlin, 1900.

BATCHELER, JOHN : *The Ainu and Their Folk-Lore.* London, 1901.

„ *The Ainu of Japan.* London, 1892.

BEARDMORE, EDWARD : " The Natives of Mowat, Dandai New Guinea " in *Journal of the Anthropological Institute.* London, 1890. Vol. XIX, pp. 450-473.

BEVERIDGE, PETER : " On the Aborigines Inhabiting the Great Lacustrine and Riverine Depression of the Lower Murray, Lower Murrumbidgee Lower Lachlan, and Lower Darling ", *Transactions and Proceedings of the Royal Society of New South Wales for* 1883. Sydney, 1884. Vol. XVII, pp. 19-74.

BLEEK, WILLIAM H. I. : *Reynard the Fox in South Africa.* London, 1864.

BLOOMFIELD, MAURICE : *Cerberus, The Dog of Hades.* Chicago, 1905.

„ *The Atharva-Veda.* Strassburg, 1899.

„ *The Religion of the Veda.* New York, 1908.

„ " Contributions to the Interpretation of the Veda ", Fourth Series, *American Journal of Philology.* Baltimore, 1891. Vol. XII pp. 414-443.

BOAS, FRANZ : *Second General Report of the Indians of British Columbia,* in *Sixth Report of the Committee on the North-Western Tribes of Canada,* in *The Report of the Sixtieth Meeting of the British Association for the Advancement of Science.* London, 1891. pp. 562-715.

„ *The Central Eskimo* in *Sixth Annual Report of the Bureau of Ethnology.* Washington, 1888. pp. 399-669.

„ *The Eskimo of Baffin Land and Hudson Bay* in *Bulletin, American Museum of Natural History.* New York, 1901. Vol. XV, Pt. 1, pp. 1-370.

„ *The Social Organization and Secret Society of the Kwakiutl Indians* in 1895 *Report of the United States National Museum.* Washington, 1897. pp. 315-733.

„ " The Origins of Death ", *Journal of American Folk-Lore.* Boston, 1917. Vol. XXX, pp. 486-491.

„ " Mythology and Folk-Tales of the North American Indians ", *Journal of American Folk-Lore.* Boston, 1914. Vol. XXVII, pp. 374-410.

„ " The Development of Folk-Tales and Myths ", *Scientific Monthly.* New York, 1916. Vol. II, pp. 335-343.

„ " Limitations of the Comparative Methods of Anthropology ", *Science.* New York, 1896. Vol. IV, pp. 901-908.

„ " Mythology of the Bella Coola Indians ", *Jesup North Pacific Expedition.* Leiden, 1898. Vol. I, Pt. 2, pp. 25-127. (*Memoir, American Museum of Natural History.* Vol. II.)

BOGORAS, WALDEMAR : *The Chukchee* in *Jesup North Pacific Expedition.* Leiden, 1904-1909. Vol. VII. (*Memoir, American Museum of Natural History.* Vol. XI.)

„ *Chukchee Mythology* in *Jesup North Pacific Expedition.* Leiden, 1910. Vol. VIII, Pt. I, pp. 1-197. (*Memoir, American Museum of Natural History.* Vol. XII.)

BONNER, T. D.: *The Life and Adventures of James P. Beckwourth* (written at his own dictation). New York, 1856.

BONNEY, FREDERICK : "On Some Customs of the Aborigines of the River Darling, New South Wales", *Journal of the Anthropological Institute.* London, 1884. Vol. XIII, pp. 122-137.

BOSCANA, GERONIMO : *Chinigchinich.* New York, 1846. [Bound with *Life in California,* by Alfred Robinson.)

BREASTED, JAMES H.: *Development of Religion and Thought in Ancient Egypt.* New York, 1912.

„ *Ancient Records of Egypt.* Chicago, 1906-1907. Vol. I.

BRETT, WILLIAM : *The Indian Tribes of Guiana.* New York, 1852.

BRINTON, DANIEL G.: *The Myths of the New World.* Philadelphia, 1896.

BROWN, GEORGE : *Melanesians and Polynesians.* London, 1910.

BUTLER, JOHN. *Travels and Adventures in the Province of Assam.* London, 1855.

CABATON, ANTOINE : *Nouvelles Recherches sur les Chams.* Paris, 1901. (Publications de L'ecole française d'extreme-Orient.)

CARTER, JESSE B.:_ *The Religion of Numa.* London, 1906.

„ *The Religious Life of Ancient Rome.* Boston, 1911.

CHALMERS (Rev.) JAMES : "Notes on the Natives of Kiwai Island, Fly River, British New Guinea", *Journal of the Anthropological Institute.* London, 1903. Vol. XXXIII, pp. 117-124.

CHAPMAN, JAMES : *Travels in the Interior of South Africa.* London, 1868. Vol. I.

CLEMENT, E.: "Ethnographical Notes on the Western-Australian Aborigines", *Internationales Archiv für Ethnographie.* Leiden, 1904. Vol. XVI, pp. 1-16.

CLODD, E.: "What's in a Name ? " *Folk-Lore.* London, 1890. Vol. I, pp. 272-274.

CODRINGTON, ROBERT H.: *The Melanesians.* Oxford, 1891.

„ "On Social Regulations in Melanesia," *Journal of the Anthropological Institute.* London, 1889. Vol. XVIII, pp. 306-313.

COLEBROOKE, HENRY T.: *Miscellaneous Essays by H. T. Colebrooke with the Life of the Author by Sir T. E. Colebrooke.* London, 1873. Vol. II.

CONYBEARE, FREDERICK C.: *Myths, Magic and Morals.* London, 1910.

CRANZ, DAVID : *The History of Greenland.* London, 1767. Vol. I.

CRAWLEY, ALFRED E.: *The Mystic Rose.* New York, 1927.

CROOKE, WILLIAM : *The Natives of Northern India.* London, 1907.

„ *The North-West Provinces of India.* London, 1897.

„ *The Popular Religion and Folk-Lore of Northern India.* Westminster, 1896. 2 vols.

CUNNINGHAM, JAMES F.: *Uganda and its Peoples,* London, 1905.

CURR, EDWARD M.: *The Australian Race.* Melbourne, 1886-1887. Vols. I, III.

DALL, WILLIAM H.: *Alaska and its Resources.* Boston, 1870.

DAWSON, JAMES : *Australian Aborigines.* Melbourne, 1881.

DENNETT, R. E.: *At the Back of the Black Man's Mind.* London, 1906.

„ *Nigerian Studies.* London, 1910.

DUBOIS, ABBE J. A.: *Hindu Manners, Customs and Ceremonies.* Oxford, 1924. Trans. by Henry K. Beauchamp.

DUTT, ROMESH CHUNDER : *History of India.* London, 1906. Vol. I.

EHRENREICH, PAUL : "Zur Frage der Beurtheilung und Bewerthung ethnographischer Analogien ", *Correspondenz Blatt der deutschen Gesellschaft für Anthropologie, Ethnologie und Urgeschichte.* München, 1903. Vol. XXXIV, pp. 176-180.

ELLIS, ALFRED B.: *Yoruba-Speaking Peoples of the Slave Coast of West Africa*. London, 1894.
  „ *Ewe-Speaking Peoples of the Slave Coast of West Africa*. London, 1890.
  „ *Tshi-Speaking Peoples of the Gold Coast of West Africa*. London, 1887.
ENDERLI, J.: "Zwei Jahre bei den Tschuktschen und Korjaken", Peter-mann *Mitteilungen*. Gotha, 1903. Vol. XLIX, pp. 175-184, 219-227, 225-259.
ENDLE, SIDNEY: *The Kachâris*. London, 1911.
FARNELL, LEWIS RICHARD: *The Evolution of Religion*. London, 1905.
FARRAND, LIVINGSTON: *Basis of American History*. New York, 1906.
FAURIEL, CLAUDE C.: *Chants Populaires de la Grèce Moderne*, 2 vols. Paris, 1824-1825.
FAWCETT, FREDERICK: "Ôdikal and Other Customs of the Muppans", *Folk-Lore*. London, 1912. Vol. XXIII, pp. 33-44.
  „ "The Kondayamkottai Maravars, a Dravidian Tribe of Tinnevelly, Southern India", *Journal of the Anthropological Institute*. London, 1903. Vol. XXXIII, pp. 57-65.
  „ "Notes on Some of the People of Malabar", *Madras Government Museum Bulletin*. Madras, 1900. Vol. III, No. 1, pp. 1-85.
  „ "Nâyars of Malabar", *Madras Government Museum Bulletin*. Madras, 1900. Vol. III, No. 3, pp. 185-322 (especially the section "Death and Succeeding Ceremonies").
FISON, LORIMER: *Tales from Old Fiji*. London, 1904.
FISON, LORIMER and HOWITT, ALFRED W.: *The Kamilaroi and Kurnai*. Melbourne, 1800.
FLETCHER, ALICE C. and LA FLESCHE, FRANCIS: *The Omaha Tribe* in *Twenty-seventh Annual Report of the Bureau of Ethnology*. Washington, 1911. pp. 33-642.
FOUCART, GEORGE: "Primitive Names", *Hasting's Encyclopedia of Religion and Ethics*. 13 vols. New York, 1908-1927. Vol. IX, pp. 129-136.
FOWLER, W. WARDE: *The Religious Experience of the Roman People*. London, 1911.
  „ *The Roman Festivals of the Period of the Republic*. London, 1899.
FOY, W.: "Menalesien", *Archiv für Religionwissenschaft*. Leipzig, 1907. Vol. X. pp. 129-149.
FRASER, JOHN: *The Aborigines of New South Wales*. Sydney, 1892.
FRAZER, SIR JAMES G.: *The Belief in Immortality and the Worship of the Dead*, 3 vols. London, 1913-1922.
  „ *Taboo and Perils of the Soul in Golden Bough*. London, 1911. Vol. II.
  „ *Psyche's Task*. London, 1909.
FRIEDLÄNDER, LUDWIG: *Life and Manners in the Early Roman Empire*, 3 vols. London. 1913.
FUSTEL DE COULANGES, NUMA DENIS: *The Ancient City*. Boston, 1901. (Translated from the French by Willard Small.)
GENNEP, ARNOLD VAN: *Tabou et Totémisme à Madagascar*. Paris, 1904.
  „ *Les Rites de Passage*. Paris, 1909.
GEORGI, JOHANN G.: *Russia or a Compleat Historical Account of all the Nations which Comprise That Empire*. 4 Vols. London, 1780. Translated by W. Tooke.
GODDARD, PLINY EARLE: *Hupa Texts* (University of California Publications of American Archæology and Ethnology). California, 1904. Vol. I, No. 2.
  „ *Life and Culture of the Hupa* (University of California Publications of American Archæology and Ethnology). California, 1903. Vol. I, No. 1.
GOLDENWEISER, ALEXANDER: "Totemism, an Analytic Study", *Journal of American Folk-Lore*. Boston, 1910. Vol. XXIII, pp. 179-293.

GOLDENWEISER, ALEXANDER: "Principle of Limited Possibilities", *Journal of American Folk-Lore.* Boston, 1913. Vol. XXVI, pp. 259-290.
„ "Critique on the History of Melanesian Society", *Science.* New York, 1916. Vol. XLIV, pp. 824-828.
„ "Mana and the Religious Thrill," *Journal of Philosophy, Psychology and Scientific Methods.* Lancaster, 1915. Vol. XII, pp. 632-640.
„ "The Heurislic Value of Traditional Records", *American Anthropologist.* Lancaster, 1915. Vol. XVII, pp. 763-764.
„ "Religion and Society: Critic of Emil Durkheim's Theory of the Origin and Nature of Religion", *Journal of Philosophy, Psychology and Scientific Methods.* Lancaster, 1917. Vol. XIV, pp. 113-124.
GRABOWSKY, F.: "Dor Tod, das Begräbnis, das Tiwah, oder Todtenfast, beiden Dajaken", *Internationales Archiv für Ethnographie.* Leiden, 1889. Vol. II, pp. 177-204.
GRAEBNER, ROBERT F.: *Methode der Ethnologie.* Heidelburg, 1911.
GRANGER, FRANK S.: *The Worship of the Romans.* London, 1895.
GRAY, LOUIS H.: "Hair and Nails", *Hasting's Encyclopædia of Religion and Ethics*, 13 vols. New York, 1903-1927. Vol. VI, pp. 474-477.
GREY, SIR GEORGE: *Journals of Two Expeditions of Discovery in North-West and Western Australia during the Years* 1837-39, 2 vols. London, 1841.
GRUPPE, OTTO: *Griechische Mythologie und Religiongeschichte*, 2 vols. München, 1906.
GUISE, R. E.: "On the Tribes Inhabiting the Mouth of the Wanigela River, New Guinea", *Journal of the Anthropological Institute.* London, 1899. Vol. XXVIII, pp. 205-219.
GURDON, PHILIP R. T.: *The Khasis.* London, 1907.
HADDON, A. C.: "Review of Ribbe's Zwei Jahre unter den Kannibalen der Salomo-Inseln", *Folk-Lore.* London, 1905. Vol. XVI, pp. 113-116.
HADDON, A. C. (Editor): *Cambridge Anthropological Expedition to Torres Straits*, 6 vols. Cambridge, 1901-1912.
HARE, AUGUSTUS J. C.: *Walks in Rome*, 2 vols. London, 1897.
HARTLAND, EDWIN S.: *Primitive Paternity.* London, 1909-1910.
„ *Ritual and Belief.* London, 1914.
HAWKES, ERNEST WILLIAM: "The Inviting In-Feast of the Dasken Eskimo", *Geological Survey of Canada, Memoirs.* Ottawa, 1913. Vol. XLV, pp. 1-20.
HENRY, A.: "The Lolos and Other Tribes of Western China", *Journal of the Anthropological Institute.* London, 1903. Vol. XXXIII, pp. 96-107.
HICKSON, SIDNEY J.: *A Naturalist in North Celebes.* London, 1889.
HILL-TOUT, CHARLES: "Report on the Ethnology of the StlatlumH of British Columbia", *Journal of the Anthropological Institute*, London, 1905. Vol. XXXV. pp. 126-218.
HIRN, YRJÖ: *The Origins of Art.* London, 1900.
HODSON, THOMAS CALLAN: *The Nāga Tribes of Manipur.* London, 1911.
HOLLIS, ALFRED C.: *The Nandi.* Oxford, 1909.
„ *The Masai.* Oxford, 1905.
HOPKINS, EDWARD W.: *The Religions of India.* Boston, 1895.
„ *India Old and New.* New York, 1902.
HOWITT, ALFRED W.: *The Native Tribes of South-East Australia.* London, 1904.
„ "On Some Australian Beliefs", *Journal of the Anthropological Institute.* London, 1884. Vol. XIII. pp. 185-198.
Imperial Gazetteer of India. Oxford, 1907-1909. Vol. I.
Indian Antiquary (The), A Journal of Oriental Research. Bombay, 1872-1926.

IYER, ANANTHA K. : *The Cochin Tribes and Castes.* Madras, 1909-1912. Vol. II.

IYER, S. APPADORAI : " Nayādis of Malabar ", *Madras Government Museum Bulletin.* Madras, 1901. Vol. IV, No. 1, pp. 66-78.

JACKSON, ABRAHAM V. W. : *Persia, Past and Present.* New York, 1906.

JACKSON, JOHN : " Narrative ", *Captain Erskine's Journal of a Cruise among the Islands of the Western Pacific.* London, 1853. pp. 411-477.

JASTROW, MORRIS : *The Religion of Babylonia and Assyria.* Boston, 1898.

JEVONS, FRANK B. : *An Introductions to the History of Religion.* London, 1914.

JOCHELSON, WALDEMAR I. : *The Koryak* in *Jesup North Pacific Expedition.* Leiden, 1908. Vol. VI. (*Memoir, American Museum of Natural History*, Vol. X.)

JOLLY, JULIUS : *Recht und Sitte* (Grundrissder indoarischen Philologie und Altertums Kunde), Band II, Heft 8, Strassburg, 1896.

JONES, WILLIAM : *Ojibwa Texts* in *Publication of the American Ethnological Society.* Leiden, 1917-1919. Vol. VII. Pts. 1 and 2.

„ " The Algonquin Manitou ", *Journal of American Folk-Lore.* Boston, 1905. Vol. XVII, pp. 183-190.

KIDD, DUDLEY : *The Essential Kafir.* London, 1904.

KING, IRVING : *The Development of Religion.* New York, 1910.

KLEINTITSCHEN, AUGUST : *Die Küstenbewohner der Gazellehalbinsel.* Hiltrup bei Münster. Westfalen, 1906.

KOCH, THEODOR : " Zum Animus der Süd-Amerikanischen Indianer ", *Internationales Archiv für Ethnographie.* Leiden, 1900. Supplement to Vol. XIII, pp. 1-146.

KOLB, PETER : *The Present State of the Cape of Good Hope,* 2 vols. London, 1731. (Originally written in High German and translated from the original by Mr. Medley.)

KROEBER, ALFRED L. : " The Arapho," *Bulletin, American Museum of Natural History.* New York, 1902-1907. Vol. XVIII, Pts. 1-2, 4.

KRUIJT, ALB : *Het Animisme in den Indischen Archipel.* Gravenhage, 1906.

KUSNEZOW, S. W. : " Über den Glauben vom Jenseits und den Todtencultus der Tscheremissen ", *Internationale Archiv für Ethnographie.* Leiden, 1896. Vol. IX., pp. 153-161.

LAMB, ROBERT : *Saints and Savages.* Edinburgh, 1905.

LANDES, A. : " Contes et Legendes Annamites ", extract from *Excursions et Reconnaissances.* Saigon, 1886. No. 25.

LAWES, Rev. W. G. : " Ethnographical Notes on the Motu, Koitapu, and Koiari Tribes of New Guinea ", *Journal of the Anthropological Institute.* London, 1879. Vol. VIII, pp. 369-376.

LEUBA, JAMES H. : *The Belief in God and Immortality.* Chicago, 1921.

LÉVY-BRUHL, LUCIEN : *Les Fonctions Mentales des les Sociétés Inférieures.* Paris, 1910.

LISIANSKY, UREY : *A Voyage Round the World.* London, 1814.

LOWIE, ROBERT H. : " Ceremonialism in North America ", *American Anthropologist.* Lancaster, 1914. Vol. XVI, pp. 602-631.

„ " Social Organization ", *American Journal of Sociology.* Chicago, 1914. Vol. XX, pp. 63-97

„ " Critical Comment on Dr. Swanson and Dr. Dixon's Primitive American History ", *American Anthropologist.* Lancaster, 1915. Vol. XVII, pp. 597-599.

„ " Psychology and Sociology ", *American Journal of Sociology.* Chicago, 1915. Vol. XXI, pp. 217-229.

„ " On the Principle of Convergence in Ethnology ", *Journal of American Folk-Lore.* Boston, 1912. Vol. XXV, pp. 24-42.

MACDONALD, Rev. JAMES : " East Central African Customs ", *Journal of the Anthropological Institute.* London, 1893. Vol. XXII, pp. 99-122.

MACDONNELL, ARTHUR A. and KEITH, ARTHUR B. : *Vedic Index of Names and Subjects.* London, 1912. 2 vols.

MALO, DAVIDA : *Hawaiian Antiquities.* Honolulu, 1903.

Man, A Monthly Record of Anthropological Science, 28 vols. London, 1901-1928. Vol. XVIII.

MARETT, ROBERT R. : The Threshold of Religion, 2nd edit. New York, 1914.

MARINER, WILLIAM : An Account of the Natives of the Tonga Islands, 2 vols. London, 1817.

MARKHAM, SIR CLEMENTS ROBERT : Narratives of the Rites and Laws of the Yncas. London, 1873.

MASPERO, SIR GASTON : The Dawn of Civilization. New York, 1901.

MATTHEWS, WASHINGTON : " Ethnography and Philology of the Hidatsa Indians ", United States Geological and Geographical Survey. Washington, 1877. Miscellaneous Publications, No. 7.

McCULLOCH, W. : " Account of the Valley of Munnipore and of the Hill Tribes ", Selections from the Records of the Government of India, 27, Foreign Department 1. Calcutta, 1859.

McGEE, W. J. : " The Siouan Indians ", Fifteenth Annual Report of the Bureau of Ethnology. Washington, 1897. pp. 157-244.

MEIER, P. JOSEF : " Mythen und Sagen der Admiralitatsinsulaner ", Anthropos. Wien, 1908. Vol. III, pp. 193-206, 651-671.

MERIVALE, CHARLES : A History of Rome under the Empire, 7 vols. New York, 1863-1866.

MEROLLA DA SORRENTO, FATHER JEROM : " A Voyage to Congo ", Pinkerton's Voyages and Travels. London, 1814. (Translated from the Italian.) Vol. XVI. pp. 195-316.

MORGAN, LEWIS H. : League of the Ho-dé-no-sau-nee or Iroquois. New York, 1922. Bks. I, II.

MURGOCI, A. : " Customs Connected with Death and Burial among the Roumanians ", Folk-Lore. London, 1919. Vol. XXX, pp. 89-102.

NELSON, EDWARD W. : "The Eskimo about Behring Strait ", Eighteenth Annual Report of the Bureau of Ethnology. Washington, 1899. Pt. 1, pp. 19-518.

NEUHASS, RICHARD GUSTAV : Deutsch Neu-Guinea. Berlin, 1911. 3 vols.

OLDENBERG, HERMANN : The Grihya-Sutras. Vols. 29-39 in Sacred Books of the East. Oxford, 1886-1892.

,, Die Religion des Veda. Berlin, 1894.

OLDFIELD, AUGUSTUS : " On the Aborigines of Australia ", Transactions of the Ethnological Society of London. London, 1865. New Series, Vol. III, pp. 215-293.

PARKINSON, RICHARD : Dreissig Jahre in der Südsee. Stuttgart, 1907.

PAYNE, EDWARD J. : History of the New World Called America. Oxford, 1892.

PERRY, W. J. : " Orientation of the Dead in Indonesia ", Journal of the Anthropological Institute. London, 1914. Vol. XLIV, pp. 281-294.

,, " Myths of Origin and Homes of the Dead in Indonesia ", Folk-Lore. London, 1915. Vol. XXVI, pp. 138-152.

POLITIS, N. G. : " On the Breaking of Vessels as a Funeral Rite in Modern Greece " (translated by Louis Dyer), Journal of the Anthropological Institute. London, 1894. Vol. XXIII, pp. 29-41.

PREUSS, KONRAD THEODOR : Die Begräbnisarten der Amerikaner und Nordostasiaten. Königsberg, 1894.

RADIN, PAUL : " Religion of the North American Indians ", Journal of American Folk-Lore. Boston, 1914. Vol. XXVII, pp. 335-373.

RAMAGE, CRAUFURD T. : Nooks and By-ways of Italy. Liverpool, 1868.

RASCHER, R. : "Die Sulka, ein Beitrag zue Ethnographie Neu Pommern ", Archiv für Anthropologie. Braunschweig, 1904. Vol. XXIX, pp. 209-235.

RATTRAY, ROBERT S. : Some Folk-Lore Stories and Songs in Chinyanja. London, 1907.

RATZEL, FRIEDRICH : " Uber den anthropogeographischen Wert ethnographischen Merkmale ", Anthropogeographie. Stuttgart, 1891. Vol. II, pp. 577-630.

RIDLEY, REV. WILLIAM : *Kamilaroi, Dippel, and Turrubul.* Sydney, 1866.
RIEDEL, J. G. F. : "The Sawn or Haawu Group ", *Revue Coloniale Internationale.* Amsterdam, 1885. Vol. I, pp. 303-321.
  „   *Die Sluik-en Kroesharige Rassen Tusschen Selebas en Papua.* Gravenhage, 1886.
RINK, HINRICH J. : *Tales and Traditions of the Eskimo.* Edinburgh, 1875.
RISLEY, SIR HERBERT H. : *The Peoples of India,* 2nd edit. Calcutta, 1915.
RIVERO, MARIANO EDWARD and VON TSCHUDI, JOHN J. : *Peruvian Antiquities.* New York, 1853 (Translated by F. L. Hawks).
RIVERS, WILLIAM H. R. : "The Contact of Peoples ", *Essays and Studies Presented to William Ridgeway.* Cambridge, 1913.
  „   "The Primitive Conception of Death," *Hibbert Journal.* London, 1912. Vol. X, Pt. 1, pp. 393-407.
  „   *The History of Melanesian Society,* 2 vols. Cambridge, 1914.
  „   *The Todas.* London, 1906.
ROSCOE, JOHN : *The Baganda.* London, 1911.
ROSE, H. A. : "Hindu Birth Observances in the Punjab ", *Journal of the Anthropological Institute.* London, 1884. Vol. XIII, pp. 122-137.
ROTH, RUDOLPH (of Tübingen) : "On the Morality of the Veda " (translated by William D. Whitney), *Journal of the American Oriental Society.* New York, 1853. Vol. III, pp. 329-349.
ROTH, WALTER E. : *Ethnological Studies among the North-West-Central Queensland Aborigines.* Brisbane, 1897.
ROUGIER, P. EMANUEL : "Maladies et Médicines à Fiji autrefois et aujourd-'hui ", *Anthropos.* Salzburg, 1907. Vol. II, pp. 68-79, 994-1008.
RUSSELL, FRANK : *The Pima Indians in The Twenty-sixth Annual Report of the Bureau of Ethnology.* Washington, 1908. pp. 17-379.
RUSSELL, R. V. : *The Tribes and Castes of the Central Provinces of India,* 4 vols. London, 1916.
SCHEFTELOWITZ, J. : "Die Sündentilgung durch Wasser ", *Archiv Religionswissenschaft.* Leipzig, 1914. Vol. XVII, pp. 353-412.
SCHMIDT, LEOPOLD : *Die Ethik der Alten Griechen,* 2 vols. Berlin, 1882.
SEIDEL, H. : "Krankheit, Tod und Begräbnis bei den Togonegern ", *Globus.* Braunschweig, 1897. Vol. LXXII, No. 2, pp. 21-25.
SELIGMANN, CHARLES G. : *The Melanesians of British New Guinea.* Cambridge, 1910.
SHAKESPEAR, JOHN : *The Lushei Kuki Clans.* London, 1912.
SHEDDEN-RALSTON, WILLIAM RALSTON : *The Songs of the Russian People.* London, 1872.
SHERRING, CHARLES A. : *Western Tibet and the British Borderland.* London, 1906.
SHOTWELL, JAMES T. : *The Religious Revolution of To-day.* Boston, 1924.
SKEAT, WALTER W. and BLAGDEN, CHARLES O. : *Pagan Races of the Malay Peninsula,* 2 vols. London, 1906.
SMYTH, ROBERT E. : *The Aborigines of Victoria.* Melbourne, 1878.
SONNERAT, PIERRE : *Voyage aux Indes Orientales et à la Chine,* 4 vols. Paris, 1806.
SOUTHEY, ROBERT : *History of Brazil,* 3 vols. London, 1817-1822.
SPENCER, SIR BALDWIN : *Native Tribes of the Northern Territory of Australia.* London, 1914.
SPENCER, SIR BALDWIN and GILLEN, F. J. : *Across Australia,* 2 vols. London, 1912.
  „   „   *The Northern Tribes of Central Australia.* London, 1904.
  „   „   *The Native Tribes of Central Australia.* London, 1899.
SPENCER, HERBERT : *The Principles of Sociology.* 3 vols. New York, 1895-97.
SPIETH, JAKOB : *Die Ewe Stamme.* Berlin, 1906.
STANBRIDGE, W. E. : "Some Particulars of the General Characteristics, Astronomy and Mythology of the Tribes in the Central Part of Victoria, Southern Australia ", *Transactions of the Ethnological Society of London,* New Series. London, 1861. Vol. I, pp. 286-304.

292 BIBLIOGRAPHY

STOLZ, — : "De Umgebung von Kap König Wilhelm", Neuhauss' *Deutsch Neu Guinea*. Berlin, 1911. Vol. III, pp. 245-286.

SWANTON, JNO. R. : *Contributions to the Ethnology of the Haida in Jesup North Pacific Expedition*. Leiden, 1904. Vol. V, Pt. 1. (*Memoir, American Museum of Natural History*, Vol. VIII.)

TAPLIN, GEORGE : *The Folklore, Manners, Customs and Languages of the South Australian Aborigines*. Adelaide, 1879.

TEIT, JAMES : *The Thompson Indians of British Columbia in Jesup North Pacific Expedition*. Leiden, 1900. Vol. I, pp. 163-390 (*Memoir, American Museum of Natural History*, Vol. II).

THOMAS, CYRUS : "Burial Mounds of the Northern Sections of the United States", *Fifth Annual Report of the Bureau of Ethnology*. Washington, 1887. pp. xxxviii-xlii.

THOMAS, NORTHCOTE, W. : *Natives of Australia*. London, 1906.

THOMSON, BASIL : *The Fijians*. London, 1908.

THURNBERG, C. P. : "An Account of the Cape of Good Hope and Some Parts of the Interior of South Africa", *Pinkerton's Voyages and Travels*, London, 1814. Vol. XVI, pp. 1-147.

THURNWALD, RICHARD : *Forschungen auf den Salomo-Inseln und dem Bismarck-Archipel*. Berlin, 1912. Vol. II.

THURSTON, EDGAR : *Castes and Tribes of Southern India*, 7 vols. Madras, 1909.

„ *Ethnographic Notes in Southern India*. Madras, 1906.

TURNER, REV. GEORGE : *Samoa, A Hundred Years and Long Before*. London, 1884.

„ *Nineteen Years in Polynesia*. London, 1861.

„ *Ethnology of the Ungava District, Hudson Bay Territory in Eleventh Annual Report of the Bureau of Ethnology*. Washington, 1894. pp. 167-349.

TYLOR, SIR EDWARD B. : *Primitive Culture*, 2 vols. London, 1903 (4th edit., revised).

URQUHART, F. L. : "Legends of the Australian Aborigines", *Journal of the Anthropological Institute*. London, 1885. Vol. XIV.

VORMANN, P. FRANZ : "Zur Psychologie, Religion, Soziologie, und Geschichte der Monumbo-Papua, Deutsch Neu Guinea", *Anthropos*. Wien, 1910. Vol. V, pp. 407-418.

WATERMAN, T. T. : "The Explanatory Element in the Folk-Tales of the North American Indians", *Journal of American Folk-Lore*. Boston 1914. Vol. XXVII, pp. 1-54.

WEBSTER, HUTTON : *Rest Days*. New York, 1916.

WEINHOLD, KARL : *Altnordisches Leben*. Berlin, 1856.

WESTERMARCK, EDVARD A. : *Origin and Development of Moral Ideas*, 3 vols. London, 1917, 2nd edit.

WILKES, CHARLES : *Narrative of the United States Exploring Expedition*, 1838-1842. Philadelphia, 1845.

WILLIAMS, SIR MONIER : *Buddhism in its Connection with Hinduism and its Contact with Christianity*. London, 1889.

WILLIAMS, REV. THOMAS : *Fiji and the Fijians*, 2 vols. London, 1870.

WILLIAMSON, ROBERT W. : *The Mafulu Mountain People of British New Guinea*. London, 1912.

WISSLER, CLARK : *The American Indian*. New York, 1922, 2nd edit.

WOLLASTON, ALEXANDER F. R. : *Pygmies and Papuans*. New York, 1912.

WOULE, KARL : *Native Life in East Africa*. London, 1909. (Translated by A. Werner.)

WUNDT, WILHELM : *Volkerpsychologie*, 10 vols. Leipzig, 1911-1920.

YARROW, H. C. : "The Study of Mortuary Customs (of the North American Indians)", *First Annual Report of the Bureau of Ethnology*. Washington, 1811. pp. xxvi-xxvii.

GLOSSARY OF TERMS
not otherwise explained in the text.

Allira : Name applied by a man to his own or his brothers', brood and tribal, and by a woman to her brothers', children.

Arunga : Grandfather or grandchild on the male side ; also the native name of the Euro which gives its name to a totem.

Betel : A leaf used in the north-western part of Melanesia ; a drink made from this ; the leaf is also chewed.

Buyulu : Mother's sister's child. English equivalent : cousin.

Chimmia : This term expresses the relationship of grandfather or grandchild on the mother's side.

Chimurilia : Chaplet of beads worn by certain women during the final mourning ceremony. This term is used by the men only ; the women call it *arumurilia*.

Gammona : All the men who may lawfully marry the daughters of a deceased man.

Gariauuna : Name given to the burial and mourning ceremonies.

Gulkan-gulkan : The evil spirit of the one who killed a Jupagalk man.

Ichchiloivichi (usually abbreviated *ichchil*) : All those who go near a corpse at a Teivali funeral become *ichchiloivichi*.

Ikuntera : Father-in-law ; the name applied by a man to every man whose daughter is eligible to him as a wife.

Intichiúma : Ceremony to increase the supply of the totemic animal or plant which gives its name to the totemic group which performs the ceremony.

Itia : Younger brother or sister, blood and tribal.

Kadi : Wife's brother. English equivalent : brother-in-law.

Kaka : Mother's brother. English equivalent : uncle.

Kaku : Male speaking or female speaking elder sister. English equivalent : Elder sister ; cousin.

Kami : Mother's father ; male speaking daughter's child ; mother's brother's child ; father's sister's child. English equivalents : maternal grandfather ; male speaking daughter's child ; cousin.

Kapuna : Parents of both father and mother and others of their generation to whom a definite relationship can be traced ; ancestors of the preceding generation are also *Kapuna*, but are *Kapuna-Kua-Kahi*.

Keno : Bathing place of the soul of the dead man.

Kupuka : Younger brothers ; father's younger brother's sons, tribal and blood ; younger sisters ; father's younger brother's daughters, tribal and blood. English equivalents : brother ; cousin ; sister ; cousin.

Latu : Exogamous matrilineal clans.

Lubra : The usual name applied by white people to a native woman.

Mia : Term applied by a man to all women whom his father might lawfully have married.

Mura : A man's wife's or a husband's, mother, blood and tribal ; thus all women whose daughters are eligible as wives are *Mura* to him.

Neyi : Male speaking or female speaking elder brother. English equivalent ; elder brother.

Ngandri : Mother ; mother's sister.

Ngaperi : Father ; father's brother.

Ngata-mura : Male speaking child ; female speaking brother's child.

Ngataria : Female speaking child.

Ngatata : Male speaking or female speaking younger brother or sister. English equivalent : younger brother or sister, or cousin.

Noa : Potential husband or wife.

Nunu : The soul.

Oknia : Term applied by a man to his actual father and to all men who might lawfully have married his mother *(Okilia-Oknia)*.

Pariarinji : Name of a male sub-class.

Sagu : Arrowroot.

Soma : A leafless shrub growing in all parts of India yielding a mildly acidulous milky juice ; a plant used at sacrifice, its sap having been used by the Vedic Aryas as a symbol of renewed life through sacrifice. The praises of *soma* are sung in the Rig-Veda and it is there deified. (In Puranic mythology : the moon or its deity.)

Tamani : Term for father, father's brother, and the husband of the mother's sister, these being the customary uses in the classificatory system.

Tarunga : A spirit, separable from the body, though not often in life separated. When a man dies, his *tarunga* becomes a *tindalo*.

Tidnari : Male speaking sister's child. English equivalent : nephew, niece.

Tindadho : A ghost, so-called after the spirit leaves the dead man.

Tindalo : Ghosts (chiefly).

Tjuanáku : Name of a male sub-class. (Binbinga tribe.)

Tjúlant júka : Name of a male sub-class. (Gnanji and Binbinga tribes.)

Ulthana : The spirit part of a dead man which is supposed to haunt the precincts of the grave until the final mourning ceremony has been carried out.

Umba : Name applied by a man to her own or his sister's children and by a man to those of his sister.

Umbirna : Wife's brother ; the term is applied by a man to the brother of any woman who is lawfully marriageable to him.

Unawa : Used by the Arunta tribe to designate men and women who are reciprocally marriageable.

Ungaraitcha : Term of relationship applied to elder sister, blood and tribal.

Unkulla : Relationship term applied to the sons and daughters of the father's sisters.

Urpmilchima : Final mourning ceremony conducted at the grave of a dead man or woman. The word means " trampling the twigs on the grave ".

Uwinna : Term of relationship applied to a father's sisters, blood and tribal.

Witia : Younger brother, blood and tribal.

INDEX

Africa, personality idea in, 119 ;
importance of name in, 143
Age, disposal of body associated
with, 13, 200, 201, 204, 205,
206 ; death from, 40, 41 ;
purification dependent upon,
126 ; mourning connected
with, 231 ; life after death
influenced by, 253 ; differences, insignificant in death-
complex, 273
All Saints' Day, 156
Allen, on attitude toward dead, 54 ;
on attitude toward evil spirits,
183
Asvalayana, 46
Atharva-Veda, charms about death
in, 37 ; disposal of the body
in, 55 ; Yama in, 167 ; future
punishments in, 169, 258 ;
suttee in, 240
Australia, use of fire, 2, 75, 76, 166 ;
tales, 3, 24, 25, 26, 27, 29, 212,
215 ; lacerations, 10, 96 ;
disposal of dead in, 15, 45,
52, 186, 200, 201, 202, 203, 204,
205, 208, 209, 210, 216, 219,
220, 221, 222, 223, 237, 265 ;
author's method applied to,
16-18 ; causes of death, 31,
32, 33, 34, 35, 37, 39, 40, 41,
42 ; driving away ghost, 63,
72, 78, 81 ; dread of the spirit,
64, 65, 66, 73 ; use of water,
74, 75 ; wailing, 78, 239 ;
desertion of house or camp,
80, 112, 113 ; spirit *vs.* ghost,
81, 183 ; just-so death situation, 82 ; attitude toward
corpse, 85, 87 ; importance of
hair, 90, 91, 92, 93, 94 ;
reversal of custom, 100, 101 ;
erection of hut on grave, 110,
111 ; destruction of property,
116, 117 ; purification, 125,
133 ; silence ban, 125, 138,
139, 236 ; importance of name,
137, 141 ; feasts, 158 ; reincarnation, 158, 173-177 ; life
after death, 165, 166, 181, 182,
246, 251, 252, 253, 256, 257 ;
orientation, 208, 209, 245 ;
mourning, 226, 227, 228, 229,
230, 231, 232, 233 ; taboos,
235, 245, 246 ; totemic cere-

monies, 239, 245, 246 ; woman's
connection with disposal, 239 ;
immolation of women, 243 ;
cult of the dead, 265

Bastian, on *elementargedanken,*
volkergedanken, 5 ; on origin
of tales, 44
Birthplace, controlling place of
burial, 123
Bloomfield, on "glance of the dog",
123 ; on uncanny character
of death, 167 ; on transmigration of souls, 168
Boas, on similarity of psychological
processes, 2, 82 ; on attitude
toward diffusion, 44 ; on
reversal of custom, 282
Bonney, on mourning, 228
Bose, on hair-cutting, 91
Breasted, reasons of, for preservation of body, 181
Brown, on causes of death, 35 ; on
feasts, 148 ; describes life after
death, 255
Brinton, on psychic unity theory,
4, 5
Burial, rites, 12, 13, 17, 18, 47, 66,
67 ; significance of, 45, 48, 49,
50, 180 ; co-existent with
cremation, 55 ; methods of,
51, 52, 53, 55, 197-199, 201-
206, 219, 222, 223, 269 ; of
children, 187, 205, 273 ; with
property, 116, 117 ; not
sufficient to prevent return of
ghost, 57 ; feast following,
147 ; priority of cremation
over, 187 ; identified with rank,
187, 197, 198, 199, 200, 201 ;
dependent upon exigencies of
occasion, 223 ; at birth-place,
223 ; associated with environment, 221, 222 ; influenced
by moral consideration, 218 ;
affected by sex, 202, 203, 204 ;
influenced by age, 204, 205,
206 ; connected with clan
spirit, 206, 207, 208, 209, 220 ;
customs connected with phratry
relations, 209 ; customs connected with kinship, 210 ;
in accordance with class, sub-
class, and local group, 211 ;
associated with Land of the